Students and External B...... | Staff & Research

STUDIES IN BRITISH POLITICS

CONTRIBUTORS

Mark Abrams
Research Services

K. J. W. Alexander
Strathclyde University

Lord Balniel
Conservative M.P.

John Biffen
Conservative M.P.

Brian Blake
BBC

Elizabeth Bott
Tavistock Institute

British Broadcasting
Corporation
Audience Research Department

D. E. Butler
Nuffield College, Oxford

Morris Davis
University of Illinois

Henry Durant
Gallup Poll

Harry Eckstein
Princeton University

Leon Epstein
Wisconsin University

Ron Hall
Sunday Times

Alexander Hobbs
Strathclyde University

H. C. Mackenzie
National Coal Board

R. T. McKenzie
London School of Economics

W. J. M. Mackenzie
Manchester University

Donald McLachlan
Sunday Telegraph

R. S. Milne
University of British Columbia

Richard Rose
Manchester University

Stanley Rothman
Smith College

Allan Silver
Columbia University

Ian Waller
Sunday Telegraph

Egon Wertheimer
Late German Journalist

Peter Willmott
Institute of Community Studies

Harold Wilson
Prime Minister

Lord Windlesham
Rediffusion T.V.

Michael Young
Institute of Community Studies

STUDIES IN BRITISH POLITICS

A Reader in Political Sociology

EDITED BY

RICHARD ROSE

University of Manchester

MACMILLAN
London · Melbourne · Toronto

ST MARTIN'S PRESS
New York
1966

By the same author

★

POLITICS IN ENGLAND

MUST LABOUR LOSE? (*with Mark Abrams*)

THE BRITISH GENERAL ELECTION OF 1959
(*with D. E. Butler*)

COMPARATIVE POLITICAL FINANCE
(*edited with A. J. Heidenheimer*)

MACMILLAN AND COMPANY LIMITED
Little Essex Street London WC2
also Bombay Calcutta Madras Melbourne

THE MACMILLAN COMPANY OF CANADA LIMITED
70 Bond Street Toronto 2

ST MARTIN'S PRESS INC
175 Fifth Avenue New York 10010 NY

PRINTED IN GREAT BRITAIN

CONTENTS

v

ACKNOWLEDGEMENTS

T HE study of political behaviour involves the gradual accumulation
of information, concepts, and hypotheses by many people over a
lengthy period of time; the debt that any worker in this field owes
to his colleagues, whether personal friends or individuals known only
through their writing, is large. An editor of a collection of articles
is more obviously indebted than most to the efforts of fellow students
of politics. It is a pleasure to acknowledge what the editor has
learned from other authors by the practical device of securing
wider circulation for their work. The editor is grateful for the permission of authors and publishers to reprint articles that originally
appeared elsewhere; the source of publication is listed at the foot
of each article and this represents the formal permission to reprint.

The original idea for this reader resulted from an after-dinner
conversation in Manchester with Professor Samuel J. Eldersveld of
the University of Michigan in 1961. The *Political Behaviour Reader*
that Professor Eldersveld cocdited was a pioneering collection of
American articles that contributed much to the education of the
editor while a research student at Oxford. Professor Eldersveld
suggested that a collection of articles on political behaviour in
Britain might be of use to a wide audience. The immediate stimulus
to edit this book came from preparing the manuscript of *Politics
in England*, which set out the editor's interpretation of politics; it
seemed right and proper that articles that influenced this thinking
and occasionally challenged it should be made available to all
interested in the subject.

By the wise and far-sighted accumulation of books and academic
journals through the decades, the librarians of the University of
Manchester greatly simplified the task of preparing this reader and
its bibliography. As new universities are founded without a heritage
of books and, perhaps, handicapped by governments unaware of the
central importance of a library to a university, it is likely that books
of this type will increasingly become a necessity, if students and
scholars are to have ready access to materials originally published
in places scattered across two continents and across a length of time.

Students in the editor's Political Behaviour course at Manchester
have served as guinea-pigs for experiments in the exposition of a
body of social-science literature. John D. Lees, now Lecturer in

American Studies at Keele, assisted greatly in compiling the bibliography. Clare, Charles and Lincoln Rose made and decorated the box that held the bibliography cards. My wife, Rosemary, has been helpful and patient in ways too numerous to mention.

University of Manchester   RICHARD ROSE
25 March 1965

INTRODUCTION

POLITICAL activity is complex; government involves many kinds of relationships between individuals, groups, institutions, and values. If we are to comprehend the politics of a country, we cannot confine our studies exclusively and narrowly to the formal institutions of government, for governments do not exist independently of the men who work them and the society around them. The difficulties which have arisen in exporting institutions of British government to Commonwealth nations clearly and unequivocally make this point. In addition to understanding the formal machinery of government, we must also understand the psychology of the men who seek influence, the particular features of society which have shaped their outlooks, the parties and pressure groups that affect government, and the informal social ties that bring some people together for political purposes and separate them from others.

The opening section of this reader presents articles which consider, in several different contexts, the political culture of Englishmen. Various social and psychological influences upon the development of political behaviour are considered in the second part. The articles on political communication in the third section consider from various perspectives the movement of opinions back and forth between government and the general public. Parties and pressure groups are the best-known institutions for channelling public opinion to government, and studies of these organizations form the concluding sections of this volume.

Any collection of articles involves the exclusion as well as the inclusion of material. This volume focuses upon political activity outside the formal machinery of government; a companion volume will concentrate upon political behaviour within the policy-making process of government. Within the area of coverage, the chief criteria for inclusion are quality, relevance, permanence, and difficulty of access elsewhere. While the emphasis on quality is self-justifying, it should be remembered that merit may take different forms; some articles are included because they are nearly definitive studies of a topic, others because they provide important interpretations of controversial problems, and others because they are pioneering attempts to develop ideas in important but understudied areas of British politics. In this context, relevance refers to the significance of an article in relationship to the main themes of the volume. The emphasis upon permanent significance has meant the exclusion of studies which concentrate upon topical issues in such a way that long-range significance is lost. Few selections are from books in print. It was assumed that books are more readily accessible to readers than journal articles, and that it is usually far better to print studies virtually full length than to give only a brief excerpt of ideas developed at book length. Because of the wide variety of approaches to the study of politics, articles of merit are published in many different types of journals and periodicals. Some journals are not available in public libraries because of their recondite appeal, while other periodicals are excluded from university libraries because they are ephemeral. Few libraries will have the great majority of the articles included here in their collection; even then, few readers would have the time and the bibliographical patience to trace back through hundreds of periodicals the occasional article worth re-reading. The editor, recalling his own efforts to assemble a working bibliography on British politics, believes that the convenience of this collection speaks for itself.

The authors represented in this volume write from a very wide variety of perspectives — political scientist, sociologist, social psychologist, journalist, and Member of Parliament. Some of the contributors would not think of themselves primarily as social scientists. The descriptive label of an author is hardly the best way to assess the quality of what he has written. An article which is unpretentiously intended to describe a relationship or institution may tell us more about political behaviour by making points of general significance implicitly than does an article which establishes an explicit and elaborate theoretical framework in order to reach trivial conclusions. Quantitative or descriptive techniques are not good or bad in themselves; rather, they are more or less relevant to particular problems in the study of politics. Although no specific prescription can be given about methods of political research, one can emphasize that certain approaches ought to be used within limited areas. For instance, a writer on public opinion or voting behaviour should not rely simply on introspection but also refer to empirical studies conducted by interviewing individuals selected by sample survey methods; a writer on social class in politics should take care to define his use of this ambiguous concept, and give an indication of what proportion of the population is being placed in the working class and the middle class. Contributions to this volume exemplify the use of techniques drawn from the study of history, political institutions, sociology, psychology, social psychology, statistics, anthropology, and, last but not least, personal observation and reflection. Methodological eclecticism results in the articles varying in their degree of 'objectivity'; even objective data, however, can be the grounds for controversy. For instance, any intelligent student of politics should be able to provide more than one explanation for facts about the relationship between occupational class and voting in Britain.

While methodological eclecticism has many advantages, it does mean that the studies in this volume are not written from a single social science viewpoint, or in a single style. In some cases, important theoretical assumptions and implications are not stated explicitly by the authors, and readers with a limited familiarity with social-science literature may not necessarily be able to place selections in context. For this reason, an introduction to each section provides a brief exposition of the social-science context into which articles may be fitted. Bibliographical notes are also provided, serving as an introduction to a large body of theoretical literature and classic empirical studies. Headnotes are given for each article, pointing out the specific significance of the selection for British politics. References to books, plus the bibliography of articles on British politics, are intended to make this book a comprehensive introduction to the literature of political behaviour in England. The reader who wishes to consider the problem of connecting findings from disparate studies is invited to turn to the editor's *Politics in England*, for a systematic book-length treatment of the subject.

Any label which may be given to the study of politics in the light of a very wide variety of social science concepts, including specifically political concepts, oversimplifies a complex set of perspectives. In the popular press the approach is often labelled 'psephology', although the study of election statistics and voting is only one specialized field within the study of politics. In university circles, the term 'political sociology' is most often used; this term, however, should not be taken to mean that politics can be reduced simply to the analyses of group and class interactions. In America, the approach is often termed the study of 'political behavior', although the approaches used are far more varied than those of behavioural psychology. More recently, in America, this approach has been labelled the 'functional approach', even though the analysis of structures and processes in terms of a very few basic political functions comprises only a small part of the literature.

Perhaps the most promising feature of the development of new methods of studying politics in recent decades is that the practitioners cannot be easily labelled. Critics who seek to pin labels upon diverse groups only show their own unfamiliarity with the literature, as well as unreceptiveness to the possibility of new ideas. The revolt against excessive concentration upon legalistic and institutional analysis has led scholars in many different directions — some have been fruitful and some have not. *Studies in British Politics* is meant to provide the necessary type of evidence for assessing the strengths and weaknesses of social science approaches to politics, namely, a collection of the best articles of this type that have been published to date about British politics. Debating the theoretical possibility or impossibility of conducting various kinds of research is sterile; the test should simply be how much different methods can add to our existing knowledge of British politics.

BIBLIOGRAPHICAL NOTE

The approach to politics outlined in this introduction is discussed at length in W. G. Runciman, *Social Science and Political Theory* (Cambridge: University Press, 1963); David Easton, *The Political System* (New York: Knopf, 1953); Robert Dahl, 'The Behavioral Approach in Political Science', *American Political Science Review*, lv. 4 (1961); and Heinz Eulau, *The Behavioral Persuasion in Politics* (New York: Random House, 1963).

Although the following anthologies about political behaviour primarily analyse politics in the context of America, the questions raised, the methods employed and the answers presented are often of relevance to the study of politics in England. These anthologies include: Nelson W. Polsby, *et al.*, *Politics and Social Life* (Boston: Houghton Mifflin Co., 1963); Harry Eckstein and David Apter, *Comparative Politics* (New York: Free Press of Glencoe, 1963); S. Sidney Ulmer, *Introductory Readings in Political Behavior* (Chicago: Rand, McNally, 1961); and Heinz Eulau, *et al.*, *Political Behavior* (Glencoe, Illinois: Free Press, 1956). In addition, there is a succinct summary of a large body of literature concerning political participation in Robert E. Lane, *Political Life* (New York: Free Press of Glencoe, 1959).

CHAPTER I

THE POLITICAL CULTURE

FOR many centuries writers on politics have been interested in the patterns of values, beliefs, and emotions shared by a nation's citizenry, and the political implications of such outlooks. Bagehot's *The English Constitution* and de Tocqueville's *Democracy in America* are well-known examples of books which analyse the political consequences of the attitudes prevailing in a society. In this century, social scientists have been studying the national character of a people by systematic empirical observations that enable complex distinctions to be made about what is termed the culture of a society. The approach was first developed by anthropologists, and has only recently been introduced into politics. The political culture of a nation consists of the characteristic attitudes of its population towards basic features of the political system — the community to be included within its boundaries, the nature of the régime, the definition of what government is expected to do and refrain from doing, and the role of individuals as participants and passive subjects of government. Culture has been studied through the writings of philosophers and politicians, and by direct participant-observation. The development of survey techniques for interviewing samples of people representative of a cross-section of the population now makes it technically possible to study cultural attitudes in an objective and quantified form; *The Civic Culture*, by Gabriel Almond and Sidney Verba, is a landmark in this field, using survey data to compare the political culture of Britain, America, Germany, Italy, and Mexico.

Although the political culture in one sense is the sum total of individual political outlooks, it is important to realize that from another perspective, individual outlooks are greatly influenced by the cultural values, beliefs, and emotions which are taught persons in the process of political socialization. Beginning in early childhood, a young Englishman learns through formal and informal instruction the basic cultural outlook of his society. This process of socialization helps to differentiate the individual Englishman from a German, Russian, or American; many cultural attitudes — an emotional response to the Queen, or a positive belief in parliamentary institutions — are not rooted in the nature of humankind or social organization but rather are specific to the political culture of a country. As generation succeeds generation, the environment and the institutions socializing people into the culture change, as do some of the basic values, beliefs, and emotions. Although cultural changes usually occur slowly, and this is particularly true of England, it is often just at those places where changes in outlook are being debated that political conflict will be greatest.

Within a large and complex society it is possible to distinguish sub-cultures, that is, groups that differ from many others in the society in terms of some significant values, beliefs, and emotions. The emphasis upon the national political culture is specially relevant when making comparisons between England and other countries; the emphasis upon the sub-cultures is relevant in making comparisons between different groups within a country. Sub-cultures may reflect differences in social position, in party affiliations, or in political roles. For instance, notwithstanding formal legal equality in politics, men and women appear to have different sub-cultural norms concerning political participation, resulting from differences in the position of men and women in society. Within the Labour Party, it is possible to distinguish a group of left-wing Socialists whose views vary sufficiently from those of the general population that they might be termed a Socialist sub-culture; within the Conservative Party, there is a distinguishable sub-culture reflecting traditional, pre-democratic values, beliefs, and emotions. Those who have the outlook of one of these two sub-cultures appear to be in a minority within both parties. Within government, appropriate outlooks might vary from role to role, or office to office; individuals moving, say, from the role of back-bencher to that of minister must learn new attitudes appropriate to the ministerial sub-culture.

If conflicting views are widely held about basic features of the culture, such as the constitutionality of the régime, then the position of the constitutional government will be precarious at best; this, for example, has long been the case in France, where sub-cultural differences concern fundamentals of political life. Within England, challenges to the basic values of the political culture have not been settled by overthrowing the Constitution since the Civil War. Consensus is not inevitable in this country; changes in Ireland and England in the nineteenth century led to deep conflict concerning a basic cultural norm — the definition of the community to be included within the boundaries of the state. This cultural conflict, the exception that illustrates the ability of British people to take unconstitutional action, was only settled by insurrection and civil war within the 'United' Kingdom.

Because cultural values, beliefs, and emotions concern basic features of the political system, they provide little clear guidance when particular issues of public policy arise. Agreement about the general principle of welfare legislation would not necessarily cause leaders of different parties to agree about the precise rate of pensions at a given time; it need not even produce agreement between all ministers within a single party. The fact that, except for the Irish controversy, England has escaped political conflict concerning basic values, beliefs, and emotions may lead persons to take the existence of consensus about the political culture for granted; when viewed from an international perspective, this enduring consensus is one of the most distinctive features of politics in England.

BIBLIOGRAPHICAL NOTE

Because of the great importance of continuity with the past in British politics, historical writing is often relevant to the study of the development of the contemporary political culture, especially the literature about the causes and consequences of the Civil War in the seventeenth century and about industrialization. A. V. Dicey's *Lectures on the Relation Between Law and Public Opinion in England During the Nineteenth Century* (1st edn., 1905) is a pioneering effort to state systematically the relations between basic political attitudes and social and political change. For an important re-evaluation of this relationship see Oliver MacDonagh, *A Pattern of Government Growth* (London: MacGibbon & Kee, 1961), and Henry Parris, 'The Nineteenth-Century Revolution in Government: a Reappraisal Reappraised', *The Historical Journal*, iii. 1 (1961). Walter Bagehot's *The English Constitution* (1st edn., 1867) provides a brilliant and enduring discussion of cultural attitudes tending to inhibit change.

Among contemporary social scientists a wide variety of approaches have been employed in analysing the culture. In addition to the articles included here, special attention might be drawn to T. H. Marshall, *Citizenship and Social Class* (Cambridge: University Press, 1950); Perry Anderson, 'Origins of the Present Crisis', *New Left Review*, no. 23 (1964), and Richard Rose, 'England: a Traditionally Modern Culture', in Sidney Verba and Lucian Pye (editors), *Political Culture and Political Development* (Princeton: University Press, 1965). In addition to presenting empirical data about Britain, Gabriel Almond and Sidney Verba in *The Civic Culture* (Princeton: University Press, 1963) discuss culture comparatively, within a conceptual framework designed to distinguish between types of political culture, and influences upon the formation of cultural outlooks.

MODERNITY AND TRADITION IN BRITAIN

By STANLEY ROTHMAN

THE study of the causes and consequences of changes in the
political culture is as difficult as it is important. Rothman's
essay ambitiously seeks to provide answers to a number of
major questions of historical political sociology, by discussing
changes on a time-scale much more sweeping than that traditionally employed by British historians. Rothman seeks to
demonstrate that twentieth-century cultural attitudes have
been greatly influenced by the persistence of a mixture of
cultural attitudes prevalent before the industrialization of this
country. Throughout the essay a comparative perspective is
implicit: why did England develop differently from France
and America in certain important respects? By simplifying
his treatment of historical processes, the author is able to
raise fundamental questions about the development of the
contemporary political culture of England.

The Englishman is tempted to believe that no-one
outside his happy island is altogether worthy to play
cricket or the parliamentary game.
  Raymond Aron, *The Opium of the Intellectuals*

WITH the increasing study of non-Western societies it is becoming
ever more apparent that the countries of the West, whatever
differences may exist among them, form part of a common European
civilization. It seems, therefore, that a fruitful approach to analysis of
the social and political systems of any Western country is to seek a
dynamic understanding of the particular combination of Western
elements that have characterized them — and thus to develop a
common set of categories for comparisons both among Western
nations and between Western and non-Western nations. In this
essay such an approach is applied to Britain. My thesis is that the
structure and dynamics of British social and political life are to be
understood in terms of the traditional society out of which modern
Britain emerged, and the particular manner in which the transition

---

Reprinted from *Social Research*, vol. xxviii, no. 3 (1961), pp. 297–317, with the
permission of the publisher. The above version omits a concluding section discussing possible future trends in British society.

to modernity developed. More specifically, it is argued that a crucial key to understanding British social and political life is the fact that Britain entered upon modernity as a *Gemeinschaft*, to use a term coined by Tönnies, that is, a collectivity whose members are bound together by *affective* ties to the collectivity itself, and to each other as members of the collectivity.[1]

I do not, of course, maintain that the development of British social and political life is to be explained solely in terms of *Gemeinschaft*. Certainly a complex combination of variables operating over time determined the pattern that emerged; in the nineteenth century, for example, important influences were such factors as Britain's economic supremacy, the role of empire as safety valve, the role of Methodism. My point is that a particular pattern of social relations did develop, and that as such it played an autonomous causal role. In effect this pattern represented the nationalization of the class structure and attitudes that had been characteristic of the medieval manor. And as a result, British political and social life has been characterized, at least until recently, by a unique synthesis of traditional elements and the forces that transformed them. For example, the emergence of democratic conceptions of authority in the nineteenth and twentieth centuries was associated, as Bagehot and later commentators have noted, with the maintenance of a deferential society and a governing class characterized by strong feelings of *noblesse oblige*.

In what follows I shall attempt to demonstrate that these propositions systematize features of British social and political life that have heretofore been explained by *ad hoc* propositions or not explained at all, and that they enable us to make meaningful and systematic comparisons between the British social and political systems and those of other Western countries. For such comparisons I shall refer primarily to France and the United States. And my analysis will focus primarily on political life.

I

The British introduced Europe, and we may say the whole world, to 'modernity'. It was in Britain that the practical, that is, industrial, use of modern science had its beginnings, and it was there that the Calvinist sects sprang up which provided the psychological basis for

---

[1] Ferdinand Tönnies, *Fundamental Concepts of Sociology*, trans. Charles P. Loomis (New York, 1940). Actually, of course, I am following Weber's use of the term; see Max Weber, *The Theory of Social and Economic Organization*, trans. A. M. Henderson and Talcott Parsons (New York, 1947), pp. 136–8.

B

capitalist entrepreneurship. It was in Britain, too, that the multiplicity of sects springing from Calvinism itself (and from the destruc-
tion of a central religious authority which was a concomitant of the
break with Rome) prepared the way for the erosion of a psychologically compelling religious view of the universe, and hence for the
emergence of the secular world view. Thus the modern outlook
sprang naturally, as it were, from British soil. This may go a long
way to explain why the rifts that developed in other countries, where
the new was introduced from the outside, and where 'modern' men
had to struggle with far 'stickier' societies, never reached full proportions in Britain. It also explains why many traditional social
patterns retained their viability in the face of dramatic change.
They could more easily be accommodated to the social–economic
and ideological revolution to which they had given birth than was
the case with other nations.

One of the key variables here is that England had developed many
of the characteristics of a modern nation before the economic and
social revolutions of the eighteenth and nineteenth centuries — indeed, much earlier. Henry VIII could consummate the break with
Rome with relative ease, in part because he no longer had to compete with a powerful quasi-independent aristocracy, and because
Britons, bound together by a common law and a set of national institutions, thought of the Roman Church as a foreign Church.[1] Thus
England escaped the religious upheavals that rent the Continent.
And, even more important, the liberal economists and political
theorists of a later period felt far less need to completely transform
traditional patterns than did reformers in other countries. Among
the aims of all continental reformers was the development of an integrated national state under a common law. Traditional English
society was characterized by both.

But the fact that England had developed national institutions before the reformers' attack on traditional modes of thought and action
meant that these institutions and the modes of thought associated
with them retained important traditional elements. Eighteenth-
century England, in practice as well as theory, was more than a
mere aggregation of atoms bound together by law or force. The
'estates' of the realm were functionally related to one another by
traditionally defined rights, duties, and attitudes. It was as if the
state were the medieval manor writ large — as if the sense of mutual
responsibilities which had theoretically characterized the manor had
been transferred to the national level. Thus the State played a con-

[1] D. L. Keir, *The Constitutional History of Modern Britain* (London, 1955), p. 57.

tinuing role in regulating conditions of work, and secular authorities took over from the Church the care of the indigent and poor through a system of outdoor relief that reached its culmination in the Speenhamland system of 1795.[1] And we find here a governing class willing, despite some grumbles, to support 'poor rates' that were quite high. Comparison with France is instructive. As Trevelyan notes: 'The worst horrors of failure, of unemployment or of unprovided old age were not suffered by the poor in England to the same extent as in the continental countries of the ancient régime. The regiments of beggars, such as continued to swarm in the streets of Italy, and of France under Louis XIV, were no longer over here . . . That is one reason . . . why through all our political, religious and social feuds from the Seventeenth to the Nineteenth Centuries the quiet and orderly habits of the people, even in times of distress, continued upon the whole as a national characteristic.'[2] I certainly do not want to suggest that English social life at this point was idyllic, but for present purposes it is the comparison that is important.

Modernity, the rapid industrialization that transformed traditional societies, came to the Western world in the form of liberal capitalism, of which the intellectual grandfather was John Locke and the most systematic British exponents were the philosophic radicals.[3] The premises of liberalism stood in direct antithesis to the assumptions of the society it sought to transform. For natural inequality it substituted natural equality, each man counting as one. For a view of secular history as a series of events it substituted a conception of history as the development towards a future in which men would become happier and more moral as they achieved increasing control over nature. For reliance on the traditional ways of doing things it substituted the method of reason and the standard of utility. It accepted and even welcomed changing patterns of social life. In economic thought it idealized the free market, and attacked all limitations on the natural play of economic laws, whether these resulted from tariffs, guilds, the regulation of wages, or poor rates. It equated the good life with the life of economic well-being, and subordinated other values to those of economic expansion. It expected continued technological and economic progress. The philosophic reaction to liberal capitalism came in the form of the rationalization

[1] See Karl Polyani, *The Great Transformation* (New York, 1944).
[2] George Trevelyan, *Illustrated English Social History*, vol ii (New York, 1942), p. 88.
[3] See Leo Strauss, *Natural Right and History* (Chicago, 1953), pp. 202–51; also Élie Halévy, *The Growth of Philosophic Radicalism*, trans. Mary Morris (London, 1928).

of tradition, that is, conservative thought, and the clash between the advocates of the new and the defenders of the old took a variety of forms.

In the United States, with its general lack of traditional social patterns, no substantial conservative orientation emerged. The premises of liberal thought were regarded as natural, and were accepted almost immediately, with an interpretation that was democratic, egalitarian, and atomistic. As Hartz points out,[1] the United States thus skipped the traditional stage of European society and began life essentially as a modern nation. As a result, American society was never characterized by the sharp ideological conflicts that developed in European nations. Ideological conflict involves basic disagreements on the nature of legitimate political authority and the goals of political action. And sharp as labour–capital conflicts became in this country, the fact is that both groups were committed to essentially a liberal–capitalist outlook, and hence the situation cannot be described in terms of ideological conflict. Compared to developments in almost every other nation in the world since the early nineteenth century, the changes experienced by the United States have been relatively marginal.

The development in France is illustrative. While Americans drew the most radical theoretical implications from Locke, these did not produce radicalism on the practical level, for they described substantially what existed. In France too the premises of liberalism yielded radical consequences almost immediately, but there the same theoretical conclusions, and the attempt to carry them out, could only mean violent social upheaval and further radicalization. (This helps explain the ambivalence with which Americans like Jefferson regarded the French Revolution: they could not help but agree with the ideas of the revolutionaries, but they recoiled from the results of those ideas and from the kind of men whom really radical social changes generally bring to power.) In France the 'stickiness' of pre-existing social patterns resulted in Jacobinism, the emergence of an intransigent conservatism, and the development of a persistent fault in French society that finds its violent echoes down to the present.[2]

British development exhibits still another pattern. Whig historians have written of the triumph of liberalism, and socialists of the triumph of the middle class and of capitalism. Actually neither of these interpretations is completely satisfactory, for the actual course

[1] Louis Hartz, *The Liberal Tradition in America* (New York, 1955).
[2] See George H. Sabine, 'The Two Democratic Traditions', in *Philosophical Review*, vol. lxi (October 1952), pp. 451–75.

of events involved an intermingling of liberal and traditional views of society. As with Calvinism itself, liberalism was transformed even as it transformed the traditional community out of which it emerged. The result was that while Britain became more and more liberal as the nineteenth century proceeded, so liberalism took on increasing traditional content. In this process the fact that Britain was already a national community played an important role: it muted the inherently radical premises of conflicting ideologies, thus permitting the pragmatic handling of issues arising from violent social changes; and in some areas it even inhibited the very conception of thought patterns that might tend to shatter the stability of the community. Thus the logical consequences of liberal premises were muted on the levels of both thought and action. The liberal attack on the Establishment was never a total attack, and conservatives never held on to the point of no return. Later, when the area of conflict shifted and a socialist movement developed, the pattern repeated itself.

The consequences of the liberal idea were many: the gradual extension of the suffrage through the great reform bills; the establishment of free trade, culminating in the repeal of the Corn Laws; the new Poor Law of 1834; and so on. Politically the result was a society that was becoming more and more democratic, with consequent shifts in the distribution of power. Economically the result was the creation of a society that for a short time approached the model of *laissez-faire* — but only for a short time and never completely, for at the same time that a new 'economic' Poor Law was being introduced, so were factory acts. And the pace of social reform of this type increased as the century wore on, to culminate in the National Insurance Act of 1911, providing for universal unemployment insurance, old-age protection, and a very extensive system of free medical care.

Again it should be emphasized that the history of social and economic change cannot be associated solely with either a party or a social class. Conservatives in Britain accept significant portions of the new economics and the new politics, and the Whigs (liberals) accepted the idea of community responsibility, despite the heavy weight they attached to the arguments of the liberal economists.[1] Classic liberalism assigned very little role to the State aside from the maintenance of law and order (and American liberals, until the New Deal period, were committed to this point of view). But British liberals, almost from the beginning, implicitly considered the state to have a creative role in transforming the will of the community into action, if only to eliminate feudal abuses.

[1] See E. L. Woodward, *The Age of Reform, 1815–1870* (London, 1938), p. 142.

A notable area in which liberal theory was quickly eroded in action was its acceptance of the legitimacy of trade-union organization. In the classic liberal view, labour was a commodity to be bought as cheaply as possible, and any limitation on free contract, in the form of associations of men, was thought to be a positive evil. Here again, however, a large number of Britons, while accepting the views of the 'economists' in theory, felt that workers had as much right to protect their interests as the masters — a reflection of the traditional view of society as made up of organized estates. This comes out quite clearly in the debates on the Combination Acts of 1824 and 1825, especially the latter. At neither time did the point of view that labour had no right to organize command substantial support. The only question really raised dealt with the limitations to be placed on trade-union activity.[1] Again the capstone was the insurance act of 1911, which, by providing that benefits be paid through friendly societies, almost compelled individuals to join unions and fostered their ever more rapid growth. In contrast to the United States, where the organization of 'interests' has always been regarded as somewhat sinister, all British governments have discussed proposed legislation with the interests affected, and have even encouraged the amalgamation of different organizations representing the same interest, so that consultations might be more readily completed.[2]

Traditional histories of the working-class movement tend to emphasize the workers' 'struggle' for the recognition of 'rights'. Without denying the fact of opposition and even sharp conflict, one is struck by the relative rapidity with which working-class organization was accepted in Britain as compared with either France or the United States. Trade unions were not legalized in France until 1884, and until 1890 the French worker had to carry a *livret* or be accounted a vagabond; he handed it to his employer when he took a job and could not take another unless his employer signed and returned the book to him, thus indicating that all obligations had been met. While legal prohibitions were not nearly so severe in the United States, there too the individualistic orientation of both employers and workers seriously inhibited the formation of trade unions. In Britain, moreover, the amount of violence attending conflicts between labour and capital was relatively small. Workers preferred letters to *The Times* and an appeal to the general will of the com-

---

[1] Hansard, *Parliamentary Debates* (second series): xi (1824), 409, 911; xii (1825), 1288, 1351.

[2] See Gilbert Walker, *Economic Planning by Programme and Control in Great Britain* (London, 1957), pp. 135–6.

munity to mounting the barricades. And capitalists were willing to
yield under pressure rather than maintain a completely intransigent
position. The willingness to compromise built on itself. British employers, in contrast to the French, did not think of trade-union
leaders as irresponsible revolutionaries, and trade-union leaders
came to expect the possibility of gains based on peaceful action. I am
aware, of course, that this picture flies in the face of conventional
discussions of the nineteenth century, but so far as I can determine,
the evidence for it, *if one takes a comparative view*, is overwhelming.

Before turning to the development of British political life, I wish
to add a word on the emergence of modern socialism. This is not
simply, in my opinion, a concomitant of industrialization or of
liberal capitalism. If it were, a socialist party of substantial size
should have developed in the United States. It seems more reasonable to search for the origins of Western socialism in the particular
relationships that characterized European society. More specifically,
following Hartz and Ulam,[1] I would argue that a key factor was the
emergence of liberal capitalism, that is, *bourgeois* society, out of a pre-
existing feudal society. According to this view, the class consciousness of European workers and their reaction to the imperatives of
industrialism and the atomism of liberalism are related to two main
factors: the tension between the continuing class consciousness of the
European *bourgeoisie* and the promise of liberalism; and the tension
between the imperatives of a liberal–capitalist society and an awareness of what had been before. Certainly socialism's intellectual attack
on liberalism combines the insights of the conservative reaction to
liberal society with the liberal promise of equality and affluence.

But if the class consciousness of the worker explains the ultimate
attraction of a working-class party, what explains the relative
moderation of British socialism as a movement? Is not part of the
answer to be found in the relative muting, in Britain, of the implications of liberal thought, from which socialism took its promise, and
in the social content that almost immediately infused British
liberalism?

In Britain the intellectuals who embraced socialism were, by and
large, far from being in total rebellion against the society they wished
to change. The fact that the State constantly intervened to amelio-
rate economic evils took the edge off social protest. And the success
of trade unions, first of the skilled and then of the unskilled, gave
workers a stake in the system. Not only did it provide a career open
to talents for the most dynamic of the workers but it gave them a

---

[1] Hartz (cited above, note 6) and Adam B. Ulam, 'The Historical Role of Marxism and the Soviet System', in *World Politics*, vol. viii (October 1955), pp. 20–45.

sense of belonging to an estate whose interests were represented. Here the history of the first and second generations of the leaders of the unskilled is instructive. The pattern is typified by the career of Ernest Bevin: beginning as a member of the Social Democratic Federation, he gradually sloughed off his radicalism as he achieved power at the head of a highly successful trade union. This was not, of course, a question of betrayal or of the 'aristocratic embrace' but rather an acceptance of the legitimacy of a system of which he had become part.[1]

British radicals, even while preaching moderate socialism, refused to attack the basic communal values of the society. Contrast, for example, Clement Attlee and Léon Blum.[2] By 1920 Blum was certainly no longer a *political* revolutionary. Yet throughout his life he mounted a fundamental attack on all of what he considered the *bourgeois* premises of French society, including conceptions of love and the family. Attlee, on the other hand, accepted all of these values; indeed he could not conceive of questioning them. Thus when Blum outlines the future that socialism will bring, his words induce the intellectual excitement of a radical and total attack, but Attlee on this subject is merely dull. In Britain fundamental criticisms of the basic values of the community are left to literati, who are always marginal politically; there, in contrast to France, literary and political criticism hardly ever meet. Radicals from other countries who find haven in England are almost always highly critical of what seems to them the insularity and stuffiness of their English comrades.

II

British politics is characterized by a disciplined two-party system. The fact of two parties it shares with the United States; the fact of disciplined parties it shares, at least in some measure, with the European continent. The combination is almost unique, and can be fully understood only in terms of the previous discussion.

It has frequently been asserted that the existence of a two-party system in Britain is primarily the result of its system of single-member electoral districts, for this system discriminates sharply

---

[1] On Bevin see Trevor Evans, *Bevin of Britain* (London, 1946); Francis Williams, *Bevin* (London, 1946); J. T. Murphy, *Labour's Big Three* (London, 1948); and Alan Bullock, *The Life and Times of Ernest Bevin*, vol. i (London, 1960). On other trade-union leaders see J. M. Clynes, *Memoirs* (London, 1938); Will Thorne, *My Life's Battles* (London, 1925); Ben Tillett, *Memoirs and Reflections* (London, 1931).

[2] On Blum see Louise Dalby, 'The Ideas of Léon Blum', unpublished Ph.D. dissertation, Radcliffe College (1956). On Attlee see Hugh Jenkins, *Mr. Attlee* (London, 1948); or read Attlee's *The Labour Party in Perspective — and Twelve Years Later* (London, 1949) and *As it Happened* (London, 1954).

against minor parties.[1] But this essentially mechanical answer is not satisfactory in and of itself, even though it may represent a factor of significance. The electoral system did not prevent the continued existence of a party that represented a geographically segregated ethnic minority, the Irish: those who continued to support the nationalist cause felt that neither of the major British parties had anything of importance to offer them. And even if a minority were not isolated geographically but felt strongly enough about certain kinds of issues, it might continue to support the party of its choice despite the discrimination of the electoral system. This was the experience of the Labour Party itself for a number of years, and also of the French Communist Party during 1924–36, when it was heavily discriminated against by the electoral system. In fact it can be argued that discrimination of this kind against powerful minority sentiments may have the result of turning them to violence. Thus while single-member districts may create a tendency towards two parties, the ultimate result may be the replacement of a party system by civil war. Apropos of this, it can be argued that the political polarization that occurred in the United States between 1852 and 1860 was not unrelated to the existence of an electoral system characterized by single-member districts and a popularly elected president.

In other words, if single-member electoral districts are to produce a successful (in the sense of working peacefully over time) two-party system, a precondition is necessary: the society in which the system operates must not be characterized by sharp conflicts.[2] Only under this condition can the major parties absorb the adherents of the minor. If single-member electoral districts have served, in both Britain and the United States, to produce a successful two-party system, they have done so because in some measure the politics of the two countries is pragmatic, founded on basic social consensus.

How then do we explain the differences between the British and American systems, specifically the difference between a disciplined two-party system and one that is not disciplined? Without attempting a total explanation of this complex problem, I would emphasize that one necessary condition for the development of party discipline is that the party be more than a party: it must be a 'cause', representing a particular *Weltanschauung*. It is notable that party discipline in Britain reached its maximum only after the emergence of the

[1] The classic American exposition is provided by E. E. Schattschneider, *Party Government* (New York, 1942); see also Maurice Duverger, *Les Partis politiques* (Paris, 1951).

[2] See the typology developed by D. A. Rustow, 'Some Observations on Proportional Representation', in *Journal of Politics*, vol. xii (February 1950), pp. 107–28.

Labour Party;[1] and what has held the Labour Party together has been the self-imposed discipline not only of the party but also of an electorate to whom party meant everything and the quality of individual leadership meant practically nothing. This has been partly true also of the communists in France and of the socialists and Catholics in Germany, but in the multi-party environments of the Continent, where the significance of party 'mission' becomes blurred by the fine shadings of political differences, even 'radical' parties, or those representing a given religious or ethnic group, have found it more difficult to maintain discipline than has the Labour Party. The discipline that has characterized the British Conservative Party in recent years has been not so much the result of a positive sense of mission as a reflex to the discipline of those who have opposed it within the framework of a two-party system. And in the United States, where a radical party has not developed, for reasons already outlined, this essential ideological basis for party discipline has not existed.

But if we grant the importance of this factor we are faced with what, on the surface, appears to be something of a paradox. Among the necessary conditions of a successful two-party system is the existence of pragmatic politics, but among the necessary conditions of disciplined parties is that, in some sense, they be more than parties — that they represent *Weltanschauungen*, divergent ideologies. How can it be held that both of these seemingly contradictory conditions have obtained in Britain? The answer lies again in the fact that ideological and class conflict has always taken place in Britain within the framework of a more inclusive attachment to the community as such. I suggest that British politics cannot be understood unless these interrelations are recognized.

It has often been argued that the key to a disciplined party system in Britain lies in the continued authority of the Crown, which devolved upon the prime minister — including, and this is what is generally emphasized, the power of dissolution. The effective institutionalization of the power of dissolution in the hands of the prime minister has also been cited — especially by Frenchmen who have seen absence of this power as one of the prime sources of the weakness of the French executive — to explain why British government has effec-

[1] James B. Christoph, 'The Study of Voting Behavior in the British House of Commons', in *Western Political Quarterly*, vol. xi (June 1958), pp. 319–40. See also Leon D. Epstein, 'British Mass Parties in Comparison with American Parties', in *Political Science Quarterly*, vol. lxxx (March 1956), pp. 97–125; W. J. M. Mackenzie *et al.*, 'Partis politiques et classes sociales en Angleterre' (mimeographed, n.d.); Leslie Lipson, 'The Two Party Tradition in British Politics', in *American Political Science Review*, vol. lxvii (June 1953), pp. 337–59.

tively become cabinet government while France, at least until the Fifth Republic, remained a parliamentary régime. Undoubtedly the power of dissolution played a role, but the answer is far more complex than this, and in fact the institutionalization of the dissolution power has itself to be explained. Why did the dissolution powers of the French monarchy not devolve upon the prime minister?

Again I would suggest that the development of the dissolution power in Britain, and indeed the whole system of cabinet government, can best be understood in terms of our previous discussion. More specifically, it was *possible* for cabinet government to emerge there because Britain's transition from traditional to modern society was associated not only with the development of class and ideological conflict and hence with the emergence of a disciplined two-party system but also with the fact that party leaders, convinced of the necessity of effective governance, continued, despite their differences, to assign a creative role to the state as the executive arm of the community. These points can be clarified by comparing British developments with those of France and the United States.

The first precondition of the emergence of cabinet government was the development of a parliamentary régime in which legislative and executive authority was derived from the same body. This occurred in all European countries as the traditional balance among king, aristocracy, and commons tipped towards the commons, and authority came to reside in the institution responsible to the people.

In the United States, however, the political separation and balance of power created by the founding fathers maintained itself. It could do so for a number of reasons. First of all it was not, as in Britain, a social balance. Thus the president, unlike the English monarch, could combine democracy with authority. But even given this, and the constitutional fetishism that quite early came to characterize American public life, the pattern still might have been different. Had the country been sharply divided into numerous splinters, as was France, we might have slipped into Caesarism. Or had sharp class divisions yielded two disciplined parties, and had Americans felt a strong need for a state capable of carrying out a relatively integrated and active public policy, it is certainly possible that some greater integration between the president and the legislature would have developed. In other words, both the structure and the dynamics of our political system are a result of our having been born a modern nation, that is, a liberal society.[1]

---

[1] On the relationship between our being a totally liberal society and our constitutional fetishism see Hartz, op. cit. The word fetishism is not used here in a pejorative sense.

In France, as in England, dissolution was originally part of the prerogative of the monarch. Under the constitution of the Third Republic the power was assigned to the president. It was not used by him after MacMahon and *le seize mai*, but there is no logical reason that the power could not have devolved upon a prime minister who was immediately responsible to a parliamentary majority. The reasons it failed to do so are not difficult to uncover. Part of the answer lies in the feeling of the 'republicans' that such authority would bring with it the dangers of 'reactionary' plebiscitarianism, but of great importance as well was the emergence of a multi-party system from a fragmented political culture.

Such was the nature of this system that in order to become prime minister one needed the support of the Assembly as against the support of one's party. Therefore if one wished to obtain office one did not force deputies to fight another election, in which the issues would, in any event, be unclear and nothing would be resolved. And, in general, those who obtained office were men with a sense of 'balance' who, despite differences of ideological nuance, liked and were liked by a reasonably substantial number of deputies. These were men who were, by and large, more oriented to office than to policy. Even during the Fourth Republic, then, when the dissolution power was specifically given to the prime minister, it was used only once. In fact, many potential ministers were forced to promise that they would not make use of this power unless the Assembly supported them. Thus, given the existence of a multiplicity of ideological parties that found it impossible to achieve their ends, individual deputies (with the exception of the communists or the very extreme right) were always tempted to seek the satisfaction of their constituents' immediate demands through mutual back-scratching and the power that comes from office. As a result, the political system was such, paradoxically enough, as to transform ideological into pragmatic politics.[1]

In Britain, finally, it was widely agreed that, whatever the balance of political forces, effective government was required. But given the acceptance of popular sovereignty, the emergence of two disciplined parties implied that an effective government could be formed only by the party that possessed a majority, rather than, as had been the case in the middle of the nineteenth century, by intra-parliamentary

[1] For discussions of the Third and Fourth Republics see H. Luethy, *France Against Herself* (New York, 1955); David Thomson, *Democracy in France* (London, 1946); R. de Jouvenel, *La République des camarades* (Paris, 1914); Nathan Leites, *On the Game of Politics in France* (Stanford, 1959); and P. Williams's very perceptive article, 'Compromise and Crisis in French Politics', in *Political Science Quarterly*, vol. lxii (September 1957), pp. 321–39.

negotiation. If the leader of that party lost his compact majority his only course, save in exceptional circumstances, was to dissolve the Parliament, since the breakdown of agreement within a party precluded effective government. And since the electoral fate of his party became bound up with the image of the Government and the prime minister, his authority was bound to increase, especially since, except in the most rare circumstances, one preferred one's own party in office, whatever one's disagreements with official policy.[1]

This relationship between Government and Parliament, which emerged with the modern party system in Britain, is what structured the present organization of the Commons. In France and the United States legislators have, for different reasons, been primarily members of the legislature rather than members of a government or an opposition, and thus legislative policy there has been largely determined by a mutual give-and-take among legislators who are anxious both to pass what they consider to be good legislation and to satisfy the interests they represent. But if the legislation that is introduced does not come from a government of trusted colleagues who have at their disposal the bureaucratic apparatus necessary for drawing up a programme, the legislature is thrown back on itself. Thus a complex system of subject-matter committees has developed, and the committees, since they acquire the authority and prestige that come from expertise and power over time-tables, have drawn to themselves the most dynamic members of the legislature. This, of course, serves to further weaken executive authority. It is no accident that in Britain the subject-matter committees that existed in the eighteenth and nineteenth centuries gradually disappeared, and that all governments today exhibit an unwillingness to restore them, even in very limited areas.[2]

If the system operates effectively in its peculiarly British manner, it is only because, tied in with all of this, are those informal agreements and attitudes that assume Parliament to be a body searching to discover and implement the general will of the community. A majority does not, as it could, ride roughshod over a minority, but, through informal channels, tries to arrange time-tables acceptable to all; and all governments, whatever the size of their majority, remain sensitive to minority desires. The symbol of this attitude is that continued cherishing of traditional procedures ('the dignified part of

---

[1] On developments in Britain see Kenneth Mackenzie, *The English Parliament* (London 1950); K. B. Smellie, *A Hundred Years of English Government* (New York 1951); C. S. Emden, *The People and the Constitution* (London 1933).

[2] Note the reaction of the present Government to the suggestion of a Select Committee that Parliament experiment with specialized committees: *The Economist*, 25 July 1959.

government,' to use Bagehot's delightful formulation) which never fails to delight American visitors and has always angered rising young radicals.[1]

The importance of the view that the state is a creative instrument whose function it is to serve the general will of the community, and that public servants have a duty to carry out this will is exemplified in the British bureaucracy. In the 1930's, when the Marxist view of history was popular, it was widely argued that the emergence of an efficient disciplined bureaucracy was tied in with the rise of the middle classes, and that if, in Britain, the bureaucracy had served several masters equally well, this was only because the masters were equally *bourgeois* parties.[2] At that time it was feared that the coming to power of a Labour government would entail a serious bureaucratic crisis. The fears did not, of course, materialize; the bureaucracy continued to serve different sets of masters with equal diligence.[3] Actually, the Marxist view was invalid in other respects as well. For example, the German bureaucracy, on which the British reforms of the mid-nineteenth century were based, was developed not by the *bourgeoisie* but by an aristocratic state. And in the United States the rise of middle-class democracy was associated initially with a complete loss of interest in the ideal of a bureaucratic apparatus consisting of competent men.

But pointing to the errors of the Marxist analysis does not tell us why the British so naturally developed a bureaucracy that combined effectiveness with objectivity. After all, in both France and Germany ideological differences did lead bureaucrats to subvert the governments with whose views they violently disagreed. Again, one cannot argue that it has been *simply* a matter of basic ideological consensus, for in the United States bureaucrats have found themselves in frequent conflict with administrations or Congressional edicts they did not like, and administrations still feel it necessary to replace top-level officials by members of their own party. Here too the difference between the United States and Britain is partly a consequence of divergent patterns of legislative–executive relationships. However, if middle-class reformers in Britain were, from the beginning, concerned with the development of an effective bureaucracy, it was, as

[1] And of course the young radicals, if re-elected often enough, generally come to cherish the tradition themselves, and are accused by a new generation of young radicals of having succumbed to the 'aristocratic embrace'. See, for example, David Kirkwood, *My Life of Revolt* (London, 1935).

[2] For a fairly typical statement of this view see J. D. Kingsley, *Representative Bureaucracy* (Yellow Springs, Ohio, 1944).

[3] See C. R. Attlee, 'Civil Servants, Ministers, Parliament and the Public', in *Political Quarterly*, vol. xxv (1954), pp. 308–15.

we have seen, because British liberals always felt the necessity for effective state action. And if they accepted the ideal of the 'gentleman' as the model of the bureaucrat, it was because they had, in part, internalized the values of the society they were changing. Finally, if in fact the British public has come to assume that Civil Servants will carry out political mandates with which they disagree, and if Civil Servants have accepted this image of themselves, it has been because of a general agreement underlying sharp political differences — an agreement that bureaucrats are the servants of a community interest transcending political conflict, and that their job is to translate the 'general will' of the community into effective action.[1]

To complete this discussion we can examine the symbols that serve as shorthand expressions of national unity. The symbols of American consensus, the founts at which we renew our faith, are the Declaration of Independence and the Constitution, documents that enshrine a set of abstract ideas — the 'liberal' view of the world. In Britain, on the other hand, the symbol of unity remains the monarchy and all the traditional paraphernalia that go with it. One may attack the monarchy because it fosters a class society, or because, as Keir Hardy and other early Labour Party militants contended, it is a 'stupid' archaic institution.[2] Or one may defend it because of its utility as a symbol or because it serves certain psychological needs. But its possible usefulness as a 'symbol' does not explain why it is a symbol, and the psychological needs it is sometimes said to fulfil (such as pageantry in a drab world) do not enable us to explain why Americans, who have similar needs, fulfil them in different ways. When all is said and done, neither defence nor attack explains the monarchy's continued attraction for the British people as a symbol of their nationality. It has no real ideological continuity with the past. At one time it was part of a certain kind of society in which it played an integral role, combining dignity with power. Today, like the smile on the Cheshire cat, only the dignity remains. Everyone knows that the prerogative of the monarchy is no more.

If the monarchy does not, like our Constitution, stand for a set of political ideas handed down from the past, what does it stand for? To raise the question in this way is to answer it. It represents the

---

[1] See F. M. Marx, *The Administrative State* (Chicago, 1957), p. 86. In Germany and France the members of the bureaucratic *élite* were also 'gentlemen' serving a 'creative' state; but they identified the 'real' state with their own preconceptions in communities that had been shattered by social and ideological upheavals (Germany under Weimar, and France throughout the nineteenth and the first half of the twentieth century).

[2] See Kingsley Martin, *The Magic of Monarchy* (New York, 1937).

British community *qua* community, not only at the present moment but in its total development. Thus the attachment to monarchy is a traditional attachment, in the Weberian sense. To be sure, the monarchy could not have survived had it not relinquished political power gracefully, that is, had it not been lifted out of the realm of politics; thus the actual fact of its survival may be, in part, the result of historical accident. However, the accident could not have occurred were it not for the cultural role the monarchy played and has continued to play.

The development of British social and political life has involved a uniquely British synthesis of traditional patterns and the forces that transformed them. The synthesis was possible not only because traditional British society was less 'sticky' than its counterparts elsewhere but because its patterns had taken on a national form before their transformation began. The result has been an organic community with its own peculiar political institutions. No wonder, then, as Aron points out in the quotation at the beginning of this essay, the British tend to regard their institutions as peculiarly their own, while both Americans and Frenchmen identify themselves with universal ideas applicable to all peoples.

CONSERVATISM, INDUSTRIALISM AND THE WORKING-CLASS TORY IN ENGLAND

By R. T. McKenzie and Allan Silver

PRIOR to the constitutional reforms of the nineteenth century, social deference was of fundamental importance in the political culture. Bagehot, writing at a time when franchise reform threatened to upset the traditional bases of authority, was greatly concerned with the question of whether the newly enfranchised industrial workers would or could be led to remain deferential towards the social classes who had traditionally provided political leaders. Nearly a century later, McKenzie and Silver have set out to reconsider the significance of deference in the working-class sub-culture by an historical and contemporary analysis. Because the authors combine the use of conventional historical materials with the use of survey data in order to study both past and present, their work is important on methodological as well as substantive grounds.

The Historical Context

SINCE 1886[1] there have been thirteen British elections which have produced a House of Commons in which a single party held a working majority of seats; and on eleven of these thirteen occasions it was the Conservative Party which found itself in this position. The most heavily — and longest — urbanized and industrialized electorate of any democracy has only twice returned a Parliament in which a party of the left has had a working majority.

The Conservative achievement is particularly striking if it is

---

[1] 1886 marks the beginning of modern electoral history in Britain since the Third Reform Act of 1884 and the redistribution of seats in 1885 carried the country almost the whole way to 'one *man* one vote' and 'one vote one value'. The Liberal Party won its only clearcut victory in 1906, although it was able to rule with the support of other parties after the election of 1892 and the two elections of 1910; Labour won its only working majority in 1945, although it formed minority governments in 1924 and 1929–31 and ruled briefly without a working majority in 1950–1.

This article is a revised version of a paper presented by the authors to the Fifth World Congress of the International Sociological Association (Washington, 1962). It is based upon a long work in progress.

recalled that the modern party was born after 1832 specifically of resistance to the idea of political equality and that it was, in its beginnings, largely out of sympathy with industrialism. In addition its leadership, always drawn overwhelmingly from the upper and upper-middle classes, has faced a preponderantly working-class electorate without the advantage of explicit religious support of the sort that has bolstered the right in the preponderantly Catholic countries of continental Europe.

What accounts for the Conservatives' success in holding power alone (or in Conservative-dominated coalitions) for three-quarters of the period since Britain became a political democracy? In part the answer lies in the fragmentation of the non-Conservative vote. At the beginning of the period the Liberals split in 1886 over Gladstone's proposals for Irish Home Rule and an important wing of the party entered what was to be a permanent alliance with the Conservatives. Meanwhile after 1900 the emergent Labour Party drained off working-class support for the Liberals; and when the latter were again racked by bitter quarrels during and after the First World War Labour was able to supplant the Liberals as the second party in the state. The Socialists, in turn, virtually fell apart in 1931; and again, twenty years later, after their only period of majority rule Labour became absorbed in internecine conflict which was to last for almost a decade. Meanwhile the Liberals, who had continued to poll a small but significant share of the electoral vote, began to re-gain marked public support (in by-elections at least) during the early 1960's. The Conservatives, although often deeply divided during the years since 1886, were a far more cohesive political force than their opponents on the left. Undoubtedly this was a major factor in enabling them to retain their parliamentary ascendency even though their share of the total votes cast in elections during the period 1886–1959 was no more than 47 per cent.

But Conservative electoral success in Britain is not solely or even primarily the consequence of the fissiparous tendencies of the British left (or of its political ineptitude, striking though that has been). A much more important consideration is the fact that the Conservatives have been one of the most successful of all right-wing parties in coming to terms with the political implications of industrialism and the 'age of democratic revolution'.[1] It can be argued that the true forerunners of modern sociology are those European conservatives

---

[1] For a perceptive analysis of the problems involved in the adjustment of western European political societies to these social and political changes see R. Bendix, 'The Lower Classes and the Democratic Revolution', *Industrial Relations*, vol. i, no. 1 (October 1961), pp. 91–116.

(like Burke in England, Bonald, de Maistre, and others on the
Continent) who were profoundly concerned about 'the poison of
social disintegration' which they saw flowing from the French
Revolution and the break-up of the old pre-industrial society.[1] They
became deeply concerned with the concept of order; they saw society
as an organic whole, not as a mere aggregate of individuals; they
stressed the interdependence of institutions, customs, and habits;
they argued that religion (and even folk beliefs and 'prejudices', in
Burke's terminology) acted as an 'emotional cement' within society.
Above all they insisted on the importance of a structured group life,
and an hierarchical social order in which each is assured of his status.

Certain of the more pessimistic (and frightened) continental Conservatives concluded that the answer to the problem of social dis-
organization raised by the industrial and democratic revolutions lay
with 'the Pope and the executioner'. But British Conservatives, who
could not rely on the Pope, were wise enough for the most part to
eschew the assistance of the executioner; they perceived that the
answer lay with the reinforcement of those institutions in British
society which would help to maintain cohesion and strengthen consensus in that society.[2]

The greatest of nineteenth-century British Conservative leaders,
Benjamin Disraeli, recognized as vividly as did his contemporary,
Karl Marx, the existence of 'the two nations' in nineteenth-century
industrial Britain. Disraeli and his followers of course rejected the
Marxist view that this division was the inevitable precursor of a
revolution out of which a new consensus would be established in a
classless society. But they also rejected the view of those Liberal
advocates of *laissez-faire* who were prepared to depend on the self-
regulating mechanisms of the market automatically to produce a
harmony of interests. Nor were they in the least attracted by the
doctrines of Social Darwinism.

The Conservatives accepted the inevitability of the class system
since they believed that it reflects the innate inequality of men. They
realized, however, that conflict was immanent in the worker–owner
relationship, and they therefore tried to redress the balance of interests when it shifted too far in the direction of the owners of
industry; hence their willingness to sponsor legislation recognizing
trade unions and governing the condition of work in factories. In

[1] The most recent exposition of this view is to be found in Leon Bramson, *The
Political Context of Sociology* (Princeton, 1961), chap. 1.

[2] It is not intended to suggest that the British Conservative Party was monolithic in its reactions to the political problems of industrialism; at many critical
periods there were acute internal tensions within the party between the advocates
of differing political strategies.

addition they, rather than the Liberals, took the initiative in bringing the urban masses within the pale of the constitution by the first major extension of the franchise to the urban working classes in 1867. But above all else the Conservatives under Disraeli's inspiration attempted to ally themselves with the forces of social cohesion within British society; they championed the monarchy and the system of 'orders' reflected in the peerage, religion, nationalism, and, towards the end of the century, imperialism — indeed, all the institutions and forces likely to eliminate domestic strife, to ensure stability, and to override sectional interests.

In what was perhaps the most important address ever made by a British Conservative leader, Disraeli in his Crystal Palace speech in 1872 declared that the fundamental purposes of Conservatism were to 'maintain the institutions of the country; to uphold the empire of England; and to elevate the condition of the people'.[1] With characteristic audacity Disraeli hereby claimed for his party a unique role as custodian of the national interest (as a contemporary Conservative publication puts it 'there is no textbook of Conservatism, except the history of Britain'); but Disraeli also demonstrated the wisdom of British Conservatism by coupling with the national appeal a concern for the welfare of the masses. This programme was to prove attractive not merely to the upper strata of British society but also to a large section of the working class which has remained unmoved by appeals to class solidarity even though, by sheer weight of electoral numbers, the working class has been in a position to control the levers of political power for the past eighty years.

From their earliest beginnings the Conservatives had been able to rely on the support of the 'squirearchy' and of a large part of 'the landed interest'; in addition, by the turn of the century they had become the acknowledged champions of the business community; and, with the decline of the Liberals, they were to inherit the preponderant part of the middle-class vote. But these sources of electoral support would not have enabled the Conservatives to maintain their parliamentary ascendancy had they not also been able to win and retain the support of a very considerable proportion of the working class, which from 1884 onwards represented two-thirds of the electorate. It would appear that at most elections the Conservatives have won about one-third of the working-class vote and that this working-class element has constituted about one-half the party's total electoral support.

The phenomenon of working-class Conservatism has long been a source of exasperation to the left in Britain. After the general election

---

[1] T. E. Kebbel (ed.), *Selected Speeches of the Earl of Beaconsfield*, vol. ii, pp. 530 ff.

of 1868 (following the passage of the Second Reform Act of 1867 which enfranchised a large proportion of the urban working class), Engels wrote to Marx:

What do you say to the elections in the factory districts? Once again the proletariat has discredited itself terribly. . . . It cannot be denied that the increase of working class voters has brought the Tories more than their simple percentage increase; it has improved their relative position.[1]

Ninety years and thirty-three elections later a considerable section of the proletariat was, in the view of the left, still 'discrediting itself terribly'. After the Labour Party's ejection from office in 1951, an official party publication brooded over the failure of universal suffrage to produce the expected result:

Once the mass of the people have the vote, Socialists were convinced that Conservatism and all that it stood for would be swept away. Their victory seemed certain for conservatism which was based on privilege and wealth was inevitably a minority creed, whereas socialism, with its appeal to social justice and economic self-interest, would recruit the big battalions of the poor and under-privileged, whom the vote would make the masters of political democracy. . . . Yet it is clear that events have falsified these pre-dictions. . . . The question which must now be asked is why the fruits of universal suffrage have taken so long to ripen. How is it that so large a pro-portion of the electorate, many of whom are neither wealthy or privileged, have been recruited for a cause which is not their own?[2]

One need not accept the assumptions underlying either of these quotations to recognize that working-class Conservatism has been a major factor in determining the distinctive pattern of modern British politics.

The Tory Worker Today

This section provides a very brief account of some findings from re-search undertaken by the present writers into the nature of con-temporary working-class Conservative allegiance in England. A sample survey undertaken in six urban constituencies — in London, Manchester, Halifax, and Coventry — yielded 604 working-class voters, including 178 Conservatives. The research was not concerned with the social psychological mechanisms of particular voting choices, nor with the effects of an electoral campaign, but rather with the relatively enduring conditions out of which party affiliations emerge under the pressures of events, issues, and propaganda.[3]

[1] *Karl Marx and Frederick Engels on Britain* (Moscow, 1953), pp. 499–500.
[2] Peter Shore, *The Real Nature of Conservatism*, Labour Party Educational Series No. 3 (September 1952).
[3] Field work was carried out during May–June 1958, a time of political quies-cence in Britain, and eighteen months before the subsequent general election.

Two kinds of approaches to the material were taken: straightforward comparisons of working-class Labour and Conservative voters, and internal analyses of the population of working-class Conservatives. In the former procedure, we ask what characteristics are associated with the frequency with which working-class electors vote Conservative. In the latter, we are less interested in the frequency of working-class Conservative voting, and more in the conditions and consequences of the social and ideological bases out of which this behaviour emerges.

The most general impression one gets from a comparison of Labour and Conservative working-class voters in this sample is of a prevailing homogeneity between the two groups. There is little difference between them in terms of sex, income, or occupational skill level, and only a moderate difference in terms of age. No comparable studies exist to provide a base line, but previous research does suggest that an earlier tendency for working-class Conservatives to be older and have lower incomes than Labour voters is disappearing, though the Conservatives are still somewhat older.

These aggregate results conceal some diverging trends: among the lower income group older voters more frequently vote Conservative than younger (Table 1); and, while age and sex separately are either

TABLE 1

Among working-class voters with below-average incomes, the older are more often Conservative than the younger

	Below-average incomes		Above-average incomes	
	Under age 44 %	Above age 44 %	Under age 44 %	Above age 44 %
Labour . .	83	63	71	70
Conservative .	17	37	29	30
N (= 100%)	72	162	150	102

moderately related or unrelated to voting Conservative, older working-class women vote Conservative with considerably more frequency than do other groups. We shall return to these findings later, in another context.

The political and social perspectives of Labour and Conservative working-class voters differ where one would expect them to — with respect to objects of partisan concern like the issue of nationalization, key power sources such as the trade unions, big business and the upper classes, and the parties themselves. Yet the differences are not such as to override an impression that Conservative values pervade much of the urban working class, including many Labour voters. There is, for example, a widespread dislike or distrust of trade unions: more than half of the entire sample agrees that unions have too much power. The unions are often perceived — even by working-class Labour voters — as unduly disruptive or officious; and there is a good deal of feeling that strikes are called too frequently, despite the far lower strike rate of Britain compared to that of the United States. The organic view of society, promulgated by the great Conservative spokesmen, Burke and Disraeli, finds a responsive echo in the contemporary urban working class. For such reasons, it is hard to think of working-class Conservatives in Britain as normatively deviant from working-class political culture; on the contrary, they seem to express aspects of a wide national consensus.

It is also difficult to think of working-class Conservatives as apathetic, ignorant, or alienated people — a kind of psychological *Lumpenproletariat*. Working-class Conservatism cannot, apparently, be ascribed to political pathology in ways analogous to the alleged link between the 'authoritarian personality' and clinical pathology. In fact, the working-class Conservatives in our sample tend to be better informed than the Labour voters in terms of political knowledge; somewhat more of them, to take but one example, knew the name of the Leader of the Labour Party. Furthermore, Conservative voters show no signs of a greater sense of political futility. In short, the Conservatives appear to be as well integrated as Labour voters into the political process in contemporary Britain.

Conservative working-class voters proved to be much more committed to their party in terms of a range of criteria than Labour voters. While Labour is widely perceived as more concerned with the interests of the common man, it is often seen as more solicitous than efficacious, while the Conservatives are widely seen as more efficacious than solicitous. In short, many working-class voters believe that the Conservatives have a capacity to get things done — a superior executive ability — which appears to offset their lesser concern with the class interests of manual workers.

'Concern for the interests of the common man' is almost the only criterion on which Labour is consistently ranked higher than the Conservatives. With respect to foreign policy, Commonwealth relations, national prosperity, and the sense of patriotism, the Conservatives are evaluated as far superior by Tory voters, and as almost the equal of or superior to Labour by Labour voters. In fact, Conservative voters in the working class appear to enjoy greater congruence between voting behaviour and broad perceptions of the parties than do Labour voters, who seem to be linked to Labour almost entirely in terms of class interest. In a political culture which values so highly the Burkean themes of consensus and national community, this suggests that working-class Conservatives may be under less ideological cross-pressure than Labour voters.

Let us turn from the analysis of working-class Conservative and Labour voters, to focus on the population of working-class Conservatives. Here, we can no longer rely upon the dichotomous choice situation imposed by a two-party system to provide the categories of analysis. Rather, it is necessary to develop analytic categories derived from the historical origins of working-class Conservatism in Britain.

Both Marx and Disraeli conceived working-class Conservatism to be based on what Walter Bagehot, in *The English Constitution*, called 'deference': the voluntary abnegation of power by the working class in favour of an hereditary, or quasi-hereditary *élite*. A reading both of Bagehot and of Conservative propaganda directed at the working class suggests the following set of characteristics of 'deferential' Conservatism:

1. Deferentials prefer ascribed, socially superior political leadership.
2. Deferentials prefer power to originate from the *élite*, rather than from the mass franchise.
3. Deferentials form and express political judgements in terms of the intrinsic characteristics of leaders, not pragmatically in terms of issues or the outcome of policy.
4. Deferentials view political outcomes benefiting the working class as indulgent or paternalistic acts by the *élite*, not as flowing from the machinery of government or the economy.
5. Deferentials prefer continuity to abrupt change.
6. Deferentials view the Conservative Party as more patriotic than the opposition.

We have also used a typological opposite to deference — perspectives which run counter to these traditional values; we called working-class voters with such outlooks 'seculars'. The question then becomes: are all, or almost all, working-class Conservatives 'deferentials' — as envisioned by observers so diversely committed as Marx, Bagehot, and Disraeli? If not, what are the conditions and consequences of these two kinds of working-class Conservatism?

It is necessary to illustrate at least the single most important criterion used to define deference and secularism. We asked respondents to explain their choice for prime minister as between two

men — one of them the son of a banker and M.P., a graduate of
Eton and Oxford, and an officer in the Guards; the other, the son of
a lorry-driver who went to a grammar school, won a scholarship to a
provincial university, entered the Army as a private and was promoted to officer rank. We have, then, caricatured but not unrealistic pictures of ascribed, *élitist* leadership and of achieved
leadership of working-class origin. A few quotations will give the
flavour of the distinctions made possible by this procedure.

Deferential responses: (Respondent prefers son of M.P.) 'Because
he should have the brains or instincts of parents. The qualities
to make a prime minister are in the breeding. When it comes to
critical questions like whether the country should go to war you want
someone with a good headpiece who knows what he's doing. It's
born in you.'

'The M.P.'s son. Breeding counts every time. I like to be set an
example and have someone I can look up to. I know the other man
has got a long way on his own merits, and I do admire that, but
breeding shows and is most important in that position.'

Secular responses: (Respondent prefers lorry-driver's son.) 'He has
struggled in life. He knows more about the working troubles of the
ordinary person. Those who inherit money rarely know anything
about real life. This man has proved he is clever and can achieve
something without any help from others.'

'Either of them because it depends upon their individual ruling
ability.'

Using this criterion alone, it was possible to compare working-
class voters for the two parties. Deference is considerably more
common among Conservative than Labour voters. Half of Conservatives, but only one-fifth of Labour voters, preferred the prime
minister of *élite* social origin. It seems that deferential perspectives
continue to sustain the Conservatism of very many working-class
voters in contemporary urban England.

When we look for social differences between these two ideological
kinds of working-class Conservatives, the factors of age, sex, and
income that failed to discriminate or do so decreasingly between
Labour and Conservative voters, come to life: deferentials strongly
tend to be older than seculars and to have lower incomes; and there
is a marked, but lesser tendency for fewer women than men to be
seculars. In so far as youth and higher incomes are linked to post-war
social change — to which women can be thought of as socially less

exposed than men — secularism may be displacing deference as an ideological basis of working-class Conservatism in Britain. It is not possible, however, definitively to establish this conclusion by means of observations at one point in time. Moreover, the themes and motifs of traditional, hierarchical Conservatism — so richly available in British culture — may well be available for resuscitation under the impact of future events.

Some political attitudes of deferentials and seculars diverge. Seculars, for example, are less often unconditionally committed to the Conservative Party: almost all the deferentials, but only half the seculars, said that they would definitely vote Conservative in an imminent hypothetical election — a result obtained long before the pressures of the campaign, and of the necessity for choice, precipitated long-standing loyalties. There is a moderate, but consistent tendency for seculars to be more frequently 'leftist' on a variety of issues and judgements. There is considerable evidence to suggest that seculars are more concerned with social mobility: many more of them than deferentials endorse a complaint that it is 'too hard for a man with ambition to get ahead in Britain'. Finally, seculars seem to be more sensitized to economic deprivation: among low income working-class Conservatives (but not those with high incomes) seculars are much more likely to identify with the working class than are deferentials (Table 2).

TABLE 2

Among working-class Conservatives with below-average incomes, seculars are more likely than deferentials to identify with the working class

Class Identification	Below-average Incomes			Above-average Incomes		
	Deferential %	Mixed %	Secular %	Deferential %	Mixed %	Secular %
Working class .	58	70	89	77	73	73
Middle class .	34	21	11	23	13	21
Other, don't know .	8	9	..	..	14	6
* $N (= 100\%)$	26	24	18	13	15	34

* The income of 48 of the chief wage-earners was not ascertained.

Keeping in mind that deferentials are considerably older than seculars, we can now suggest why, as we have reported, low income has a conservatizing effect among older working-class voters, but seems to move younger ones in the direction of Labour. Low income may be tolerated by deferential Conservatives and, indeed, experienced as calling for increased reliance upon the traditional *élite*. But for seculars, low income may represent a severe strain upon their commitment to the Conservative Party — a commitment based upon pragmatic rather than traditional grounds. The political impact of low income, then, depends on the values and perspectives upon which party loyalty is based. Analogous reasoning may account for the uniquely high level of Conservative voting among older, working-class women: both their age and sex combine to leave them relatively unexposed to 'secularization' among Conservative voters; hence, they are less able to withdraw support from the traditional *élite*.

We can also suggest why the typical correlates of working-class rightist voting — age, sex, and income — do not obtain, or are decreasing, in contemporary Britain. We are, perhaps, witnessing a shift from the politicized ethos of earlier working-class protest to what has been called the 'post-political' age. In the earlier context, traditionalist ideologies like deference were linked, in the working class, to low income (among unskilled rural migrants from traditional backgrounds), to women (relatively insulated from change), and to the older (who had been socialized into traditional values); hence, these characteristics in turn were often linked to 'rightist' voting. But as working-class Conservatism is stabilized in Britain on the basis of ideologies more appropriate to industrial culture, like secular Conservatism, the earlier empirical correlations between working-class rightist voting and these attributes begin to diminish.

Does this mean that something like Jacksonian, or more generally egalitarian, perspectives are emerging in the working-class electorate? Not necessarily. Even in the United States, as Robert Lane has suggested, inegalitarian values have important functions for the industrial working class.[1] And, as Gabriel Almond has argued, traditional elements in modern political culture can be seen not as deviant, anachronistic, or atavistic, but as serving critically important expressive and symbolic purposes.[2] Where would these things be more likely to persist than in the peculiarly and triumphantly mixed political culture of Britain, in which traditional themes bear so close a relationship to the very sense of nationality?

The data contain other suggestions as to the future of working-

---

[1] R. E. Lane, 'The Fear of Equality', *American Political Science Review*, vol. liii, no. 1 (March 1959), pp. 35–51. See also his *Political Ideology* (New York, 1962), pp. 57–81.

[2] G. Almond and J. Coleman, *The Politics of the Developing Areas* (Princeton, 1960), pp. 20–5.

class deference. For example, as younger working-class Conservative voters appear to move away from deference — at least for the present — younger Labour voters do not; indeed, they may be moving towards it. Thus, proportionately more younger than older Conservatives prefer the lorry-driver's son as prime minister, but somewhat more younger than older Labour voters prefer the candidate of *élite* social origin (Table 3). It is possible that, while secu-

TABLE 3

Older working-class voters are more likely than younger to prefer a prime minister of élite social origin among Conservative voters, but not among Labour voters

Prefers Prime Minister of	Labour Voters		Conservative Voters	
	Under age 44 %	Above age 44 %	Under age 44 %	Above age 44 %
Working-class origin . .	70	80	54	39
Élite origin .	27	17	40	53
Neither, don't know .	3	3	6	8
N (= 100%)	207	218	65	113

larism is 'modern' for working-class Conservatives it is less so for Labour voters. It is as if deferential predispositions among working-class voters for both major parties are converging towards a common level.

It may be, then, that as recent social change in Britain — expanded working-class horizons, improved access to education, higher incomes, the slow erosion of class boundaries — is diluting deference among Conservatives, the resulting greater integration of the working class into British society is confronting Labour voters with traditional themes to which they had previously been unexposed or hostile. Such themes, deference among them, may in the Britain of the future begin to lose their intimate connection with the Conservative Party and become more than ever norms for the good citizen, regardless of party loyalty. Indeed, the data show that the connection between deference and Conservative voting is far stronger among older than among younger workers (Table 4). Thus deference may be declining among Conservative working-class voters, increasing or maintaining itself among Labour voters, and thus becoming less factional and more consensual among the working-class electorate.

At the moment, however, it appears that post-war social change in

IS A PRICK

TABLE 4

Deference is more closely linked to Conservative voting among older than younger working-class voters, regardless of income

	Below-average Income				Above-average Income			
	Under age 44		Above age 44		Under age 44		Above age 44	
Prefers Prime Minister of	Élite origin (deferential) %	Working-class origin (secular) %	Élite origin (deferential) %	Working-class origin (secular) %	Élite origin (deferential) %	Working-class origin (secular) %	Élite origin (deferential) %	Working-class origin (secular) %
Labour . .	70	86	36	76	64	75	48	81
Conservative .	30	14	64	24	36	25	52	19
N (= 100%)	19	51	47	105	44	95	33	63

urban Britain has acted less dramatically to change the frequency with which working-class electors vote Conservative than to shift the social and ideological basis of working-class Conservative allegiance from the older and poorer to the younger and better-paid, from deferentials to seculars. The Conservative Party is well prepared by its history to cope with this change. But one hundred years after the Reform Act of 1867, the decline of deference among working-class Conservatives sharpens the party's need to attract the increasingly prosperous descendants of the Victorian working-men whom Disraeli and his followers enfranchised.

Five years after that reform, Bagehot, fearing the domination of the 'poor ignorant people', saw deference as crucial to 'the happy working of a delicate experiment'.[1] As working-class Conservatives come to include fewer of the poor and the deferential, the shape of the party's relationship to its working-class voters remains to be clarified by time, research, and the course of events.

[1] *The English Constitution* (introduction to the 2nd edn., 1872), Fontana Library (London, 1963), p. 275.

PORTRAIT OF THE LABOUR PARTY

By EGON WERTHEIMER

LABOUR and Socialist parties are a common phenomenon of modern European states. Among these, the British Labour Party has been unusual historically in its readiness to work within the broad traditions of the political culture; it is also unusual historically in its relative freedom from Marxist influences which have formed within the working class of some countries a sub-culture in fundamental conflict with the dominant political culture. Egon Wertheimer, a German Social Democratic journalist stationed in London, published a remarkable study of the Labour Party in 1929, specifically contrasting the cultural outlook of British Socialists with their German counterparts. The excerpts reprinted below show how Wertheimer ingeniously linked his generalizations about cultural attitudes to detailed considerations of political and social institutions. Although some of the author's remarks refer to practices no longer characteristic of the Labour Party, they are important to recall because relevant to an understanding of the development of a political culture free from the conflicts which have divided the left in Germany, France, and Italy in this century.

IN *substance*, British socialism differs on one important point from the socialism of the rest of the world. So far as can be gathered from the authoritative statements on the subject, British socialism will regard its main task as fulfilled when the transfer of the means of production to the ownership and control of the community (that is, when a radical change in the distribution of income) has been effected. It appears to be prepared to acknowledge the old traditional distribution of work, within the framework of the capitalist machine, between the organizers and directors of the apparatus of production, on the one hand, and manual workers with no direct influence on the direction, on the other, provided that the former capitalist monopoly of education is abolished and equal opportunities to rise are thus guaranteed to all young people. In other words, its aim is not to alter the position of the individual worker in the productive process

Reprinted from *Portrait of the Labour Party* (London: G. P. Putnam's Sons, 1929), pp. 89-95, 111-19, 135-50.

but merely to sweep away the dividend hunter, and to afford every gifted schoolchild the chance of obtaining the education necessary to qualify for posts as managers and organizers.

The Marxian socialism of the Continent, on the contrary, regards it as one of its chief tasks to alter the relationship of the individual workman to the productive process in which he participates; that is to say, within his factory or works. It does not, therefore, stop at an alteration in the organization of property and the distribution of wealth as such but seeks, directly and indirectly, to secure for the individual worker an increased influence on production in the industry in which he is employed. The struggle for the works council as a first step towards this change in the position of the worker within industry is the external expression of this side of continental socialism. From it continental socialism derives one of its strongest psychological impulses. It is curious to find that British socialism (especially since the collapse of the guild socialist movement) seems to have relegated entirely to the background this psychologically important element of the socialist system of the rest of the world. This is particularly evident in the remarkable abandonment of the works council movement in Great Britain.

If the Birmingham programme is compared with those issued latterly by the continental parties, and in particular with the Social Democratic 'Heidelberg' programme, one point of difference apart from fundamental theoretical divergences positively leaps to the eye. The continental programmes, almost without exception, contain a certain group of demands, not in themselves socialistic but which for historical and sociological reasons have formed a kind of chemical affinity with the Labour movement. Under this heading come all that series of cultural demands which have their being in the consciousness of a conflicting socialist and capitalist morality and which turn on problems of sex, the prevailing marriage laws, and the relation of Church and State. Even the Heidelberg programme, which touches upon these matters with a certain reserve, contains clauses demanding disestablishment of the Church, co-education of both sexes, and removal of the stigma of illegitimacy. And in addition to the points explicitly touched upon in programmes, in all continental socialist parties there is a widespread tacit agreement on the necessity for a change in attitude towards questions of contraception, interruption of pregnancy, and revision of medieval legislation on homosexuality, etc.

Here, more than upon any other point, the difference between the continental and British Socialist parties becomes apparent, and the close connection of British Labour with British national culture and tradition revealed. Otto Bauer, in the 'Marxian Studies', has classified a process in a certain stage of working-class evolution which, owing to special circumstances, has been operative in the British movement from its very beginnings. 'Just as the working-class in any country', he wrote, 'in approaching power must adapt the methods and practices of their struggle to the special peculiarities of the national terrain, so must its theories, as they take in more and more culture be coloured by its national culture.' This close affinity of the Labour Party with traditions of national culture has been especially favoured by the circumstances of its tardy birth, the lack of a class-struggle ideology, and a historical period of conflict with state and society. Separated by no class barriers from the mental and spiritual concepts of capitalism, which would otherwise have given birth to an exclusively proletarian way of life and morality, and deep-rooted in national religious tradition, the Labour Party has never been able to make a clean breakaway from capitalist culture. The widespread religious non-conformity of the working class and close affinity with the Puritan traditions of the dissenting churches, militated effectively against the rise of any radical proletarian culture. In the words of a young American Socialist writer, the average English Labour Party member would be no less indignant at the attitude of the continental socialist towards religious questions than the average Anglican bishop!

The formation of a common cultural front between the Labour Party and continental socialism is therefore only feasible within very narrow limits. And it is by no means the case, as is so frequently believed on the Continent, that the divergency of the two attitudes on these cultural questions is due merely to expediency on the part of the Labour Party, an expediency dictated by electoral necessities and the desire to present the least possible vulnerability of front to attacks that must inevitably be delivered in a strongly puritanical country. The indignant disgust which the attitude of continental women socialists towards legalization of abortion aroused should have opened the eyes of many who believed these differences merely superficial or tactical. Those who participated in the International Women's Conference in Brussels will still remember the veiled but unmistakable condemnation uttered by Dr. Marion Phillips, speaking in the name of the Women's Organisations of the British Labour Party. The attitude prevalent among continental women socialists towards 'compulsory motherhood,' she pointed out, would arouse the greatest opposition among the women of Great Britain, and the whole idea would only wound and outrage their tenderest sensibilities.

For the continental the most illuminating (and I trust to be forgiven if I say entertaining) light shed upon this very subject was the discussion published in the autumn of 1928 in the *New Leader*, that always interesting organ of the I.L.P. An anonymous author, writing under the pseudonym '27', delivered himself with terrific emphasis in a series of articles on the collapse of puritanism among the new generation, the dangers of sexual abstinence, and the justification of extra-marital sex experience, etc. '27', evidently fired with convert enthusiasm by first contact with crude psycho-analytical conclusions long regarded as *vieux jeu* on the Continent, gave triumphant vent to commonplaces rendered rather comic by their overstatement. The general trend of his case represented what has long been common opinion among continental socialists, but here in England a socialist clergyman joined in the discussion with every sign of horror and indignation. A mother of a family wrote and described how she had been compelled secretly to destroy the current copy before it made appearance at the family breakfast table, and another letter, bearing every evidence of emanation from a panel doctor's consulting-room, bore an eloquent medical plea for pre-marital chastity. Another letter to the editor made no bones about the fact that such moral bolshevism could only bode the direst consequences for the political fate of the Labour Party.

Here yawns most ominously and evidently the deep gulf that divides British and continental Socialism, but to clear away all possibilities of misunderstanding it must be stated that among the younger generation of Socialists, not only in Germany and Austria but also in France, there are strong signs of a neo-puritanical movement which is perhaps one of the most interesting phenomena to be observed at the present moment in the development of continental socialism.

Generally speaking, it can be stated with all certainty that opinions such as those published by '27' are by no means in accord with those of either organized Labour or its leaders in Britain. British Labour and its leaders are essentially Puritan. Such statements, so far as they can be regarded as a definite tendency, are not representative of an individual party but rather of a certain section of the new generation, although British public opinion may not be prepared to admit this as a fact. On the contrary, the foreign observer can better imagine the Liberal Party, even though we underestimate its Nonconformist prejudices, as champion of these concepts than the Labour Party. To generalize, in comparison with the Marxist socialism of continental parties, the Labour Party in cultural questions is a neutral, not to say conservative, body.

*   *   *

D

All observers of the British Labour movement in the last quarter of the nineteenth century are agreed that its specific form of organization represented a departure from continental development. In the year 1899 it was not a question of choice between federal organization or individual membership but between federal organization and the existence of a Labour Party. This opinion of all historians of British socialism would seem to be confirmed by the failure of every attempt on the part of the Social Democratic Federation and the Independent Labour Party to build up a large national organization on a basis of individual membership.

However this might be, with the founding of the Labour Representation Committee there came into being that form of organization which remained in the main unaltered during the next two decades, until it began in 1918 to approximate more closely to the continental form. If on the one hand the federative structure of the Labour Party emanates directly from the character of the Labour Party as an electoral machine, then this exterior feature at the same time reacts on the further destiny of Socialism in England. Here, and I think for the first time, an attempt is made to show what special and particular influence the form of Labour Party organization has had upon the spiritual and intellectual development of the party and its consequences for the political life of Great Britain.

To understand the special and peculiar form taken by Labour Party organization, it is necessary to compare the divergent methods adopted, in each case for very practical reasons, in building up the Social Democratic Party in Germany and the Labour Party in Great Britain. One difference is immediately striking. The German party grew from its local parties and district units. The whole organization had its basis in these cells, and from these it drew its whole strength. Herein lies the secret of German Social Democratic power, a power which the political opponents of German socialism have never been able to understand during times when, to their amazement, its strength has remained unimpaired despite severe trials and inner crises. The present-day character of 'paying-in' night, the monthly meeting of the smallest party unit, is by no means disproof of this contention, although it has largely lost its original vitality, and has degenerated into empty routine.

In contrast to the German party, the British started life as a federal organization, to which the large trade-union groups and Socialist societies were affiliated collectively. These groups did not relinquish their own identity on affiliation. They preserved their own form, function, and tradition intact, and the life of the larger party found its greatest expression within their confines. In other words, a trade-union branch meeting differed only from the meeting of a local Labour Party in the latter's agenda. Until 1918 the local trade-union branches and the constituent socialist organizations provided the only common meeting-places for Labour Party members.

It is quite clear that this divergence of organization has had much influence on the outlook and mentality of the members of the two national parties. The continental worker's membership was the outcome of a personal decision. From the moment of registration the party organization surrounded him with a whole series of duties and obligations, demanded certain services from him and, to a certain extent, determined his mode of life. Were he at all an active member, his own personal, spiritual, and extra-vocational freedom became the more curtailed. The party absorbed the greater part of his private life. It did not stop at that point where the individual ceases to be solely a political entity but penetrated into his cultural existence, organized him in musical societies and workers' choirs, placed an educational apparatus at his disposal, determined his reading and his mental outlook, through the party library, and obliged him to subscribe to party newspapers. Nor was he free in his sporting associations. He must join, if so inclined at all, workers' sports clubs.

By all these threads he was bound to a common group life which offered him that happiness which comes from participation in a community of interests, and, in so far as he was an organized manual worker, enriched his life with an intensity of experiences before unknown. His entry into the party had a decisive reality that did not fail to influence every aspect of his life.

The virtues of this form of organization for the intellectual and for those who enter the socialist movement from the ranks of the middle and upper classes are rather problematical. In the period before the war more than now, entry into the party meant not only a rupture with all his social connections, but, in many cases, of all close association with his non-socialist professional colleagues.

His conviction and devotion to socialist faith and ideals, especially if they are not fired by political ambitions, are subjected to a severer test than the worker's. The worker entering the party, accepting its programme and thus acknowledging the class struggle, finds himself sharing in a common life of which he approves instinctively, and which satisfies more than his purely material and political interests. The organization is flesh of his flesh and spirit of his spirit.

The socialist coming from the capitalist ranks finds his acknowledgement of the class struggle opposed not only to his interests, but also to his instincts. The atmosphere of the party is not congenial.

But his convictions are stronger than his instincts, and he is determined to maintain loyally the change in outlook which his entry into the party involves. There is bitter conflict with the family and social circle in which he formerly moved, and to avoid social boycott he must sever all connection with it. Only in cases where he has chosen politics as a career does the group life of the party offer recompense for that which he has lost. In contrast to the attitude of the British Labour Party towards its intellectuals, he meets mistrust and coolness, for unlike the British, the continental Labour movement lacks entirely any belief in the inborn superiority of the upper classes. Far too often it has seen the ruling class fail at decisive moments; too often it has seen its own forecasts confirmed by the tide of events. The term 'our betters' has no place in the phraseology of the continental working-man.

The situation in Great Britain is quite different. Entry into the Labour Party, at least until 1927, followed as a matter of course for all trade unionists (and therefore the majority of the party membership) not as the result of an individual decision but following upon a majority decision of the union, sometimes taken years before. Membership is therefore most frequently only an attribute of loyalty to the union, and by no means the result of personal inner conviction as on the Continent. In addition, the union remains the chief centre, and party life is merely a reflection of union life. For some 98 per cent the party represents nothing more definite to the trade unionists who compose it than an outside body which appeals to him at election times. The party does not make any extra-political demands upon its members. Here and there they may be united in workmen's clubs and choirs, but these are not the result of systematic organization on the part of headquarters. Here and there attempts have been made to give sport a definite working-class complexion, as on the Continent, but usually this has been shown to be impracticable, nor is it deemed desirable by the majority of socialist leaders. That sport, for instance, can be a matter of class division is an idea foreign to the average English socialist. Party membership for the overwhelming majority in Great Britain represents nothing more in the way of personal obligation than his passive acceptance of the obligation to pay the political levy and to vote (if he chooses, which he does not always choose) for Labour candidates. It makes no moral demands on the private life of the individual.

In these circumstances the position of the intellectual in the Labour Party is much simpler than on the Continent. On joining the Fabian Society or the I.L.P. — the usual procedure until 1918 — he needed to make no acknowledgement of the class war, and was

therefore under no moral obligation to break off all his social connections. His private life remained his own affair, and he was thus
spared all those problems of conscience which afflict the continental
middle-class socialist.

That passion for justice, which gives to British socialism its main
characteristic, lays only a very indefinite and general moral obligation on his shoulders. It is to be admitted that the very facility which
attends their entry into the Labour Party and the few demands either
of soul or body that are made upon them, renders the absorption of
the upper-class recruits into the life of the party far less real than on
the Continent. In many cases their private life and the cause they
have at heart stand in glaring contradiction, and the press has not
failed to capitalize the fact by repeated attacks on the 'millionaire'
members of the Labour Party. But, as on the Continent, these
attacks seem to produce greater effect on the Liberals and Conservatives than on the workers.

*   *   *

EDITOR'S NOTE: Wertheimer's discussion of different types of
middle- and upper-class recruits to the ranks of Labour politicians
concludes thus:

It is not intended here to analyse the subjective motives that have
led certain members of the aristocracy to transfer their affection to
Labour: suffice it to say that these may not always have been purely
idealist; rather, shall we say, a certain personal vanity that felt itself
circumscribed and frustrated within the older parties, unfulfilled
ambition, or political adventurousness may all have played their
part, not to mention what Trotsky has termed 'the attraction of
power'.

It would, however, be unjust to judge the problem on the personal
merits or demerits of these few. The motives mentioned above may
either consciously or unconsciously influence these men in their
profession of socialist faith, but they provide no satisfactory explanation of the phenomenon. Those who are really representative have
entered the Labour Party as a body for reasons which cannot be
egoistic. The majority have been keenly aware of the injustice of the
present system of ownership and distribution of power, and have
been imbued with the chivalrous wish to help the underdog, to aid
the weak in their struggle against the powerful and mighty. This
impulse has ever found individual champions in the British ruling
class, and has always been an honourable tradition among a small
minority. This, together with that aspect of the national character,

a readiness for compromise that is almost second nature, explains much in the history of Great Britain that must otherwise remain a mystery. Neither the history of Great Britain itself, nor the reception accorded to these aristocratic converts on their admission to the Labour Party, can be grasped if these factors are overlooked. Possibly if the impulse is regarded objectively there is a certain amount of patronage that could be detected in this impulse: a variation on the theme of 'Ich Dien' which serves the Prince of Wales for his motto — last survival of the feudal outlook. It would be interesting not only to examine the connection between the Labour Party and liberal radicalism, to whose inheritance the Labour Party has succeeded, but also to inspect the paths that lead from British conservatism to British socialism. But more important still is to try and visualize what the English working class itself sees in this accession of un-accustomed aristocratic strength. There is here a definite contrast with the continental attitude. The party statutes on the Continent preclude any outsiders or recruits such as these from any effective participation in the party councils and policy. To obtain a nomina-tion to the party conference three years' ordinary membership must be served; a parliamentary candidate must have five years' or-ganized service in the German Social Democratic Party. Further he must overcome mistrust and endure slights, be jealously supervised and often deliberately superseded. This has the result that certain men of strong personality with socialistic tendencies either fail to find their way into the party ranks, or, because of the obstacles that are set them, are forced to leave them. Often only the weakest person-alities have the necessary patience and desire to pursue their humble way in the continental parties, a fact which their present weak leadership reflects to a certain extent. In the years 1918 and 1919 this was clearly visible. The sudden overthrow of the monarchy, and with it the revelation of the hollowness of all that it had before made sacred, led thousands of capable men from the middle and upper classes into the Social Democratic Party, thus opening up the world of socialist thought to all. No use was made of them, nor was any attempt made to consolidate their loyalty by making them delegates and M.P.s. Party traditions were too rigid to adapt themselves to this new situation with any effectiveness. Continental socialism frittered away its one and only great opportunity, and in so doing suffered its greatest defeat.

In contrast with Germany, in England the party machinery and the affection of the rank and file were tendered them with every cordiality. All technical difficulties that lay in their path were smoothed and — or so it appeared to the foreigner — candidatures were offered them with an excessive timidity and a timid excessiveness. Compared with the Continent, they met with no obstacles. In the circumstances the lack of opportunity for the young and rising man in the Labour Party stated for a fact by a young Conservative in *The Times* correspondence columns seems highly improbable.

A variety of motives have led to their acceptance on the part of the workers themselves. In Great Britain, more than in any other country, there is a strong element of what might be termed proletarian snobbery. The number of workers, organized in trade unions and owing political allegiance to the Labour Party, who feel themselves rather flattered by the presence of members of the ruling class in their midst must run into hundreds of thousands. A certain amount of moral responsibility for this lies at the door of the yellow and illustrated press circulating in millions among the working class, which has aroused this condition of mind by its insistence on interest in its columns of society gossip and twaddle. For the foreigner the columns devoted to this form of social activity even among papers with an exclusively working-class and *petit-bourgeois* circulation is a thing calculated to arouse astonishment. And especially as to him it must appear that they are not concerned with the doings of the real aristocracy but with the vulgarities of the plutocracy. Into this category fall the extreme interest and excitement which the nuptials of high society seem to arouse among the masses. The spectacle presented by a queue, formed almost exclusively of working-class women, braving wind and rain to catch a glimpse of bride and bridegroom as they emerge from the portals of a West End church and enhancing the glamour of a rather ridiculous parade of vanity, is among the most peculiar that ever strikes the foreigner in London. It must ever remain for him impossible to reconcile the great measure of self-respect possessed by the British working class, a self-respect which cannot fail to strike him, with this tenderly wistful interest in the vacuous doings of the upper ten thousand.

In the second half of the nineteenth century there were similar phenomena to be observed on the Continent. In Vienna, for instance, the proletariat took tremendous interest, not in the marriages, but in the funerals of the great ones of the earth. The arrival of the socialist parties, their powerful press and their ceaseless propaganda, at last knocked the shamefulness and ridiculousness of this attitude into the heads of the working class and actually made their realization of it the touchstone of their proletarian culture. Possibly the continued existence of this proletarian snobbery in England is due to the fact that there is no clear dividing line between the mental and spiritual outlook of the working class and the *bourgeoisie*, a division rendered a matter of course to the workers on the Continent by Marxist teaching. On the Continent any worker showing interest in the social round would be certain to be found in a non-socialist party. In England loyalty to the Labour Party has nothing to do with these reactions and display, if at least unconscious, of lack of class pride.

This state of mind, however interesting a phenomenon to the foreign observer, is no more a decisive factor in the fate of the upper class members of the Labour Party than is their egotistic motive. Far more important is the degree of class trust aroused by the 'under-dog' tradition observed by a certain section of the ruling class in a way impossible in any other country outside England. This trust is extended far more definitely and spontaneously to the recruits from the landed aristocracy than to those from the industrial capitalist class. The British working class trust the country gentleman far more than the descendant of the manufacturing capitalist, but even these latter have affinities which would be unthinkable on the Continent. In many cases personal animosities have been tempered by worship at the same chapel. Nonconformity has often given worker and master a common interest; the Anglican Church until recent times was too representative of the ruling class to form a basis for mutual trust. The worker worshipping in the same dissenting chapel with the pious son of a Nonconformist manufacturing family, avowing the same strict puritanism and seeing in his master's home the same moral discipline and way of life that material necessity imposed upon his own, felt bound to him by spiritual ties whose strength must not be underestimated. The Quakers, alone among the capitalists of the world, have succeeded in observing a 'double loyalty' — loyalty to their own immediate interests and to the interests of their workers. And it must not be forgotten that a great part of the lack of a social revolutionary impulse in the British working class during the last fifty years has only been made possible by the tact of the ruling class. Their higher standard of life, their luxuries have never been flaunted in the faces of the working class as in many continental countries. Here are meant the real upper and middle class and not certain of the *nouveaux riches*, whose extravagant vulgarity vies with that of any ruling class in Europe. The manufacturers of Bradford, for decades the 'millionaire' city of England, during the last half of the nine-teenth century, lived as modestly as their 'hands' and avoided any parade of pomp or circumstance that might serve to rouse and wound their local workers. And this was not due to mere cant and hypocrisy as continental critics are pleased to imagine, but had its origin in a real discipline; the 'millionaires' of Bradford preferred to abjure luxury rather than challenge the poverty of their workers. The tact of the English propertied classes is as much responsible for the ineffectiveness of the class-struggle theory in England as the extravagance and profligacy and lack of any human fellow-feeling with the worker among the Russian aristocracy and upper classes before the war for the cruelties and atrocities of the Bolshevik revolution.

Judging the phenomenon of middle- and upper-class converts to Labour as a whole, it must not be forgotten that the Labour Party is following an old tradition. Contrary to continental usage, change of party in England, even though the selfish motive be but thinly veiled, has never been regarded as immoral. The interlopers, not only those whose idealist motives could not be misinterpreted but even the praetorians with fingers itching for the fattest plum, met with a certain amount of consideration on entering the party. The British worker believes to have learned from the history of centuries that he may expect no less valuable service for his cause from the careerist than from the just and upright. The careerist is no new phenomenon in English politics. Since the time of the notorious 'Gentleman Wilkes' who, in spite of his doubtful character, rendered unquestionable service to the lowest classes, they have flourished in dozens. Disraeli is not the least among them, nor is Lord Birkenhead, a man whose abilities seem ridiculously overrated in England. All these careerists and political adventurers having given valuable service to Empire, Great Britain, and their parties, the English are not inclined to inquire too closely into motives. Here, as in other aspects of political life, the Labour Party is following an old tradition.

In addition to a general respect of the upper classes, a whole series of impulses and motives accounts for the hearty welcome accorded these newcomers by the party. A desire for fresh blood (one wholly foreign to the rapidly stagnating continental movement) ensured them rapid popularity. This may be taken as the expression of the healthy instinct of a healthy organism seeking an antidote against the dangers of autoparalysis and the conviction that these men possess qualities indispensable in the present phase of the party's development. It feels — of course never consciously in the mass of members — that with the rise of the party to place as official Opposition and alternative Government a new type of official is necessary for certain new functions in place of the agitator and organizer within the party. It is the conviction that proletarian conditions within a dominant capitalist society are not fitted or likely to produce the administrator, the 'governing' type, capable of thought and action on a grand scale. Their presence at the political and diplomatic helm serve to increase confidence and raise the party's prestige.

But perhaps the decisive factor was that which urged it in the present phase, where Labour finds itself confronted for the first time by the realities of government, to limit itself to secure first steps rather than embark upon unlimited experiment with unskilled hands. The psychological processes of the Labour Party, directing its energies to the point immediately attainable, find here their full reflection and contrast to the continental Labour movement.

The alternatives facing both movements were exactly the same — either to surmount the situation with leaders of their own class, with men whose abilities, apart from the leaders of the great trade unions, had only been proved within narrow limits or to promote the new-comers to immediate leadership regardless of length of party service.

These alternatives automatically confront any Labour movement on its rise to parliamentary power. Alone in the world and without any hesitation, the British Labour Party chose the latter; and this the more surprisingly as no other movement is so heavily laden with trade-union influence, usually inimical to the intellectual. In con-trast to their continental colleagues, the British workers feel that it is more advantageous for socialism's fate in this decade to make use of men born with an understanding of tradition and a ruthless will to power than to limit their choice to men of their own class who have not had the advantages of education in the ruling class.

This point of view was easily discernible in the 1928 Birmingham Conference, where not only were two newcomers elected to the Party Executive but the entire discussion on foreign politics given over to their speeches. For the foreigner accustomed to an executive's animosity displayed to any interloper who has not twenty-five years' party service, this debate was astonishing. George Lansbury, the old class warrior and most endearing figure among all the English left and by whose side a man like Cook cuts a pitiful figure — it was Lansbury himself who gave the Mosleys, Kenworthys, Bakers, and Wedgwood Benns free rein. The old champion of the British working class and of society's outcasts let these men take the field in a body as though he, and with him the whole conference, wished to show England that liberalism and conservatism had no longer the sole monopoly of Oxford and Cambridge men.

Generally speaking the moment was favourable for their recep-tion; technical and organizational considerations gave them added favour. The weakness of party organization pointed out in the pre-vious chapter, its character as a depot for the collection of election funds, permitted the passing over of local officials and organizers.

The local bodies in the constituencies were allowed wide scope in their choice of candidates, and here again tradition played its important part. And here again a tradition that the Labour Party has taken over from the capitalist parties without hesitation: the sole aim of local Liberal and Conservative parties was to win the local seat for their candidate; his party loyalty and reliability were in these circumstances secondary considerations. To ensure winning the seat all efforts were made to secure some national figure as candidate or, failing this, one who in addition to personal charm was possessed of either title, rank, or money. Especially desirable was one who possessed a combination of all three.

It cannot be denied that the Labour Party has followed the tradition with all fidelity, and in doing so was not disturbed by any feeling of disaccord with its most sacred principles or aims. Money, rank, and title in addition to personal service have been determining factors in the choice of the party's candidates. In dozens of cases constituencies have been allotted to such men or women who declared themselves ready to finance their own election costs either wholly or partially. In practice therefore a plutocratic element has crept into the party, a state of affairs that could neither exist nor be tolerated in any other socialist party. By passing over members of the working class in this manner we find a whole series of men and women of the middle class and aristocracy representing the Labour Party in the House of Commons. This state of affairs must astound every continental socialist, and the more so when he finds the party headquarters, because of the relief given to the party funds, apparently lending the practice tacit approval. But neither can it be said that the men and women elected in this manner have in any way brought dishonour upon the socialist movement in Great Britain. Indeed, among them are to be found the most influential among the younger leaders.

Paradoxically enough this practice of personally financing election contests is due to the trade union's custom of supplying funds for its own candidates in order to strengthen its influence in the parliamentary party. With logic peculiar enough it is felt that what has been allowed the trade unions without question for more than twenty years cannot be denied the individual. Similar circumstances on the Continent, and especially in central Europe, are unthinkable. The rank and file would see in it every sign and proof of a dishonoured corruption and would flock *en masse* to the Communist Party as answer to their betrayal. In the one case known to me in Germany, the mere attempt led to the ignominious cancellation of a sure and certain candidature and the close of a political career.

It cannot in the scope of this small volume be touched upon how nearly these recruits from the ruling class, of whom I take Sir Oswald Mosley as an outstanding personality, have influenced the party and affected its character for good or evil; or how far they have falsified it and introduced factors in its policy which should or must be foreign to it. Without entering into the controversy that rages about them, I would say that far from these men having weakened the socialist character of the movement, it is they who have given new life and impulse to the socialist side of the agitation. For them, in contrast to those trade union leaders become sceptic, this newly discovered socialism is not a remote ideal with scant connection with the day's routine but a standpoint from which to judge every aspect of the daily economic and political struggle.

In the election struggle they have lent new glamour to the party. The personal attraction they possess for a most numerous electorate has gained votes and seats that must otherwise have fallen into enemy hands. They have psychologically facilitated and influenced the *petit-bourgeois* vote, in every country the most difficult to win for socialism, in favour of Labour candidates by making the Labour Party 'respectable'. The very fact that men and women of a high social standing could stand as candidates on a Labour platform has led to electoral gains, and therefore to an increase of political power without the loss of the working-class vote.

On the other side an element of snobbery has been introduced which, if the portents are not deceptive, may in the next five years constitute one of the most serious problems within the party. Were there the slightest possibility of a Communist expansion in Great Britain, here is the point which would afford them the most successful material for agitation. As long as the Labour Party does not abjure the monarchy and is prepared to tolerate the House of Lords as a political institution, thus giving tacit approval to hereditary social distinctions, it cannot well fight against the attractive advantage conferred by titles, rank, and social qualifications possessed by its own party members. It would place itself in a position contrary to its actual political practice.

At the present moment only a provisional balance can be struck, and one which is temporarily to the credit of its aristocratic converts. At the moment everything is in a state of flux; it cannot exactly be foreseen to what extent they will be assimilated by the party or to what extent they will change the party.[1]

---

[1] For a detailed study of this group, see Catherine Ann Cline, *Recruits to Labour* (Syracuse: University Press, 1963) — Editor's note.

CHAPTER II

FACTORS IN POLITICAL SOCIALIZATION

SINCE politics involves individual and group activities, both sociological and psychological factors are important as influences upon
the political behaviour of Englishmen. The factors influencing
political behaviour are many, including the family, education,
neighbours, friends, churches, political parties, and class. Influences
operate gradually, beginning in early childhood and potentially
extending throughout an individual's adult life. In this process of
political socialization, an Englishman learns the prevailing political
values, beliefs, and emotions of the political culture and what kinds
of political attitudes and activities are appropriate for a person in
his position. In traditional language, one would say that a young
person is prepared for his 'station in life'. All stations do not imply
the same political behaviour: a youth at a major public school may
learn that he could or should aspire to a prominent national political
role; a youth in a secondary modern school will be taught implicitly
or explicitly, that the appropriate position for him in the political
system is much different.

Studies of political behaviour have emphasized that a single factor
cannot be treated as the sole determinant of political behaviour.
Neither personality, a psychological attribute of an individual, nor
class structure, a sociological attribute of a society, can explain
fully the complex motivations which lead some individuals into
political activity and others to shun it. Both types of influence inter-
act upon each other. Certain character traits of individuals, e.g.
a 'public-school manner' or 'bluntness' in political controversy,
may be developed by educational institutions or by trade unions
respectively. Factors in political socialization have a cumulative
influence, and in England often operate in a single direction. A
person born into a middle-class home, with a grammar-school
education and a middle-class job is likely to vote Conservative; a
person born into a working-class home, with a secondary-modern-
school education and a job as an unskilled worker is likely to vote
Labour. By studying the influence of factors, either individually or
in combination, it is possible to make significant statements about
the probability that a group of individuals will act in a certain way

49

politically. Statements about probabilities are helpful for they give predictions more accurate than those produced by chance. Because they are statements of probabilities, however, they cannot be accurate in every instance; all individuals exposed to similar social experiences do not respond identically. In some individuals the process of political socialization produces cross-pressures; they are exposed to conflicting political outlooks by their particular combination of social experiences. Typical examples are wealthy businessmen who have risen from humble social origins with little education, and middle-class teachers who have risen from working-class backgrounds by virtue of scholarships.

Voting provides an ideal situation for studying the importance of social and psychological influences. Because the great majority of the adult population votes, the number of cases on which one can base generalizations is large, and a series of elections provides repeated tests of conclusions. In this country, studies have usually emphasized the importance of social class, although surveys have also provided evidence that approximately one-third of the electorate deviates from the party preference that class influence would be expected to produce; in other words, subjective psychological attitudes must also be at work. Studies of political participation, particularly of recruitment into Parliament and the higher civil service, have clearly delineated the extent to which class and educational backgrounds tend to limit the types of people who seek such offices, and thus the types who obtain offices. By intensive study of political biographies, W. L. Guttsman in *The British Political Elite* has been able to show subjective psychological differences within the broad categories of upper- and upper-middle-class political recruits. Because of the important role of the educational system in differentiating English youths, many works by educational sociologists are also of relevance to the study of political socialization; Brian Jackson and Dennis Marsden's *Education and the Working Class* is an outstanding example of a study of a process of socialization which gives conflicting cues for adult political behaviour.

While social and psychological factors operating upon an Englishman in childhood and adolescence clearly influence political behaviour, they do not determine the behaviour of all adults. An Englishman's political actions will reflect a wide variety of influences, some of which were prominent in the political system long before his birth, and have been transmitted to him by parents, childhood friends, and early education. By the time a young Englishman is old enough to vote he will have had sufficient indication of what is expected of him so that there will be predispositions towards certain forms of political activity. But adult influences, particularly for those involved actively in political parties and government, can be effective in teaching new attitudes towards politics or altering old ones. Political socialization occurs throughout an individual's lifetime; in many instances, however, what is freshly learned serves primarily to reinforce what was learned previously.

BIBLIOGRAPHICAL NOTE

For a systematic introduction to findings on the influence of social and psychological factors upon political behaviour in England, see Richard Rose, *Politics in England* (London: Faber, 1965) chaps. 3–4. Graham Wallas's *Human Nature in Politics* (1st edn., 1908) is full of insights derived from the author's own experience of politics. Among modern writers, a pioneering study by a psychologist is H. J. Eysenck, *The Psychology of Politics* (London: Routledge, 1954). W. L. Guttsman's *The British Political Elite* (London: MacGibbon & Kee, 1963) is excellent on the historical pattern of recruitment to Cabinet offices. Rupert Wilkinson's *The Prefects* (London: Oxford University Press, 1964) studies the influence of public schools upon political attitudes and politicians. *The Civic Culture* by Gabriel Almond and Sidney Verba is also relevant. A general introduction to the use of class categories is provided by *Class, Status and Power* (Glencoe, Illinois: Free Press, 1953), edited by Reinhard Bendix and S. M. Lipset. Margaret Stacey's *Tradition and Change* (London: Oxford University Press, 1960) analyses in detail the co-existence of deferential and industrial models of class relationships in a single English community, Banbury.

Among voting studies, special attention should be given to Robert Alford, *Party and Society* (London: Murray, 1964), because the author seeks to assess the relative importance of class, religion, and regional influences upon voting behaviour over a number of general elections, by comparing Britain with America, Australia, and Canada. Studies in the context of a single election include R. S. Milne and H. C. Mackenzie, *Straight Fight* (London: Hansard Society, 1954) and, by the same authors, *Marginal Seat, 1955* (London: Hansard Society, 1958); Mark Benney, *et al.*, *How People Vote* (London: Routledge, 1956); and Joseph Trenaman and Denis McQuail, *Television and the Political Image* (London: Methuen, 1961). John Bonham's *The Middle Class Vote* (London: Faber, 1954) studies one section of the electorate in several general elections. Data from a variety of sources is summarized and discussed in Jean Blondel, *Voters, Parties and Leaders* (Harmondsworth: Penguin, 1963).

Introductions to the substantial American literature can be found in James C. Davies, *Human Nature in Politics* (New York: Wiley, 1963); Robert Lane, *Political Life*; and Herbert Hyman, *Political Socialization* (Glencoe, Illinois: Free Press, 1959). All the anthologies referred to in the bibliographical note for the introduction have sections devoted to social and psychological influences upon political behaviour. Among American studies of voting behaviour, the most significant are Angus Campbell *et al.*, *The American Voter* (New York: Wiley, 1960); Bernard Berelson *et al.*, *Voting* (Chicago: University Press, 1954); P. F. Lazarsfeld *et al.*, *The People's Choice* (New York: Duell, Sloan & Pearce, 1944); and W. M. McPhee and W. A. Glaser, *Public Opinion and Congressional Elections* (New York: Free Press, 1962).

THE FAMILY BACKGROUND OF ETONIANS

By RON HALL

OF the many factors that can influence behaviour, family background comes first in time and, some psychologists would argue, it is most lasting in effect. Studies of political recruitment in England have consistently found that a small number of high-status families furnish a very disproportionate number of those in national political roles. Family background facilitates entrance into status-conferring and status-confirming public schools, universities, and occupations where high political aspirations may be encouraged. Ron Hall's methodologically ingenious analysis of the family backgrounds of contemporary Etonians is of interest to students of political behaviour, since Eton furnishes a very disproportionate number of those who go into politics from a public school background. Hall's study makes clear that Eton families are socially as well as politically atypical of the upper and upper-middle classes in England.

WITH the possible exceptions of Royal Yacht Squadron ensigns and Brigade of Guards bowlers, the Old Etonian tie is generally considered to be the most definitive status-symbol of the British aristocracy. This belief is not without justification. Two-thirds of Britain's dukes, marquesses, and earls went to school at Eton. So did the heads of most older baronial houses. About a half of all Etonians are armigerous. No other school has anything like so many old boys in high office. In the Cabinet, Etonians outnumber their nearest rivals, the Wykehamists, by seven to two. In the Court of Directors of the Bank of England, the proportion is even greater. About a quarter of all Tory M.P.s were educated at Eton. And Etonians have an absolute majority in that other bastion of established power — the Jockey Club.

Nevertheless, the use of an Eton education as a social indicator is open to an objection — it takes no account of any rise or fall in social status after schooldays are over. For an Old Etonian on the decline, the moment of truth comes when a place cannot be found for his

Reprinted in an adapted and abridged form from *Time & Tide*, 28 December 1961, pp. 2187–92; the article was originally entitled 'The Status Seeker's Guide to the Eton Home Counties'.

son. And a *parvenu* can consider himself 'arrived' on the day his
son is offered a place. Clearly a more exact indicator of present
social status is whether or not you are accepted as an Eton *parent*.

In order to analyse the family background of Etonians, information about two thousand parents whose sons have entered Eton in
the last ten years was taken from a random sample of persons
named in the 'parent or guardian' column of the *Eton College
Chronicle*'s school lists.

To attempt to classify parents of Etonians in terms of occupation
is somewhat misleading, for the sample immediately reveals that
Eton parents often do not have jobs in the conventional sense.
Research indicates that one-third have no identifiable occupation,
or are *rentiers*. Another third have been military officers, and continue to use their service rank after retirement, as befits an officer
and gentleman. (This figure includes a few parents who may still
be on active military service, and thus employed as career officers;
for these, almost certainly, a military career will not be the sole or
necessarily even the primary source of earnings.) An additional
7 per cent are 'gentleman farmers', an accepted occupation for the
squirearchy for generations. Six per cent are engaged in older
professions, half as clergymen, scholars, barristers, etc., and the
other half as senior Civil Servants, M.P.s, or Cabinet ministers.
Only one-fifth are in industry, commerce, or finance; this group is
largely formed by directors of banks and financial institutions.

The social status of Eton parents can better be assessed by examination of standard reference books listing those who have inherited or earned prestige. In this way, one can discriminate between different types of prestige within the small but heterogeneous
section of British society known as the 'upper' and 'upper-middle-
class' (Table 1).

TABLE 1

Status of Eton parents

Name Listed in	%
Debrett's (peerage or baronetage) . .	40
Debrett's (knightage or companionage)	4
Burke's Landed Gentry	19
Who's Who (but not in any of the above)	2
The Directory of Directors only . .	14
None of the above	21

More than three-fifths of Etonians have parents from whom they inherit social status; in the great majority of cases, their parents will also have enjoyed inherited social status. Only one-seventh have parents whose primary distinction is that they are rich, that is, directors of companies; parents listed under other headings in Table 1 may also be rich, but that is not their sole claim to social status. Only one Eton parent in fifty may be said to be a meritocrat, that is, someone who has achieved a place in *Who's Who* without having inherited or also acquired a traditional form of social prestige, such as a peerage, knighthood, or landed gentry status.

The social distinctiveness of Eton parents is also shown by the types of residence in which they live. Only one-sixth of Eton parents have a house with a number on its door, and less than 1 per cent live in a house with a suburban-type name. One-half live in a residence styled 'Manor', 'Hall', 'Court', or by a similar name, and 3 per cent live in a castle, abbey, or stately home. The remainder give a variety of country addresses.

In sum, this data shows quite clearly that Etonians do not come from 'ordinary' middle-class homes, for the majority of middle-class children do not go to boarding-schools. Contemporary Etonians do not come from 'ordinary' upper-middle-class homes, for Eton is only one of more than one hundred boarding-schools for the sons of this class. The bias in admission to Eton is clearly in favour of boys from families which have been long established in society; the families are so well established that the parents do not need to strive to secure high status, because they are born with high status. The information about occupations suggests that many Eton parents have not tried to convert their initial social advantages into powerful positions within society, for one-third are not distinctively employed, and another third are or have been content with a conventional period of service as a middle-rank officer. Slightly less than one-third of Eton parents occupy significant positions within the old professions or in finance. Etonians and their parents are not representative of the top 5 per cent of the population; rather, they appear to be a socially distinctive enclave within this group.

The social distinctiveness of Eton families is further demonstrated by an analysis of their geographical dispersion around the British Isles. An index of the social status of each county and London postal district (that is, the number of Eton parents resident there) was found by calculating the number of addresses of Eton parents per hundred thousand of population. Counties and postal districts could then be grouped into A, B, C, D, or E status, according to their index numbers.

A striking thing about Table 2 is the general consistency of the results. Counties of similar social status are clustered together in large geographic areas. A-status areas are surrounded mainly by B-status areas, the Bs blend off into the Cs, and so on. Also all the extremities of Britain — the Northern Highlands, Norfolk, Kent, the

TABLE 2

The geographical dispersion of Eton parents by county

GROUP A

(more than 15 per 100,000 population)

Berkshire . . . 28·8	Roxburgh . . . 21·7
Rutland . . . . 28·0	Argyll . . . . 19·0
Oxfordshire . . . 25·8	Selkirk . . . . 18·2
Berwickshire . . . 24·0	Buckinghamshire . . 17·3

GROUP B

(more than 7 per 100,000)

Hertfordshire . . . 14·6	Dorset . . . . 8·3
Perthshire . . . 13·3	Gloucestershire. . . 7·7
Montgomery . . . 13·0	Yorkshire (North Riding) . 7·7
Kirkcudbright . . . 12·9	East Lothian . . . 7·7
Wiltshire . . . 12·7	Shropshire . . . 7·6
Sussex . . . . 12·4	Westmorland . . . 7·5
Suffolk . . . . 12·0	Cambridgeshire . . 7·4
Radnorshire . . . 10·0	Surrey . . . . 7·2
London . . . . 9·5	Moray and Nairn . . 7·1
Hampshire . . . 8·3	Sutherlandshire . . 7·0

GROUP C

(More than 3 per 100,000)

Northamptonshire . . 6·9	Fife . . . . 4·6
Peebles . . . . 6·7	Kincardine . . . 4·2
Anglesey . . . 6·0	Banffshire . . . 4·0
Pembrokeshire . . 5·5	Caithness . . . 4·0
Norfolk . . . . 5·0	Cornwall . . . 4·0
Ross and Cromarty . . 5·0	Devon . . . . 3·9
Kent . . . . 4·9	Herefordshire . . . 3·9
Somerset . . . . 4·9	Flint . . . . 3·5
Inverness-shire . . . 4·7	Bedfordshire . . . 3·2
Dumfries . . . 4·7	Wigtown . . . 3·1

Group D

(more than 1 per 100,000)

Huntingdon	.	.	.	2·9	Cheshire	. . .	2·0
Essex	.	.	.	2·7	Leicestershire	. .	1·9
Midlothian	.	.	.	2·5	Northumberland	. .	1·9
Merioneth	.	.	.	2·4	Cumberland	. . .	1·8
Aberdeenshire	.	.	.	2·3	Denbigh	. . .	1·7
Angus	.	.	.	2·2	Warwickshire	. .	1·4
Ayrshire	.	.	.	2·2	Derbyshire	. . .	1·3
West Lothian	.	.	.	2·2	Yorkshire (East Riding)	.	1·2
Worcestershire	.	.	.	2·1	Nottinghamshire	. .	1·2
Stirlingshire	.	.	.	2·1	Dunbartonshire	. .	1·2
					Lincolnshire	. . .	1·0

Group E

(less than 1 per 100,000)

Middlesex	.	.	.	0·6	Staffordshire	. . .	0·3
Yorkshire (West Riding)	.			0·6	Durham	. . . .	0·3
Renfrew	.	.	.	0·6	Lancashire	. . .	0·2
Glamorgan	.	.	.	0·6	Lanarkshire	. . .	0·1
Monmouthshire	.	.		0·4			

Less than 0·1 or none: Brecknock, Caernarvonshire, Cardigan, Carmarthen, Clackmannan, and Kinross.

South-West, Pembrokeshire, and Anglesey — are of similar status. But despite the similarity between adjacent counties, there is a massive difference between the highest and the lowest. Eton parents are one-hundred and fifty times more dense (purely numerically, of course) in Berkshire than in Lancashire, and two-hundred and fifty times more dense in Berwickshire than in Lanarkshire.

Table 2 reveals three distinct focal points of top-status living: the upper Thames valley counties, which, although rural, are within Rolls-ing distance of Harrods; the Scottish Borders, which still retain the more pleasant features of feudalism; and the central and western Highlands, where, contrary to popular belief, there are still a few great estates, castles, and deer parks not yet bought by Americans. In addition there are two minor focal points. Shropshire, traditionally the most 'county' of the Midland counties, forms a B-status group with the two adjacent Welsh counties. And, spreading across the socially-barren North of England, is a B-status belt taking in Westmorland and the North Riding of Yorkshire. Most of the remaining B-status counties form a large broken ring around

London, extending along the south coast, and up into East Anglia. Sussex, not surprisingly, is the smartest of the south coast counties. It contains Worthing, Hove, and Eastbourne — the resorts which came highest in status in a statistical study done by the Centre for Urban Studies.[1] And, even more to the point, it has more ducal seats than any other county in Britain. Suffolk, the smartest of the East Anglian counties, owes its high rating mainly to the horsey folk round Newmarket, and its plethora of population-unchanged-since-the-original-Domesday-Book villages.

The status-pattern of the rest of Britain can best be explained in terms of urbanization. There is nothing remarkable in the discovery that it is smarter to live in country rather than town. What is more surprising is the extent of the difference revealed by the Eton lists. Excluding London and Edinburgh, there are sixty-eight British towns with more than 100,000 inhabitants — accounting, between them, for roughly a third of the total population of Britain. In the sample of two thousand Eton parents, only thirty-four (or 1·7 per cent) lived in these towns. York and Birmingham each had six Eton parents; Northampton had five; Brighton and Reading, three; Bristol and Ipswich, two; Cardiff, Derby, Leicester, Liverpool, Newcastle, Nottingham and Plymouth each had one. The other fifty-four towns had none at all. None in Leeds. None in Glasgow. None in Sheffield. None in Southampton. None in Manchester or any of the Lancashire cotton towns.

Table 3 shows that, in Britain as a whole, an upper-crust person is

TABLE 3

The rural basis of Eton families'
place of residence %

Country	.	.	. 78
London or Edinburgh	.		. 17
Medium-size provincial town		.	3
Large provincial town	.		. 2

nearly fifty times more likely to live in the country than in a large provincial town. Taking the North of England alone, the comparison is almost grotesque. The postal area of one tiny market town, Malton (population 4,438), which nestles by the River Derwent in the North Riding of Yorkshire, has produced more Etonians in the last ten years than have all the great Northern industrial cities

[1] C. A. Moser and Wolf Scott, *British Towns* (Edinburgh: Oliver & Boyd, 1961), fig. 2, opposite p. 80.

put together. The capitals, Edinburgh (index 2·8) and the County of London (index 9·5) are, of course, much smarter than most provincial towns — roughly comparable in status with the surrounding semi-rural areas. Out of the 351 addresses in big towns, 305 were in London. This explains why, in the kind of society where one is likely to own more than one residence, the phrase 'town house' means a house *in London*. In effect, there is only *one* town in which one could possibly live.

The direct effect of urbanization on the status of counties is obvious. Those which contain a number of large towns are, almost without exception, at the bottom end of the scale. The lowest English county, Lancashire, has twenty-one towns of more than 50,000 inhabitants (including Bootle and Wigan, which, so far as I can discover, have never produced an Etonian in their history). The West Riding — much less smart than the North Riding — would have been as low as Lancashire, but for the saving grace of the Harrogate district. Also at the bottom end of the list are the North-Eastern counties, which, although not quite so densely populated, make up for it by the squalor of their seaboard towns (Gateshead, for example, was the lowest town in England in the Centre for Urban Studies survey).[1] And Lanarkshire, which contains a third of the population of Scotland, crammed into the tenements of Glasgow and Motherwell, has the lowest index of all the larger British counties. The scattering of industrial towns across central England, holds nearly all the Midland counties down to C or D status. Even areas with quite a large rural gentry, such as the hunting country of Leicestershire, and the 'county of spires and squires', Northamptonshire, are lower than might otherwise have been expected — as, too, are Warwickshire (Coventry and Birmingham) and Gloucestershire (Bristol).

There is also a secondary effect of urbanization due to commuters. Counties in the commuting areas of the main cities tend to be lower in the social scale than their outward prosperity indicates, even though they may contain no large cities of their own. The problem of commuters — mainly middle-class businessmen — is that they not only swell the populations of the commuting counties but they also drive out the indigenous gentry. They buy up their halls and manors, talk stocks and shares at the Hunt Ball, drag party politics into council meetings, produce all sorts of new-fangled ideas on the magistrates' bench, and even try to marry into local families. The understandable desire to escape the commuters has already led to a noticeable decline in the gentry of such counties as Cheshire (the

---

[1] C. A. Moser and Wolf Scott, op. cit.

commuting area for Manchester and Liverpool), Surrey (London),
Ayrshire (Glasgow), and Worcestershire (Birmingham).

This process was evident from the survey. As the London commuting circle has spread outwards, so the number of Etonians from
the home counties has decreased. During the ten years covered by
the sample, the number of Eton parents in Surrey fell by a quarter,
and Hertfordshire dropped from A to B status. Simultaneous with
this was an increase in Etonians from Suffolk and Sussex – out of
range for all but the most ardent commuters. So far, the number of
Etonians from the upper Thames valley counties has remained consistently high. It is possible that with the improvement of London's
road access from the West, these counties may begin to get a bigger
share of commuters, but they have not yet shown any sign of going
into a social decline.

Eton itself is, of course, just inside this top-status area, and it is
arguable that this may have biased the results in its favour. A pre-
caution taken against this was to omit from the sample those parents
who were also members of the school staff or who were officially
connected with the school. It is unlikely that many other local
parents have an advantage in obtaining places for their sons. Four
years ago, Berkshire was given the Queen's permission to call itself
the Royal County. The county council includes: three baronets, a
baronet's widow, two peer's sons, a general, seven retired colonels,
five retired majors, a captain, two naval commanders, an air-
commodore, and five double-barrelled names. At least eleven of the
council appear in Debrett, and six hold the Military Cross, socially
speaking the highest status military decoration.

At first sight, the two oddest results of the survey are those of
Rutland and Middlesex. These two counties represent the opposite
extremes of urbanization. Rutland, England's smallest county, is
completely rural. The nearest thing it has to a town is Oakham,
which consists of a castle, a hunting inn, and a village population of
4,000. Also, it is outside the commuting circle of any large town. The
effect is to make it very much a top-status county. Rutland's index
of 28·0 has, of course, to be treated with caution, since the statistical
significance of results decreases, the smaller the county. But previous Eton lists show that tiny Rutland has consistently produced
almost as many Etonians as, say, the whole of Lancashire.

The Middlesex index might seem even more surprising. On almost
any measurement, it is one of Britain's most prosperous and highly
developed counties. The rateable value per head, for example, is
higher than any county outside London. Yet it has produced less
than a score of Etonians in the last ten years. Middlesex is, in fact,

Britain's mecca of mod-con. and semi-detached. The posh residential suburbs — like Southgate and Twickenham — which are Middlesex's main (and only) feature, give the county a particularly strong middle class. It is not short even of upper middles: the 1951 census showed that only three counties have a higher proportion of professional people. And in most counties with a large number of upper middles, there is also a substantial aristocracy. Why not in Middlesex?

As a general rule, the aristocracy have little in common with the upper middle class. Relatively few of them are professional men themselves, apart from soldiers and politicians. Professor Ross and Nancy Mitford have pointed out that they don't even speak the same language.[1] The traditional aristocratic way of life is more dependent, in a complementary sense, on the presence of a large peasantry of the kind found in East Anglia, the Borders, and the Western Highlands. The only reason why upper middles and aristocrats are so often found together is that the middle class want to live among, and adopt the attitudes of the aristocracy, rather than that the aristocracy want to live among the middle class. So far as Middlesex is concerned, the aristocracy seem quite convinced that they do not want to live there. Apart from the odd Labour peer and industrialist knight, there is scarcely a title in the county. And there is only one retired colonel on its huge county council.

Generally speaking, if an upper-crust person decides to take up town life, he will go the whole hog and live in central London. Middlesex is, in fact, an extension of the London status-pattern. The ability to place a town address in its correct position on the social scale is one of the most instinctive and widely held social accomplishments. True, not everyone is capable of the subtleties of Oscar Wilde's Lady Bracknell, who poured scorn on 'the unfashionable side' of Belgrave Square.

London addresses show that, although smart society is no longer confined to the north-west corner of Belgrave Square, upper-bracket town houses are still extremely localized within London. This is even more remarkable in view of the national figures for town houses. Of the top-status city-dwellers in all parts of Britain, scarcely one in three lives more than a couple of miles from Harrods in Knightsbridge. Table 4 is divided by postal districts, instead of boroughs, since the postal district is the first (and usually the most revealing) social indicator looked for in an address. Most of the map is completely blank — ninety of London's 115 postal districts have failed to produce a single Etonian in the last ten years. This means that if a

---

[1] Nancy Mitford (ed.), *Noblesse Oblige* (Harmondsworth: Penguin, 1959).

TABLE 4

Concentration within London of Eton families

Postal district	Parents per 100,000 people	Postal district	Parents per 100,000 people
W.8 (Kensington)	179	N.6 (Highgate)	16
S.W.3 (Chelsea)	160	N.W.1 (Regent's Park)	15
S.W.1 (Westminster, Pimlico)	138	N.W.3 (Hampstead)	13
S.W.7 (South Kensington)	100	S.W.15 (Roehampton)	13
W.1 (Mayfair, St. Marylebone)	72	S.W.5 (Earl's Court)	12
N.W.8 (St. John's Wood)	67	N.W.11 (Hampstead Garden Suburb)	9
W.14 (West Kensington Fulham, etc.)	27	W.11 (Notting Hill)	8
S.W.10 (Chelsea)	21	W.6 (Hammersmith)	3
W.2 (Paddington, Bayswater)	19	S.E.3 (Blackheath)	3
		W.4 (Chiswick)	3
		W.9 (Maida Vale)	3
		S.W.19 (Wimbledon)	2
		Ninety other districts	0

(*Note:* City of London addresses, E.C.1 to 4, are not included in the above table because the residential population of the district is extremely small, and most of the addresses given turned out to be business premises, mainly of banks and financial institutions of which Eton parents were directors.)

postal district has an index at all, it is well above the general social level.

The rough boundaries of the top-status area are the Thames (an Eton parent is forty times more likely to live north than south of the river) and a line drawn north and south through Piccadilly Circus (an Eton parent is three-hundred times more likely to live west rather than east of this line). These are both traditional status divisions. The south bank of the Thames, never very smart, went completely to the dogs with early Victorian property speculation; and the line through Piccadilly Circus is the product of the movement westwards of London's fashionable residential districts since the days of Wren. This westwards movement appears still to be continuing. During the period covered by the survey, there was a noticeable fall in the number of Eton addresses in Westminster (S.W.1), Chelsea (S.W.3), and Mayfair and St Marylebone (W.1), while there was a sharp rise in Kensington (W.8 and 14) and Earl's Court (S.W.5). A few Eton parents have gone even so far as to cross the Thames into Roehampton (S.W.15). This, presumably, is not directly due to the rise in central London house values — which would tend to increase social stratification — so much as to the conversion of many central town houses into offices and sub-family-size flats. Although, in Mayfair for example, there is still no shortage of dowagers, wealthy celibates, and divorced peers, it is becoming rapidly denuded of top-status family men.

What of north London? The only social focal point of any note is Regent's Park. Because of the park, and the additional attraction of the Members' Pavilion at Lord's, N.W.8, is easily the smartest postal district outside the Harrods hinterland, N.W.1 is distinctly on the Wrong Side of the Park, but has a few Eton parents and will probably get more, now that Nash's parkside terraces are being expensively reconstructed. Despite its pretensions, Hampstead (N.W.3) is surprisingly low. The rest of London can be discounted completely. The 3,000,000 people who live in the north, east, and south-east postal areas include only a handful of Eton parents — all in Highgate (N.6) and Blackheath (S.E.3), both favourite residential districts for lesser stockbrokers. Even the newly voguish districts of Dulwich (S.E.21), Southwark (S.E.1), and Islington (N.1) have no Eton parents.

Postal districts, as a means of assessing the quality of addresses, are of course open to a few ambiguities. A curious symptom of London's historical growth is that *many* of the finer social distinctions *within* postal districts can be explained in terms of railway lines. In S.W.1 there is a sharp status-division marked off by the line running south-westwards from Victoria Station. The Belgravia side, taken individually, is London's smartest area, with an index of about 200; the Pimlico side (whose houses are almost identical in architecture, if not in the same state of repair) is below the tracks in more senses than one. W.2 is fairly smart around the north side of Hyde Park, but falls to E status around Paddington Station. And N.W.1 is the most ambiguous of all, with its abrupt transition from the elegance of Regent's Park to the squalid surroundings of Euston and St. Pancras Stations. These finer divisions still further increase the localization of top-status town houses.

There is no reason to suppose that this kind of social pattern is peculiar to London. The county status map also showed a high degree of localization. And if suitable indexes could be found for provincial cities, the people of power and influence would, no doubt, be found to live in the same select districts or on top of the same hill. All of which shows that the aristocracy is as determined as ever to cling together.

THE FAMILY BACKGROUND OF
HAROLD WILSON

A BBC interview with BRIAN BLAKE

STATISTICAL studies of family background and recruitment
into national politics usually emphasize the influence of
mutually reinforcing socialization factors — upper-middle-
class parents, public school education and upper-middle-class
occupational status. But the influence of individual families
can also be important in helping a young person to compensate
for the disadvantages arising from a less-prestigious family
background, by consciously guiding ambitions in a political
direction. In a BBC interview with Brian Blake shortly before becoming Prime Minister in 1964, Harold Wilson provided an excellent illustration of the influence of family pre-
disposing an individual toward a political career. In his
remarks he also showed that as he matured and went to
Oxford, social factors — especially those differentiating
Northerners and Southerners, and grammar-school boys
and public-school boys — became increasingly salient in the
development of his individual political outlook.

*The following is an abbreviated version of a broadcast with Mr. Harold
Wilson, by Brian Blake of the BBCs North Regional staff. It was recorded
12 February 1964 at Transport House, London.*

Blake. I think, Mr. Wilson, that you are the first Prime Minister
of this country to come from a provincial grammar school. Are you
our prototype for the sixties and the seventies, the efficient man, the
classless man ?

Wilson. I remember I was asked that question on television the
night I was elected leader of the Labour Party. I was asked what
class I thought I belonged to, so I said, 'Well, someone who started
at an elementary school in Yorkshire and became an Oxford don —
where do you put him in this class spectrum ?' I think these phrases
are becoming more and more meaningless. In the advanced technological age many of those who were called workers are becoming
highly skilled technicians, people mastering techniques of science,
mathematics that would have made a Senior Wrangler blench

Reprinted in an abridged form from *The Listener*, 29 October 1964, pp. 653–5.

fifty years ago. I don't think we can really talk so much in those terms.

A politically minded family

Blake. Are you a strong family man?

Wilson. Yes. My mother, who died four years ago, had a very big influence on me. Most of her family emigrated from Manchester to Australia. Her brother, who was very politically conscious when he was in England, left at the age of twenty and became Speaker of the West Australian Parliament. My mother went out to visit them and I went with her when I was a very small boy, and I think I got the political bug from seeing them perform in that West Australian Parliament there. My father also was very politically minded. He voted Labour in Manchester in the 1906 election. But I think my biggest influence as far as they were concerned — and this was true of my grandparents as well as my parents — was the church or chapel background, the Nonconformist background. They regarded politics as a practical, secular expression of the religious views they held, the passionate, Nonconformist views, and in common with a large number of my own people I came to politics from that approach, the moral approach, based on our religious upbringing.

Blake. It occasionally seems that you've come to politics through the influence of people, and teachers, rather more than any strong emotional feelings.

Wilson. I think I was born with politics in me; I think the influence of friendly teachers and others has been considerable, but merely guiding me in the direction I wanted to go anyway. The emotional feeling began when I was living as a boy in a pretty depressed textile area, seeing the parents of a lot of my friends unemployed, my own father unemployed for a time, though we were never in real poverty. Seeing some of the boys who had been at school with me themselves unable to get work after they left school began the passionate feeling; but maybe I didn't really feel passionately about these things till I got away from them and found out how unaware people in other parts of the country were of what was going on in the North. I had that feeling particularly when I was at Oxford.

Blake. Let's stay with your family for a moment because all your life you have been accused of a tremendous amount of self-confidence. And I'm wondering if this came from this early strong family link?

Wilson. I don't think I really have had this self-confidence. I remember when, for example, I was first a Minister, in the Labour Government after the war, and decisions had to be taken, I weighed them up and sometimes talked round them with the senior officials, perhaps for hour after hour; at the end we would take a decision, I sometimes felt 'I'm about 51 per cent certain that that decision is right'. Not often more than that. I think perhaps the doubt I had about it made it more likely that one did reach the right decision. Those who were able always to make a quick decision — everything was a straight yes or no or straight black or white — often made bad mistakes.

Blake. An old friend of yours in Huddersfield when somebody asked 'What do you think of your old mate being Prime Minister?', said 'Well, he said he would'. That's all.

Wilson. Yes, I remember when we were kids we used to talk about what we were going to be and what we were going to do. I'd been brought up to feel that a job like Prime Minister, or any other job, was not one that should be reserved for the products of a particular school. I was interested in politics. Another ambition I had at the time was to be editor of the *Manchester Guardian*, as it was then. Indeed, I was still pursuing that aim at a much more advanced age.

Blake. It is reported that your father once said to a headmaster: 'This school ought to do a good job on Harold and then it will be remembered'.

Wilson. It was when I left Yorkshire and went to the Wirral: my father decided that I should go to a new school, the new local county school, later grammar school, where there were very young keen teachers, all under thirty except the head-master, and my father said: 'The school has got its name to make; if you make it with my son I'll be very happy, and so will you'. That was really the approach of it. He'd no idea whether I would get any scholarships or not.

Blake. No, but there's been a lot of luck, hasn't there — the luck of your father taking your photograph on the steps of 10 Downing Street; was this luck or . . . ?

Wilson. That was when I was eight. No, the luck was that after I'd had my wallet pinched in 1950, with what we thought was the only copy in it, the negative of it turned up last year. Of course I've been lucky: I was lucky in my schools, I was lucky in my teachers, I was lucky in getting that scholarship to Oxford, which neither I nor anyone else expected me to get, I was lucky in the people I met, I was lucky that as soon as I had taken my degree I was researching with a man like Sir William Beveridge who taught me a lot of the method of work and what hard work meant; I've been lucky all along, of course. I was lucky in politics, lucky to be given a chance by Clem Attlee as a Minister when I was only twenty-nine: and of course luck plays an enormous part in this. What I am trying to suggest is that there are millions of others who, given a chance, have got something to contribute, and many of them have not had the lucky breaks that I've had, and who have been held down to some extent by the sort of system under which we are living.

Almost magical luck?

Blake. In so many ways this luck that you talk of is almost magical, in view of what your father said, of the confidence that your family had in you. Have you ever felt that there was some sort of destiny behind it?

Wilson. Well, this is a philosophical question; what you mean by destiny or what you mean by luck. Napoleon once said he couldn't afford unlucky generals; he felt that luck was a question of seizing the opportunity when it came. This is true up to a point. On the other hand, one can't deny there is such a thing as luck, and there are many people who do not get the opportunities to show what they have in them.

Blake. Wouldn't you say that the more obvious way to trace it, or to chase it, is to look at your single-mindedness, at your ambition?

Wilson. Single-mindedness is important; hard work is important. I didn't work all that hard perhaps when I was about thirteen or fourteen or fifteen; I got into a bit of trouble at school about that. But when I went to the Wirral school, where I was the only boy in the sixth form getting individual tuition, I had a real incentive to work, and again at Oxford. Again, with Beveridge, as I said, one learnt to work, and if you are interested in the work, you aren't interested in the number of hours you work, you are at it all the time; it becomes a hobby as well as work, and indeed your biggest danger then is that you are unable to put it down and you may get stale.

Blake. In between school and Oxford what impressed you? Did the general strike of 1926 make any impact on you?

Wilson. I was very young then, I was only ten: I didn't know very much about it at that time. It was the unemployment and the depression that made much more impact. A friend of ours was a weaver; he lost his job, and I was about fourteen. It was my first lesson in economics to realize that this friend couldn't get a job, couldn't afford to buy much coal because they couldn't sell the cloth he could have produced, whereas in Barnsley, a few miles away, the miners were out of work — they couldn't sell their coal and they couldn't afford to buy suits made of the cloth he could have made. That was a simple, challenging problem in economics; it's one that has stayed with me ever since, and I've never found an answer to it, except in the sort of things that I believe in.

Blake. From the economic point of view rather than from the emotional, personal point of view?

Wilson. It started emotionally; it started personally by seeing the difference it made to our friend's life, and his home and his family, that he was out of work: then you began to query the system, not merely as an inefficient, wasteful system, as a system that wasn't working very well; you began to query it as something that was essentially evil in forcing, as it was, millions of people into those conditions of living.

Blake. How did the Spanish Civil War affect you?

Wilson. I was never a Marxist, I never have been a Marxist, and never a theoretical socialist, I've always been a pragmatic socialist, and many of the things that have affected my socialism I took for granted in those days: for example, the educational system, the scholarship system and all the rest of it. It wasn't until one sort of got outside and was able to take a look, that one realized how many fundamentally decent people were getting the wrong end of the stick from our economic and our social system. With regard to the Spanish Civil War, we all felt strongly about it at that time, politically. I was at Oxford for the greater part of it. We felt strongly particularly about the Hitlerite aggression, the Munich period, and all the rest of it, though I think I would be right in saying that most of my passionate feelings at the time were in terms of unemployment and home affairs, rather than foreign affairs.

Blake. It was at this stage in a way that you separated from the ordinary young man who is worried and anxious and toys with Marxism, who thinks of going to Spain even if he never goes?

Wilson. I reacted against Marxism at Oxford. I come from a northern nonconformist Liberal–Labour tradition, and when I found — I was wrong, looking back on it, but this was perhaps the insularity of my time and my background — when as I saw it, all these public-school Marxists, many of them communists, most of them knowing absolutely nothing of the conditions in which we in the north were living or had been brought up, I reacted so strongly against it that I felt the Oxford Labour Club wasn't for the likes of me and for a short time I joined the Liberal Club, hoping vainly to convert them to my ideas of radical socialism. That didn't last long. I soon saw there was no hope of that. But certainly I never had any common cause with what I regarded as a public-school Marxist.

A college without the 'old-boy' network

Blake. What sort of effect did Oxford have on you?

Wilson. Different colleges at that time were very different. The college I went to was a college that drew a large proportion of its undergraduates from, mainly, grammar schools in Wales, by closed scholarships confined to those who were born or educated in Wales; and certainly in my college I never got the idea of what has now come to be regarded as Oxbridge. I think the number of public school boys in that college was certainly less than 10 per cent. One wasn't aware of the fact that one was moving with different people from those one had been at school with. I went to a college that did not reflect the 'old boy' network. I saw more of that when I became a lecturer at New College, which was much more orientated on the Wykehamist tradition. For the first time I began to realize that side of Oxford life; perhaps I hadn't seen very much of it in my first three years.

Blake. I have a feeling that instead of rebelling against it and arguing with the top table, you enjoyed it so much that you really became an Oxford man in this sense.

Wilson. Arguing with the top table? I used to argue with them in the tutorials; I had always such a healthy respect and fear for them that I didn't argue very hard on subjects they knew so much more about than I did. But no, I regard it as a great place for one to do some work, and for one to become a master — a limited master — of the subject one was studying to fit oneself to deal with these problems, unemployment and the rest, when one got into the outside world. But I didn't see much of the social life at Oxford; I didn't have much time for it, frankly.

F

Blake. A lot of young socialists wouldn't have had your modesty in saying 'they knew so much more than I did' about these things; they would have said, 'they look at them from a different point of view, an establishment point of view, and they are wrong'.

Wilson. I must say, when I became a young don I found I had pupils who certainly thought they knew a lot more economics than I did, but I began to judge whether they did or not by the effectiveness of their essays and whether they had done their homework. They had much more self-confidence, I think, because of their kind of upbringing, than I had. I have always felt that these were very difficult problems, and, to use the old phrase, I used to wish I was as certain of anything as they were of everything. I have felt that many times since, with the products of a similar upbringing in different walks of life.

THE UPPER CLASS

By LORD BALNIEL

DISTINCTIONS of birth, education, style of life, occupation, and wealth combine to produce a small group of people who are variously referred to as the 'upper class', the 'professional class' or even as the 'ordinary [*sic*] middle class'. Members of this class are prominent in a number of national political roles, as ministers, M.P.s, Civil Servants, and chairmen or members of many Government committees and commissions. Lord Balniel, Conservative M.P. from Hertford since 1955, is of the stratum of which he writes. He is the elder son of the 28th Earl of Crawford and 11th Earl of Balcarres and the nephew of the 5th Marquess of Salisbury; he was educated at Eton and Trinity College, Cambridge. His article concentrates attention upon the influence of an upper-class background upon those who go into politics, particularly those who, in Bentham's terms, are 'lay gents' or, in contemporary terms, amateurs rather than technocrats.

AT the turn of the nineteenth century, the Duke of Wellington declared that 'Nobody cares a damn about the House of Lords'. He was partly right. At the turn of the twentieth century Matthew Arnold could write that the aristocracy 'have a more significant part in English life during the past and today than in almost every other country'. He also was right. Both these statements could be repeated today. Both would contain a large element of truth.

What is the influence of the aristocracy? What is the influence not only of the peerage but of that whole section of society, intangible because it is not a caste defined by any form of privilege but whose members in their hearts regard themselves as being 'upper class'? What is the influence of this class which opens its doors to anyone who possesses the acceptable mixture of hereditary status, social conformity, money, education, talent, property, or self-confidence? This article touches on some aspects of their influence.

Mere rank or title — the O.B.E. or a baronetcy — is not quite enough as an entry card. As King James I rather bluntly replied when being asked by a lady whether he would make her son a

---

Reprinted from *The Twentieth Century*, no. 999 (1960), pp. 427–32.

gentleman — 'I could make him a nobleman but God Almighty could not make him a gentleman.' The boundaries of the class are not defined, indeed each member of the class has a different estimation of where they are; there are no title deeds which can buy entry, except perhaps big money; but one minute of association will enable a member to recognize a colleague as surely as Jeanne d'Arc picked out the Dauphin. As one of the expert Mitfords has said, class is a subject for intuition rather than conversation.

In so far as there is a single common denominator of experience which is confined to the class, it is the educational system through which most of its members pass. About 2 per cent of the population are educated in public boarding-schools, and a high proportion of these people would look on themselves as upper class. At an early age the system divorces a small section of the community from the main stream of national life. It removes children from their home and local environment; inculcates a sense of separateness; fosters an ignorance of life in the wider community, and is a vehicle by which a sense of class differentiation is strengthened. Of course, the system has its compensatory advantages — educational and social. Indeed what must appear as a kind of educational apartheid and a weakness, at least to those whose objective is a classless society, is in fact in some ways a source of considerable strength to the nation. For the system gives to its members a cohesive strength which otherwise they would lack — as instinctive and as valuable as the cohesive strength of, for instance, the trade-union movement.

The cement of the class is not so much a sense of common purpose (as is the case in the trade-union movement) as a sense of common experience. At one time indeed the upper class had a sense of common purpose. The nineteenth century saw the preservation of property rights as a bond which united a class, otherwise torn in twain on every other political issue. This all-embracing purpose kept the cohesion of the class, both nationally and internationally. It was a source of social stability. It contributed to the peace of Europe, for the ruling class of all nations had a common interest to maintain. Today there is no such bond. Instead a common educational experience, not shared by the mass of the community, gives to the class a sense of mutual understanding, loyalty, and tolerance.

This is of value. Although the class has long ago shed the mantle of a ruling class, it has inherited a tradition of public service which gives it influence in the higher reaches of political and executive government. To demonstrate this one has only to look at the educational background of the Cabinet (fifteen out of the nineteen members having attended public school) or the diplomatic corps, or the colonial service, or the commissioned ranks of the army. An established position in society blunting the edge of ambition, mutual trust and loyalty, tolerance, all contribute in political circles to the relaxed, almost instinctive, and sometimes excessive cohesion of the Conservative Party. It contrasts with the chronic disarray and apprehension of betrayal within the Labour Party, whose membership cannot draw on such a wide degree of common experience.

The same benefit accrues in other fields. The understanding within the class oils the entire machinery of government. It may blind men to the defects of their colleagues — as the Foreign Office discovered with the defection of some of their members to Russia. Tolerance of weakness and fault may be stretched to dangerous lengths. But the mechanics of the higher administration and executive action are eased by there being a perceptible sentiment of social unity over and above the bonds of nationality and the good will which grows between men practising the same profession.

This is not, of course, to say that all senior civil servants or military officers think of themselves as being upper class. But most men honourably aspire to the highest social status that lies within their reach. If talent drives them to the top of their profession they will imperceptibly but automatically acquire on their way up the characteristics which enable them to meet any colleague or antagonist as a social equal.

The trappings of seniority help the ego a good deal — the grades of furniture in a Ministry are as subtly indicative of status as any blazon in an heraldic court — or for that matter as indicative of status as a Gauguin in a millionaire's flat. These kinds of things may help in establishing social status — but they are merely outward symbols. It is the assumption of power, the acceptance of responsibilities, the exercise of influence which gives to a character some of the self-confidence necessary to enter the charmed, but not charming, circle. Real quality of some kind or other is required of the entrant. None is required of the man who was born in the purple.

The educational system contributes to the cohesion of the class. It also contributes to one of the happier traditions which this section of society gives us — the tradition of the amateur. Specialization is left until the universities are reached — and even then it is more often than not specialization in the humanities which is no direct training for any profession.

The tradition of the amateur grows out of the varied duties that were expected of the ruling class. Its representative provided the government — both nationally and locally. He was expected to look after his country estate, to be a sportsman, to administer justice from the magistrates' bench, and patronize the arts. From among the ranks of his colleagues were drawn the personnel of the Church and the fighting services.

The class has never abandoned this diversification of interest. The specialization of the Junkers in the military field; the abandonment of country life by the Court of Versailles or the hidalgo of Spain did not occur in England. Instead, our ruling class maintained a wide diversification of interest which, while it did not preclude moderate specialization in any particular field, created an attitude of mind in which the amateur was respected. Passions were not aroused by single objects. Fanaticism was not a characteristic of the class. And although we no longer are ruled by those who devote their leisure in amateur fashion to politics — we still have a society in which the amateur wields greater influence than the professional.

In Britain perhaps more than elsewhere there is a widespread dislike of a society where the dominating posts are held by specialists. One sees the most important responsibilities within society entrusted deliberately to those who are amateur, unpaid, and often part-time. The departments of state have their policies determined by ministers who do not have a lifetime's interest in their functions. The local magistrate is amateur, part-time, and unpaid. The police are controlled not by Prefects but by locally elected councillors who are also amateur, part-time and unpaid. The boards running the hospitals, the nationalized industries of coal, electricity, the airways, atomic energy, the authorities building the new towns, the BBC, are all to some degree controlled by men and women who are amateurs and undertaking the task as a part-time occupation.

The tradition of the amateur is an inheritance from the leisured aristocrat of the past. But its maintenance by the less leisured upper class of today is of continuing benefit to the country. It fosters the sense of national unity. The amateur has a wide understanding of general matters. He is more capable than a specialist of understanding the problems of other professions. The strength of the amateur tradition helps to develop a mutual esteem between professions which is less apparent elsewhere. We don't have the anti-clericalism of France; nor the mutual dislike of public and egghead in America; nor the tension between politician and judge in South Africa; nor the distrust between military and civilian in Germany. Instead there is a tendency to live and let live, to tolerate the foibles and irritations of the other professions, to respect their privacy and not to interfere in their working. This mutual esteem and toleration helps to preserve the balance of our society.

With this inheritance from the past there has come another. Just as respect for the way of the life of the aristocrat of yesterday (or at least of some of them) has brought respect to the amateur tradition of today, so respect paid to the aristocracy of yesterday has imparted to the institutions of Government with which they were so long associated an aura of aristocracy.

For generations, both before 1832 and after, membership of the House of Commons and the House of Lords was drawn from the same class. This is no longer true. But the hierarchical structure of Government still remains. Crown, Lords, and Commons still exist. And indeed even in the democratic element of the Constitution — Members of the Commons, whatever social class they themselves may belong to, have today absorbed many of the traditions, and retained the privileges won for them by the old ruling class. And Government as a whole, being associated with a hierarchical structure, in particular with its apex the Crown, commands deference from the public. It is not only the institutions of Government, but all that complex of society, fashionably called the Establishment, which commands a certain deference. This respect for authority is of great value in maintaining the stability of our society. It stems partly from the respect which once was paid to the aristocracy and the gentry, and is today paid to their legatees.

Whether or not that old deference paid to the upper class is deserved today is another question – and a question which is not commented on here. But the danger which faces an established class is that its members may feel that they are entitled to a respect based not on their individual merit but on the status of their class. They may feel, perhaps rightly, that their social status is widely envied even in this democratic age. They may feel that an egalitarian society is neither achieved nor wanted. And in accepting their unearned social status, and in rejecting any move towards an egalitarian society, they may be tempted to consolidate the society we have inherited irrespective of its quality. They may like to think nostalgically of the upper class as 'the great oaks that shade a country', instead of building a country in which the hopes of all men have an equal chance of growing to full maturity.

The danger to the upper class of looking to the past rather than the future has grown in recent years. When every other section of society has 'never had it so good', the upper class (and to some extent also the professional class) is not so sure. For them it wasn't so bad in the good old days. The natural desire of a still well-off class, whose fortunes have suffered a relative decline, is to turn its back on the present, and the future. It is more comfortable than to meet the challenge of a changing society. It is easier to allow old forms to ossify, to become colleagues in complacency, rather than to make the conscious effort required of leadership. Nowhere, for instance, is stagnation more marked than in the failure of the public schools to adapt themselves in the second half of the twentieth century to keep the educational lead for the upper class they won in the nineteenth.

Whatever their attitude to the future, there is among the upper class a sense of certainty that they have deserved well of the country in the past. They inherit the tradition of a class which thought of itself as being born to rule; and which did in fact rule not only over our own people but over the greatest Empire that the world has ever seen. Out of this has grown an instinctive self-confidence which serves the country well — in marked contrast, for instance, with the never-ending guilt which plagues the conscience of so many intellectuals.

An established class does not often question the social structure which gives it a comfortable place. Ours is perhaps almost unaware of some of the wrongs which exist in that structure. But this complacency protects them from excess. They do not strive to maintain their position. Indeed a great merit of our upper class is that they do so little to remain 'upper'. It makes them a difficult target to hit. The peers with inherited titles, with a few exceptions, appear perfectly content to allow the House of Lords to die of inactivity. And just as Norman blood had to be enriched with American money — so the pulse of the Lords has had to be quickened, not by their own efforts but by the efforts of new arrivals. Indeed, the entire Establishment is preserved not so much by the conscious efforts of the well-established but by the zeal of those who have just won entry, and by the hopes of those who still aspire.

SOCIAL GRADING BY MANUAL WORKERS[1]

By MICHAEL YOUNG and PETER WILLMOTT

CLASS is one of the central concepts of sociology; it is also one of the most difficult to use. Sociologists often define class in terms of categories of occupations. But studies have shown that individual Englishmen do not always employ occupational rankings when subjectively placing themselves in a class structure; furthermore, these studies have found that occupational rankings may vary somewhat as between individuals. The study of social classification conducted by Michael Young and Peter Willmott indicates very clearly variations that can occur in the way individuals rank occupations. It is also important because it suggests that for some respondents political partisanship influences social attitudes, rather than vice versa.

THE studies of social mobility carried out at the London School of Economics included a pioneering inquiry into the social grading of occupations by John Hall and D. Caradog Jones.[2] The inquiry showed, in the words of the critique by C. A. Moser and J. R. Hall in the final report,[3] that there was a 'substantial measure of public agreement' on the social prestige of different occupations. There were, however, as Moser and Hall pointed out, certain limitations in the original inquiry; in particular, the samples under-represented manual workers. This paper reports a small research project in East London, repeating the Hall–Jones inquiry with two differences — first, that the sample consisted mainly of manual workers; secondly, that personal interviews were used rather than written questionnaires. After they had graded occupations, people were asked the reasons for their decisions.

The manual workers questioned in the original inquiry were

[1] The authors are greatly indebted to Mr. Philip Barbour who undertook the statistical tabulations incorporated in this paper, and to Mr. C. A. Moser and Professor Richard M. Titmuss, who gave valuable advice on a number of points.

[2] J. Hall and D. Caradog Jones, 'Social Grading of Occupations', *British Journal of Sociology*, vol. i, no. 1 (1950), 51.

[3] C. A. Moser and J. R. Hall, 'The Social Grading of Occupations', p. 50, being chap. 2 of *Social Mobility in Britain*, ed. D. V. Glass (London, 1954).

Reprinted from *The British Journal of Sociology*, vol. vii, no. 4 (1956), pp. 337–45.

chosen from what Moser and Hall called an 'arbitrary selection of organizations'.[1] Since none of those mentioned by name was an organization of manual workers, it is perhaps somewhat surprising that the combined general and pilot samples yielded as many as 55 men and women in the survey's bottom two occupational categories of semi-skilled and unskilled manual workers. There are no manual workers in the trade unions listed as among the organizations which co-operated: they are all composed of non-manual workers, namely, insurance agents, civil servants, and local government officers. 'Members' of the Trades Union Congress also took part, but since its only members are the affiliated unions such as the Amalgamated Engineering Union, this must mean members of the *staff* of the T.U.C., none of whom are manual workers, with the exception of a few liftmen and cleaners. Most of the manual workers both in the pilot and the general samples must presumably have come from members of adult education classes and their friends. But the few manual workers who attend such classes may rather share the attitudes of the non-manual workers, who form the majority of class members,[2] than of manual workers in general. The pronounced agreement in the ranking of occupations between the manual workers and the others may therefore have been partly due to the way in which the manual workers were selected; the very fact that they were associated (either as members or friends of members) with adult education classes, which are themselves predominantly 'white collar' organizations, may have made their views on occupational prestige much more similar to the opinions of non-manual than of manual workers in general.

The small research project described here was an attempt to find out whether manual workers chosen at random from electoral registers and the like would give different answers from the manual workers associated with the Hall–Jones' organizations. We had no resources for any substantial study of social grading and all that could be done was to add some questions on the subject to interviews whose primary purpose was to elucidate the structure of the kinship system in an East London borough. The samples were very small and, being chosen for this different purpose, were far from ideal for a study of social grading. The inquiry was local, and the respondents may not have been representative of manual workers in general. Despite these disadvantages, we were encouraged to proceed because

---

[1] C. A. Moser and J. R. Hall, op. cit., p. 37.

[2] The percentage of 'manual workers' among Workers' Educational Association students during 1953–4, the last year for which figures are available, was 16·9 (*Annual Report*, 1954, W.E.A., Table 3, pp. 80–1).

in one important respect our survey was of the kind recommended by Moser and Hall: they suggested that further study of the subject, in particular of the criteria used by rankers, should rely not on written questionnaires but on personal interviews.[1]

The informants were made up from two sets of 50 married men. To get the first set a random sample of every 36th person was drawn from the borough's electoral register and, from the 933 people interviewed, a sub-sample of 50 people of either sex who had 2 or more children under 15 was selected for more intensive questioning. The rankers were the men, and also the husbands of the women, who figured in this sub-sample. There were 7 refusals, leaving 43 men who answered all the questions on social grading. To get the second set, a further sample of 50 was drawn from a list of all the tenants on an L.C.C. housing estate on the Eastern outskirts of London, being people, again with 2 or more children under 15, who had recently moved from the borough to the estate. 47 of them responded at a first interview in 1953; 42 men were still on the estate in 1955, and of these 39 granted a second interview. The questions on social grading were put at the second interview, so that altogether there were 82 respondents. Since there were no very marked differences between them, the results of the two sets of interviews have been amalgamated. The only difference worth noting is that there were more 'deviants' (see below for definition) on the housing estate.

The distribution of occupational classes in our sample, as compared with the East London borough, Great Britain and the two Hall–Jones samples, is shown in Table 1. The classification is the Registrar-General's.

It is not possible to find out from the published report the proportion of manual workers in the Hall–Jones samples since skilled manual and 'routine' non-manual workers were included together in two of their occupational categories. But it is clear that manual workers, and particularly the less skilled manual workers, are much more largely represented in our sample. In respect of age, our sample, consisting as it does of fathers with young children, contained fewer very young and fewer very old people than did the Hall–Jones sample. We explained the purpose of the questions, verbally, on the same lines as given in writing in the Hall–Jones inquiry,[2] saying that

[1] C. A. Moser and J. R. Hall, op. cit., p. 47. A. F. Davies had also suggested that it might be useful to collect 'subjective reports' from informants on their ranking task, and that it would be easier to evaluate past studies if this had been done. We were in a position to collect such 'subjective reports'. A. F. Davies, 'Prestige of Occupations', *British Journal of Sociology*, vol. iii, no. 2 (1952), p. 144.

[2] The exact form of words was set out in J. Hall and D. Caradog Jones, op. cit., p. 51.

TABLE 1

Comparison of Occupational Classes of Respondents
(Percentages)

Class	East London Inquiry	Census 1951 East London Borough	Census 1951 G.B.	Hall–Jones Inquiry (Males — general sample)	Hall–Jones Inquiry (Males — pilot sample)
I . . .	1	1	3	52	42
II . . .	5	6	15		
III Non-manual .	7				
		55	53	44	51
Manual . .	49				
IV . . .	20	13	16		
				4	7
V . . .	18	25	13		
Number in samples	82	..	..	710	219

our interest was in social class and what made for class differences, that occupation was one of the things that determined a person's class, and that we wanted to know in what order, as to their *social standing*, the informant would grade the occupations in our list. We then presented the alphabetic list of occupations[1] to the informants. The informants were, as in the original study, asked to start by classifying the occupations into five main classes, lettered A, B, C, D, E, and then to arrange the occupations in descending numerical order within each of these classes, tieing those they considered to be on the same social level. After the form had been completed we asked additional questions about the criteria informants had in mind in ranking specific occupations in the way they had.

[1] Exactly the same description of occupations was used as in the Hall–Jones list (op. cit., p. 52) except that by an error 'coal-hewer' was, on our form, rendered as 'coal-miner'. In any further inquiry it would be as well to substitute some new titles, for instance 'primary school teacher' for 'elementary school teacher (assistant)' and 'lorry-driver' for 'carter' since these two occupations more or less disappeared several years ago. 'Business manager (10–99 hands)' has a somewhat archaic flavour, especially to those who are themselves 'hands' and 'Civil Servant (Executive Grade)' is liable to be misleading to people who do not know the peculiar nomenclature of the British Civil Service. A recent American report was misled, presumably by the 'Executive Grade', into classing these fairly humble Civil Servants along with a head of department in State government in the U.S.A. although just above a Japanese priest in a Buddhist temple who was regarded as equal to a Nonconformist minister! A. Inkeles and P. H. Rossi, 'National Comparisons of Occupational Prestige', *American Journal of Sociology* (1956), p. 336.

Comparison of Grading

The rankings have been analysed by the same methods as those used in the original study. Results are compared in Table 2. In

TABLE 2

Comparative social grading of occupations in the two inquiries

Hall–Jones Inquiry (Median Ranking A.M. of Group Judgements: Males – general sample)		East London Inquiry		
Males		Median ranking	Quartiles	Quartiles difference
Medical officer . . .	1·3	Medical Officer of Health .	1	1/5	4
Company director . .	1·6	Chartered accountant .	5	3/13	10
Country solicitor . .	2·6	Company director . .	5	1/12	11
Chartered accountant .	3·2	Country solicitor . .	6	3/13	10
Civil servant . . .	6·0	Farmer	6	4/10	6
Business manager . .	6·0	Business manager . .	7	3/12	9
Works manager . .	6·4	Works manager . .	7	5/11	6
Nonconformist minister .	6·4	Elementary school teacher .	10	4/16	12
Farmer	7·3	Jobbing master builder .	10	6/13	7
Elementary school teacher .	10·8	Minister (nonconformist) .	11	4/18	14
Jobbing master builder .	11·4	Civil servant . . .	11	6/17	11
News reporter . . .	11·8	News reporter . .	12	9/15	6
Commercial traveller .	12·0	Coal-miner . . .	13	6/12	12
Chef	13·8	Policeman . . .	13	7/18	11
Insurance agent . .	14·6	Fitter	13	10/17	7
Newsagent and tobacconist.	15·0	Carpenter . . .	14	9/18	9
Policeman . . .	16·1	Chef	15	9/21	12
Routine clerk . . .	16·1	Bricklayer . . .	16	9/19	10
Fitter	17·6	Newsagent and tobacconist	19	13/22	9
Carpenter . . .	18·6	Commercial traveller .	19	14/25	11
Shop assistant . . .	20·2	Insurance agent . .	20	15/23	8
Bricklayer . . .	20·2	Agricultural labourer .	21	8/25	17
Tractor-driver . . .	23·0	Routine clerk . .	21	18/23	5
Coal-hewer . . .	23·2	Tractor-driver . . .	21	13/24	11
Railway porter . . .	25·3	Dock labourer . .	22	14/25	11
Agricultural labourer.	25·5	Shop assistant . .	24	22/26	4
Carter	25·8	Carter	25	23/28	5
Barman	26·4	Railway porter. . .	27	23/28	5
Dock labourer . . .	27·0	Road-sweeper . .	27	23/29	6
Road-sweeper . . .	28·9	Barman	28	25/30	5

the Hall–Jones list occupations are ranked according to the median rankings of various groups into which the whole sample was divided for purposes of analysis. Since final rankings are the arithmetic mean of the group median rankings, they are not whole numbers, as they are in the East London list. Manual workers in the two bottom categories of the Hall–Jones general sample are excluded from the groups whose judgements are shown here, as they were from the original published report, but their views were stated to be in close conformity.

In the order of the median rankings there is a good deal of similarity between the two sets of results.[1] The Medical Officer of Health

[1] To apply one test, the rank correlation coefficient is 0·90.

is at the top of both lists.[1] Immediately below is a group of professional occupations which are in more or less the same order in both
lists. But the middle and lower ranges of the list show some considerable differences. In general, the East London rankers have
elevated the more skilled manual jobs and depressed the non-
manual occupations. Agricultural labourer, bricklayer, carpenter,
coal-miner, dock labourer, farmer, fitter, and policeman are all
higher in the scale. Chef, civil servant, commercial traveller, insurance agent, newsagent and tobacconist, routine clerk and shop
assistants are all appreciably lower. In so far as the inquiries are comparable, despite the difference in time, it would seem there is a
tendency for manual workers to grade manual jobs more highly than
they are graded by the non-manual workers who predominated in
the Hall–Jones study. Although it was too slight to disturb the conclusion that members of the 'general public' did not differ much in
their 'judgement of social class', such a tendency was also noticed
in the original report.[2]

A much more striking difference between the two sets of results
is in the range of variability of the rankings. Hall and Jones remarked that 'there appeared to be a tendency for the judgement
about the social class of selected occupations to become more variable and, to that extent, less reliable as we descended the occupational scale among those whose opinion was canvassed'. There was,
in other words, less agreement among manual workers. The East
London study more than confirms this finding. In the Hall–Jones
inquiry the average difference between the upper and lower quar-
tiles was about $3\frac{1}{2}$ for all groups, and just over 4 for the two lowest
occupational classes. In the East London study the average quartile
difference (shown in detail in Table 2) was, at 8·8, more than twice
as great. This difference is so substantial that the informants cannot
be regarded as being agreed in their judgements.

Another measure of consensus is the extent of agreement about
the allocation of occupations to a specific one of the five initial
grades, A, B, C, D, and E. In the Hall–Jones inquiry, for about half
the occupations at least 60 per cent of the rankers were agreed on

---

[1] The high ranking of the medical profession does seem to be something common,
not only to different occupational groups, but even between countries. In the
U.S.A. Physician (although not of course the same as M.O.H.) ranks just below a
U.S. Supreme Court Justice, equal to a State Governor, and above a Cabinet
Minister. National Opinion Research Centre, 'Jobs and Occupations: a Popular
Evaluation' in *Class, Status and Power*, ed. R. Bendix and S. M. Lipset (London,
1954), p. 411.

[2] J. Hall and D. Caradog Jones, op. cit., p. 42. See also C. A. Moser and J. R.
Hall, op. cit., p. 41.

the initial grade;[1] in the East London survey such a degree of consensus — that is, 60 per cent of the rankers agreeing — was reached for only 5 out of the 30 occupations.

Sub-division of the Rankers

The East London informants ranged from those with views very like the general opinion of the Hall–Jones sample to others whom, in the course of the interviewing, we came to think of as 'upside-downers'. These were the people who generally put non-manual jobs such as company director and chartered accountant towards the bottom and manual jobs, such as agricultural labourer, coal miner, and bricklayer, towards the top of the scale. How were we to distinguish these 'deviants' from the others for purposes of analysis? We wanted a group large enough for separate analysis and identified by the extent of deviation from the Hall–Jones ranking. The expedient we adopted was to calculate each informant's deviation and then to place it graphically on a scale from 0 to 450. We calculated each person's deviation by adding the differences between the order of ranking of each occupation in the ranker's own list and in the Hall–Jones ranking. Thus a person who put M.O.H. last and road sweeper first, but otherwise followed the Hall–Jones order precisely, would have a deviation of 58·6. We found that, when the scale was set out, there was a break in it around 225, with clusters of informants (totalling 22) having deviations greater than this and other clusters less. We decided therefore to treat as deviants the 22 informants with deviations above 225; 22 was a large enough group for our purpose and the gap in the scale at this point seemed to give some justification to what would otherwise have been a completely arbitrary decision. The ratings of the deviants are compared in Table 3 with the 60 respondents whom we shall style 'normal'.

Here is part of the explanation for the difference between the results for the Hall–Jones rankers and those for the East London sample as a whole. The rankings by what we have called the deviants are so far from the Hall–Jones model, and the range of variability so great (the average quartile difference is 8·9), that the results for our total sample must obviously have been influenced considerably. But all of the differences between the results of the Hall–Jones inquiry and our own cannot be explained in this way. As one would expect, the rankings of the normal group are closer to the Hall–Jones model than are the rankings of the East London sample as a

[1] C. A. Moser and J. R. Hall, op. cit., p. 39.

TABLE 3

Grading by normal and deviant respondents

	Normal			Deviant	
	Median	Quartile difference		Median	Quartile difference
Medical Officer of Health .	1	3	Agricultural labourer .	3	4
Company director . .	3	7	Medical Officer of Health	3	6
Chartered accountant .	3	4	Farmer . . .	4	4
Solicitor . . .	5	6	Coal-miner . . .	4	6
Business manager . .	6	7	Policeman . . .	4	8
Works manager . .	6	4	Tractor-driver . .	5	10
Farmer	7	6	Bricklayer . . .	6	7
Nonconformist minister .	8	11	Elementary school teacher	8	11
Civil servant . . .	10	9	Carpenter . . .	9	8
Jobbing master builder .	10	7	Dock labourer . .	9	6
Elementary school teacher .	10	10	Jobbing master builder .	10	8
News reporter . . .	10	7	Fitter . . .	11	9
Chef	13	8	Works manager . .	14	11
Coal-miner . . .	14	9	Road-sweeper. . .	15	16
Fitter	15	7	Solicitor . . .	16	10
Policeman . . .	15	8	News reporter . .	16	11
Carpenter . . .	16	8	Company director . .	16	13
Bricklayer . . .	18	7	Newsagent and tobacconist	17	8
Commercial traveller.	18	9	Chartered accountant .	17	11
Insurance agent . .	19	9	Nonconformist minister .	17	19
Newsagent and tobacconist.	19	8	Business manager . .	18	10
Routine clerk . . .	21	6	Civil servant . . .	19	7
Tractor-driver . . .	22	5	Carter . . .	19	10
Dock labourer . . .	23	6	Routine clerk . .	21	6
Agricultural labourer.	24	9	Railway porter . .	22	9
Shop assistant . . .	24	3	Insurance agent . .	22	12
Carter	25	3	Shop assistant. . .	23	8
Railway porter. . .	27	4	Chef . . .	25	16
Barman	28	5	Commercial traveller .	26	6
Road-sweeper . . .	28	4	Barman . . .	29	4

whole,[1] but the average quartile difference for the normal group, at 6·6, is still significantly higher than those of the Hall–Jones samples. Furthermore, even the normal group shows striking differences, in its final ranking, from that of the Hall–Jones rankers. Skilled manual occupations — coal-miner, fitter, carpenter, and bricklayer — are still judged to be higher than the non-manual commercial traveller, insurance agent, clerk, and newsagent. The normal group among these East London manual workers, in contrast with the Hall–Jones respondents, also put both agricultural labourer and dock labourer above the shop assistant. Thus, though they more or less agreed with the Hall–Jones rankings of occupations at the top and bottom of the scale, they disagreed about the relative standing of the middle range of occupations — and disagreed particularly about

[1] The rank correlation coefficient of the rankings of the normal group with the Hall–Jones rankings is 0·93, compared with 0·90 for the East London sample as a whole. For the deviants it is −0·073.

the standing of skilled manual occupations as against that of routine non-manual. It is clear, therefore, that even if we excluded the extreme group of 'upside-downers', whom we discuss below, the final rankings of the East London sample would still not concur with those of the Hall–Jones inquiry. We do not, however, know how far the differences represent different 'models' of the occupational structure and how far they result from generally recognized changes in the prestige of skilled manual as against non-manual occupations in the period between the two inquiries.

Criteria of Ranking

One of the purposes of the interview was to explore informants' attitudes to their task and to occupational prestige generally. After the forms had been completed, we asked the informants why they had graded the occupations in the way they had and where they would place their own jobs. We decided, after examining the reports in detail, that the answers could be classified into one or other of five groups according to the main criterion stressed. Allocation of those who mentioned more than one criterion and of some of the less articulate informants to one group rather than another was arbitrary, but, despite this, we consider that this fivefold classification does reasonable justice to the variety of opinions expressed.

The meaning given to the five criteria is illustrated in the words of some fairly typical respondents.

1. *Ability.* 'My idea was to put them according to the ability needed. If you've got ability you'll get on well. In my job a man with a bit of brain and common sense could pick it up in a few moments; another man wouldn't learn it in a lifetime.'

'To my mind it's a question of how much intelligence you have. I'd measure them more or less intellectually.'

2. *Education.* 'Education is what counts. If I was an educated man I would know how to speak and everything, and I dare say I wouldn't have the sort of job I've got.'

3. *Remuneration.* 'I think it's money today — that's the important thing today.'

'I'm going by the money — which would bring their standard of living in line.'

4. *Social milieu.* 'I've put the business manager at the top because the social standing of the business manager's very high, and I put the minister alongside him because these old parsons have got a high social standing — they're all right anywhere they go.'

G

5. *Social contribution.* 'The general idea was what good the people do. What they put into the country. The Medical Officer of Health is putting the most into the country and I don't suppose he's getting all that money.'

'Those I've put at the top — they're actually working. They're doing something essential.'

The answers of our informants, classified according to these five criteria, are set out in Table 4. This table indicates, in effect, the meaning given to the key term, 'social standing', by our informants. The deviants are shown separately from the normal group.

Most of those in the normal group employed the kind of criteria that one imagines were employed by the bulk of Hall–Jones respondents. They were thinking primarily of the ability, education, and skill which people required for particular jobs.

TABLE 4
Criteria of ranking

	Normal	Deviant
Ability	30	1
Education . . .	8	0
Remuneration . .	9	0
Social milieu . .	4	0
Social contribution . .	9	21
TOTAL . . .	60	22

Most of the deviants, on the other hand, judged according to the social contribution made by the various occupations. The reason for their being 'upside-downers' was not that they made their judgements haphazardly; on the contrary, they seemed to have made their choices according to a principle which they were able, on the whole, to formulate more readily than those whose views were nearer to the Hall–Jones scale. Their principle was the value of the job to society, its usefulness,[1] its importance, and in this light they rated manual occupations higher in the main than non-manual. As one man said: 'I've put all people who do physical labour at the top.

[1] A previous investigation showed that Modern School-boys of manual worker origin employed this criterion when grading jobs. 'There was a tendency for the Modern School-boys to refer more frequently to the usefulness of the job (e.g. the bricklayer (miner) is important because people need houses (coal)) and for the Grammar School-boy to stress the power and responsibility which an occupation commands.' H. T. Himmelweit, A. H. Halsey, A. N. Oppenheim. 'The Views of Adolescents on some Aspects of the Social Class Structure,' *British Journal of Sociology*, vol. iii, no. 2 (1952), p. 160.

They're absolutely essential.' The manner in which they applied their criterion to particular jobs can be illustrated from their remarks.

Agricultural labourer came out top in the deviants' classification (see Table 3) because his job of food production was thought to be of first importance to the country. 'Agricultural labourer,' said one man, 'up at the top — you can't do without grub.' Farmer and tractor-driver were highly placed for the same reason. Likewise the Medical Officer of Health — 'He's essential for health. Without that man you've got no foundation to build on.' Likewise the coal-miner — 'without coal, industry stops'. Likewise the bricklayer — 'You've got to have food and after that you've got to have houses. That's why I put the farms and the builders at the top.'

Non-manual occupations — what one man referred to as the 'old collar and tie jobs' — were on the whole placed low because they were considered to be of less value to society. Here are some remarks on particular jobs.

Clerk: 'In our factory half the workers are clerks. They're doing the Government's work — P.A.Y.E. and all that caper.'

'Anybody can push a pen along.'

Chartered Accountant: 'He does more fiddling than anything.'

Business Manager: 'They're not doing anything. They get their money for walking around.'

Company Director: 'There have to be Guv'nors, but I can't see there's any use in these people who act as directors on fifty companies or so. He goes right down at the bottom.'

'I put company directors and all those at the bottom. Usually people are nominated to these positions. There might be a thousand people working for a company. No one of that lot would become a company director. Actual people who form the company never get the chance of becoming company director. They come from outside and then they get a fat cheque for attending once a month.'

Insurance Agent: 'Now we've got the family health lark, from the cradle to the grave, you know, we don't need him.'

Civil Servant: 'I could find other ways of using my money.'

The group among our informants whom we have described as 'deviants' adopted with one exception this criterion of usefulness, and ranked occupations accordingly. Those in the normal group applied in the main other criteria and came to different decisions. Can we say anything about the characteristics which differentiate one group from the other? The deviants were, by and large, drawn from the manual workers in the sample, and to a slightly larger extent from the unskilled and semi-skilled workers than from the skilled. This is shown by Table 5. The occupations of the informants are categorized according to the Registrar-General's Classification,[1] and

TABLE 5

Relation of occupational class of rankers to their judgements

	Normal	Deviant
Non-manual (R.G. I, II, and III)	10	1
Skilled manual (R.G. III) . .	30	10
Semi-skilled and unskilled manual (R.G. IV and V) . .	20	11
TOTAL	60	22

the manual are divided from the non-manual workers contained in the Registrar-General's Class III.

With one exception, the deviants were manual workers. They also assigned high ratings to manual workers. They therefore on the whole assigned high ratings to themselves, higher than did manual workers in the normal group. This is shown by Table 6 which records the distribution of the initial grades to which people assigned themselves.

TABLE 6

Self-grading of rankers

Initial Grade		Normal	Deviant
A		4	14
B		19	1
C		22	6
D		10	0
E		5	1
TOTAL		60	22

Naturally, few of the people in our sample happened to have jobs identical with those in the Hall–Jones list. One way in which the deviants managed to accord themselves high standing and maintain their self-respect was to associate their jobs with the occupations in

[1] *Classification of Occupations, 1950*, General Register Office, H.M.S.O., 1951. The informant's occupation could not be categorized according to the Hall–Jones standard as their classification of jobs other than the 30 has not been published.

the list to which they had given high ratings on the grounds of their usefulness. Here are a few examples of the process at work. A butcher said: 'Well, it's to do with the farmer and the land, so I think I'll put it in A along with the agricultural labourer, the farmer and the tractor-driver. It's all to do with food, you see. If the farmer didn't grow the animals, we wouldn't have a job and it wouldn't be any good people breeding animals unless we were there to kill them and turn them into meat.' Incidentally, his son, who was at a grammar school, scoffed at his father afterwards and said, 'You ought to go down in E.'

A thermometer-maker did the same. 'Our job, making thermometers, is very important. They're used for every trade, hospitals, and everything. Health is really the most important thing. My job is linked up with the doctors.'

A bookbinder, one who has a high regard for the minister, said: 'I've put my own job well up. It's bookbinder and we bind Bibles. It's to do with religion, and that's important.'

A postman put his own job on a level with the policeman and commented: 'Postmen do a lot of hard work for the public. The public doesn't realize what we do for them. I was speaking just the other day to a fellow-postman who was an ex-mayor of Hackney. That's the sort of person you meet in the Post Office.'

A dustman had no doubts about his status in his own eyes. 'I'd put dustman right at the top alongside the Medical Officer of Health. He helps to keep health and that's essential.'

Politics and the Deviants

Many of the deviants revealed that their opinions about occupational prestige were closely related to their opinions about politics.[1]

'Does that mean the Guv'nor? If it does then he's got to go in the top rank. You've got to have a Guv'nor or there wouldn't be any jobs for the other people to do. I'm not all that Communistic that I think you can do without Guv'nors. Of course if I was Communistic, I suppose I'd put people like that right down at the bottom.'

He then proceeded to put company directors, at any rate, right down at the bottom. Another informant, a charge-hand in a tailoring factory, stated:

'Of course politics are bound to come into this. The answers which

[1] They were in effect adopting the 'power model' of class (employed by people who strongly identify themselves with the working class) which is distinguished from other models in a stimulating article by Elizabeth Bott, 'The Concept of Class as a Reference Group', *Human Relations*, vol. vii, no. 3 (1954), pp. 259–85.

you give will depend on what your politics are to a certain extent. For instance, if you don't think much of the people like business managers and company directors and that, you'll put them pretty low down.'

This association between occupational grading and political attitudes is no more than one would expect.[1] In the British labour movement both Marxists who hold to the labour theory of value and the predominant non-Marxists who stress the 'dignity of labour' have united to assert that manual work is, if not superior, certainly not inferior to any other. When the Labour Party in its 1918 constitution pledged itself 'to secure for the workers by hand or by brain the full fruits of their industry', the workers by brain did not come first, and even though it may well be much less distinctive than in the past, the labour movement still has a separate ideology of its own. The classic doctrine that first shall be last, and the last first, still holds sway. Unless one appreciates its influence it is impossible to understand the continuous pressure from manual workers for redistribution of money and power. If everyone recognized the Hall–Jones ordering of status, putting business managers above road-sweepers, the right of the business manager to more power and more money than the road-sweeper would not be open to challenge. But in so far as manual workers deny the superiority of the business manager, they also deny his right (and affirm their own) to higher reward.

The deviants still adhere to the ideology of the labour movement, an ideology whose existence may give rise to much more disagreement about occupational prestige in Britain than in the United States. The influence which this ideology has upon occupational grading (and indeed upon educational aspirations, political behaviour, and industrial relations) would be worth exploring fully in any future investigation.

To do this effectively it would be necessary to put at least two different questions to the informants. Hall and Jones asked a single question, one which was not free from ambiguity,[2] and since we

[1] It would be interesting to relate studies of voting behaviour and social grading. What one would expect is that voters of our deviant type would be Labour voters. The answers to a simple question about the standing of a few jobs, like company director, chartered accountant, bricklayer, and dock labourer, might provide the evidence for predicting the votes at an election of some of the people who were doubtful before.

[2] The rankers were asked to grade occupations according to their social standing, but it was not made fully clear in the main survey (as distinct from the preliminary inquiry into the views of prominent people) whether they were to go by their own personal opinions or whether they were to follow what they believed the *general* opinion to be. Cf. pp. 50 and 51 of J. Hall and D. Caradog Jones, op. cit.

wanted our results to be comparable with theirs we asked the same single question. In future inquiries it would be as well to ask people not only for their view of the general opinion about the standing of jobs but also for their own personal opinion. The first question would be designed to discover what *is* the general prestige scale, the second to discover the views of people about what it *should be*. This could be done by asking the two questions either of the same people at different stages of an interview or of matched samples of different people, on the lines recommended by Moser and Hall.[1] Such an inquiry would reveal the extent to which people regard non-manual work as superior to manual, and show how far their views about what *should be*, colour their views about what *is*.

Summary

1. The Hall–Jones inquiry found a high degree of consensus on the grading of occupations. By contrast, this East London inquiry finds a considerable measure of dissensus among the manual workers in its sample.

2. The East London respondents are divided into two groups. The ordering of occupations even by those in the normal group is not the same as the Hall–Jones classification.

3. The deviants grade occupations according to their 'social contribution', that is to say, according to their usefulness to society. Manual workers are on the whole ranked above non-manual.

4. The deviants are influenced by their political attitudes. In so far as they refuse to recognize the superiority of 'workers by brain' over 'workers by hand', their views belong to the distinctive ideology of the labour movement.

In conclusion, we would stress the limitations of this inquiry. It was on a very small scale, and a much larger sample is plainly required. It was made in East London, and the residents in it may not be at all representative of manual workers in general. The validity of the findings can only be tested by a full-scale inquiry. A full-scale inquiry into the views of a cross-section of the population, using verbal interviews and generally proceeding on the lines recommended by Moser and Hall, and Davies, could reveal the measure of dissensus — consensus on the status of occupations, and, beyond that, lay the foundations for a study of an important aspect of political ideology in contemporary Britain.

[1] C. A. Moser and J. R. Hall, op. cit., p. 48.

CONCEPTS OF CLASS

By ELIZABETH BOTT

ALTHOUGH politicians sometimes describe class relationships in conflict terms, conflict is only one of a number of
possible relationships between persons in different classes in
society. Elizabeth Bott's study of how English people conceive of class structure is a pioneering effort to explore the
nature and number of class categories that individuals use.
The study makes clear that the conflict model, while sometimes employed, is characteristic of individuals in only one
type of social situation.

A FAMILY does not live directly in the total society, or even, in
many cases, in a local community. The effective social environment
of a family is its network of friends, neighbours, relatives, and
particular social institutions. This is its primary social world. But
this does not mean that families have no ideas about their society
as a whole or about families in general. The couples surveyed
differed widely in their views on these matters. These differences are
interpreted here as a result of varying social experience and personal needs.

The couples' ideas about class structure give a good, though by no
means complete, indication of their conception of the society as a
whole and their own place in it. Much of the literature on class
suggests that social classes are concrete entities in the sense of being
actual groups, and that most members of a society agree in their
description of what these entities are and what criteria should be
used to describe them. Our data suggest, on the contrary, that people
disagree profoundly in their views on class, so much so that we sometimes wondered if they were talking about the same society. Our
conclusion is that in certain important respects they were not.
Although a finisher in Bermondsey and an account executive in
Chelsea are both members of the larger British society, they live in
different worlds; they have different jobs, different friends, different
neighbours, and different family trees. Each bases his ideas of class
on his own experience, so that it is hardly surprising that each has a

Reprinted from *Family and Social Network* (London: Tavistock Publications,
1957), pp. 159–78.

different conception of the class structure as a whole. In these circumstances it would be naïve to assume that people's ideas about class will be a valid representation of the 'real' or 'objective' class structure of the society as a whole. Their ideas do, however, reveal information about the people themselves and their primary social experience. In this chapter an attempt is made to describe how people construct their ideas about class and how they use them in making comparisons and evaluations.

Questions about class were asked as part of a general inquiry into each couple's *Weltanschauung*. Various matters associated with class, prestige, and power came up spontaneously in the course of conversation about other matters. Direct questions about class were asked towards the end of the interviews. Information was sought on seven topics:

1. What classes each couple thought there were?
2. What criteria they were using in defining these classes and also what criteria they used to place individuals in them?
3. What they thought about the mobility of individuals?
4. What they thought about changes in the class structure as a whole in the past and probable changes in the future?
5. Where they placed themselves?
6. What aspirations they had for their children?
7. Whether they thought family life varied according to class?

The material on class ideology was not central to the main aim of the investigation, so care was taken not to put an unnecessary strain on the relationship between the field worker and the couple for this purpose. As a result, four early families were not asked about class at all. Of the remaining sixteen, five were not asked about self-placement because the field worker thought the couple would be too anxious to deal with such a question without embarrassment. The spontaneous material is therefore uniformly rich and detailed, but the systematic probing of this material by direct questioning could not be carried out to the same degree in all cases.

The research families varied considerably in socio-economic status, although there were no unskilled workers. The incomes of the husbands before tax ranged from £330 to over £1,800. The occupations of the husbands in families with loose-knit networks were: deputy fire manager of an insurance firm, pottery designer working as an occupational therapist in a mental hospital, statistician in a welfare agency, account executive in an advertising agency — he was in charge of relations with several important clients — and temporary clerk in the Gas Board. The occupations of husbands in families with medium-knit networks were: skilled repairer of optical instruments, establishments officer in Public Health Department of a local authority, sundry supplies buyer for a medium-sized industrial firm, manager of health food shop, clerk in insurance firm, painter and decorator, general commercial manager of a light engineering firm, self-employed repairer of radio and television sets, and police constable. The husband in the family with the most close-knit network was a finisher in a large boot and shoe repair firm. The occupations of the husbands in families with transitional networks were: draughtsman in a firm of architects, clerk in a large department store, W.E.A. lecturer, owner-operator of a small tobacco and sweet shop, and plumber.

A. *The Processes by which Individuals Develop Their Concepts of the Class Structure*

In this chapter I discuss only class ideology, not the class structure of the society as a whole. The method adopted did not provide the data necessary for a study of class structure as such, and as the study progressed it became clear that a detailed knowledge of the class structure of the society as a whole was not a necessary prerequisite for understanding the way in which individuals construct and use their own ideas about class. If one's aim were to compare and contrast the class ideology of a large number of informants, it would be helpful to use some measure of their position in the total class structure as a yardstick against which their class ideology could be compared. Various theories and definitions of class might be used for this purpose. In my opinion no one of these theories is valid for all purposes although each is appropriate to particular problems. If one is studying social and economic change, a useful definition is the Marxian one of classes as actual or potential corporate groups recruited on the basis of position in relation to the means of production. If one is studying the distinctions of prestige in a small community, Warner's definition of social class is useful (Warner and Lunt, 1941). If one is comparing the attitudes of a large sample of people one is likely to treat class as a socio-economic category. For the purposes of the present study, however, the most important point about the class structure is its extreme complexity. The various institutions and groups involved in social differentiation are not tightly fitted together so as to form a small number of closed, corporate classes easily identified by all members of the society. It is this complexity and loose articulation that makes possible the variation in class ideology that was found among our informants.

There have been several studies, notably that of Centers, in which political and social attitudes have been compared with 'objective' class position and with 'subjective' self-placement in a pre-defined class (Centers, 1949 and 1952). Hammond has extended this approach very considerably by comparing people's ideology about class with their objective class position. Instead of asking his informants to place themselves in pre-defined classes, he asked what they thought the classes were and then compared the different types of ideological model with objective class position (Hammond, 1952). His results are in line with the present study, but instead of concentrating on large-scale comparisons of ideology with objective position, the aim here is to understand the processes and mechanisms by which particular individuals arrive at their ideas of class.

To tackle such a problem, it is not enough to know the individual's position in a socio-economic category or objectively defined class. People do not experience their objective class position as a single, clearly defined status. They do not report any direct, immediate experience of belonging to a class as a membership group, except on the now rare occasions when classes act as corporate groups. But people do have direct experience of distinctions of power and prestige in their places of work, among their colleagues, in schools, and in their relationships with friends, neighbours, and relatives. In other words the ingredients, the raw materials, of class ideology are located in the individual's various primary social experiences, rather than in his position in a socio-economic category. The hypothesis advanced here is that when an individual talks about class he is trying to say something, in a symbolic form, about his experiences of power and prestige in his actual membership groups and social relationships both past and present. These experiences have little intrinsic connection with one another, especially in a large city, and each of the groups and networks concerned has its own pattern of organization. The psychological situation for the individual, therefore, is one of belonging to a number of unconnected groups each with its own system of prestige and power. When he is comparing himself with other people or placing himself in the widest social context, he manufactures a notion of his general social position out of these various experiences. He reduces them all to a sort of common denominator. This is not a very accurate procedure. The experiences are not differentiated and related to one another; they are telescoped and condensed into one general notion. But it is accurate enough for orientating him in a complex society.

Most people are hardly aware of performing these acts of social conceptualization. Thus a plumber, whose class ideology is reported in detail below, combined together his experiences in several

groups to arrive at a general model of two interdependent but conflicting classes. The most important experiences he was using in
constructing this model were his membership in a closely integrated
neighbourhood during his childhood, his experience of unemployment, his experience in his present job, with his colleagues, with his
superiors at work, with neighbours, with acquaintances in various
clubs, together with some more indirect information about the 'idle
rich'. But he was not aware of the precise contribution of each of
these separate group memberships, even though he had talked about
each of them separately and agreed with the field worker's suggestion that his experience in them provided the basis of his own view
of the class structure.

Very occasionally an informant pointed out that the various
group contexts were separate and should not really be combined into
a notion of general status or class. Thus the clerk in an insurance firm
dealt with the situation by saying that prestige depended on the
context of evaluation. Quoting from the interview record:

. . . He went on to say that it made a difference if you were looking at the
thing nationally or locally. If you looked at a man's position from the point
of view of his neighbourhood, any professional man would be at the top of
the tree. But if you looked at the profession as a whole, from the national
point of view, it might not be the top of the tree. . . . Most doctors work in
one local area and live in another. Among other doctors, their position
would depend on how well they did their work, etc. In their neighbourhood,
it would depend on where they lived. Take Golders Green, for example.
That was predominantly a Jewish neighbourhood. Also it was mostly an
area of professional people. He said it wouldn't give a man any particular
prestige to be a doctor in Golders Green because everyone else was a doctor
there too.'

Most informants reduced their own unconnected relationships and
group memberships to a notion of general position without worrying
about such niceties of evaluation, and many individuals seemed to be
hardly aware of the fact that they were using their own experiences
as a basis for their model of the class structure.

The individual performs a telescoping procedure on other people
as well as on himself. If they are people who have the same, or
similar, group memberships as himself, he is likely to feel that they
have the same general position and belong to his own class. If they
are outsiders, his knowledge of them will be indirect and incomplete
so that there is plenty of room for projection and distortion. Thus
several individuals who placed themselves in the 'middle class'
made two or three differentiations in their own class but spoke of
the 'working class' or 'manual labourers' as an undifferentiated

mass. Similarly some people who placed themselves in the 'working class' made differentiations within it but lumped together everyone else as 'the rich'. The more remote the people of another class, the less opportunity there is for checking fantasy against fact, so that the individual can see in such people what he wants to see, and what he wants to see will depend on his perception of their position relative to his own.

In brief, the individual constructs his notions of social position and class from his own various and unconnected experiences of prestige and power and his imperfect knowledge of other people's. He manufactures classes, assigns norms and values to them, and then uses them in various contexts to make comparisons and evaluations. He is not just a passive recipient assimilating the norms of concrete, external, organized classes. He creates his own model of the class structure and uses it as a rough-and-ready means of orientating himself in a society so complex that he cannot experience directly more than a very limited part of it.[1]

B. The Concept of Reference Group in Relation to Class Ideology

Although the term 'reference group' has been very rapidly adopted by sociologists and social psychologists during the past ten years, there appears to be considerable disagreement over its definition,[2] I use it to mean *any group, real or fictitious, that is thought by an individual to have a real existence and is employed by him to compare or evaluate his position with that of others, and to justify or explain his actions*. He may belong to the reference group; he may not. He may be positively identified with it and want to belong to it; he may not. The 'group' concerned may not even be a real group; it may be a category con-

[1] Cf. Bartlett's general theory that perceiving and remembering are active processes in which the individual not only receives information but also constructs it in accordance with his own attitudes (Bartlett, 1932).

[2] Hyman, who introduced the term, uses it to mean any group with which the individual compares himself (Hyman, 1942). Newcomb uses it to mean any group with which the individual is identified; the identification may be positive, negative, or ambivalent but cannot be neutral (Newcomb, 1948, 1950, and 1952). Merton and Kitt use the term very generally, to refer both to groups used for comparison and to groups with which the individual is emotionally identified (Merton and Kitt, 1950). Sherif restricts the term to groups with which the individual is positively identified (Sherif, 1953). Keller and Stern use it only for groups to which the individual does not belong (Keller and Stern, 1953). Eisenstadt is concerned with the way norms and values become linked to a particular group (Eisenstadt, 1954). Kelley points out that the term is sometimes used to mean any group with which the individual compares himself, sometimes to mean any group with which he is emotionally identified (Kelley, 1952). I find it convenient to use the term in the most general sense, adding qualifying adjectives where necessary.

structed by the individual. At this point I go beyond the literature, for most authors assume that reference groups exist *sui generis* apart from the individual. Such sociologically real groups have independent norms that can be internalized by the individual, and that can then be used by him in perceiving and evaluating himself and other people; the norms of the external group become the attitudes of the individual. I think the reverse process occurs too; individuals do, of course, internalize norms that exist in actual external groups, but they also project some of their own attitudes and values back into the external situation. Reinterpretation and projection occur to some extent in all cases of assimilating norms, but such processes are particularly important in the construction and use of classes as reference groups.

Many authors have mentioned in passing that individuals use classes as reference groups. Newcomb goes into the matter in some detail in discussing the work of Centers and Steiner (Newcomb, 1950, pp. 228–32). According to the work of Centers, one can predict political attitudes from the individual's subjective class identification about as well as from his occupational status as objectively defined (Centers, 1949 and 1952). According to Steiner, students who are middle class by objective criteria but working class by self-placement have attitudes similar to those of students who are working class both by objective and subjective criteria. In the language of reference group theory, one would say that the individual expresses attitudes that are in accordance with the norms of the class which is a positive reference group for him. If he uses his own class as a positive reference group, he will adhere to its norms. If he uses another class as a positive reference group, he will express attitudes in accordance with this group of which he is not a member.

Such an interpretation assumes that classes are actual groups with interlocking social roles and distinctive norms, so that norms can be directly internalized by the individual. This amounts to a reification of the concept of class; classes, at least as defined in the above studies, appear to be categories rather than actual groups, so that their norms cannot be internalized directly. My suggestion is that there are three steps in an individual's creation of a class reference group: first, he internalizes the norms of his primary membership groups — place of work, colleagues, friends, neighbourhood, family — together with other notions assimilated from books and the various mass media; second, he performs an act of conceptualization in reducing these relatively unconnected and often contradictory norms to a common denominator; third, he projects his conceptualizations back on to society at large. This is not a conscious, deliberate process; it happens for the most part unwittingly. Moreover, modifications and revisions are constantly being made, and there are often inconsistencies and contradictions between the constructions made at different times and for different purposes. The main point is that the individual himself is an active agent. He does not simply internalize the norms of classes that have an independent external existence. He takes in the norms of certain actual groups, works them over, and constructs class reference groups out of them.

It is useful to make a distinction between *direct reference groups* and *constructed reference groups. Direct* reference groups are those in which the referent is an actual group with interlocking roles and distinctive norms that can be directly internalized by the individual; there is a relatively small amount of construction of the group and projection of norms into it by the individual. Such direct reference groups may be membership groups, or they may be non-membership groups whose norms have been internalized by the individual. The crucial point is that they are actual groups that exist independently of him. *Constructed* reference groups are those in which the referent is a concept or social category rather than an actual group; in this case the amount of construction and projection of norms into the constructed group is relatively high.

Classes are constructed reference groups. They are used by individuals to structure their social world and to make comparisons and evaluations of their own behaviour and that of other people. Although these concepts may not be objectively real, they are psychologically real, in the sense that they affect the behaviour of the individual. Among the research families, there was considerable variation in the extent to which people believed in the external reality of their class reference groups. Some informants were deeply convinced that classes had a real, objective, external existence; others were very sceptical and said that classes were really figments of people's imaginations; the most common attitude, although not expressed in these words, was that classes were rather like stereotypes, not to be taken too seriously, but virtually indispensable for making comparisons and evaluations.

C. The Use of Class Reference Groups and Models of the Class Structure

All the research couples made some use of class reference groups in the course of informal conversation. In addition, most couples produce a model of the total class structure in reply to our direct questions. There were two wives who denied the existence of classes, but they did it so vehemently as to suggest that they thought classes existed, but wished for various reasons that they did not. Several people were hardly aware that they were operating a model of the class structure, and they experienced some pain in the course of making it explicit, and realizing that it was full of contradictions and inconsistencies. Many couples pointed out that the various criteria of class membership they were using — occupation, income, control of people through wealth or industrial power, education, family background, manners, accent, etc. — did not fit together closely so as to form a neat hierarchy, and they were not sure which should be given first priority. At this point several people remarked that classes were not real groups and that people who believed in them were snobbish and unpleasant.

In ordinary conversation, people never used their whole model. They used bits and pieces of it as reference groups in particular contexts of comparison and evaluation. Nearly everyone talked about classes when discussing the society as a whole and the social and political changes in it. Classes were also used for placing strangers and for contrasting other people's social lot with one's own in a wide social context. Apart from these universal usages, couples varied greatly in the extent to which they used class reference groups in ordinary conversation. The couples who used them most frequently were those who were dealing with unfamiliar situations, making relationships with new people in different social or physical surroundings. Some had been mobile socially, some only physically, but they were all faced with the problem of sorting people out, of placing themselves in relation to other people. They were all structuring their social world. Couples who were more settled talked about prestige and power in more particular terms without generalizing them into concepts of class.

It appears, then, that everyone operates a model of the class structure, but that the models are fluid and variable and are used differently in different social contexts. It is this fluidity which explains the fact that one gets such different results about class ideology when using different methods of inquiry. Several studies show that if a large number of people are asked to rank occupations and to place them in pre-defined classes, they will agree, more or less, in their rankings (Centers, 1949 and 1952; Form, 1946; Hall and Caradog Jones, 1950; North and Hatt, 1947). In spite of some contradictions between these studies, it seems clear that there is some general agreement about the social status of occupations, but it is difficult to tell how much of this agreement is a function of the methods used and how much is a reflection of social stereotyping or of genuine consensus. In any case, such agreement does not necessarily mean that these rankings or classes are used by the rankers in their everyday social life.[1]

Our method of open-ended questioning, like Hammond's (1952), turned up far more variation than studies made by questionnaire. Although some features were common to all versions, and it is possible to define several main types of model, each version had some unique features of its own. Furthermore, it is always necessary to remember that an informant's responses were strongly influenced by his immediate social situation, particularly by his relationship with the field worker. At times this was very obvious, as when a woman revealed her snobbishness, or what she thought was snobbishness, and then asked if the field worker thought the same way. On another occasion one of the field workers asked a man what type he meant by 'semi-professionals' and was told, 'Well as a matter of fact I was thinking of you. You aren't an ordinary office worker, but you aren't like a lawyer or a doctor either.' At other times people were less consciously aware of the immediate situation. But it always had some effect on the presentation of the model and it was necessary for the field worker to use his understanding of it in the analysis of each couple's ideas about class.

In ordinary conversation, as has been stated above, people used only parts of their model. There were sometimes discrepancies between these bits and pieces and the tidied-up version presented in reply to direct questions, but the differences were usually variations in emphasis and detail. For example, the sundry supplies buyer and his wife used a model of upper, middle, and working class with three subdivisions in the middle class, placing themselves in the 'middle-middle class'. On other occasions when they were discussing general social and political changes and comparing certain neighbourhoods, they spontaneously used the terms 'middle class' and 'working class' much as they used them when formally outlining the whole model. Sometimes they used the phrase 'the lower income groups' — always spoken with inverted commas — as a synonym for 'working class', partly as a gentle dig at surveys and research work, and partly

[1] Cf. Eysenck's statement that answers to forced-choice questions need not represent the subject's attitudes as expressed in more unstructured interviews. 'It has generally been assumed that stereotyped replies to questions on "national characteristics" indicate stereotyped thinking on the part of the respondents; our results suggest *per contra* that the majority of respondents have no particular views on the subject at all, and are perfectly aware of the fact that any replies they can make are merely the result of cultural and social indoctrination. In other words, the results of studies of this kind are predetermined by the methodology used; when we look for stereotyped views, and give the subject no chance to reply in any non-stereotyped fashion, we should not be surprised that the answer we get is a stereotyped one' (Eysenck and Crown, 1948).

H

as a way of getting around the embarrassment of talking directly about people lower in the hierarchy than themselves. In talking spontaneously about friends, neighbours, and colleagues, they introduced a number of additional concepts: 'suburbanites', 'bohemians', 'intellectuals', and 'intelligent people'. All of these concepts were concerned with social status to a greater or lesser degree, and all had some connection with their class reference groups; they were refinements within the middle-class reference group, although they cut across the three sub-divisions within the middle class.

In brief, people use class reference groups for making both comparisons and evaluations in the widest social context, but their usages vary according to the immediate social situation and the specific purpose of the comparisons and evaluations. It follows that there is no one valid way of finding out what people *really* think about class, for each method will reveal slightly different reference groups, although there is a strain of consistency and continuity running through each couple's usages at different times.

D. Discussion

As has been stated above, all the couples used class reference groups, and everyone operated a model of the class structure, at least implicitly. With two exceptions, informants agreed that classes existed and that society could be divided up into layers differing in power or prestige, or both. In spite of all the individual variations, there was some general consensus about these layers, particularly about contrasts between extremes. Thus, most informants said, or implied, that very rich people or big industrialists or professionals belonged in different classes from people who worked with their hands. There seemed to be some agreement, too, about the terms 'middle class' and 'working class', although not everyone used the words, and the usages were not precise. There were two common definitions of 'the working class'; first as 'anyone who works for a living,' and second as 'people who work with their hands', although there were several informants who included clerks in this second category. It was more difficult to find any general agreement on the term 'the middle class'; it usually meant people above the working class, and those people who used the term generally thought there was an upper class as well.

Consensus disappeared when informants began to deal with occupations or people who were close together. Should clerical workers, for example, be included in the 'working class' or the 'middle class'? Is a doctor in the same class as a large factory manager? Is a small shopowner in the same class as a highly skilled tradesman? In such cases, which were brought up by various informants, there was no general agreement; different individuals dealt with these problems in different ways.

There was general agreement that occupation was the most important criterion of an individual's class membership, although some informants did not mention it directly and a few insisted that money income was more important than occupation. (These were individuals who considered themselves to be relatively well-off financially.) In spite of the agreement on occupation, however, it soon became evident that informants meant different things by the term; some thought of occupation as a source of power, others were thinking of its general prestige, others of the income attached to it. Three informants distinguished the occupational placement of individuals from the industrial and occupational system in general, but most informants did not bother about the causes of the class system as distinct from the placement of individuals in it; similarly they did not distinguish sharply between the mobility of individuals and changes in the class structure as a whole.

All informants agreed that there had been a great deal of 'levelling-up' and that this was a good thing, especially for the working class. A few couples spoke rather regretfully of their loss of income and domestic servants, comparing their situation with that formerly enjoyed by their parents. (None of the families had severe current problems concerning taxation and industrial investment.) The levelling-up was variously attributed to the war, to the militant activities of trade unions and the Labour Party, to the Welfare State, to full employment, or to national solidarity in the face of England's decline as an international power. The most cautious statement was that the old classes remained but the economic and social inequalities between them were less sharp; the most radical version was perhaps the statement by one of the clerks to the effect that 'there used to be a middle class but it seems to have gone out now'. Descriptions of levelling-up depended on the experiences of the speaker. Thus the wife of the sundry supplies buyer mentioned the rise of the working class and then went on to say that, as regards the middle class, it used to be a terrible thing to be 'in trade' but it didn't matter now, and the wife of the occupational therapist said that before the war you would not have been accepted socially (in her parents' class) if you had an accent even if you had money, but that nowadays accent and manners did not matter so much. People who placed themselves in the working class were more inclined to discuss the decline of the bosses' power and the breakdown of the distinctions between clerks, skilled

workers, and unskilled workers. Before the war, the clerks in particular were said to have lived in a different world; now they earned
about the same amount of money as manual workers, or even less,
lived in the same housing estates, and sent their children to the same
schools. Indeed, although only one or two informants mentioned the
increase in numbers of clerical workers, many people talked about
their uncertain status and about general flux in the class structure as
a whole. Several people made remarks such as the following: 'It
might have been simple in the Middle Ages, everything being so
definite you knew exactly what your place was and did not expect to
be anything else. Now it is all uncertain and you don't even know
what your place is.'

Such were the main areas of general agreement. The data do not
provide enough cases or suitable conditions of contrast to allow conclusions to be drawn about the conditions under which people's class
models will resemble one another. It seems likely that the degree of
resemblance will vary directly as the degree of similarity in primary
social experience. If people have radically different experiences, they
will have different class reference groups. If their experiences are
similar, they are more likely to have similar class reference groups.
But if their experiences are not only similar but also shared — that is
if they form a close-knit network or an organized group — they are
even more likely to converge on a common definition. Thus one
would expect to find more consensus in a mining village than in a
mixed working-class area where experiences were similar but not
shared.

Four models of the total class structure were used by the informants:

1. Two-valued power models.
2. Three-valued prestige models.
3. Many-valued prestige models.
4. Mixed power and prestige models.

These four models are sufficient to explain the views of the sixteen
couples who were questioned about class ideology. More extensive interviewing would doubtless lead to modifications and
additions.[1]

[1] Cf. Hammond (1952) whose method of comparing class models with 'objective'
position for a larger number of subjects is more appropriate to this type of analysis.
The models discussed in the present paper are similar to Hammond's, although
there are some differences in definition and criteria. For example, many of his
'composite frameworks' would probably be included in the 'prestige models' of the
present paper rather than in the 'mixed power and prestige models'. Hammond
also places less stress on numerical valuation as an intrinsic component of the
different types of model.

1. *Two-valued power models* were used by people who identified themselves strongly with the working class and felt no desire or compulsion to be socially mobile. They conceived of classes as interdependent but conflicting groups; their idea of bettering their position was by organizing the working class to get more out of the bosses, although they usually added that the boss class had lost a good deal of its power because of full employment. The use of the two basic classes is a logical consequence of using the ideas of power, onflict, and opposition, since two units represent the smallest number required for a conflict. However many classes are actually mentioned, these models are basically two-valued. For example, one man made an overall division into two classes and then made a further sub-division within his own class — again in terms of conflicting opposites; another man made a sub-division in the boss class in which professionals were allied with the bosses proper. Neither of these men felt any embarrassment about placing themselves in the lower of the two classes. They did not feel that the other class was morally superior — it had more power but not more prestige.

Two-valued power models were used by the plumber, the tobacconist, and, by implication, the radio repairer. It is possible that the wife of the radio repairer was beginning to operate a prestige model, although she denied the existence of classes.

2. *Three-valued prestige models* were used by people who placed themselves in the middle class. They divided society into three classes, upper, middle, and working, with two or three sub-divisions in the middle class. If they made three sub-divisions in the middle class they put themselves in the middle division. If they made two, they put themselves in the upper division. No mention was made of class conflict, nor indeed of any relationship between classes as organized groups. Individuals were never described as acting on behalf of their class. It was assumed that individuals could move from one class to another without being traitors. Although classes were described as 'groups', it is evident that they were conceived as categories. Each category was thought to be composed of similar people, and each differed from the others in sub-culture and prestige. The categories were arranged one on top of the other to form a prestige hierarchy. Attention was focused on the placement of individuals in these categories, i.e. their position in the hierarchy. The basic idea seemed to be that individuals in one class, if they happened to meet, might associate with one another as equals in informal interaction. Various criteria of class membership were used, but all were aimed at defining those similarities of taste and interest that would determine

the boundaries of social equality and possible friendship. The women tended to place most stress on manners, accent, taste, and social acceptability, whereas the men talked about occupation and income. The women were thinking primarily of entertaining, whereas the men were thinking about their occupations and colleagues as well. But both men and women suggested that individuals bettered themselves by acquiring the education, occupation, sub-culture, and personal friendship of people in a superior class. Over half the informants who used this model remarked on the lack of it among the various criteria of class membership. Nearly all of them also said that snobbishness was bad and that people who thought about class all the time were snobbish.

If the basic criterion of potential friendship had been systematically followed out, the class structure would have been conceived as an interlocking network of relations among friends. But in place of this conception one finds a notion of three separate classes. The use of a three-valued model is a logical consequence of thinking in terms of prestige. In order to conceptualize prestige — not only general class status but any form of prestige — one must represent one's equals, one's superiors, and one's inferiors. Three groups is the natural number for such a representation. All informants put themselves in the middle group. No one put himself in the bottom group or the top group; two informants put themselves in the upper division of the middle group. All informants were making a symbolic representation of their own status together with their equals in the middle position, with their social superiors above and their inferiors beneath.[1] Status was not conceived in relative terms as a continuum. Each class was given a specific sub-culture. By endowing each of the three groups with a distinctive set of norms and values that distinguishes it from the others, one gives concreteness and substance to the symbolic expression of superiority, equality, and inferiority, so that relativity is removed from the system.

Three-valued prestige models were used by the commercial manager, the W.E.A. lecturer, the sundry supplies buyer, the draughtsman, and one of the clerks. By implication, the statistician and his wife also used this model, although they denied the existence of classes. In all these cases both husband and wife used the same sort of model. While, however, the wives of the account executive and

---

[1] Cf. Barnes: 'I think that in some, at least, of the many instances in which people of widely varying economic position say that they belong to the middle class in a system of three (or more) social classes, they are merely stating that they are aware of these three sets of persons — superiors, equals, inferiors. It does not of itself imply that society can be divided into three groups with agreed membership' (Barnes, 1954, p. 46).

the occupational therapist used three-valued prestige models, their husbands used mixed power and prestige models.

3. *Many-valued prestige models* were used by people who placed themselves in the working class but felt some incompatibility in their position. In three cases they said they were working class by occupation, but regarded themselves as intellectually and culturally different. Intellectuals and professional people were their positive reference groups; businessmen and rich people were ignored or given lower status. In one case a man placed himself in the working class though he admitted some obligation to be mobile at least physically if not socially, and had to justify his desire to stay where he was. All four couples thought of class in terms of prestige rather than power, but they did not use the three-valued model. They listed from four to eight classes, and put themselves in the class second from bottom.

I think they multiplied the number of classes because of their adherence to the points of general consensus mentioned earlier. The term 'middle class' is not completely relative; it carried an agreed absolute connotation such that these individuals did not feel justified in placing themselves in it. If they had used the three-valued prestige model, they would then have had to place themselves in the bottom class, and this is something that no one was willing to do, presumably because it would have meant acknowledgement of absolute rather than relative inferiority. The solution adopted was multiplication of the number of classes with self-placement in the class second from the bottom. The process was not conscious and deliberate.

Many-valued prestige models were used by two of the clerks, the optical instrument repairer, and the painter and decorator.

4. *Mixed power and prestige models* were the most complex. No basic numerical value appeared, one individual using three classes, another four, and another eight. All were 'intellectuals' and they discussed the causes of the class system in general. They phrased their explanations primarily in terms of economic power. In informal conversation, however, they often talked about particular forms of status and skill in terms of equality, superiority, and inferiority, and traces of this prestige framework appeared in their formal presentations of class structure. Their models were not only complex but also unstable. Even in the course of presenting the model in reply to direct questions, these informants tended to shift from a mixed model to a two-valued power model or a three-valued prestige model. Models of this type were used by the occupational therapist and the account

executive, although their wives used three-valued prestige models. Both the deputy insurance manager and his wife, however, used a mixed model.

REFERENCES

BARNES, J. A., 'Class and Committees in a Norwegian Island Parish', *Human Relations*, vol. vii, no. 1 (1954), pp. 39–58.

BARTLETT, F. C., *Remembering* (London: Cambridge University Press, 1932).

CENTERS, R., *The Psychology of Social Classes* (Princeton: Princeton University Press, 1949).

CENTERS, R., 'The American Class Structure: A Psychological Analysis', in Swanson, G. E., Newcomb, T. M., and Hartley, E. L. (eds.), *Readings in Social Psychology* (New York: Henry Holt, 1952), pp. 299–311.

EISENSTADT, S. N., 'Studies in Reference Group Behaviour: I — Reference Norms and the Social Structure', *Human Relations*, vol. vii, no. 2 (1954), pp. 191–216.

EYSENCK, H. J., and CROWN, S. (1948) 'National Stereotypes: An Experimental and Methodological Study', *Int. J. Opin. Attitude Res.*, vo. ii, no. 1 (1948), pp. 26–39.

FORM, W. H., 'Toward an Occupational Social Psychology', *Journal of Social Psychology*, vol. xxiv (1946), pp. 85–99.

HALL, J., and CARADOG JONES, D., 'Social Grading of Occupations', *British Journal of Sociology*, vol. i, no. 1 (1950), pp. 31–55.

HAMMOND, S. B., 'Stratification in an Australian City', in Swanson, G. E., Newcomb, T. M., and Hartley, E. L. (eds.), *Readings in Social Psychology* (New York: Henry Holt, 1952), pp. 288–99.

HYMAN, H. H., 'The Psychology of Status', *Archives of Psychology*, no. 269 (1942).

KELLER, S., and STERN, E., 'Spontaneous Group References in France', *Public Opinion Quarterly*, vol. xvii, no. 2 (1953), pp. 208–17.

KELLEY, H. H., 'Two Functions of Reference Groups', in Swanson, G. E., Newcomb, T. M., and Hartley, E. L. (eds.), *Readings in Social Psychology* (New York: Henry Holt, 1952), pp. 410–14.

MERTON, R. K., and KITT, A. S., 'Contributions to the Theory of Reference Group Behavior', in Merton, R. K., and Lazarsfeld, P. F. (eds.), *Continuities in Social Research: Studies in the Scope and Method of 'The American Soldier'* (Glencoe, Illinois: Free Press, 1950), pp. 40–105.

NEWCOMB, T. M., 'Attitude Development as a Function of Reference Groups: the Bennington Study', in Sherif, M., *An Outline of Social Psychology* (New York: Harper, 1948), pp. 139–55.

NEWCOMB, T. M., *Social Psychology* (London: Tavistock Publications, and New York: Dryden Press, 1950).

NEWCOMB, T. M., and CHARTERS, W. W., 'Some Attitudinal Effects of Experimentally Increased Salience of a Membership Group', in Swanson, G. E., Newcomb, T. M., and Hartley, E. L. (eds.), *Readings in Social Psychology* (New York: Henry Holt, 1952), pp. 415–20.

NORTH, C. C., and HATT, P. K., 'Jobs and Occupations: A Popular Evaluation', *Opinion News*, vol. ix, no. 1 (1947), pp. 3–13.

SHERIF, M., and SHERIF, C. W., *Groups in Harmony and Tension* (New York: Harper, 1953).

WARNER, W. L., and LUNT, P., *The Social Life of a Modern Community* (New Haven: Yale University Press, 1941).

WHAT INFLUENCES LABOUR M.P.s?

By K. J. W. ALEXANDER and ALEXANDER HOBBS

THE persistence through the centuries of religious conflicts in
British politics is a reminder that ideas may have an independent influence upon the political behaviour of individuals. As the influence of religion has been declining in
this century, the influence of Socialist theorists appears to
have increased. The study by Alexander and Hobbs of
religion, of books and of political personalities as formative
influences upon contemporary Labour M.P.s illustrates the
variety of sources that may affect political behaviour. Because
the authors are repeating questions put by W. T. Stead to
Labour M.P.s in the 1906 Parliament, the article is also
valuable as an analysis of trends in this century.

THE 1906 general election brought the first significant influx of
Labour members into the House of Commons and there was
naturally very great interest in what manner of men they were. The
radical editor, W. T. Stead, wrote to each of the fifty-one Labour and
Lib-Lab members asking for information about the books which had
influenced them. Forty-five replied and the information they gave
was published in *Review of Reviews* (vol. xxxiii, June 1906) together
with details of their religious and educational backgrounds thus
giving an invaluable and fascinating insight into the intellectual
background of these early Labour leaders.

In more recent years there have been considerably more sophisticated and thorough investigations made of the backgrounds of
M.P.s. For examples, J. F. Ross (*Parliamentary Representation* and
Elections and Electors) has accumulated much comparative evidence
of changes through successive parliaments in this century; Finer,
Berrington, and Bartholomew (*Backbench Opinion in the House of
Commons, 1955–59*) have related many background variables to
back-bench 'motion-signing' in the 1955 House of Commons; and
more recently Cohen and Cooper ('The 1959 House of Commons' in
Occupational Psychology, October 1961) have collected by questionnaire
a considerable amount of information concerning the 1959 House.
There is a sense, however, in which such work merely complements
rather than supersedes the need for studies like Stead's, for while

Reprinted from *New Society*, 13 December 1962, pp. 11–14.

we now have available many figures and tables of education, age, sex, and father's occupation, the intellectual background which interested Stead remains relatively unexplored.

As a small contribution to bridging this gap we have attempted to bring Stead up to date. Questionnaires were sent to all Labour M.P.s (including the small group expelled from the parliamentary Labour Party early in 1961) asking eight questions. Three questions dealt with the influence of books and writers, three with the influence of religion, one with the possible influence of any historical or contemporary figure, and one with university education (the last being included as a check on the sample obtained). Respondents were also given an opportunity to give any additional information they wished. This questionnaire was a compromise between a desire to get as much specific and detailed information as possible and the suspicion that the larger and more searching the questionnaire the smaller the response was likely to be. The questionnaire is thus open to severe criticism, some of which (e.g. that the questions are too general) was made by a few of the respondents. It is arguable that a more rigorous approach would have yielded a larger response but we doubt it. As it was we received 110 completed questionnaires, which is approximately a 40 per cent sample. This figure compares unfavourably with the return of the Cohen and Cooper questionnaire (88 per cent) but this is only to be expected. The present questions are of a considerably more personal nature. This applies particularly to the questions on religion, traditionally a dangerous subject politically. Though complete anonymity had been promised, one agnostic M.P. wrote particularly requesting it. One member who did not reply wrote later saying: 'One is always suspicious.'

The intrinsic interest of the group and of the replies makes the results of value despite the relatively low return and the consequent possibility of bias. In fact, two checks on the sample provide little evidence to suggest that it deviates from the whole population of Labour M.P.s in any important way. First, university education: Cohen and Cooper, working with substantially the same group but a bigger sample, found that 42 per cent of Labour M.P.s had been to university. Our figure (45 per cent) agrees fairly well with this. Second, party alignment: as this has been a time of considerable debate and dissension within the Labour Party we were anxious to compare our replies with the respondents' position within the party. The problem here was to find some suitable criterion of, say, left and right in the party — other than a subjective appraisal by us of their positions. There are several possible short lists of left-wingers (e.g. voting against defence estimates) but these would not be big enough to provide evidence of general trends. We therefore chose the list of seventy-eight members who signed a letter (*Tribune*, 24 March 1961) objecting to the expulsion of the five M.P.s (plus the five themselves) as being roughly 'the left'. It contains some names not normally associated with the left, but in the interests of objectivity and because the questionnaire was sent soon after the signing of the letter (May–June 1961) we have resisted the temptation to tamper. The terms 'left' and 'right' are always vague, and we may at least plead that here we have defined clearly what we mean. The eighty-three of our left make up approximately 32 per cent of all Labour M.P.s. Of the ninety-five M.P.s who gave their names on their replies, twenty-seven were in the left group, i.e. 28 per cent. Despite this apparent lack of bias, however, we must interpret the results with caution. Percentages and specific figures are given only for accuracy of presentation; any extrapolation to the whole body of Labour M.P.s must be tentative.

Influence of books:

Has the reading of books played a significant part in influencing your political beliefs and actions?
What books or authors have had the greatest influence on your political beliefs?
Has any book published in the last five years particularly impressed you?

Naturally enough, the great majority of M.P.s said that the reading of books had had a significant influence on their politics. Only sixteen said *no*, though even then some of them mentioned influential books. Several others made a point of mentioning other factors, mainly personal experience, as being more important.

The general trend in answering the second question on reading, was to refer to authors rather than books (and usually more than one). Few specific books were mentioned often, apart from the Bible (eighteen times). There were a few references to *The Ragged Trousered Philanthropists*, Bellamy's *Looking Backwards*, Morris's *News From Nowhere* and Paine's *Age of Reason*. The author most commonly referred to was undoubtedly Shaw. The eight most-mentioned authors, clear above the rest of the field, are listed in Table 1. Other political writers were also mentioned several times: Strachey, Bellamy, the Webbs, Durbin — and Jack London. There are few surprising references: Disraeli, Rabelais, and Samuel Smiles might be mentioned here. In an attempt to see if any particular authors were specially favoured by special groups, we looked separately at the reading of the left and non-left groups and of those who had and had not been to university. Shaw, Wells, Cole, and Marx emerged high in all lists, Shaw always first. Tawney was

TABLE 1

The eight most Popular Authors

Shaw	.	.	.	.	. 32 mentions
Wells	.	.	.	.	. 26
Cole	.	.	.	.	. 22
Marx	.	.	.	.	. 19
Tawney	.	.	.	.	. 16
Blatchford	.	.	.	.	. 15
Morris	.	.	.	.	. 14
Laski	.	.	.	.	. 13

mainly a university members' writer, as were Strachey and Laski, though Laski was also characteristically favoured by the left. Jack London was most mentioned by the non-university left, Blatchford and Bellamy by the non-university right. The Webbs, Durbin, Koestler, and Orwell were all characteristically 'right' authors, the last three being mentioned *not at all* by the left group. The most striking difference between these replies and the 1906 results is the relative lack of creative writers in the list (although Shaw's influence was in part due to his playwriting). The first eight in 1906 were Ruskin, Dickens, Henry George, Carlyle, Mill, Scott, Shakespeare, Bunyan. There are no authors in common between the two top eight lists, the 1961 list being predominantly twentieth century. In 1906 the Bible was mentioned more than any author other than Ruskin; now it has fallen below Marx! The progress of Marx (mentioned by only two of the 1906 M.P.s) may be compared with the decline of Henry George (one mention in 1961).

In contrast to the apparent ease with which most respondents could name influential authors, recent books were mentioned by less than half (46 or 42 per cent). There seem three possible explanations for this. One the enforced concern with immediate problems indicated by one wistful reply (and echoed by others): 'Alas only blue books and pamphlets'. It is also suggested by one or two others that books are relatively unimportant creators of opinion now compared with the mass media. A third suggestion, perhaps related to the second, is that 'there does not seem to be any author imbued with any real political zeal whose present day writings could stir people's conscience or imagination'.

No recent book or author stands out in the way that Shaw does as a general influence. Three authors receive multiple mention and together are cited (either separately or as a group) by 18 of the 46: Galbraith, Crosland, and Strachey. Bullock's *Life of Bevin* is mentioned twice, his *Hitler: A Study in Tyranny* once, and Raymond

Williams' *Culture and Society* and *The Long Revolution* are each mentioned once. No other book or author occurs more than once. Most of the other books mentioned are vaguely sociological, for example, *Battle for the Mind*, *The Hidden Persuaders*, *The Roots of Crime*, *The Rise of the Meritocracy*, largely, though not completely, popular and fashionable sociology. Apart from Raymond Williams, the books of the left show up poorly: Foot's *The Pen and the Sword*, Bevan's *In Place of Fear*, published in 1952, and little else. Complementary to this is the fact that the left's recent reading does not show up as strikingly different from the rest, except for the lack of reference to Crosland and Strachey. Only one M.P. mentions books relating to one of the major political issues, nuclear warfare (*Brighter than a Thousand Suns* and King-Hall's *Defence in the Nuclear Age*), perhaps reflecting the fact that the debate has been mainly conducted in other media. Religion gets a little interest (The New English Bible and *The Phenomenon of Man*) as do the problems of underdeveloped countries (*Western Dominance in Asia, Jungle in Retreat*). The few works of creative literature included *Look Back in Anger, Dr. Zhivago, Exodus*. Perhaps some respondents assumed we were interested only in political works.

It would appear from comparison of the two questions on general influence and recent works that whereas in the past the clearly leftist writers Marx and Laski could hold their own, in recent years there are no authors on the left wing of socialist thought who have made as much impact among M.P.s as those on the right, Crosland and Strachey.

Influential figures:
In the early stages of your political life, did any one contemporary figure stand out as an influence on you?

Again the great majority of respondents gave an affirmative reply, only twenty-five said *no*, some indicating an *embarras de choix*, only a few making remarks like 'I am not much influenced by people', or 'at an early age I realized it was silly to expect too much of anyone, in any walk of life.'

The affirmative answers serve to remind one of the political origins and age of many M.P.s still active. Not unexpectedly, Keir Hardie comes out on top with 17 mentions, but he is only just ahead of Lloyd George (16 mentions). These two are well ahead of the rest. Leading Labour Party and trade union figures predominate in the rest of the higher places: Cripps 8, Bevan 7, Maxton 6, Bevin 6, followed by Henderson, W. Graham, Cook, Laski, and Shaw. Few non-British figures make much of a showing: Lincoln 4, Lenin 3,

Gandhi and F. D. Roosevelt 2 each. Two are mentioned as having a particularly negative influence, Marx and Hitler, but Marx has the compensation of a positive mention as well; Attlee, Robert Owen, Ramsay MacDonald, Arthur Greenwood, and Tillett show up poorly with one or two mentions. There are few that could not have been fairly easily predicted: Conrad Noel, Kropotkin, Churchill, Harry Pollitt, Asquith, Disraeli, and Weizman might be mentioned in this class.

Hardie and Lloyd George vary somewhat in the nature of their followers. Those mentioning Hardie are mainly without a university education, 15 without, 2 with. Lloyd George on the other hand is mentioned by 10 with a university education, 6 without. Eight of Lloyd George's followers are in the left group, only 4 of Keir Hardie's. Thus their supporters are characteristically left/university and non-left/non-university respectively. The occurrence of Lloyd George near the top of the list of outstandingly influential figures is probably to a large extent due to several M.P.s having started their political lives as Liberals. We should also note however a point made by one of the left group who mentions him: '. . . But not so much his thought as his general public demeanour.'

Religious upbringing:

Were you brought up in any particular religious denomination? If so what?

A summary of the replies to the question on religious upbringing is in Table 2.

TABLE 2
Religious upbringing

		'Left'*	Non-left*	Anon.†	Total
Anglican, Episcopalian	.	9 (33%)	20 (28%)	2	31 (28%)
Methodist	. . 19⎫				
Presbyterian	. . 13⎪				
Baptist	. . . 11⎬ 13 (48%)	34 (48%)	8	55 (50%)	
Congregationalist	. . 8⎪				
Unspecified Nonconformist.	4⎭				
Roman Catholic	. .	0	2	1	3
Jewish	. . .	2	4	2	8
None	. . . 4⎫				
Mixed	. . . 6⎬ 3	7	0	10	
Swedenborgian	. . 1⎫				
Quaker	. . . 1⎬ 0	2	1	3	
Humanist	. . . 1⎭				

* 'Left'—left-wing M.P.s as defined above; Non-left—all other Labour M.P.s.
† 'Anon'—M.P.s who preferred anonymity.

Exactly half of the respondents were brought up as Presbyterians or Nonconformists, Methodism being the largest of Nonconformist groups (nineteen members). Almost a third of the respondents were brought up as Anglicans or Episcopalians. It will be noted too that the proportions of Anglicans and Nonconformists for the left and non-left groups are similar, i.e. there is no difference in the religious origins of the two political wings of the party.

In 1906 at least 60 per cent of the group replying fell into the Non-conformist–Presbyterian group and information is not given for some members. This is almost certainly a considerable underestimation. Only three out of forty-five had been brought up in the Church of England. There therefore seems to be a considerable trend away from the dominance of Nonconformism. This trend is probably connected with a general shift in the class basis of Labour parliamentarians. In particular it is connected with the trend towards more and more Labour M.P.s having had a university education. In 1906 none of the Labour members had been to university. The general rise in the proportion has been demonstrated by Ross and by Cohen and Cooper. Table 3 shows the relationship between

TABLE 3

Religious upbringing and university education

	At Univ.	Not
Anglican, Episcopalian	20 (65%)	11
Nonconformist, Presbyterian	19 (35%)	36

TABLE 4

Social mobility of Labour M.P.s

	Professional (%)	Manual and blackcoat
1945 PARLIAMENT*		
Father's occupation	15	76
Own first occupation	26	59
1959 PARLIAMENT†		
Father's occupation	20	63
Own first occupation	27	62

* Robertson and Waites, *British Journal of Psychology*, vol. xxxvii, 1947.
† Cohen and Cooper, op. cit.

religious upbringing and university education. Almost two-thirds of those brought up as Anglicans went to university, just over a third of the Nonconformists went. Probably connected with the shift from Nonconformity and the shift to university educated members is the position of M.P.s with respect to their father's occupation and their own first occupation (Table 4).

Thus the Parliamentary Labour Party is by no means completely working class in origin, unlike the position in 1906. Taking this into account, the shift in the position with regard to religious upbringing is probably a by-product of the general shift in social composition.

Influence of religion:
Has religious belief played a significant part in influencing your political beliefs and actions?
What is your religious denomination now?
(including agnostic, etc.)

Answers to the question of the influence of religious belief were put into four categories, *clear yes, qualified yes, qualified no, clear no.* Results are given in Table 5. The trend overall is slightly towards the

TABLE 5
Influence of religious belief

	'Left'		Non-left		Anon.		Total	
'Yes' . .	11	⎫ 48%	35	⎫ 61%	4	⎫ 43%	50	⎫ 55%
Qualified 'Yes' .	2	⎭	7	⎭	2	⎭	11	⎭
Qualified 'No' .	4	⎫ 52%	3	⎫ 39%	2	⎫ 57%	9	⎫ 45%
'No' . .	10	⎭	24	⎭	6	⎭	40	⎭

two *yes* answers. On the whole, those who felt they had been influenced by religion were more forthcoming than those who felt they had not. Some quoted texts or referred to their experiences as lay preachers, etc. Others affirmed a belief in the relationship between Christianity and socialism: 'I regard democratic socialism as the political expression of Christianity.' Remarks of the opposite sort were less frequent: 'My early days in socialism seemed to bring me into conflict with my church.' 'Religion — yes, but contrawise.' Nevertheless the results do suggest a wide range of attitudes to religion with neither positive nor negative feelings clearly predominating. The political subdivisions vary somewhat in their replies to this

I

question, the left group being split almost equally in *yes/no*, the non-left group showing a clear tendency to *yes*. This difference between the two wings of the party with regard to religion becomes clearer

TABLE 6

Present religious denomination

	'Left'	Non-left	Anon.	Total
Religious . .	9⎫	34⎫	4⎫	47⎫
	⎬ 41%	⎬ 77%	⎬ 36%	⎬ 63%
Vaguely religious	2⎭	19⎭	1⎭	22⎭
None . .	4	3	1	8
Vaguely agnostic	3⎫	2⎫	0⎫	5⎫
	⎬ 44%	⎬ 19%	⎬ 57%	⎬ 30%
Agnostic . .	9⎭	11⎭	8⎭	28⎭

when the answers to the question on present denomination are considered (see Table 6). We have divided the answers to this question into the five following categories:

1. Those simply stating a particular religious denomination.

2. Those indicating a denomination but indicating that their adherence is formal or that they do not practise, *plus* those indicating a general non-denominational religious position ('ecumenical', 'vaguely C. of E. with Free Church sympathies', 'Christian agnostic', 'Christian in a general sense', etc.).

3. Those saying *none* without indicating whether they have a leaning towards religion or away from it.

4. Those saying 'agnostic' but qualifying it ('reverent agnostic', 'religious agnostic', 'mildly agnostic', etc.).

5. Those saying 'agnostic' unequivocally or similar ('atheist', 'humanist', etc.).

It was naturally difficult sometimes to place a reply into a category if it was long. Since, however, the trend of results seemed to be away from specific religious denomination, we usually gave religion the benefit of any doubt. Table 7 gives a breakdown into denominations of those in category (1). It will be noted that 63 per cent claim some sort of religious adherence as opposed to 30 per cent claiming to be agnostic. There are two reasons for believing that this may well give an inflated estimate of religious adherence. One is that writing 'agnostic' or 'humanist' probably has more weight than simply writing 'ditto' or 'same' under the denomination stated for upbringing (as several respondents did). Furthermore some M.P.s may

TABLE 7

Present religious denomination: breakdown

	'Left'	Non-left	Anon.	Total
Anglican, Episcopalian	1	9	1	11 (23%)
Methodist . 13				
Presbyterian . 7	6	19	2	27 (57%)
Baptist . . 5				
Congregationalist 2				
Roman Catholic	0	2	0	2
Jewish . .	1	2	1	4
Christian Spiritualist	0	1	0	1
Unitarian . . .	1	0	0	1
Quaker . . .	0	1	0	1

have assumed we were interested in formal adherence rather than belief. The second reason is the high proportion of clear agnostics in the anonymous group of replies. This suggests an easily understood reticence on the part of M.P.s to be associated with a non-religious position. This might have affected some of those replying and may have led to a higher proportion of agnostics not returning the questionnaire.

Whether this surmise is correct or not, however, it is clear that there is a wide divergence of views in the party *vis-à-vis* religion. Of our respondents, the unequivocal agnostics (28) are equal in strength to the largest denominational grouping (Nonconformists 27). More striking than this however is the political split already referred to. Whereas in the case of the left the two religious categories and the two agnostic categories have roughly equal numbers (11 and 12 respectively) the non-left group is predominantly religious (53 to 13). Thus while it cannot be said that the left is not religious, it can be said that the right pretty clearly is.

TABLE 8

Religious upbringing and present denomination

	Upbringing*	Present Denomination	Fall†
Anglican, Episcopalian .	31 (28%)	11 (10%)	20 (65%)
Nonconformist, Presbyterian	55 (50%)	27 (25%)	28 (51%)
Jewish	8	4	4
Roman Catholic . .	3	2	1

* Percentages referred to are percentages of *all* respondents.
† Percentage of original total (i.e. upbringing).

One other feature of the influence of religion may be mentioned, namely, the relationship between present belief and upbringing. Table 8 shows a comparison between the two sets of figures for the main religious groups. Although not all members adhering to a particular denomination were brought up in it, the great majority were. We therefore have what amounts to figures of the extent to which members brought up in a denomination hold to their faith or fall from it. Anglicans appear to have considerably less staying power than Nonconformists.

A comparison of university education and party alignment showed an interesting lack of influence. As can be seen in Table 9, there is

TABLE 9
University education

			Attended University		Total
'Left'	.	.	13	(48%)	27
Non-left	.	.	29	(42%)	69
Anon.	.	.	7	(50%)	13
Total	.	.	49	(45%)	110

little difference between the groups; a slightly higher proportion of the left group have been to university but the difference is small. It would seem that a man's education has less influence on his position in the party than does his religion.

No attempt was made to explore many of the other possible influences on an M.P. such as, for example, his experience at home or in his occupation. Many interesting points were made by respondents nevertheless and some may be mentioned here. Several members mention a radical or socialist father as having a profound influence on them. Perhaps related to this is the fact that while many mention sordid home conditions almost none mention their own conditions of work. Where experience at work was mentioned it is usually with reference to the conditions of others:

Had I not been a socialist my experience as a teacher in Glasgow during the thirties would have made me one. The effects of years of unemployment on the children were devastating.

I was a general medical practitioner in an industrial town and arrived at the conclusion from my own observations that the policy

of the Labour Party was the one needed to alleviate the suffering
I saw.

The remarks made may be biased in some way but the altruistic
motive to take up politics is mentioned more frequently than those
of self-help often supposed to underpin the Labour movement.
Some respondents made brief statements of faith which seemed to be
of special importance to them. A few were religious texts or affirma-
tions ('I believe God's commandments solve the riddle of life'),
others were more pointed views of politics:

Politics should act as a midwife and deliver the next phase of
civilization without destroying the mother.

The influences which we attempted to explore through this questionnaire are difficult to pin down. There is no satisfactory way of establishing the influence of a book, a man, or a religion, and the person
subjected to the influence may be as uncertain as the onlooker. Our
results in no way can be said to establish any points about these areas
of influence. What such an investigation can do, perhaps, is give
some clues to the self image of the person replying, i.e. how he explains the person he believes himself to be.

Within our self-imposed limits we may have established a little
of the outline of that self-image of Labour M.P.s. Some characteristics seem quite widely spread among them. They were readers of
Shaw, Wells, Cole and Marx and influenced by them in the past,
though much less influenced or impressed by books now. They have
no outstanding contemporary literary influences, though on the
right of the party there are Crosland and Strachey. In their youth
the greatest influence was probably a Labour leader such as Keir
Hardie, or possibly Lloyd George. On the right of the party there is
the feeling that religion has been an influence on politics and most
members retain their religious beliefs. This is much less the case on
the left of the party.

VOTING BEHAVIOUR IN BRITAIN, 1945-64

The Gallup Poll — HENRY DURANT, Director

WHILE an election campaign is on, attention is fixed upon public opinion polls as a device for anticipating the result. Once an election is concluded, the data is significant in a different way — as evidence of how different social groups divided in their party preferences. By comparing the party preferences of different social groups from election to election, one can see to what extent relationships between various characteristics and party preferences are durable or simply the product of a particular configuration of influences at a single general election. The British Gallup Poll has a unique historical collection of voting behaviour data, since it pioneered political opinion surveys in England in 1938 and has conducted surveys at every general election since 1945.

THE Gallup Poll data presented here are derived from interviews with quota samples of the electorate immediately before and after the day of a general election. Replies from several surveys taken at almost the same time are often grouped together to provide tables for a single election; in this way, the numbers of persons interviewed from different subsections of the population can be made large enough to give estimates of the party preferences of relatively small social groups (e.g. persons aged twenty-one to twenty-nine). Because samples of any population, including the electorate, vary slightly from survey to survey, small fluctuations of a few per cent in the following tables should be disregarded. In the six general elections since 1945 the Gallup Poll has forecast the distance between the two parties with an average error of 1·9 per cent, in its final pre-election survey; it has always forecast the winner correctly.[1]

Gallup Poll surveys show that while there is a persisting relationship between voting and social class, this relationship is not equally strong within all classes (see Table 1). The upper-middle class is the most class-conscious politically, that is, the most homogeneous in

[1] On survey methods generally, see C. A. Moser, *Survey Methods in Social Investigation* (London: Heinemann, 1958).

The data in this article are from the files of the Gallup Poll. The commentary is by the editor.

TABLE 1

*Class differences in voting behaviour**

UPPER-MIDDLE CLASS

Party	1945 %	1950 %	1951 %	1955 %	1959 %	1964 %
Conservative .	76	79	90	89	87	77
Labour . .	14	9	6	9	6	9
Liberal . .	10	12	4	2	7	14
Labour lead over Conservative	−62	−70†	−84	−80	−81†	−68†

MIDDLE CLASS

Party	1945 %	1950 %	1951 %	1955 %	1959 %	1964 %
Conservative .	61	69	73	77	76	65
Labour . .	24	17	22	21	16	22
Liberal . .	15	14	5	2	8	13
Labour lead .	−37	−52	−51	−56	−60	−43

WORKING CLASS

Party	1945‡ %	1950 %	1951 %	1955 %	1959 %	1964 %
Conservative .	32	36	44	41	40	33
Labour . .	57	53	52	57	54	53
Liberal . .	11	11	4	2	6	14
Labour lead .	25	17	8	16	14	20

VERY POOR

Party	1945‡ %	1950 %	1951 %	1955 %	1959 %	1964 %
Conservative .	32	24	31	44	25	32
Labour . .	57	64	67	54	68	59
Liberal . .	11	12	2	2	7	9
Labour lead .	25	40	36	10	43	27

* For a description of class categories, see the text.
† Liberals second to Conservatives.
‡ 1945 figures in these columns are for working class and very poor respondents grouped together.

voting, favouring the Conservatives over Labour by margins ranging from about $5\frac{1}{2}$ to 1 up to 16 to 1 at general elections since 1945. The upper-middle-class group, described as Average Plus in Gallup reports, constituted 6 per cent of its 1964 sample. The Average category in the Gallup classification system, corresponding to what sociologists call the middle-middle class and a large segment of the lower-middle class, is also pro-Conservative, though much less so than the upper-middle class. This grouping, 22 per cent of the 1964 Gallup sample, has favoured Conservatives over Labour by margins ranging from $2\frac{1}{2}$ to 1 up to $4\frac{1}{2}$ to 1 at post-war general elections.

Working-class voters consistently favour the Labour Party, but by much smaller margins than middle-class voters favour the Conservatives. The Average Minus category of the Gallup Poll, 61 per cent of its 1964 sample, includes the vast majority of manual workers interviewed. It has not favoured Labour by a margin as great as 2 to 1 at any post-war general election; this group has favoured Labour by a margin of less than 5 to 4 up to a margin of slightly less than 2 to 1. The Gallup method of classification includes some routine non-manual workers in its Average Minus category; if an allowance is made for the probable pro-Conservative weighting which this minority might introduce, the manual workers in the group would be slightly more cohesive politically, but at a maximum, less than 7 to 3 Labour. The Very Poor category, 11 per cent of the Gallup Poll sample in 1964, includes the poorest manual workers, and also a disproportionate number of pensioners. Hence, while it is an exclusively manual-worker category, the presence of a large number of old people introduces a second influence into the grouping. At post-war general elections, it has favoured Labour by margins ranging from 5 to 4 up to 11 to 4; it has not been as strongly Labour at any election as the middle-class or upper-middle class groups have been Conservative.

The relative importance of class as an influence upon British voting, notwithstanding the fact that it is not the sole influence, is emphasized by a comparative international study by Robert Alford, *Party and Society*.[1] Alford used Gallup Poll data from Britain, America, Australia, and Canada to compare the extent to which the Labour or left party in each of these countries was exclusively working-class in its electoral support; because this data extended back to the Second World War, he was also able to examine the persistence of this form of class voting. Alford found that Britain had the highest level of class voting in terms of his index, and that

[1] (London: Murray, 1964.)

this level was more stable than that of any of the other three nations; furthermore, religious and regional differences appear to reduce class voting much less in Britain than in either Canada or America.

When voter preferences in Britain are analysed in terms of sex differences, men show a consistent bias in favour of the Labour Party, and women in favour of the Conservatives (Table 2).

TABLE 2

Sex differences in voting behaviour

MEN

Party	1945 %	1950 %	1951 %	1955 %	1959 %	1964 %
Conservatives .	35	41	46	47	45	40
Labour . .	54	46	51	51	48	49
Liberals . .	11	13	3	2	7	11
Labour lead .	19	5	5	4	3	9

WOMEN

Party	1945 %	1950 %	1951 %	1955 %	1959 %	1964 %
Conservatives .	43	45	54	55	51	45
Labour . .	45	43	42	42	43	39
Liberals . .	12	12	4	3	6	16
Labour lead .	2	−2	−12	−13	−8	−6

Quantitatively, the bias is much smaller than the bias of the middle class towards the Conservatives and of working-class voters towards Labour. Because the electoral system tends to magnify the consequences in terms of parliamentary seats of relatively small advantages in votes, politicians may be specially concerned with these small differences. It is important to note, however, that while sex differences in voting persist, and may also be found in a number of other Western countries,[1] the differences are so small proportionately that sex has very little accuracy as a predictor of the vote of an individual.

Analysis of the influence of age upon voting is complicated because it is necessary to review figures over a period of time, as in Table 3, to ensure that apparent differences are not simply the consequence

[1] See S. M. Lipset, *Political Man* (London: Heinemann, 1960).

TABLE 3

Age differences in voting behaviour

YOUNG VOTERS, 21-29

Party	1945 %	1950 %	1951 %	1955 %	1959 %	1964 %
Conservatives .	29	36	44	43	46	39
Labour . .	57	52	53	54	47	47
Liberals . .	14	12	3	3	7	14
Labour lead .	28	16	9	11	1	8

MIDDLE AGE, 30-49

Party	1945 %	1950 %	1951 %	1955 %	1959 %	1964 %
Conservatives .	36	43	48	49	48	42
Labour . .	52	45	48	48	47	45
Liberals . .	12	12	4	3	5	13
Labour lead .	16	2	0	−1	−1	3

LATE MIDDLE AGE, 50-64

Party	1945* %	1950 %	1951 %	1955 %	1959 %	1964 %
Conservatives .	43	50	57	56	53	44
Labour . .	47	38	39	42	40	40
Liberals . .	10	12	4	2	7	16
Labour lead .	4	−12	−18	−14	−13	− 4

OLD-AGE PENSIONERS, 65 PLUS

Party	1945* %	1950 %	1951 %	1955 %	1959 %	1964† %
Conservatives .	43	40	48	54	44	46
Labour . .	47	47	51	45	51	44
Liberals . .	10	13	1	1	5	10
Labour lead .	4	7	3	−9	7	−2

* 1945 figures in these columns combine the 50–64 and 65 plus age groups.

† National Opinion Poll random sample figures give Conservatives a 13 per cent lead over Labour in 1964, and suggest that quota samples may be biased by selecting a disproportionately small number of old Conservatives.

of particular political situations, or of attitudinal differences between age cohorts which have reached political maturity in different political circumstances — e.g., before the First World War, the Depression, post-1945 austerity, and post-1955 prosperity. Furthermore, in the youth category, aged twenty-one to twenty-nine, the membership will change completely in a decade; in successive decades, one is not comparing differences in the voting behaviour of the same persons, but rather of different young persons. In the age group over sixty-five, mortality operates slightly more slowly in changing the characteristics of the members. A small number of old people included in the category in 1945, born before 1880, would still be represented in the 1964 figures; the category in 1964 would also include men who were not old enough to vote until after the First World War.

Because of changes in the composition of young voters, the sizable shifts recorded in this category are understandable. While Gallup findings have shown voters aged twenty-one to twenty-nine favouring Labour at every post-war election, the margins have varied from 1 per cent to 28 per cent. Except for the 1945 general election, Labour's only sweeping victory at the polls, the two middle age groups have been relatively stable in their party preferences, with those aged thirty to forty-nine dividing virtually evenly, and those aged fifty to sixty-four consistently favouring the Conservatives. Among old age pensioners and others above the age of sixty-five, Gallup Poll data indicate that preferences have shifted back and forth between the parties, and shifted counter to national swings at the same election. This volatility may well be due to the behaviour of a section of pensioners who are influenced to shift votes much more readily than other social groupings because of their particular concern with only one political issue — the value which the Government gives to their old age pension.

Study of these tables makes clear how misleading are attempts to explain voting behaviour in terms of a *single* social characteristic of voters. While observable differences in voting do exist and persist between men and women and different age groups these differences in partisan allegiance are far too small to be explained away simply as consequences of social differences. Even objective social class, which correlates with party preference at all levels of class structure, leaves unexplained the voting behaviour of that third of the British electorate which does not vote in agreement with its objective class. The tables in this article can provide evidence for a tentative body of generalizations about social factors influencing voting behaviour, but more complex analysis would be required to increase the explanatory power of these data; such analysis would assess not only the effect of combinations of characteristics (for example, of old age and sex, or objective class and age) but also the effect of a variety of attitudinal factors, such as subjective social class assessment, involvement in politics and perceptions of politics.[1]

[1] For an example of complex analysis, including attitudinal influences as well as simple social characteristics discussed in this article, see A. Campbell, *et al.*, *The American Voter* (New York: Wiley, 1960).

SOCIAL TRENDS AND ELECTORAL BEHAVIOUR

By MARK ABRAMS

THE study of voting behaviour gains in significance as voting
is related to a wide range of social and psychological factors
which influence individual political activity and inactivity in
the years between elections. Mark Abrams' study provides data
about the extent to which voters are interested and informed
about politics and the relationship between involvement and
party preferences. It indicates how dangerous it is to draw
inferences about the political opinions of voters on a wide
range of public issues, because so many voters have such
limited amounts of political interest and information. Inasmuch as some party preferences shifted to Labour between
the time data was collected and the 1964 general election, it
also illustrates the difficulties of extrapolating trends into the
future.

BEFORE attempting to link the two parts of the title to this paper
I would like to discuss them separately. For the great majority of
British citizens electoral behaviour consists almost entirely of voting
for a party candidate or not voting at all at a parliamentary general
election, and it is with this form of behaviour that I shall be mainly
concerned.

We know from official statistics for all contested constituencies the
total turn-out, but for anything more revealing than this we are
dependent upon the findings of sample surveys. From these, however,
we are able to establish with a fair degree of reliability the turn-out
rate for various sections of the electorate and to see that within the
total figures there are considerable and politically important variations. The survey figures used here are drawn very largely from two
nation-wide inquiries; one was carried out in the summer of 1959
shortly before the general election of that year and used a probability
sample of just under 1,000 adults; the second was completed in
January 1960 (i.e. shortly after the election) and this used a quota
sample of 750 adults. Both surveys asked about voting behaviour at
the 1955 general election and the later one also inquired about the
1959 election. The fact that both surveys were within two or three

Reprinted from *The British Journal of Sociology*, vol. xiii, no. 3 (1962), pp. 228–42.

months of the 1959 general election meant that few respondents thought in terms of supporting the Liberal Party.

In 1955, with an electorate of 34 millions in Great Britain (the survey area), 26·1 million votes were cast, i.e. 77 per cent of the electorate voted. By 1959 almost 2½ millions of this electorate had died. Nearly two-thirds of these casualties came from a section of the electorate with usually a low turn-out (i.e. those aged seventy or more), and we would therefore expect that a survey among the survivors in 1959 would show for them a turn-out of approximately 80 per cent at the 1955 election. In fact, in both the 1959 and 1960 surveys, of those old enough to have voted in 1955, some 85 per cent said they had voted at that general election.

Inflation of this kind and of this order is, unfortunately, not uncommon in surveys which question people about their voting behaviour at past elections. Bearing this in mind one may cautiously but reasonably conclude that:

1. There was in 1955 very little difference in turn-out between men and women.

2. The turn-out was lower among young electors (aged thirty-four or less) than among older voters (aged fifty or more).

3. The turn-out was slightly lower among semi- and unskilled manual workers and their wives than it was among skilled workers and middle-class electors.

4. The turn-out was much lower among people who between elections have not made up their minds to vote for either the Labour Party or the Conservative Party. Among supporters of the two parties, Conservatives had a slightly higher turn-out.

5. The turn-out was very much lower among people who are not members of a political party, do not support one of them, and do not even feel that they 'lean' towards one of them. These completely non-political electors form roughly 12 per cent of the electorate (i.e. over 4 million electors); but in spite of their detachment half of them do, in fact, vote at a general election. The difference in total votes between the two major parties in both the 1955 and 1959 general elections was little more than 1 million.

6. But apart from this fringe of detached electors it is clear that among the rest of the electorate there is, in every sub-group, a turn-out of at least 80 per cent — and in some the rate is over 90 per cent.

Side by side with this very high turn-out rate outside the small detached fringe there is one other remarkable feature of British electoral behaviour — the average person's high stability of party voting from one general election to another. Table 2 is based on the

TABLE 1

1955 Turn-out rates in various sections of the 1959/60 electorate

Sections of survivors of 1955 electorate	*Claimed turn-out in 1955*	*Size of each group in the 1959 electorate*
	%	%
Men	86	47
Women	85	53
Aged under 35	76	26
„ 35–49	81	30
„ 50 or more	86	44
Middle class	87	32
Skilled working class . . .	87	33
Semi- and unskilled working class . .	83	35
Conservative intending voters in 1959/60 .	91	38
Labour intending voters in 1959/60 . .	89	40
Other electors in 1959/60	67	22
Party members in 1959/60 . . .	95	15
Party supporters in 1959/60 . . .	92	45
Party 'leaners' in 1959/60	83	28
No party identification in 1959/60 . .	51	12

TABLE 2

1955 voting behaviour of 1959 electorate aged twenty-five and over

Party supported in 1955 election	*1959 electorate*		
	Conservative %	*Labour* %	*Rest of 1959 electorate* %
Conservative .	87	3	22
Labour . .	3	86	31
Liberal . .	1	*	11
Abstained . .	9	11	36
TOTAL . .	100	100	100

* Less than 0·5 per cent.

earlier survey and shows, for those old enough to vote in both elections, the 1955 voting behaviour of the 1959 electorate; almost 90
per cent of the 1959 Conservatives had voted Conservative in 1955;
and almost 90 per cent of Labour supporters had voted Labour in
1955.

In Table 3 there is shown for those who supported the Conservatives in the 1960 survey their answers to a series of questions that

132

MARK ABRAMS

TABLE 3
General election behaviour of 1960 Conservatives*

	1959 %	1955 %	1951 %
Voted Conservative .	86	75	69
Voted Labour . .	3	10	11
Voted Liberal, etc. .	1	1	1
Don't remember . .	†	4	7
Information refused .	1	1	1
Abstained . . .	9	9	11
TOTAL . . .	100	100	100

* Excluding at each election those too young to vote.
† Less than 0·5 per cent.

TABLE 4
General election behaviour of 1960 Labour supporters

	1959 %	1955 %	1951 %
Voted Labour . .	89	88	86
Voted Conservative .	3	1	1
Voted Liberal, etc. .	*	1	..
Don't remember . .	..	2	4
Information refused .	1	1	1
Abstained . . .	7	7	8
TOTAL . . .	100	100	100

* Less than 0·5 per cent.

TABLE 5
General election behaviour of 1960 rest of electorate

	1959 %	1955 %	1951 %
Voted Conservative .	23	17	9
Voted Labour . .	26	31	37
Voted Liberal, etc. .	11	12	10
Don't remember . .	2	10	20
Information refused .	14	15	15
Abstained . .	24	15	9
TOTAL . . .	100	100	100

asked them how they had voted in each of the three preceding general elections (1959, 1955, 1951). Table 4 gives the answers of 1960 Labour supporters, and Table 5 gives the answers of those who in 1960 supported neither of the two main parties.

From these tables it will be seen that:

1. Among the Conservatives, the party that had grown in electoral popularity over the period (and therefore had probably attracted into its ranks former opponents and waverers), nearly three-quarters of the 1960 supporters were people who were Conservative voters three general elections earlier.

2. At the beginning of 1960 support for the Labour Party had probably reached its lowest point since 1945; it is therefore not surprising to find that at the time of the survey older Labour supporters were almost entirely people who had voted Labour throughout the 1950's and stood fast even after three successive electoral defeats.

3. Even among the 1960 fence-sitters there was a high degree of long-term consistency in their detachment; probably half of them had not voted for either of the two major parties at any of the three elections.

Taken together the two features of British electoral behaviour so far discussed — the very high turn-out and the high stability of party loyalties — might suggest that most British electors are keenly interested in politics, and that the supporters of the two main parties see the Conservative Party and Labour Party as sharply unequal in their ability to handle the nation's problems. Neither of these conclusions would appear to be justified.

The first of these possibilities was examined in a survey carried out by Research Services a few months after the last general election. In the summer of 1960 we interviewed a quota sample of 1,500 persons aged sixteen and over; this sample was selected so that in many of its main socio-demographic traits — age, sex, occupation, income, terminal education age, etc. — it matched the total adult population of England and Wales. The main purpose of the inquiry was to measure the extent to which people discussed the sort of material that normally appears in their newspapers and their interest in such material. At one point in the interview they were asked: 'How would you describe your interest in politics?' And their answers were recorded in terms of four levels of interest — very interested, interested, not really interested, not at all interested. Only 15 per cent of all respondents said they were very interested in politics.

Between various sections of the sample there were, however,

K

considerable differences in the responses to this initial question. The proportion claiming to be very interested in politics was much higher among men than among women, higher among people aged forty-five or more, among those who had received some higher education, and among middle-class adults. But even in these groups the proportion claiming to be very interested was quite small; it was usually below 20 per cent, and only among men did it rise to 21 per cent.

Within the sample of male respondents the other features of the pattern already described broadly repeated itself. Thus, among middle-class men aged forty-five and over, and with some higher education, 22 per cent said they were very interested in politics; and among working-class men aged below forty-five, and with no higher education, only 13 per cent claimed to be very interested.

Since a claimed high interest in politics is largely concentrated among men we have in the rest of this account of the survey restricted ourselves to the replies from the men in the sample.

TABLE 6

How would you describe your interest in politics?

	Total sample %	Men %	Women %	Age Under 45 %	Age 45 and over %	Middle class %	Working class %	Terminal education age Under 16 %	Terminal education age 16 or more %
Very interested	15	21	8	10	19	17	14	14	19
Interested	37	39	35	41	34	52	30	32	53
Not really interested	33	29	38	35	31	22	38	37	22
Not at all interested	15	11	19	14	16	9	18	17	6
TOTAL	100	100	100	100	100	100	100	100	100
NUMBER	1,496	762	734	736	760	472	1,024	1,147	349

To assess the quality of claimed interest in politics, all respondents were asked about their attendance at meetings during the twelve months preceding the interview. Over the year, of all the men with little or no interest in politics, only 6 per cent had been to a political meeting. Among those 'interested in politics' as few as 1 in 6 had taken part in a political meeting at least once in twelve months. Only among the 21 per cent of men who claimed to be 'very interested in politics' was there anything like large-scale attendance; and even among this minority less than half claimed they had atten-

ded a political meeting during the year. (It should be remembered
that the year covered included the 1959 general election.)

The answers to one of the questions included in the survey carried
out just before the 1959 general election similarly suggest that it is
not false modesty which leads so many people to disclaim any lively
interest in politics. Here each respondent was asked to name three
leaders of the Conservative Party, three leaders of the Labour Party
and one leader of the Liberal Party.[1] Within these limitations only 30
per cent of all respondents gave at least five correct names, and 20
per cent were unable to provide even one correct name. Moreover,
this total position was not the outcome of a mixture of complete
knowledgeability among the 15 per cent of the sample who were
party members and complete ignorance on the part of those who
felt they did not even 'lean' towards one of the political parties.

TABLE 7

Able to name party leaders

	Type of respondent				
	Party member %	Party supporter %	Lean towards a party %	Others %	Total %
7 correct* .	9	5	4	3	5
6 ,, .	16	11	8	8	11
5 ,, .	18	13	17	6	14
4 ,, .	18	13	12	13	14
3 ,, .	11	13	12	13	12
2 ,, .	8	15	12	12	13
1 ,, .	9	13	11	11	11
None,, .	11	17	24	34	20
	100	100	100	100	100

* Within the limits set, i.e. three from each major party and one Liberal; most
people were defeated by the task of naming a Liberal leader.

Knowledge and ignorance were well distributed among all sections
of the electorate. Even among party members nearly 40 per cent
could think of only three or even fewer correct names, and among
those totally detached from party sympathies as many as 30 per
cent were able to produce four or more correct names.

It seems reasonable, in the light of this and much similar evidence,
to conclude that our high turn-out and persistent party loyalty do

[1] The definition of a 'leader' was generous; we accepted as correct the names of
19 Conservative Ministers, 18 Labour Front Benchers and 3 Liberal M.P.s.

not stem from a widespread, deep, and informed interest in politics. What about the other possibility — that they are the products of a sharp awareness on the part of the electorate that the two main parties differ substantially in their competence to manage the nation's affairs? Here again, the two surveys conducted round the 1959 general election lead one to doubt this explanation.

In the 1960 inquiry respondents were given a card listing sixteen political ends and party traits and told: 'Here are some of the things that have been said about the two main political parties. Would you tell me, for each statement, whether you think it applies more to the Conservatives, or to the Labour Party? You may say that some of the statements apply to both, or do not apply to either party.' For four of the statements roughly half or more of the respondents indicated that they were not aware of any difference between the two parties (these were concerned with the prevention of a nuclear war, fair treatment for all races, a concern for the nation as a whole, and the maintenance of world peace). On a further eight issues between 33 and 45 per cent of the respondents were unable to detect any difference between Conservatives and Labour. And on only four of the statements was there a clear-cut attribution of the goal to either Conservatives or Labour by at least two-thirds of the total sample. (These were: stands mainly for the middle class, would give more chances to the person who wants to better himself, would make the country more prosperous, and stands mainly for the working class. The first three were clearly recognized as marks of the Conservative Party, and the last was seen as overwhelmingly a Labour Party preoccupation.) In short, a clear-cut partisan view of the two parties seems to be limited largely to class images and the opportunities for personal and general material advancement.

Naturally, the supporters of each party are able to discern a greater degree of conflict between the two parties, and this discrimination is greatest among those respondents who in 1960 supported the Labour Party — even after its three successive defeats. But even among these die-hards between 44 and 55 per cent of them said they could see no difference in the competence of the two parties when handling seven out of the sixteen listed traits and objectives. And these seven included such apparently important items as fair treatment for all races, concern for the nation as a whole, and the prevention of nuclear war. Indeed, these Labour stalwarts were able to discriminate sharply between the two parties on no more than three or four of the listed issues; three-quarters or more of them were able to identify one or other of the two parties as standing mainly for the working class, concerned to help the underdog, or ready to raise the standard of living of ordinary people. Usually they thought it was the Labour Party which distinctively had these interests at heart.

The Conservatives, thanks largely to the broadmindedness of those of its supporters with comparatively recent roots in the party, showed a greater readiness to attribute competence and good intentions to both parties when they came to consider the prevention of nuclear war and fair treatment for all races. On another six issues between 35 and 46 per cent of them were unable to discriminate between the two parties. But, unlike Labour supporters, nearly all Conservatives claimed to be able to recognize a difference between the Conservative Party and the Labour Party when it came to finding a party which would make the country more prosperous, would satisfy the man with ideals, and would really respect British traditions.

Not surprisingly, it was among the 17 per cent of respondents who refused to support either main party that readiness to discriminate

TABLE 8

Political ends: proportion saying 'applies to both'
(or 'to neither' or 'don't know')

| | | Supporters of | | |
Statement	All respondents %	Con. %	Lab. %	Rest %
Would really work to prevent nuclear war	63	67	52	74
Believes in fair treatment for all races and creeds	63	62	54	69
Would do most for world peace	49	46	49	63
Is out for the nation as a whole	49	39	54	68
Has a clear-cut policy	44	31	50	66
Would try to abolish class differences	42	43	36	50
Really respects British traditions	41	29	51	55
Would extend the Welfare services	39	44	31	38
Is out to help the underdog	37	42	22	50
Is most satisfying for the man with ideals	36	29	36	56
Would raise standard of living of ordinary people	35	35	26	53
Has united team of top leaders	33	20	44	48
Stands mainly for the middle class	31	32	26	41
Would give more chances to person who wants to better himself	31	27	28	53
Would make the country more prosperous	29	16	38	48
Stands mainly for the working class	19	24	8	27

between Conservatives and Labour was lowest. In commenting on thirteen of the sixteen listed statements roughly 50 per cent or more of these fence-sitters said that either party would be equally competent or equally incompetent.

Further evidence that a large part of the electorate are prepared to attribute good intentions and reasonable competence to both parties is provided by the findings of the 1959 pre-general election survey. Informants were asked: 'Do you think the Conservative Party's policies would ever endanger the country's welfare?' Two-thirds said they thought they probably would not. Even among Labour supporters over half were of this opinion, and only 10 per cent were reasonably sure that Conservative policies were a potential danger to the nation's welfare.

TABLE 9

'*Do you think the Conservative Party's policies would ever endanger the country's welfare?*'

	Conservatives %	Labour %	Others %	Total %
Probably would .	2	10	6	6
Might . .	9	32	25	22
Probably wouldn't	87	52	57	66
Don't know .	2	6	12	6
TOTAL . .	100	100	100	100

Not quite the same high measure of forbearance was extended to the Labour Party when informants were asked: 'Do you think Labour Party policies would ever seriously endanger the country's welfare?' But even so, almost half the sample said they thought they would not. Even among Conservative supporters over a quarter thought the danger unlikely and only one-third considered the threat to be probable. These views are all the more striking when it is seen that over a quarter of Labour's supporters thought their Party's policies might seriously endanger the nation's welfare.

One remarkable feature of this unwillingness on the part of the 1959 electorate to translate party defeat into national disaster was the above-average magnanimity of working-class Labour supporters: 54 per cent felt that Conservative Party policies would probably not endanger the country's welfare. At the same time middle-class Conservatives failed to match this tolerance; only 24 per cent of these said that Labour policies constituted no probable threat to the nation's welfare. In other words, within the Labour Party middle-class deviants are slightly more fearful than others of Conservative policies; but within the Conservative Party the middle-class regulars are more suspicious than others of their opponent's policies. In other words, while mutual tolerance is generally quite high there seems to be a little more of it among working-class party supporters than there is among middle-class party supporters.

TABLE 10

'Do you think the Labour Party's policies would ever seriously endanger the country's welfare?'

	Conservatives %	Labour %	Others %	Total %
Probably would .	34	3	10	16
Might . .	37	24	34	31
Probably wouldn't	26	68	42	47
Don't know .	3	5	14	6
TOTAL . .	100	100	100	100

However, too much should not be made of this appearance of middle-class political truculence. A survey carried out by us in the summer of 1960 was specifically concerned with the intra-party groupings of middle-class people who were under forty-five years of age and had a terminal education age of at least sixteen years of age. After they had indicated the party they supported they were then asked to indicate their relative position within the party.

TABLE 11

Location within party: middle class under forty-five years of age

	Conservatives %	Labour %	Liberals %
Left .	23	34	28
Centre .	59	39	38
Right .	18	27	34
TOTAL	100	100	100

Almost one-quarter of the Conservatives said they were on the left flank of their party and over a quarter of the Labour supporters considered themselves to be on the right flank of their party. In each case the biggest single group chose for themselves a central position.

It seems reasonable to conclude that normally there is comparatively little tension between the mass of supporters of the two main parties and that therefore voting stability and high turn-out must spring from other causes.

The early-1960 survey throws some light on one of the main causes of voting stability. Respondents were asked how their parents voted before the war. The replies suggest that most people acquire their party loyalties by inheritance. Of all the fathers described by informants, 32 per cent were known by their offspring to have been Conservatives, 31 per cent Labour, 10 per cent Liberals, 5 per cent

TABLE 12

Inter-generation voting behaviour

| Respondents' party choice | Father's pre-war voting behaviour | | | | |
	Con. %	Lab. %	Lib. %	Not known %	Never voted %
Conservative .	71	28	36	48	44
Labour . .	15	61	24	31	44
Other* . .	14	11	40	21	12
TOTAL .	100	100	100	100	100

* Includes Liberals, don't knows, and would abstain.

had never voted, and of the remaining 22 per cent the present respondents said they had never known their fathers' political loyalties. Among the children of Conservative fathers, over 70 per cent are now Conservatives and only 15 per cent support Labour. Among the children of Labour fathers, over 60 per cent are now Labour supporters and only 28 per cent are Conservatives. Only the children of pre-war Liberals and the children of secretive fathers received no clear-cut guidance on political thinking for the post-war world. At present, just over one-quarter of them are completely detached from both the main parties, another 30 per cent vote Labour and 45 per cent are Conservatives. (It is possible that both these rootless groups are potential defectors from their present parties.)

While these figures show the considerable importance of parental socialization in the acquisition of party loyalties they also make clear that the matching between generations is not complete. Rebels, especially in the households of Labour fathers, have appeared in the post-war years. The recent survey among third-year students at

four London colleges shows, for one small group, the inner pattern
of this breakaway movement. All the students in the survey could
be considered, because of the jobs they will take up after graduating,
to be middle class. Not all of them, however, came from middle-
class homes. Of the 740 students of British nationality, 23 per cent
in giving their fathers' present occupations described them in these
terms as working class. This quarter of the students could therefore be
regarded as having moved up the social scale. The relationship between fathers' and children's social class and politics is shown in
Table 13. Of all the students with working-class parents, 65 per

TABLE 13

Social class and inter-generation voting behaviour: London University students

Students' party ties	Students with middle-class parents who vote:				Students with working-class parents who vote:			
	Con. %	Lab. %	Lib. %	D.K. %	Con. %	Lab. %	Lib. %	D.K. %
Conservative .	52	16	18	32	43	20	33	35
Labour . .	15	54	22	22	5	43	17	22
Liberal . .	15	12	60	24	32	10	50	19
Other and D.K..	18	18	—	22	20	27	—	24
TOTAL . .	100	100	100	100	100	100	100	100

cent said they knew the political loyalties of their fathers; over half
(55 per cent) of these fathers were described by their offspring as
Labour supporters, but little more than two-fifths (43 per cent)
of these children of working-class Labour-voting fathers currently
support the Labour Party; another one-fifth support the Conservative Party. This inter-generation move to the right is clearly associated with upward social mobility; there is no rightward move of comparable dimensions among the children of middle-class Labour-
voting fathers. In this group more than half (54 per cent) follow in
father's Labour footsteps, and only one in six has become a Conservative.

It seems reasonable to conclude, therefore, that while current
political loyalties have been mainly determined by parental
socialization, complete repetition between the generations has been
prevented largely by upward social mobility which has generated a
net movement towards the centre and the right.

Table 13a underlines the need to talk about a net movement since

it shows that a handful of middle-class Conservative fathers have
produced Labour-supporting sons and daughters. The table also
indicates that in both groups — the socially stable and the socially
mobile — the biggest net movement in party support has been towards the centre. This latter shift shown in the student survey ties in

TABLE 13a

Inter-generation voting behaviour: London University Students

	Voting of middle-class fathers %	Voting intentions of their children %	Voting of working-class fathers %	Voting intentions of their children %
Conservative .	49	38	27	32
Labour . .	16	23	36	25
Liberal . .	5	20	2	20
Don't know .	30	19	35	23
TOTAL . .	100	100	100	100

consistently with the findings already discussed of the two earlier
general surveys — that is, the readiness of supporters of both main
parties to admit a wide range of virtue and competence among their
opponents.

This mutual tolerance by party supporters can be shown by
sample surveys to be a comparatively recent development in modern
British political attitudes. In the late 1940's the electorate was convinced that there were sharp and irreconcilable differences between
the two parties. For example, in one of our own surveys carried out
in July 1949, among all electors, except Conservative supporters,
substantial minorities were convinced that a Conservative victory in
the next general election would mean mass unemployment, the dis-
mantlement of the Welfare State, more industrial disputes, and an
abrupt extension of private enterprise. Simultaneously, all but
Labour supporters feared that another Labour victory would lead
to a much wider application of nationalization, the neglect of
national material prosperity, and excessive class-oriented legislation;
one-third of all Conservatives, in answer to another question, asserted
that in its four years of power the Labour Government had done
nothing that was worthy of approval.

The lowering of tension since then has various sources. One of
them, of course, is that since the late 1940's the average standard of
living has risen appreciably in this country. Another, and more

stable source springs from the changes that are taking place in the way people earn their living. Between 1950 and 1960 the total number of workers in the whole of British manufacturing industry increased by slightly under one million; but of these additional employees only one-third were manual workers and the remaining two-thirds were white-collar workers — i.e. those with clerical, administrative, or technical jobs. Within industry there are still many more manual workers than white-collar workers, but the balance between them is changing steadily. Ten years ago the manpower of an average factory was made up of one white-collar worker for every six manual workers on its payroll; but today it apparently needs one white-collar worker for every four manual workers in the factory.

But this is not the whole picture. There are many millions of workers who are employed outside the scope of manufacturing industry. For example, there are those in the distributive trades (shop assistants, wholesalers, etc.), those in banking, insurance and finance, those in public administration (working for both local and central government), those in the professional and scientific services (education, medicine, etc.), and, finally, there are those who are described in the statistical tables as being employed in the 'miscellaneous' service trades — hotels, laundries, entertainment, garages. Today, the number of people working in these five groups of non-factory occupations is larger than the number of workers — both manual and white-collar — in the whole of manufacturing industry. And, what is more important, over the past ten years two out of every three people added to the nation's total working population have been absorbed by these five non-industrial occupations.

In effect, then, in post-war Britain there has been a double movement in the way people earn their living: most new workers have gone into non-industrial jobs, and, secondly, most people who have gone into industry have taken up white-collar jobs. These employment changes are slowly, but persistently and fundamentally, affecting our non-working lives. For example, they largely account for the much greater concern today with higher education and particularly with technical and professional training. Again, as more and more people work at jobs which are not physically exhausting home life and family life have taken on a new importance and a new vitality. Compared with a generation ago, people today show a greater interest in their homes, in home-ownership, in moving to the suburbs, and in the family 'doing things together'. In politics one consequence of the shift in jobs is that more and more voters move away from the extremes of both right and left and prefer policies of moderation.

There is a growing interest by the ordinary man and woman in
local matters and local needs — schools, hospitals, town planning,
roads, youth clubs, old people's clubs, smoke abatement, etc. Most
of these are problems better tackled by professional skill rather than
by ideological slogans, and this shift further encourages moderation
and discourages extremism. In industry and business the white-
collar workers are replacing the manual workers as the key group
which determines society's productivity and growth. So in politics
they are replacing them as the group whose interests and needs increasingly determine the direction and climate of political discussion
and controversy. Both political parties have been slow to see and to
accept these changes — although one party has been much slower
than the other. Their procrastination has been encouraged by the fact
that voting behaviour, based as it is largely on early socialization
and a sense of duty, has not, so far, been affected sharply by changing
political attitudes. However, the gap between political attitudes
and voting behaviour is steadily hardening and even politicians are
coming to realize that complex changes in the class structure of post-
war British society threaten in the not too distant future to end the
old ideological simplifications about politics.

THE FLOATING VOTE

By R. S. MILNE *and* H. C. MACKENZIE

WHEN an effort is made to relate social and psychological differences to party loyalties, there is little difficulty in defining 'Conservative' and 'Labour'; this is *a fortiori* true if one concentrates attention upon a single point in time. All electors cannot, however, be fitted into these two categories, plus the category of stable Liberal voter. The term 'floating voter' is familiar, but precise definition is not as easy and unequivocal as casual usage might suggest. One advantage of empirical survey studies is that they confront students of politics with the practical significance of varying definitions, and provide evidence of the quantitative difference between broad and narrow definitions of a concept. R. S. Milne and H. C. Mackenzie, authors of two book-length studies of general elections in Bristol, show to what extent modifying the definition of the term 'floating voter' can increase the size of the group whose behaviour is to be explained. A comparative analysis of the problem of floating voters is contained in H. Daudt, *Floating Voters and the Floating Vote* (Leiden: H. E. Stenfert Kroese, 1961).

THIS note is concerned with possible definitions of the 'floating vote' in Britain and with estimates of its size according to each definition, at the general election in Bristol North-East in 1951.[1] In everyday usage, the term 'floating vote' is often restricted to those electors who switch their vote from one major party to another at two successive elections. Not many people switch their votes in the course of their whole lives;[2] therefore, the number changing in the short period between any two successive elections is necessarily small. On this definition, only 4 per cent of the electors in the Bristol sample were floaters: just over 3 per cent changed from Labour to Conservative; fewer than 1 per cent changed in the other direction.

[1] These estimates are derived from interviews with random samples of the electors, and are, of course, subject to sampling error. A full acount of the survey on which they are based is given in the special issue of *Parliamentary Affairs*, December 1954, reprinted in book form as *Straight Fight*.

[2] *Behind the Gallup Poll* (*News Chronicle*, 1951), pp. 19–20.

Reprinted from *Political Studies*, vol. iii, no. 1 (1955), pp. 65–8.

An alternative definition of the floating vote would refer to all differences in recorded voting (including non-voting) between two successive elections. On this basis the floating vote in Bristol North-East, between the 1950 and 1951 elections, was about 25 per cent (Table 1). The comparable figures for the constituency of Droylsden (Lancashire) are shown in the same table.[1]

TABLE 1

Electors with vote in 1951 different from vote in 1950

| | Percentage of all electors | |
Category	Bristol N.E. %	Droylsden %
A. Changed — Con. to Lab. or Lab. to Con.	4	5
B. Changed — Lib. to Con. or Lab. . .	6	5
C. Voted 1951, not 1950 (too young) . .	3⎱	6
D. Voted 1951, not 1950 (other reasons) .	9⎰	
E. Voted 1950, not 1951	3	3
	25	19

Two qualifications should be borne in mind in the interpretation of Table 1. First, the number of categories and the size of each are functions of the number of different parties putting up candidates and of the change in the number of candidates at successive elections. In both Bristol North-East and Droylsden the withdrawal of the Liberals in 1951 reduced the number of candidates from three to two. Secondly, the period between the elections was short — less than two years. In an inter-election period of four or five years category C would certainly be larger. It should also be noted that category E is necessarily incomplete. On the above definition, the category should include the changes in recorded votes due to the death of persons who voted in 1950, but who died before the election in 1951. About 4 per cent of the electors had died since 1950[2] but the proportion of them who voted in 1950 is not known; if they had still been alive in 1951 they might not have changed, or they might have figured in categories A, B, or D, or even E.

Another definition of the floating vote would use the criterion of

---

[1] This is the only other constituency for which similar figures have been published, 1950–51. See P. Campbell, D. Donnison, and A. Potter, 'Voting Behaviour in Droylsden in October 1951' in *The Manchester School*, vol. xx, no. 1 (January 1952).

[2] This figure is based on the fact that 2 per cent of the sample died between the compilation of the register in November 1950 and the election in October 1951.

all actual changes in voting, or between voting and non-voting, as in Table 1, but would include only electors whose change in voting resulted wholly from a change in their own inclinations. On this view, 'floating' is regarded as an entirely voluntary process, and therefore it would be inappropriate to include all the people in Table 1 in estimates of the floating vote. To begin with, there are some persons included in the table who were physically or legally unable to vote at one of the two elections. 1951 electors in category C were legally unable to vote in 1950. Some in categories D and E were physically unable to vote in 1950 or in 1951 (for example, through sudden illness), and so were the people who died between the two elections; some were legally unable to vote because not included in the register. These persons may be split into three groups; some may not have wanted to vote anyway on the occasion when they were physically or legally unable to do so, that is, the change was in accordance with their inclinations. A second group may have wished on that occasion to vote differently than they did at the other election; they also had wanted to change, although not in the direction of non-voting. A third group, however, may have wanted to vote the same way at the two elections; their change was therefore forced upon them.[1] It is impossible to estimate the numbers in this group accurately except to say that about half of the 12 per cent in categories D and E claimed that they were unavoidably prevented from voting and consequently from supporting the same party as at the other election.

Table 1 also includes persons whose voting changes did not result wholly from a change in their own inclinations, but primarily from a restriction in their field of choice in 1951. Some of the 1950 Liberals in category B (just over one-third of the 6 per cent) said they would have voted Liberal again in 1951 if there had been a Liberal candidate, and so did two 1950 Liberal voters in category E (one-sixth out of 3 per cent). These people were still able to choose deliberately whether to vote Labour or Conservative or to abstain, but, because their first preference had been removed, their change can be regarded as voluntary only to the extent that they had a choice of second preference.[2]

[1] Those prevented legally or physically from voting in 1950 may have made a voluntary *choice* in 1951, but not a voluntary *change*.

[2] In the Stretford Survey (A. H. Birch and P. Campbell, 'Voting Behaviour in a Lancashire Constituency', in *The British Journal of Sociology*, vol. i, no. 3 (September 1950)) the authors give a basic definition of the 'floating vote', distinguishing it from habitual non-voters and from that section of the electorate which is 'consistent in allegiance in all reasonable circumstances' (p. 199). For the purpose of their survey, however, they measure the floating vote in terms of those who voted

It is possible to think of more complicated changes, but it would be a long task to catalogue them exhaustively. For instance, a change might be explained by a combination of the two sets of circumstances just listed. A 1950 non-voter who voted Conservative in 1951 might turn out, on examination, to be a staunch Liberal unavoidably prevented from voting at the first election and restricted in his choice at the second by the absence of a Liberal candidate. The general point is that not all the changes in Table 1 are wholly the result of changes in inclinations. At a rough guess, as many as 10 per cent of the electors in Table 1 may have had to change their behaviour for reasons not entirely in accord with their inclinations.

A distinction has now been introduced between changes in voting resulting wholly from changes in inclinations and other changes in voting. If inclinations are to be considered, however, why should not *all* electors whose voting inclinations or intentions change over a

TABLE 2

Electors whose vote in 1951 election differed from intention 2½ weeks previously

Category	Percentage of electors %
A. Intended to vote for one major party but voted for the other	3
B. Undecided whether to vote, but voted . . .	2
C. Intended to vote, although undecided how to vote, and voted	8
D. Intended to vote, but did not vote . . .	2
E. Intended not to vote, but voted . . .	0
	15

period, whether or not they actually vote differently at successive elections, be defined as floating voters? For instance, should not electors who seriously consider changing their vote be counted as floaters, even though they continue to vote for the same party? This is quite a sensible definition, although accurate measurement is difficult because an elector may change his voting intention at any

for different parties at the 1945 and 1950 elections. This calculation includes those who voted Liberal in 1950, but Conservative or Labour in 1945, *when there was no Liberal candidate*. Many of these 1950 Liberals may not have been voluntary changers, in so far as they would have preferred to vote Liberal at *both* elections, if it had been possible to do so. In the light of the basic definition, it seems wrong to count them as floaters. The circumstances in 1945, namely, the absence of a Liberal candidate, make it impossible to apply the only reasonable criterion of consistency in allegiance — voting for the same party at both elections.

time, and any number of times, between two elections. An interesting period for the measurement of changes in intentions is the campaign period, the critical weeks just before an election. The order of magnitude of changes over this period in 1951 in Bristol North-East is indicated in Table 2.[1]

In compiling Table 2 electors who had not completely made their minds up, but were 'leaning' towards a party, were classified as intending to vote for it. Electors who reported themselves as completely undecided were included in either category B or C, but in a few cases it is possible that this kind of response was merely a polite refusal to answer.[2]

From this brief analysis it is evident that the size of the floating vote varies greatly according to its definition. At one extreme is the figure of 4 per cent, the proportion of electors who voted for one major party in 1950 and for the other in 1951. The upper limit is less definite; it might be set at 25 per cent, the number who voted differently irrespective of reasons, or, if changes in intentions are taken into account, it could be some other figure depending on the period of time considered. The imprecise use of the term 'floating vote' is therefore liable to lead to confusion, since different persons may interpret it in different senses. The statement: 'It is the floating vote which decides elections' is a tautology if the floating vote is defined as the total number of persons who changed their voting behaviour or intentions over a particular period. But, on a narrower definition, such as that of changes from one major party to another, the statement is erroneous. From time to time, therefore, those who favour the narrower definition feel bound to point out the 'error' in statements which emphasize the floating vote, and lay stress on the role of ex-Liberals, non-voters, and the other dramatis personae of tables on voting behaviour. It would seem that the only safe rule, when trying to make any precise statement about the floating vote, is to be equally precise about the sense in which the term is being used.

[1] This is a special case of changes in intentions, since the end of the period over which changes are measured coincides with polling day. On this day, the choices available may not include the one corresponding to the elector's inclinations, for example, there may be no Liberal candidate.

[2] See e.g. Mosteller (Ed.), *The Pre-Election Polls of 1948* (The Social Science Research Council, 1949), p. 168.

CHAPTER III

POLITICAL COMMUNICATION

GOVERNMENTS must be able to communicate rapidly and effectively with their subjects if political decisions are to be known and enforced; citizens must be able to communicate directly or indirectly with those who make public policy, if they are to exert active influence upon decision-making in the intervals between general elections. The process of political communication is a continuing one, and involves a two-way flow of messages. In outline, the process of communication is simple; it requires a sender, a message, a channel, and a receiver. For centuries prior to the advent of universal suffrage, there was little concern with the problem of communicating the views of large numbers of the adult population to government, for there was no cultural expectation that they would take an active part in government. The reform movements which began in the nineteenth century agitated for a greater voice for the general public in government, and proposed reforms intended to enable the mass of the adult population to influence government, either by voting or through representatives. A. H. Birch's *Representative and Responsible Government* succinctly analyses changing cultural attitudes towards the attention which should be given the views of ordinary citizens.

In the past generation, the development of sampling methods for assessing the attitudes of large numbers of people has made it possible for academic students of politics and for electioneering politicians to study empirically the views of representative crosssections of the mass electorate. The rethinking prompted by efforts to analyse public opinion, and by the data obtained from such analyses, has concentrated on evidence emphasizing the extent to which it is misleading to ascribe any single opinion, or even a few alternative opinions, to the whole of the electorate, for many voters have very little information or interest in major issues of public policy. There is not a single 'public' with which the Government seeks to communicate; there are a variety of 'publics', distinguishable by their degree of organization, by their policy preferences, and by their knowledge and interest in political issues. The implications of this evidence are discussed very carefully by V. O. Key in *Public*

Opinion and American Democracy; many of his comments are also relevant to this country.

The enormous technological changes in the forms of mass communication in this century, such as the introduction of motion pictures, radio, and television, have given rise to an enormous amount of speculation about the possibility of these new media of communication being employed by governments to 'brain-wash' the general public. These fears have been further stimulated by the use of the media with such intent in totalitarian countries. Since the fear represents a tribute to the supposed power of the mass media, it is hardly surprising that many journalists and broadcasters have chosen to discuss this alleged danger. The discussion of the alleged power of the media has, however, proceeded with very little empirical analysis of the actual reaction of mass audiences to political propaganda disseminated through such channels. The major British study to date, Joseph Trenaman and Dennis McQuail, *Television and the Political Image*, found only a very slight influence of television upon politics in the 1959 general election. Joseph Klapper's *The Effects of Mass Communication*, a review of a large body of American research, generally confirms the negative findings of the British study. These studies suggest that in future less attention should be given to content analysis of press reporting and television programmes, and more attention to the audiences, and to the producers of media propaganda, as in Richard Rose's *Influencing Voters*.

BIBLIOGRAPHICAL NOTE

A detailed schematic outline of the subject of political communication is given in Richard Rose, *Politics in England*, chap. 8; this study also contains detailed bibliographical references. *Television and the Political Image*, by Joseph Trenaman and Dennis McQuail, is the first book from the Granada Television Research Unit at Leeds University. The present research director, J. G. Blumler, has analysed media influences in 'British Television — the Outlines of a Research Strategy', in *The British Journal of Sociology*, vol. xv, no. 3 (1964).

A voluminous literature of empirical studies of communication in many forms exists in America. Of particular relevance to students of politics are: V. O. Key, *Public Opinion and American Democracy* (New York: Knopf, 1961); Walter Lippmann, *Public Opinion* (1st edn., 1922); Joseph Klapper, *The Effects of Mass Communication* (Glencoe, Illinois: Free Press, 1960); Karl Deutsch, *The Nerves of Government*

(New York: Free Press, 1963); Douglass Cater, *The Fourth Branch of Government* (Boston: Houghton Mifflin, 1959); and the files of *Public Opinion Quarterly*. *Communications and Political Development* (Princeton: University Press, 1963), edited by Lucian W. Pye, is a wide-ranging treatment of a variety of communications processes in both non-Western and Western nations.

CAN PUBLIC OPINION INFLUENCE GOVERNMENT?

By Lord Windlesham

WHILE in very general terms the basic preferences of the general public may limit the range of alternative policies that a government considers, it is much more debatable whether and to what extent these preferences may influence or veto a policy decision in a particular instance. In such an analysis, the way in which the term 'public opinion' is defined is of major importance in determining the type of answer given. Lord Windlesham's case study carefully delineates the variety of views offered by a variety of groups in the name of a variety of 'publics' in the debate on British entry into the European Common Market.

AT Harvard in 1898, halfway through a final lecture on law and opinion in nineteenth-century England, Dicey remarked almost casually: 'Public opinion itself is, after all, a mere abstraction; it is not a power which has any independent existence; it is simply a general term for the beliefs held by a number of human beings.' Sixty-three years later this warning could usefully have been circulated round any organized group or newspaper which aimed to influence public opinion in Britain for or against the Common Market. Events between 31 July 1961 — the date of the Prime Minister's statement that negotiations for entry were to be opened — and the breakdown in January 1963 provide contemporary evidence that the conclusion of this hard-headed old Oxford lawyer is still not yet out of date.

The episode raises four questions: What is public opinion? How did pressure groupers and newspaper proprietors try to influence it over the Common Market issue? How far did they succeed? And what effect did public opinion have on Government policy?

The first obstacle in trying to define public opinion and isolate its causes is the confusion which results from a situation in which the target of public opinion is itself a principal cause of that opinion. In

---

Reprinted from *The Listener*, 22 August 1963, pp. 259–61. The article forms part of a larger study by Lord Windlesham, *Communication and Political Power* (London: Cape, 1966).

this instance Government initiative and Government action were themselves powerful forces in the creation of a climate of opinion. Parliament, Whitehall, the City, and Fleet Street were other open-ended interests not only influencing opinion but at the same time influenced by the opinions, actual or supposed, of others. Public opinion can be broadly described as what people think ought to be done; in a democracy even what they think of what is being done. On those matters of public policy which touch on the interests or emotions of many people it is likely that enough individuals will react in the same way for their collective private opinions to constitute a manifestation of public opinion. In these circumstances governments, if they wish to survive, customarily find it prudent to take such opinions into account.

Since public opinion is not a democratic affair of one man, one vote, the quality of opinion may give more weight than the number of people holding it. This was the basis of the Victorian notion of public thought: the opinions of a small group of people who took an interest in public affairs and whose opinions could directly influence events. Even with the development of the mass media, public opinion today usually has a positive role only when it originates from an informed *élite* group. In the sense of popular opinions widely held, public opinion is more of a negative, limiting factor: a way of estimating what the public will stand for rather than an expression of what the public wants.

Both varieties of public opinion — positive, informed opinion, and negative, popular opinion — had been tested by the Government in 1960 and 1961. Working parties were set up inside Government departments, special interests were consulted, diplomats reported, opinion polls were studied, and back-bench opinion in the House of Commons was sounded out. In each case the government concluded that majority opinion within all the *élite* groups, which could by convention expect to be consulted, was, if not always in favour, at any rate not implacably hostile towards British entry, providing special terms could be negotiated to the benefit of the Commonwealth, the European Free Trade Association, and British agriculture. A number of forward-looking businessmen in particular were urging closer association with Europe.

The most significant item of evidence on the influence of popular opinion was a claim made on behalf of the *Daily Mirror*. Mr. Woodrow Wyatt, M.P., has recorded that two members of the Government assured him that when the *Daily Mirror* burst out in support of a pro-European policy in June 1961 it was 'the tip over factor which had decided the Government to stop havering about it and really start the negotiations. Because they thought that if they had the *Daily Mirror* behind them, well, then they would probably be all right.'

'Then they would probably be all right.' Behind this prosaic fragment of conversation lies the fundamental calculation that any government has to make when it decides to implement policy: 'If we do this, can we get away with it?' In this sense popular opinion, or what is taken for popular opinion, is a common element in the practice of politics. The art of government, it can be argued, is the ability to estimate when too many people will say no before they have actually been given an opportunity to do so.

There is nothing to suggest that the three conditions for entry — the special terms for the Commonwealth, EFTA, and agriculture — were imposed by popular opinion. They were accepted as interests to be safeguarded, following consultation with the appropriate *élites* representing each interest, before the decision to open negotiations was final. Thereafter a majority of opinion leaders followed the Government, and a majority of opinion holders followed the opinion leaders. From July 1961 to January 1963 the role of popular opinion was no more than a residual check on any extravagantly novel extensions of pro-Market policy.

The Gallup Political Index

The Gallup Political Index accurately nailed down the nature of the choice before opinion holders in the wording of their question on the Common Market: 'If the British Government were to decide that British interest would be best served by joining the European Common Market, would you approve or disapprove?' It was complained by opponents of the Market that this was a loaded statement; that it did not directly pose the basic question whether Britain should join at all. Yet it was a factual description of the situation. The Government had decided to join if it could. The important thing to know was whether a majority of people would accept this decision or not.

Answers to the Gallup question repeated over eighteen months suggest a remarkably constant level of popular opinion. In late July 1961, 38 per cent of respondents said they would approve of such a decision, 23 per cent said they would disapprove, and 39 per cent had no opinion. A year later, in August 1962, opinion was moving against the Market although the approvals still had a 10 per cent lead over the disapprovals. By January 1963, when the negotiations ended, the position was much the same. At no time did the disapprovals outnumber the approvals, but at no time did the approvals have an overall majority over disapprovals and 'don't knows' combined.

On these findings it was the high proportion of 'don't knows' which provided a potential threat to the Government and an opportunity to the anti-Market lobbies. It is possible to consider the 'don't knows' as an inert, inactive residue; inattentive and ill-informed; sitting on the shelf like a sort of gold cup waiting to be claimed by the most vigorous participant in the opinion game. But to think in this way, apart from causing great distress to the ghost of Dicey, is to overlook the shifting and ephemeral nature of public opinion. Not far below the surface there are continual currents of movement: approval turning into disapproval; certainty falling back to uncertainty; muddle-headedness resolving into clear thinking. If at any time in 1961 or 1962 the currents had all begun to run strongly in one direction, then the basis on which the Government's policy rested could have been swept away. It can happen that political opinion can come to be shared by an overwhelming majority of the population, and it can happen quickly. The question is always how? How can popular opinion be mobilized so that opinions lying latent are activated; so that back-sliding is checked; and so that timid opinion holders become multiplicators, passing on their precious seed to people they rub up against in the routine of everyday life?

This was the problem facing, not for the first time, Lord Beaverbrook and the *Daily Express*. Their aim was a simple one: to confront the Government with such evidence of popular opposition that it would be compelled to put the *Daily Mirror* on one side and say, 'It looks as though we are not going to be able to get away with it after all.'

The spearhead of this campaign was the 'fact a day'. From June 1961, as a matter of editorial policy, one carefully selected fact, often vetted by Lord Beaverbrook personally, was regularly displayed in a box on the front page. The appeal was aimed at those holding no opinions or weak opinions, and thus potentially open to influence by means of an apparently feet-on-the-ground, no-nonsense approach pointing out what readers had to lose.

If the *Daily Express* did not convert many people outright, and it would surely not have been slow in making the claim if it had been possible to uncover any favourable evidence, at least it did duty as an emotional anchor for anti-Market opinion. No one likes to be alone with an unpopular opinion, and once people begin to relinquish an opinion because they feel isolated, the snowball can begin to roll. The daily advocacy, vigorous and self-assured, of the *Express* made it certain that no one unhappy about the Market need ever feel alone.

There it stood, the brave standard of opposition, and without it the pressure of Government action on public opinion might well have drawn in much more support from people who either had no opinion or whose opinions wavered between 1961 and 1963. So, in preventing defections and fortifying the anti-marketeers, the *Daily Express* can claim to have had some influence on popular opinion in this period.

At the same time as the mass circulation newspapers were concentrating on popular opinion, special interest groups had differing targets. Some, the National Farmers' Union, the T.U.C., and the Federation of British Industries, permanently entrenched around Whitehall, had been consulted before the Government decided to open the negotiations. Others, notably the United Kingdom Council of the European Movement and the Commonwealth Industries Association, which already existed to promote pro-European or pro-Commonwealth policies, found themselves tied by a history or a committee superstructure which prevented them from militating as single-minded pressure groups for or against entry. As a result the gate was open, and by the end of 1961 six new organized groups were in possession of the field. All aimed to become rallying points for the like-minded, while at the same time putting pressure on the Government by pointing to the demands of public opinion, popular or informed.

Common Market Campaign

In the centre of politics, drawing its support from moderates in all parties, was the Common Market Campaign. Led by Lord Gladwyn and managed by three M.P.s, Roy Jenkins and John Diamond (both Labour), and Peter Kirk (a Conservative), the Campaign was intended to show the Government and the informed public that a substantial body of respected business, trade-union, and parliamentary opinion was strongly in favour of British entry on appropriate terms. With continual access to Government, Parliament, Fleet Street, and Whitehall, the Common Market Campaign never attempted to become a mass movement. Its first and most successful enterprise was to collect the signatures of one hundred and forty well-known public men for a *Statement on Europe* published on 25 May 1961. After one or two discouraging experiments mass meetings were abandoned and the Campaign settled down to a less conspicuous routine: providing speakers for other people's meetings; issuing publications, declarations, and statements; and organizing select little briefing conferences. The extent of its direct audience is suggested by the maximum circulation of about 6,000 which by the end of 1962 had been achieved for a regular broadsheet.

Two other pro-Market interest groups set up in this period were the United Europe Association, an offshoot of the United Kingdom Council of the European Movement especially intended to activate regional support outside London, and Britain in Europe, a research and information service for business men. Each of these pro-Market groups shared three characteristic features: all-party support, access to centres of power, and a policy of concentrating attention on the opinions of well-informed *élites*. The anti-groups in contrast were distinctively one-party extremists, lacking access, and aiming to become mass movements. Disgruntled Conservatives, under the leadership of John Paul, launched the Anti-Common Market League in October 1961; R. W. Briginshaw, General Secretary of NATSOPA, started and ran the Forward Britain Movement to cater for any socialists or others who wished to protest, if appropriate by march or demonstration; and Oliver Smedley, an ex-Liberal candidate and veteran pressure grouper, founded Keep Britain Out, while at the same time acting as general liaison officer between the anti-organizations.

The Anti-Common Market League was the largest of the three. Almost self-consciously amateur in its approach, this South Kensington-based pressure group, spiritually as well as geographically remote from the more familiar corridors of power, built up a recorded membership of 30,000 between October 1961 and the end of 1962. From the start the League was concerned to present its message directly to the general public. Faced by the same problem as Lord Beaverbrook but without the convenience of a mass-circulation newspaper, the method of communication chosen was a programme of public meetings, backed by leaflets distributed from door to door. Two hundred and thirty-seven meetings were addressed by League speakers in 1962, ninety-six of them by its Chairman John Paul. Thirty thousand copies of a booklet, *Britain Not Europe*, had been sold by the end of the year, and 1,000,000 leaflets in the form of a quiz, followed by a further 500,000 at the time of the Commonwealth Prime Ministers' conference, had been distributed.

An unusual feature for a large organized group was that until Lord Sandwich accepted honorary office as President in January 1963 the League was without any national name as patron, officeholder, or committee member. Notable Conservative opponents of the Government's Common Market policy, such as Sir Derek Walker-Smith and Robin Turton, had spoken on League platforms, but had avoided any more formal association with an avowedly anti-Government pressure group with such a decidedly amateur look to it.

Yet the characteristic of amateurishness if it is coupled with competence can be an advantage to an organized group in its relations with the general public. A sort of sympathy towards the obviously non-professional can help to dispel some of the suspicion which attaches to the more noticeable attempts to put pressure on public opinion. And 30,000 recorded members, propaganda sheets counted in millions, and a meeting two days out of three are certainly no 'amateur' achievements.

What Was the Lesson?

So what can be learnt about public opinion from this episode of contemporary history? What effect did organized activity have on public opinon? And what effect did public opinion, popular or informed, have on Government action? Let us go back for a minute to the framework within which these events were contained. Government initiative led *informed* opinion in the first stage when the implications of entry were being considered. Then, after consultation with established *élite* groups, the Government decided to negotiate. At the same time *popular* opinion was sized up, as the Government asked themselves the question, 'If we do this, shall we be able to get away with it? Will public opinion stand for it?' On inspection in 1961 public opinion appeared quiescent: no specially established interest groups, no widespread popular concern.

Throughout the eighteen-month period the climate of opinion did not dramatically alter. No doubt in response to the activities of newspapers, publicists, and special interest groups people already holding an opinion on the desirability or folly of joining the Common Market came to hold it stronger. To this extent it can be said that existing attitudes on the Market were reinforced by organized activity. It is less easy to find support for the claim that issues were clarified with the result that the undecided or previously ignorant moved over on to one side or the other. The conclusion must be that public opinion had little directly attributable effect on what actually happened. But both at Westminster and in Whitehall there was a general awareness of opinion.

In the judgement of the Government a sufficient body of public opinion, informed and popular, was in favour of negotiations at the start and continued to be favourable towards the idea of entry until the breakdown. Whether this evaluation was good or bad we shall never know; the episode was beheaded; the climax of acceptance or rejection never came.

Finally it needs to be said that although public opinion did not significantly affect Government policy, it was not because the individual opinions were themselves insignificant or poorly presented, indeed the evidence is that the Government was unusually sensitive towards them, but because, in Sir William Haley's words, 'the climate of a nation's opinions is more important than the opinions themselves'. The climate did not change so the policy did not change. Public opinion remained a power without independent existence; a power too elusive to be cornered, taken, and delivered up as a solid political advantage.

THE PRESS AND PUBLIC OPINION

By Donald McLachlan

In many historical studies, the views of newspapers are treated by historians as expressions of public opinion. Politicians too may assume that editors and readers share a common outlook, or that the political views of the readers are shaped by editorial policies. Donald McLachlan's article is unusual because he turns attention to the factors influencing the editorial policy of a newspaper, rather than discussing the consequences of this policy. The article makes clear that the factors which influence editorial policy include technical and commercial problems which have nothing to do with matters of political principle.

THE business of producing newspapers and periodicals is a deeply personal one, in which different factors play powerful parts at different times. Among them do not overlook illness, chance, carelessness, whim or misunderstanding. If you wish for examples I suggest you examine such records as the *History of 'The Times'*, especially the last volume, or any detailed political biography where the subject's relations with the press are recorded in detail. It is, perhaps, because of this personal quality in journalism that so little has been written about what goes on in the minds of editors and their assistants. A true account would need a most subtle and frank description of human beings working in circumstances which make deliberation very difficult. I cannot give you this account; I do not know who could. All I can do is to suggest a kind of prolegomenon to the study of the press as an opinion-forming influence.

First let me emphasize the importance of distinguishing between different but complementary journalistic functions. Comment is made by a newspaper on news, generally but not always on the news of the day. That news has not only to be collected by reporters at home and abroad; it has first to be ordered. I do not say that every item in a newspaper has been asked for by an editor or his assistants; that is not so. Many items will be sent in by news agencies. But some of the main items will have been asked for; and those that have not

Reprinted in an abridged and slightly updated form from *The British Journal of Sociology*, vol. vi, no. 2 (1955), pp. 159–66. The article was prepared as a talk for a conference on public opinion and foreign policy.

been asked for will have been sent in or fetched because experience
has shown the reporter or correspondent that his editor will be interested in them. In a sentence, there is selection of news at the
earliest stage of daily newspaper production; and in the selection of
news every trait in the character of a newspaper office has its influence: tradition, political tendency, emphasis given to home or
foreign news, standards of taste and judgement, readers' preferences,
proprietors' preferences, and so on. These traits often exercise their
influence without individuals being conscious of them. They are
part of the office's pattern of behaviour, if I may be allowed to use
a sociological term of which I do not altogether approve.

I need not dwell on this point about selection. Once it is grasped,
its importance is easily imagined. Now follows the process of presentation which includes sub-editing and cutting. Five hundred
words of type can look completely different according to the size and
number of headlines put on them. Convention demands that a paper
has what is called a lead — the dominating story of its front or main
news page. Every journalist knows that a lead can be thoroughly
misleading, especially on a night when important or exciting news is
scarce. But there is no escaping the need for a lead, because every
front-page has its architectural requirements. As readers unfold their
paper they expect a certain familiar appearance, a certain impact, a
certain impression of restraint or liveliness. To give it them, even the
most sober newspaper has sometimes to inflate the importance of
some of its contents. It may be significant that newspapers, like
women, attach importance to make-up.

What the effect of this on the public is I do not know. Certainly
there is evidence to suggest that the more sensational the treatment
and the bigger the headlines, then the wider the circulation. Clearly
the public can be led to believe that whatever appears in certain
positions in their favourite newspaper is important. So that the
impact on opinion, the forming of views, the creation of moods of
inquisitiveness or resentment or fright, begins at this stage of presenting the news. And anybody engaged in the kind of inquiry that
you are following must take note of this fact. For it is likely that in
some newspapers, not in all, the decisions about presentation are
taken by persons who are not concerned with thinking and writing
about policy.

That news and comment should be separately handled is a well-
known principle. Ideally, there should be perfect co-ordination of
presentation and leader-writing or other comment. But in practice it
is not easily attained, partly because of the speed at which both jobs
have simultaneously to be done (three to four hours at the most),

partly because men concerned with presentation and men concerned with policy-making and writing often have very different equipments of knowledge, experience, and judgement. Indeed, they may have widely diverging views of what the public wants to know or should be told about foreign affairs. I cannot stress too strongly the importance of presentation. Remember that the reader probably looks first at the news and afterwards at the comment; unless, of course, the comment is so designed as to save him the trouble of reading the news — which sometimes happens. And remember that interest in foreign affairs and foreign policy is rooted in anxiety about prospects of war or peace, prosperity or slump, safety or danger. The reader's emotions have been aroused by the news before the leader-writer can apply the cool hand of his argument — if it is a cool hand. It is sometimes a hot and feverish one.

Now we come to comment — whether it is in leaders, or in special articles, or in personal contributions by columnists. Only leaders, generally anonymous, can be definitely attributed to office policy; that is true of periodicals as well as daily papers. It is generally the practice, and an excellent practice, that a man writing under his own name or pseudonym, will express an independent point of view. Outstanding examples have been Walter Lippman in the American press, Sir Beverly Baxter in the Beaverbrook press, Raymond Aron in the Paris *Figaro*, and John Grigg in the *Guardian*. They are unlikely to urge views diametrically opposed to those of the paper they work for; but they will have all the latitude that a reasonable man needs. And it will be that quality in their articles among others that has won them a following.

The leader-writer's position is different. He is at once paid advocate, student, inquirer, and adviser. He will have joined the paper knowing its tradition and general political line. He will have opportunities to modify or even change that line, if he has the personality, skill, and knowledge to put his case across. He is more likely to be told what not to say than what to say. He will be expected to understand the general outlook of the office and to interpret events in the light of it. He will not normally receive the kind of directives that Goebbels gave the Nazi press or which Moscow sends by teleprinter to the Soviet press.

Here we begin to see the crux of your problem — the general outlook of the office. What is it? How is it formed? Does it ignore or respect public opinion? How does it work in the special sphere of foreign affairs? What factors influence it which you can analyse and describe? These are extraordinarily subtle and difficult questions, although it is quite clear to most newspaper readers interested in public affairs what is the general outlook of their favourite organ. Each has a style, a manner, a habit of reacting which is unmistakable and sometimes even predictable. But to explain how these characteristics are acquired and maintained would need a long and close investigation, much of which would have to be in camera; for the press would be no more willing than the Old Vic Company, or a university college, or a regiment, or a football team to reveal all those personal factors which help to form a style and pattern of behaviour.

So I must take refuge in generalizations as best I can. But first let me recapitulate for a moment. I have drawn attention to the process by which news and views reach the public through the ordering, collecting, selecting, presentation, and editing of news. Throughout that process there is an interplay between personalities, practical requirements, and what I have called the office line. The stream of effort is continuous; one cannot intervene at any one point and say 'here policy is made' — except in cases of real crisis or quite unexpected happenings. Then it would be possible to say that so-and-so took a decision at such-and-such a time which determined the policy. But in most instances the journalists concerned know from precedents, from inquiry, from their own common sense what the policy is likely to be.

Now for the generalizations. The first influence on the policy of a paper will be its tradition, which is a vital part of its goodwill as a business. I do not need to explain to you what is the tradition of each of our national newspapers; it is sufficient to say that the tradition can be good or bad according to the standards of judgement one applies. Next important factor is the readership's character and the circulation. A paper that is read standing in the train, costing 4d., giving special attention to the interests of women, punters, and filmgoers, will not have space to inform its readers adequately about foreign affairs. To get such information they must pay more; and that very fact restricts the number of those people who will have an intelligent and well-informed interest in foreign affairs. Mind you, I do not wish to disparage with this remark the simple but sound judgements of people who are ill-informed. One of the problems you will have to consider later is why clever and well-informed people can have such obviously silly views while ordinary, ignorant people can have very sensible views. And in view of the fact that the ordinary people are the vast majority, you will have to consider what is the influence on foreign policy of their indifference, phlegm, and patience, or if you like, of their fears, illusions, and lack of public spirit. The fact that their newspapers do little to inform or instruct them on foreign matters may, for all we know, be a good thing. They have time to think. Perhaps the fewer people who really know about foreign policy the better; I am not sure.

Third in my list of influences in a newspaper office comes the experience, educational background, sense of responsibility of the editor and his editorial staff. Whatever the policy of the paper, their special interests and bias will be reflected in it. That is bound to be so. The man who has met Mr. Nehru and has had the privilege of private conversation with him will write about him in a manner quite different from that of the journalist who has never seen him. That bit of personal experience will have its subtle effect on everyone concerned with foreign news, through the arguments and casual conversations that take place daily in every newspaper office. Likewise a foreign editor who really knows history and foreign countries will have an immense influence on colleagues who do not; and a man who is in regular contact with ministries and officials will have a considerable influence on policy if he wishes. I mention these rather trivial examples merely to show you how much a newspaper office is like any other establishment making a collective effort. And I can perhaps rub the impression in by quoting a remark once made to me by an older colleague on a famous newspaper where I once worked: 'Policy,' he said, 'is made in this office by a committee which never meets.'

The next factor to consider is contact with readers. Do readers guide newspapers or is the opposite true? It is impossible to give a hard judgement. I am inclined to think that in the long run newspapers guide readers, at any rate the more serious ones. Each day the newspaper thrusts ten to twenty pages in front of its reader; he will write or telephone to the editor at the most fifty times a year — and that would be a record. The newspaper can influence the reader by a multitude of stories, ideas, recommendations, and services. The reader can only refuse his pennies.

Circulation is, of course, very important. Without it advertising dies, and the paper dies with it. But I doubt whether it would be possible to trace any special connection between the foreign policy of a paper and its circulation. I can imagine that happening at times like 1938, or during the war, or even during some very controversial crisis of our own time. It is known that the *Observer* in 1956 lost circulation heavily because of its views on Suez. But generally speaking, the paper's attitude in foreign affairs will be a secondary factor in the reader's choice of reading. I should qualify this by saying that papers like *The Times, Guardian, Daily Telegraph*, and periodicals like *The Economist* and the *Round Table* are clearly bought by many people

M

who have professional reasons for wishing to be well-informed on foreign affairs. But they are the *élite* minority, and I do not regard them as readers in the ordinary sense of the word. Of the part they play in forming public opinion I shall speak shortly.

Now what about the leading articles? Here is a subject well worth investigation. Do people read leaders? If so what effect do they have? Do they provide the reader with arguments and facts for his day's conversations? Are they a kind of arsenal for those who are politically or intellectually active? Do politicians take notice of them? I can answer only some of these questions. I am quite sure that influential people do use leading articles in papers they respect. On several occasions I have heard phrases used in public whose authorship I knew at first hand. I am also sure that politicians, particularly those in office, take notice; and so do their officials and advisers. It frequently happens in Whitehall that a minister will ask his officials to provide him with the answer to some charge or argument that he has seen directed against himself in the press. There is an important circular flow of ideas between Whitehall and Fleet Street. I also know that writers in lesser papers crib from writers in greater papers. To the daily writer the deeply-pondered 1,500 word articles of the weekly press can be of great assistance in his task of producing 600 words regularly and at short notice. The influence of leading articles on television commentators is considerable. So in a very real sense the good and well-informed leader-writer on a respected and influential paper is influencing public opinion. And this is not only true of his own country. Foreign correspondents in London study very carefully the leading newspapers and periodicals in order to make their own assessments of public opinion for reporting back to their own papers. And I know of at least two diplomatists of high rank and distinction who based their political despatches on certain articles they have come to rely on.

But, you may ask, what is the leader-writer up to? Is he expounding, explaining, exhorting, exposing, clarifying, analysing, or preaching? I think the answer varies from paper to paper; but generally he is ready, if not equipped, to do all these things. I think myself that his chief jobs are three: to clarify, to simplify, and to concentrate thought. That is to say he should reduce the situation or event he is examining to its essential elements; then he should simplify the issues that have to be decided; then he should make it clear what his view is — unmistakably clear. It is not, in my view, part of a leader-writer's job to imagine himself in the place of the Foreign Secretary or Prime Minister. For most of us that burden is too great; we shrivel under it and become evasive, indecisive, and end up sitting on the

fence. Nor should a leader-writer think of himself as addressing the
chancelleries of the world, tempting though it may be to have that
illusion. His job is to address the readers of his paper. If great men
like to overhear what he is saying so much the better.

Now I can imagine you saying: but on whose behalf is the leader-
writer assuming all these functions? What right has he to take the
pulpit day after day? Is he expressing public opinion or imposing his
own views? I find it extremely difficult to answer for my colleagues.
I must ask you to be content with a sequence of impressions, based on
personal friendships, experience, hearsay, and reading. First I think
leader-writers enjoy writing for its own sake. Writing is, after all, an
art; and the art, even in our most lowbrow papers, is more difficult
and deliberate than many people think. The leader-writer enjoys the
opportunity of expressing himself in a manner which shows his skill,
clarity, command of language, wit, insight, and so on. He may be
seeking power and influence; few intellectual workers are not, in my
experience. But he is also seeking to engage attention, to say something memorable, to entertain — if you like. People generally come
into journalism because they like writing; and leader-writing can be
a very enjoyable occupation, even if it is anonymous. This is an impression I would ask you to keep firmly in mind during your
investigation. The good and keen journalist is doing a turn, whether
it be serious or light. But to this exercise he brings a sense of public
responsibility, some desire to attain wisdom, a normal wish not to be
proved wrong or thought stupid. These are some of the restraints
that act on his judgement of foreign affairs. How do they work in
fact? How do they work when he is writing that we must stand up to
Hitler, or throw Chiang over, or build the hydrogen bomb, or not
build it?

I think the answer is along these lines. He will try, in most cases, to
think what is the national interest. In doing so he may of course
come to a conclusion completely opposed to that of another leader-
writer working next door in Fleet Street. But that will be due to the
different political premises and intellectual attitudes from which
they start, in fact to the personal factors which led each to join the
paper he does work for. Then our leader-writer will weigh what is
politically possible. He is unlikely in most cases to advocate a point
of view deeply different from that of the political party that his newspaper supports. That will sometimes happen, and it is a great virtue
of our papers that it does happen. But it is the exception rather than
the rule. Then our leader-writer will be influenced by what the
diplomatic correspondent has told him of the facts behind the scenes;
by messages from colleagues abroad to whom he can talk on the

telephone; by conversations he has had at lunch with people in the know; by what he has read in other papers. (I need hardly say that leader-writers read one another with the most critical zeal.) Then he will have in his mind the talk he has had with his editor on this and previous occasions. And then he will write.

Now where, in all this, does public opinion come? Some reflection of it comes in readers' letters; but they are neither emphatic nor voluminous save on special issues which are specially controversial. And in such cases the newspaper's side may be already chosen, so that the readers' views can have only limited effect. Some reflection of public opinion also comes from other newspapers. By reading them one can see to what arguments and facts public opinion is being exposed. The fact that those arguments and facts may not have reached one's own readership is sometimes overlooked. Then there are those things called political trends which everyone knows about but no one can adequately define. I have in mind the swift, and to my mind unthinking, adoption of the phrase 'peaceful co-existence' during the summer of 1953. No one knows how or why it happened, although we all know the part that the Prime Minister played in his speech of May 11 in that year. The trend began, grew and was clearly visible to any observer of public affairs.

If you ask me how these trends and moods are noticed and appreciated, I have to say, rather tamely, that it is all part of the journalist's job. You will not think me conceited if I say that we are experts in that kind of thing. A journalist who is responsible for the policy of his paper is always on the alert. He is at his job all day, even during his leisure. Like every other citizen he is influenced by what he hears, sees and reads in the hours preceding the moment when he has to write. His antennae are unusually sensitive. Moreover, in his office he is talking and arguing with others of the same interest and make-up. They, too, have been listening, reading, arguing, inquiring and they may disagree entirely with his view of what public opinion is. Between them they will probably reach a quite good, if rough-and-ready, view of what the public are thinking and feeling.

I agree that this is very rough-and-ready. But what is possible in the circumstances of daily journalism? Polls will help; for all I know they may be very valuable. But they seem to me to be taken after, not before, the event; and by the event I mean the newspaper's policy decision. I can think of no case in which a newspaper has changed its view on a matter of importance after learning through a poll that public opinion disagreed with it. On the other hand I can think of a case, a very striking case, in which a popular illustrated paper guessed what would be a popular, selling, political line, and proved sensationally right.

It seems to me that the art of editing and writing is something like the art of politics. Success depends on a combination of experience, intuition, guessing, and knowledge. And it is important to realize that newspapers, like politicians, will quite often defend lost causes, or losing causes, because they believe in them. Even if Fleet Street went to great lengths to discover more accurately what the public think, I doubt whether the policy of its chief newspapers would be very much affected. And I doubt whether it is desirable that it should be.

POLITICAL REPORTING IN BRITAIN

By D. E. BUTLER

THE great majority of the electorate must rely upon the mass media — the press, radio, television, periodicals, and books — as their major sources of information about the actions of those in national politics. Only a very small minority can privately acquire information about what is going on in Westminster by conversation, telephone, or letter. What the mass media report and are allowed to report about national politics is thus a major limiting factor on the quantity and quality of political information in circulation. D. E. Butler's article succinctly considers three controversial questions — in what ways might the press be said to give inadequate coverage to politics? to what extent are conventions of government responsible for faulty information? and, to what extent might public policy be improved by fuller reporting of national politics? Butler's controversial answers to these important questions have been challenged strongly by working journalists — see e.g. David Wood, 'The Parliamentary Lobby', *Political Quarterly*, xxxvi: 3 (1965) and Ian Waller, *infra*, pp. 177–190.

RECENT events have focused an unusual degree of attention on the political role of the press. The Vassall and Profumo affairs brought to light a great deal about the methods of newspapers and journalists; they stimulated discussion of the techniques of news-gathering, of the ethics of sensationalism, and of the rights of politicians to privacy. But I have been struck by the superficiality of most of the criticism. It has long seemed to me that the reporting of British politics needs much more and much deeper examination than it normally receives — and that the examination should be devoted primarily to the so-called serious press. The mass-circulation papers, which have been receiving most of the recent brickbats, are, after all, avowedly out to entertain; they do not even pretend to give all the facts which an intelligent voter would need in order to form a reasonable judgement on the conduct of the men who are governing him. The serious press, which claims to provide a full record of relevant events, seems to fall much shorter of its goal. Many years

---

Reprinted from *The Listener*, 15 August 1963, pp. 231–3.

ago when I first crossed the Atlantic and read widely in the American press, I felt that I was getting far closer to the heart of politics than I had ever done by the most assiduous scanning of newspapers here. Then I had never seen anything 'from the inside'. But now that I have occasionally had the chance to do so, both in London and in Washington, I have become convinced I was right. The outsider who takes the trouble can get a great deal nearer to what is really happening in the United States than he can in Britain.

I want to argue that the blame for this lies partly with the press, but still more with the way in which we run our public life. However, before analysing the underlying causes, let me illustrate the kinds of story which have been so lacking in the reporting of British politics.

Many Things Unreported

Scoops are surprisingly rare. Consider Mr. Thorneycroft's resignation in January 1958: it followed four days of comings and goings in Downing Street, but the press was taken completely by surprise when the story hit the wires just when the first editions were going to press. The *Daily Mail*'s scoop in forecasting the great Cabinet purge of July 1962 was chiefly remarkable for being so remarkable.

Informed atmospheric stories are also in short supply. Another change at the top illustrates this. In the eighteen hours following Sir Anthony Eden's resignation from the premiership the press had a golden opportunity to pick his successor — but all the serious papers, with more or less confidence, tipped Mr. Butler. We now know that Mr. Macmillan was the undoubted choice of the majority of the Cabinet and of the Conservative back-benchers. Why, then, were the lobby correspondents and newspaper editors so ill-informed about the state of opinion in the party that was, after all, governing the country?

Then there is little in the way of Whitehall stories. There is a shortage of journalists with departmental beats, who talk with Civil Servants and pass on to the public what is the common currency of the clubs where the administrative class forgather. The leaking of a document is astonishingly rare: the report of the National Economic Development Council, which reached the *Guardian* so prematurely last February, stands out as a striking exception to the rule that Whitehall's secrets go untapped by the press.

Political portraiture, too, is oddly unenterprising. The picture which the public has of the top party leaders derives far more from television than from print. The men three or four down the hierarchy are almost completely unknown. Those strengths and weaknesses so

universally appreciated by their friends and their foes at Westminster rarely seep out to the politically inquisitive public. The
physical condition of one of our leading politicians has long been a
subject of compassionate comment round the lobbies, but it is unknown to those who have had no chance of seeing him at a party
conference or from the gallery of the House of Commons. It is true
that during the leadership struggle between Mr. Wilson and Mr.
Brown the press touched a new level of personal candour — but,
even so, what was published differed widely from the things being
said by M.P.s and journalists. There is also the failure to exploit the
opportunities offered by the full-scale political interview. A notable
break-through in the last year or two has been made by Kenneth
Harris in the *Observer*; his extended conversations with Lord Home
(now Sir Alec Douglas-Home) and Harold Wilson seem to me important political documents.

Again, there is a shortage of 'case-study' reporting, of analyses of
the way in which the routine operations of politics are carried out
— the work of pressure groups, for example, or even the processes of
lobby journalism. There have been pioneer ventures by Ian Waller
of the *Sunday Telegraph* and by some others, but the contrast with the
best of American muck-raking journalism needs no underlining.

A final shortcoming is in the background story, the retelling of how
a situation developed. I remember particularly, during the tribula-
tions of the Labour Party in 1960 and 1961, the failure of the press
to offer clear summaries of the course of events or of the role of individuals as that long drawn-out struggle developed. Recently some
of the 'Sundays' have taken to offering admirable blow-by-blow
descriptions of the week's events — the Common Market breakdown
or the Profumo case — but a longer time-span is often needed.

In almost all the areas I have mentioned there have been marked
improvements in recent years: and I should mention one counter-
poise to these weaknesses in reporting — the full parliamentary summaries, the semi-verbatim record of what is said in the House of
Commons on any important question.

Why the Omissions?

Let us turn to the explanations for the state of British political reporting. Why are there these gaps? The basic answer seems to lie in
national customs, in the fact that our public life is conducted in a
much more private fashion than that of almost any other democratic
country. Rules and conventions prevent lobby correspondents from
securing, or at any rate from publishing, the most elementary political information.

First, there is individual ministerial responsibility — the rule that for every act of a Civil Servant some Minister of the Crown is personally responsible to Parliament. Ministers, not bureaucrats, take the blame publicly. Civil Servants, in return for this anonymity, give discretion; they are exceedingly inhibited about talking to journalists. A leak from them would be a usurpation of their minister's privilege. The London journalist cannot hope to find any-where in Whitehall the sort of unofficial assistance that every Washington newsman counts on from a thousand different sources in the Administration. Collective Cabinet responsibility provides a complementary barrier. Cabinet ministers accept the convention that they all hang together; once the Cabinet has made a decision, they must not even hint to journalists their reservations or disagree-ments. Inklings of Cabinet dissension do occasionally leak out but only on a very small scale. A prime minister would take firm action if he suspected any minister of appealing over the heads of the Cabinet to a wider public. Another, lesser, barrier is the primacy of Parliament. M.P.s feel they have the right to be told first of any Government plans, and the journalist who is too successful in scooping announcements to the House may well find himself in difficulties when he goes to the same quarters for another story.

Parliamentary privilege provides yet another stumbling-block. Frank comment on the behaviour of M.P.s, or of Parliament as a whole, may be interpreted as contempt of Parliament. Since the war, no fewer than three editors have been called to the Bar of the House to apologize formally for derogatory remarks appearing in their papers.

A much bigger barrier is the law of libel — or rather the way in which British courts interpret the law of libel, for I am told that the U.S. law is in a formal sense little different from the British law. 'Fair comment on a matter of public interest' is seldom an adequate defence and the prudent American convention that it is almost im-possible to libel a politician certainly does not activate British judges, still less British juries: British juries indeed seem to regard the press as fair game when it comes to assessing damages. Last March Mr. Profumo demonstrated how powerful the threat of libel actions can be; he intimidated the whole of Fleet Street into total, if often scep-tical, silence by saying that he would institute proceedings against anyone who hinted at facts which he later admitted to be true.

Yet another barrier to frank reporting is the Official Secrets Act. This was originally devised to defend State secrets from the enemy but it has been extended to cover much of the ordinary business of government: if a Cabinet document which bore no relation to state security were to fall into press hands its publisher could well be sent to prison — even if the document were thirty years old. There is no comparable prohibition in America; indeed no other democratic country is as restrictive as Britain in this respect.

Self-censorship by the Pressman

I have stressed the technical, constitutional obstructions to full and frank reporting; but there are still bigger obstructions inherent in the manner, or the manners, of our public life. Our politicians and Civil Servants, the public men, the 'insiders' who govern us, have their own way of running affairs in which they accord only a small part to the press. Anybody who is anybody has access to almost anybody else who is anybody without the need for the intermediacy of the newspapers. They conduct their discussions in Whitehall, in their clubs, in the lobbies at Westminster, on a confidential personal basis, in which the leaking of private conversations would be in the very worst of taste. Anyone suspected of such conduct would be liable to a large measure of social ostracism. Journalists abusing the confidences that came their way would find themselves barred from the contacts which are essential to their livelihood. A pressman who wants to write honestly and candidly of all that he hears and sees can mingle with the people who are making decisions, and listen to them discussing ideas still in embryo, only if he is willing to accept a remarkable degree of self-censorship.

Yet one more barrier lies in the routes of advancement in British life. Civil Servants have every incentive to be discreet; but politicians are in a similar position in that a politician's advancement depends far more upon the opinion of his senior colleagues than upon the esteem in which he is held in the outside world. The path to the top in British politics does not lie in adroit self-publicizing or in winning the goodwill of journalists by discreet indiscretions. It depends upon impressing one's party leaders. Therefore the self-advertising leak which is so invaluable a source for informed Washington correspondents is largely missing in British public life. It is not that our politicians are instinctively more moral and more discreet; it is just that, compared with congressmen, their self-interest demands a different pattern of conduct towards the press.

But the problem goes beyond constitutional law and social convention. The structure and habits of the serious press contribute to the frustrations of candid political reporting. To some extent it is a matter of social status. The proprietors and, in large measure, the editors of the serious national press are members of the Establishment who move with reasonable freedom among those with power

— but they can become too involved with their sources to pass on their information to their staff for publication. The political writing is done by lobby journalists, an able group of men who none the less do not rank enormously high in the hierarchy of their newspapers. A chairman of the Conservative Party is alleged to have complained that they were not the sort of people one could invite down for the week-end. Certainly while Parliament is in session, lobby correspondents are overworked men who have to spend the great bulk of their time labouring in the House of Commons in difficult conditions; thanks to the custom of evening sittings they have to contend with short deadlines and to cover three or four stories simultaneously; they have little leisure to dine out, to meditate about their stories, or to think in general terms about the development of English politics. This at least is true of the correspondents for the dailies. A special opportunity does rest with the correspondents of the weeklies and the 'Sundays' and they do, to an increasing extent, manage to fill some of the gaps left in the rush of daily reporting.

A Challengeable Assumption

Underlying all that I have said, there is an assumption that many will challenge — an assumption that politics would be improved if the serious press were able to report them more fully and more frankly. There are many who argue that premature publicity is an enemy to wise decision making. When the Labour Party was in disarray, the leaks from the meetings of the Parliamentary Labour Party and other bodies contributed a lot to the friction. Today the Conservatives are expressing indignation at the leaks from meetings of the 1922 Committee; in some cases they have gone so far as to impugn the accuracy or even the integrity of the reports that are published, and in some cases to challenge the propriety of an attempt to inform the public of what has happened in meetings intended to be private. One M.P., Mr. Percival, complained in a letter to *The Times* of the view of the paper's political correspondent that if a journalist thinks 'he has obtained information as to what was said at a meeting where those present were speaking to one another in confidence and where *ex hypothesi* the giving of information is a breach of confidence, he is entirely free to disregard the element of confidence and to publish as fact what he has been told'. This is but one example. The challenges to the goal of candid reporting are far-reaching. Have politicians no rights of secrecy? Would decisions be made better if journalists were listening at every keyhole in Whitehall and Westminster? Are not all the barriers I have mentioned safeguards to governmental efficiency or personal privacy? Do we want the self-interested leaks, the organized disloyalty, which is inherent in the system of reporting in Washington?

My answer is that, while press freedom may be abused, press restriction is still more of a danger. There is no need to sweep away all defences against embarrassing, or one-sided, or premature disclosures of policy. But, to my mind at least, there is no doubt that more detailed and critical reporting of what goes on 'on the inside' would, in fact, improve the quality of decision-making 'on the outside'. Certainly once the whipping system began seriously to limit the free debate and voting, once issues ceased to be settled in the public proceedings of Parliament, the content of private party meetings became a legitimate source of public interest: no responsible reporter could let himself be choked off from revealing what he could of the feelings of the Parliamentary Labour Party meetings and the meetings of the 1922 Committee.

That is the answer to Mr. Percival's claim that such gatherings should be left in obscurity. There is a real danger that public issues decided in private by limited groups are decided badly, in ignorance of possible reactions 'on the outside'. Fear of the press has led governments to be altogether too negative in their handling of the press. They have failed to recognize that vigorous informed criticism can be positively helpful, warning of trouble ahead. The contempt for some of the shabbier things done in popular journalism has led, especially on the part of politicians, to excessive and ill-judged criticism of the press as a whole. What is really needed is a much more detailed criticism of the way in which the press, and particularly the serious press, covers specific political events. Extraordinarily little is written about press coverage. Anyone who has tried to prepare a bibliography on the methods of political reporting will find that almost nothing has been printed on how lobby correspondents work, on how political stories, true and false, have emerged, have been suppressed, have been distorted, have been inflated.

This, then, is my theme: we need better political reporting (not better political reporters, for there is nothing much wrong with the lobby journalists themselves). But we shall get better political reporting only when more readers express frustration with what they are offered, when they complain more vigorously of the indirect censorship which the rules and routines of Westminster and Fleet Street impose on the news they get; and when more professional observers of politics and the press turn their attention to serious analysis and criticism of the way in which political news is obtained, is selected, and is presented.

THE PRESS AND POLITICIANS

By IAN WALLER

IT is a familiar proposition of behavioural studies that the viewpoint of an individual varies with his position in a social situation. In the preceding selection, D. E. Butler, writing from the perspective of an avid consumer of political news, analysed obstacles to political communication through the press. In the selection below, Ian Waller replies, from the viewpoint of a parliamentary lobby correspondent, one of the objects of Butler's analysis. Waller agrees with Butler that British Government is organized to obstruct the communication of political information to the general public, but he challenges some of Butler's criticisms and lists more obstacles to the free flow of information about the deliberations of government. Yet the author also emphasizes that while in conflict, political journalists and politicians must rely upon each other in order to achieve their different goals.

HIGH standards of political reporting — both the ability of the press to supply it and the willingness of Government and Parliament to facilitate it — are an essential prerequisite of good government. I believe — writing with twelve years experience as a Lobby correspondent — that there are good grounds for dissatisfaction although, unfortunately, a good deal of the criticism seems to me to be either misconceived or based on ignorance.[1] None the less there is an urgent need for a change in the relationship between press, Government, and politicians — and also in the quality of political reporting and comment and the attitude of newspaper offices to it.

But this must be firmly said at the start: it is no use politicians complaining about ill-informed writing if they are not prepared to

---

[1] The chief criticisms are, in addition to D. E. Butler's article, reprinted *supra*, pp. 170–6, Anthony Howard, 'The Role of the Lobby Correspondent', *The Listener*, 21 January 1965, pp. 93–5, and Boyce Richardson, 'The Whitehall Press Scandal', *New Statesman*, 22 January 1965, p. 102.

In addition to Waller, another Lobby correspondent, David Wood of *The Times*, has also discussed the points in dispute; see 'The Parliamentary Lobby', *Political Quarterly*, xxxvi. 3 (1965), pp. 309–22.

Reprinted in slightly edited form from *Encounter*, June 1965, no. 141, pp. 73–80, where the article appeared under the title 'The "Lobby" and Beyond'. Footnotes by the editor.

recognize that the fullest possible flow of political news — and not just the pre-packed material produced by public relations officers — is in the public interest; that the press is a partner in the business of government and politics in exactly the same sense that a vigorous and critical Opposition is vital to Parliament. This, unfortunately, is not a view that is widely held in British political life, particularly in the Conservative Establishment and the higher reaches of Whitehall. All too often the press is regarded as something either to be made use of or ignored; its role no more than the reporting of decisions arrived at. The press, of course, does not accept this. But the barriers that exist, and the reluctance to accept that the press and public have a right to share in the formulation of policy, mean that far too much comment is based on inadequate knowledge, and that political writers are forced back on to speculative writing, vague guesswork, spurious forecasting, and the irrelevant personalization of issues.

The moment, I believe, has come for Fleet Street, as well as politicians, to have a fresh look at the whole problem of the coverage of politics and, indeed, public affairs generally. My immediate concern is with Parliament and Government although the issue goes, of course, much wider. There is, for example, the voluminous reporting of trade unions, with every minute detail of their activities recounted, but too little of the activities and responsibilities of managements or their group organizations (e.g. the Federation of British Industries). Industrial correspondents see themselves too much as mere trade-union correspondents. Nor can anyone be happy about the extent to which the diplomatic correspondents have succumbed to the Foreign Office's news-management techniques, its pernicious system of 'trusties' and the subtle but very powerful pressure put on journalists who cause 'embarrassment' (i.e. adopt a critical attitude to the conduct of British foreign policy or draw heavily on other sources of information beyond the F.O. and a handful of Western embassies). The Foreign Office has always regarded the press as an instrument of diplomacy; Fleet Street, it seems to me, is all too ready to comply.

The initiative for change must come from Fleet Street. It must be prepared to use its power and authority to break down the barriers of secrecy, the mysticism and aloofness that surround so much of our public life. But first it must set its own houses in order. One important factor is the calibre, authority, and status of its specialist writers. Another is the attitude of the press to authority — be it political, governmental or industrial — and its implicit acceptance of the role of supplicant. Again, there is the use that is made of news. The in-

tense competitive pressures in the newspaper industry lead to demands for hard news, an original angle, the exclusive forecast
(which has to be close enough to the event for everyone to remember
that the *Daily Q* had it first, and is therefore as likely as not to have
been deliberately leaked to prepare public opinion — the scoop that
causes real embarrassment is much rarer). All this competitive pressure can be a healthy stimulus, but it also leads to over-emphasis and
exaggeration that damage the prestige of the press. It is, of course,
far from easy to maintain a balance between producing popular
readable papers and conveying the subtler nuances, ideas, and
undercurrents in their right perspective. But cannot more be done?
And would not the prestige and authority of the press benefit?

I want to deal with the particular problem of the reporting of
politics. There is no lack of political news in the press. It is no use
comparing (as many politicians do) the press today with that of fifty
years ago when it was produced for a minority of politically involved
readers, avidly following the minutiae of debate and with the time
and inclination to read endless columns of speeches. Nor is it any use
complaining, like Mr. David Butler, that the popular press is primarily concerned with entertainment and 'not even pretending to
give all the facts that an intelligent voter would need to form a
reasonable judgement on the men who are to govern them'. The
picture presented by the popular press is sharp, often over-written,
and with a tendency to concentrate on the sensational. There are
plenty of criticisms to be made of it. None the less a picture does
emerge which has played a part in helping to make Britain one of the
most politically conscious countries in the world. The point at issue,
however, is not the overall coverage of politics but the extent to
which the press fulfils its other vital functions of investigating, probing, and analysing.

David Butler is scathing in his criticism of the failure of Lobby
correspondents to report the 'real news' or get 'scoops'. A favourite
example of this is the way no one realized, in a space of a mere
twenty-four hours, that Mr. Macmillan rather than Mr. R. A.
Butler would get the premiership in 1957. David Butler had as it
turned out a splendid opportunity to demonstrate his superiority
when he was covering the 1963 Blackpool conference for the BBC at
which Mr. Macmillan's resignation was announced. In spite of the
most assiduous lobbying of the much-despised Lobby correspondents
as well as of politicians, his comments on the ten o'clock news each
evening revealed none of the insight I would have expected. The decision to allow R. A. Butler to make the final speech he described as

'most important . . . the most ceremonial enthronement of a party leader the Conservative Party can do'; on the Friday he dismissed the suggestion that 'if Lord Home wants it he can have it' as being 'not as simple as all that'; his final comments on the Saturday included every possible name — even Mr. Iain Macleod. I make these points simply to show that political reporting is not as uncomplicated as some academic critics like to suggest. I would have thought, on the other hand, that Mr. Walter Terry's disclosure in the *Daily Mail* of Mr. Macmillan's intention to reshuffle his Cabinet in 1962, which preceded the famous purge, and Mr. Francis Boyd's disclosure in the *Guardian* that Lord Home was to be appointed Foreign Secretary, were two memorable and genuine Lobby scoops. In another field, the *Sunday Telegraph* can claim credit for revealing and pursuing — at considerable risk both in terms of libel and Parliamentary privilege — the East German and other politico-business pressure groups at Westminster.

The comparison so frequently made with the American press — or with the best American political reporting, which is another thing — is misleading for a different reason. It completely ignores the difference in the role of the British and American political journalist, a difference that stems from the fact that British Ministers are answerable to the country through Parliament while the American press provides the link between the Administration and the nation.

Here, in fact, lies one of the real problems. It seems to me that a most serious weakness in our democracy today is that the enormous expansion in the range of governmental activities has swamped the critical resources of Parliament as well as those of the Press. While power and decision-making have moved from Westminster to Whitehall, the political journalists remain centred on a Parliament that, as it is organized today, is incapable of obtaining the information it needs to form a proper judgement of the issues it is asked to decide on. The jealously guarded right of the Commons to know first what the executive's intentions are is intended to assert Parliament's paramountcy over the executive. The fact that it is increasingly losing effective control positively facilitates the executive's natural predilection for secrecy. It is Parliament as much as the press that must reorganize itself if the executive is to be subjected to the critical examination it should receive. But it raises most immediately for the press the question of whether its organization is adequate and, in particular, whether Westminster-based Lobby correspondents are any longer appropriate as the main source of political news.

The 'Lobby' derives its name from the right, first granted by resolution of the Commons in 1884, for 'a gentleman of the Press' to enter
the Members' Lobby to talk to M.P.s. This was extended to the
House of Lords in 1963. Until the war the Lobby was comparatively
small, limited to the national and certain provincial daily papers, the
London evening papers, and the news agencies. The rest of the provincial press was admitted after the last war; now the BBC and ITV
are represented and, more recently, the Sunday papers. Most newspapers now have two Lobby men with the result that the total
strength is now one hundred and twenty-one, of whom perhaps sixty
to eighty are likely to be at work at any one time. In addition to meeting Members individually in the lobbies for private talks, there are
regular collective meetings with the Prime Minister's Press Officer,
and Ministers or Opposition front-bench spokesmen, either on
specific subjects or general policy. The meetings are held at the in-
vitation of the Lobby in a room provided for them and are presided
over by the Lobby Chairman — an important symbol of its independence of the parties or Government.

A fairly full account of the work of the Lobby is given by Lord Hill
of Luton in his autobiography *Both Sides of the Hill,* and much was
said about it during the recent Vassall Tribunal. Lobby men accept
an obligation never to disclose the sources of their information received on 'Lobby terms' — which covers both formal meetings and
private discussions at Westminster. On this basis a good deal of confidential comment is given by M.P.s, enabling the Lobby man to
present an informed account of thinking and attitudes to the issues of
moment at Westminster. He does not, as Mr. Michael Foot once
suggested, take an oath of secrecy. But he accepts the Lobby rules
and a deliberate breach would justify his colleagues requesting the
Serjeant-at-Arms to withdraw his permit — although this has never,
so far as I know, been done.

The fact that the Lobby is more formalized than other journalistic
groups, with written rules and an ultimate power of sanction — to
say nothing of a slight element of mystery and privilege about its
activities — accounts for some of the hostile criticism. But, of course,
the same general principle of informal discussion and protection of
the sources of information applies to all journalists. It is indispensable
to a well-informed press that those in authority should be able to
talk frankly to journalists without fear of being quoted. The phrase,
'Lobby terms', which attracts so much abuse, is no more than an
ordinary journalistic convention.

The Lobby had its origins in the days when the party battle at
Westminster was the essence of politics and when the actions of the

N

executive were on a comparatively limited scale and capable of easy perception and explanation. The party battles and the internal party tensions are still of great importance and are dealt with by the Lobby with skill and perception. It is, in fact, in this field that the Lobby is most expert, but today it is not the only one.

Lobby journalists include some of the shrewdest and best-informed political writers in the country and they have the advantage, lacking in some political commentators, of being in close touch with day-to-day movements of opinion both on the floor of the House and behind the scenes. The questioning at Lobby meetings can be among the most penetrating to be heard at any British press conference, and the mass of material that a Lobby man has to deal with is handled with a high degree of professional accuracy and perception. They have, too, a unique opportunity for assessing the worth of Ministers or Opposition leaders.

But its post-war growth has greatly weakened the Lobby's potential. The extent to which politicians are willing to talk frankly at a meeting must diminish with the size of the audience. Even worse is the enormous diversity of interests among its members, ranging from the serious national press to small provincial evening papers whose representatives are primarily concerned with a local angle to a national story. Collective news-gathering is anathema to a live independent press, but it has grown in all fields since the war, and the Lobby is an example of it — no worse, perhaps, than many others but, like all others, susceptible to skilful news management. But the Lobby has avoided one thing that some of the other groups have not been free of: it has refused to allow any attempt by the Government or parties to discriminate between papers or individuals. In 1951, for example, the Conservatives attempted to provide special facilities for the 'friendly Press,' which was rightly resisted by all.

The Lobby suffers, too, from the characteristic English tendency to 'clubbability' and can all too easily become part of the Parliamentary establishment, a tendency encouraged by the fact that it lives and works at Westminster. But increasingly the best Lobby journalists are, rightly, going back to personal contacts — to individual rather than collective enterprise. Perhaps the greatest single weakness in the Lobby system derives from the excessive amount of work the Lobby man is expected to do. It is absurd that representatives of the quality papers should be turning out often up to several columns a day ranging over the minutiae of political movements; summaries of endless flows of bills, white papers, reports; comments on the parliamentary situation and party matters; interpretations of front-bench speeches and questions as well as (what should be their main task) watching the development of policies and attitudes behind the scenes. It grossly overburdens them, inevitably lessens the impact of their work, and gives them insufficient time for investigation or considered comment. The status of the political correspondent, has been steadily reduced to that of a political reporter at the beck and call of his news-room. It is absurd, too, that the one man (even if now assisted by a deputy) should be expected to be an expert on all aspects of domestic policies, as well as to follow the party manoeuvring.

The real cause of the trouble, I believe, lies in this: neither newspaper offices, nor the Lobby, have adjusted themselves to the immense post-war expansion in the range of government activity. Not only has this grown but every department, as well as the political parties, has built up huge public relations departments to present its cases. Most seek to channel their efforts through the Lobby to ensure stories being handled by politically experienced journalists. At the same time the vigour, and in some respects the importance, of the party battle and internal party affairs has grown. The party battle is followed in detail by the Lobby — but the executive goes unwatched.

While I believe that newspaper offices, the Lobby, and individual journalists, as well as the attitudes that have grown up over the years, have all a part to play in affecting the quality of political reporting, the most important obstacle of all is far more deeply rooted and one which, whatever other mistakes he may have made, Mr. David Butler has put his finger on. It is the traditional lack of openness in British politics; the feeling that politics and government are a matter for the insiders and nothing to do with either the press or public — except for the former to report faithfully what has been decided.

It is not, of course, only the press that suffers this exclusiveness — as Iain Macleod's famous *Spectator* article on the Tory leadership struggle revealed,[1] the 'Magic Circle' kept its secrets even from many members of the Cabinet. But so far as the press is concerned, this exclusiveness is fortified by two formidable weapons always at the disposal of the executive: the Official Secrets Act and the rules of Parliamentary privilege — to say nothing of the ultimate weapon, the Tribunal of Inquiry.

No one who had any experience of the Vassall Tribunal[2] two years ago could doubt that the press, and not the incompetence that let

[1] 'The Tory Leadership,' *The Spectator*, 17 January 1964.
[2] Cmnd. 2009 (1963).

yet another spy loose in Whitehall, was the primary target. I was subjected to hours of cross-examination by the Treasury solicitors in private and then by the then Attorney-General, Sir John Hobson, because I reported allegations that the fact that Vassall was known in Moscow as a homosexual had been reported on to his superiors in London and ignored there. At no time did Sir John or any of his minions seem to show the slightest signs that what really mattered was whether or not this was *true* — as indeed they must surely have known by that time and the Tribunal's report eventually showed. Instead their interest centred on who had told me — to reveal, I suppose, who it was who had helped to show up the incompetence of the machine his colleagues were supposed to be running. Sir John Hobson, a member of a Government that had made more use than any other administration of the Lobby and its conventions, even had the audacity to ask that I should be directed to disclose my sources.

I have no doubt at all that the existence of these powers — the Official Secrets Act, Parliamentary privilege and the Tribunal of Inquiry — however rarely they may be invoked, limit the free flow of well-informed news and comment, and inhibit the political journalist. The Official Secrets Act can, if authority so desires, be interpreted to cover virtually everything that is said or done within the Government service. It provides a wall which protects Whitehall from probing inquiry and critical analysis. Formal rules, as well as ministerial responsibility, restrict communication between Civil Servants and the press. It is slightly anomalous that the journalist can discuss policy freely with an official of a nationalized industry — whose impact on the economy may be far greater than his opposite number in the civil service — yet he may have only the most limited and unofficial contact with the Civil Servant!

The worst features of the Official Secrets Act are its blanket nature and the fact that the use of its powers is wholly at the discretion of the executive — with the journalist virtually defenceless if they are exercised. The 'leaking' of Cabinet decisions is now a routine public relations exercise in Whitehall in order to prepare public opinion or stimulate discussion in advance of the formal announcement; but an embarrassing leakage could lead to the Act being invoked, as I believe happened at least once between the wars — until it was discovered that a Minister had done the talking. Mr. Randolph Churchill boasts, in *The Fight for the Tory Leadership*, of having seen the Cabinet paper in which Mr. Macmillan laid down how his successor was to be chosen; and he gives a full summary of it. I often wonder whether such a considerate view would have been taken of this by the Government had the book caused offence? This incident is also a curious commentary on the difficulties that genuine historians have in seeing ministerial papers covered by the fifty-year-rule. Miss Barbara Fell, it will be recalled, received two years' jail for disclosing Central Office of Information briefing material which no one even attempted to argue had the slightest security value — indeed one had already been published. However foolish her behaviour may have been, the prosecution seemed to have a wider purpose than discouraging female foolishness.

Parliamentary privilege is an obstacle in another sort of way. Discussion by the press of the proceedings of a Select Committee could expose the writer to a charge of breach of privilege, however appropriate the subject might be for public discussion. Consideration was, for example, given to such action following an account of a development in the Committee on Lords reform. Of greater importance is the inhibiting effect it has on Ministers who face complaints from the House if they give information — and this is frequently extended to indications of general policy — to the press before announcing it to Parliament. The House is properly jealous of its rights and suspicious of anything that would appear to derogate from its authority or indicate lack of respect by the executive. But one cannot help feeling that its hyper-sensitivity provides the executive with a valuable shield.

Is this merely a matter of satisfying journalistic curiosity? Is it not imperative to a well-informed democracy that as much as possible should be known of what is being thought and planned in its name? The interaction of comment and discussion is as valuable to the leaders as to those being led. This point is well argued by the Fabian Group, writing from the viewpoint of enlightened Civil Servants, who prepared the recent pamphlet, *The Administrators*. They also point out the excessive extent to which secrecy is imposed on Government actions:

Secrecy is an obstacle to good policy-making when it prevents the tapping of a sufficiently wide range of expert opinion and advice and when it narrows public discussion of policy issues. . . .

In the fields of defence and foreign policy, secrecy mainly depends on considerations of national security. In the field of economic policy the practice of secrecy seems mainly to stem from the tradition that Parliament should be told things before the public. But this should apply only to policy decisions and to statements and statistics (such as budget accounts) of immediate topical relevance.

There seems no good reason why it should inhibit the release of information or the stimulation of discussion and work in the earlier stages of planning and policy-making. The danger is that secrecy, for whatever reason it starts, becomes a habit. It becomes an excuse for preventing others from looking over your shoulder and a way of avoiding 'trouble' and escaping postmortems.[1]

The same argument applies to party policy-making. It is, for example, difficult to see the justification for the wall of secrecy Mr. Edward Heath has put round the Conservative policy review, in opposition, to the point of refusing even to name the politicians on his various groups. It is also true of the weekly meetings at Westminster of the Conservative and Labour Parliamentary parties and their policy committees. Much of the time of Lobby correspondents is spent trying to establish what has gone on, particularly when a controversial issue has been under discussion, and a rather ridiculous cat-and-mouse exercise is played in the corridors of Westminster between journalist and politician, the former seeking to piece information together from hints and leaks, the latter sometimes leaking with a heavy emphasis on the view he happens to hold.

The attempts at secrecy usually either fail because of the skill of the Lobby men or are self-defeating. If, as is often alleged, the reports that do appear are selective or distorted — and personally I believe they usually present a fair picture of the stresses in a party — it is because secrecy plays into the hands of those with an axe to grind and an interest in ensuring that a particular point of view is publicized. The journalist, pressed by edition times, has inevitably to rely on a few hasty contacts.

Many politicians will argue, of course, that these meetings are private affairs and that the press has no right to inquire into them. But this is to ignore the fact that they are concerned with public policy on which party attitudes may have the most profound effects — far more so than the subsequent debates on the floor of the House. The public has the right to know. Obviously there are some matters which the parties will want to discuss in private and to open the committees to the press would simply lead to the discussions being transferred elsewhere. But far more could be done openly. What is really wrong is that so much debate has been removed from the floor of the House to secret enclaves.

The fundamental solution must lie in breaking down the barriers that surround Government and the parties. In part this is a matter of changing attitudes as well as modifying the legal barriers. I believe that in the Conservative Party changes are coming as the old exclusive caste system breaks down: younger Conservative M.P.s are undoubtedly more open in their attitudes, more willing to discuss

[1] Fabian Tract no. 355 (1964), p. 22.

issues, more aware that the public has a right to share in policy-making. Within the government machine itself I think changes are coming — the influx of advisers brought in at high levels from industry and the professions since the election of the Labour Government has introduced a leavening of men less inhibited than the traditional Civil Servant. Among the younger generation of Civil Servants, too, one detects the feeling that freer interchange of opinions and thinking would be of benefit to all.

The impetus, of course, must come at ministerial level and here, again, the impact of a Labour Government, with the party's more open tradition — the natural corollary, perhaps, of being a crusading movement — is beneficial. The political journalist undoubtedly finds greater ease of access to Ministers and more readiness to discuss issues and thinking. The Prime Minister — partly because he is the first occupant of 10 Downing Street ever to show any signs of understanding the press and of knowing those who work for it — has had much greater personal contact, largely through the Lobby, than any of his predecessors. The tradition that the Prime Minister is an aloof, distant figure (Clement Attlee as much as any Tory) has ended and can probably never again return in quite the same degree.

It would be naïve to imagine that Mr. Wilson does it from pure altruism (as naïve as Mr. David Butler's apparent belief that state secrets pour out across the dinner tables in Washington for uninhibited reproduction in next day's press — President Kennedy's famous dispute with the *New York Herald Tribune* should dispose of that notion). All politicians wish to project themselves and their policies in the most favourable light: the task of the press is to submit them to critical examination. But the readiness of Mr. Wilson to take part in this process personally can only be welcomed provided that political journalists do not allow themselves to be dazzled by the novelty of it.

The breaking down of the barriers can only be a gradual process encouraged by the pressure of public opinion through the press. It is, perhaps, beginning to dawn on politicians that it is of benefit to them too, for secrecy breeds distortion. There is constant contrast between the pretence of a Government that it is a monolithic whole, always in absolute unison, and of the press presenting what it discovers of differences of opinion in terms of personal clashes. A recent case in point is the so-called 'Brown–Callaghan clash' over the shape of the Budget. Had more been known of the real nature of the different interpretations of the economic trends in the two departments, a more intelligent discussion might have taken place, not least to the benefit of the public which has to bear the consequences of the policies.

The press has a part to play, too, in its treatment of political news, its willingness to present ideas and thinking in less vivid terms. But the real problem for the press is how to organize itself in such a way as to ensure that it is properly equipped to keep the Government under constant, well-informed scrutiny. It has broken down partly because the centre of power has moved from Westminster to White-hall (something politicians themselves have the duty to rectify) while the Lobby remains the prime channel of political news. The Lobby is still basically geared to the more limited scope of pre-war govern-ment, it is overstretched, and its authority and status reduced — although, incidentally, many of its members are of far higher calibre and education than their pre-war counterparts.

The solution advocated by some is greater specialization. Mr. David Butler, for example, advocates a corps of journalists attached to each department and virtually, as in America, living in it. This already exists to some extent. There are now special writers on economics, defence, science, the Commonwealth, education, the Common Market (when the negotiations were on), in addition to the older specialized groups. It has, however, one grave disadvantage. It places the correspondent in the hands of one department, making him wholly dependent on one source for his news, and it can assist the process of news management; one already finds departments refusing to discuss matters with other than their accredited specialist. Another drawback is that it inevitably attracts the enthusiast who can become so emotionally involved with his subject that his critical faculties are blunted; a great advantage of the Lobby is that its members are not so personally involved. Not least of the reasons, I believe, for the shock the nation suffered from the collapse of the Common Market negotiations was that so many of the corre-spondents in Brussels believed they should and would succeed that they closed their minds (and their reports) to the possibility of failure.

None the less, it is obviously true that greater specialization is in-evitable and necessary, and there are many distinguished specialist writers who avoid these pitfalls. Much depends, obviously, on their calibre and the standing they have. But the danger is there, and many are aware of it. There are two further difficulties: specialists are not always equipped to see the political implications of an issue and, more important, there is the risk of fragmenting the front that Fleet Street, or the individual paper, can present to the massive machinery of modern government. Logic might suggest special-ization, with the Lobby increasingly confined to the political battles at Westminster. But this, I think, would weaken rather than strengthen.

The *Sunday Times*' appointment of Anthony Howard as 'Whitehall correspondent' seems at first sight an important move both to cover Whitehall more comprehensively and also to avoid the dangers of over-specialization. But it implies a separation of Whitehall from Westminster which is wrong. Nor could anything be more calculated to stiffen the barriers than the idea of appointing a journalist specially to cover civil servants and report their gossip. Nor am I impressed by what I call the 'H.P. Sauce' school of political journalism (exemplified by *The Making of the Prime Minister*),[1] the attempt to create the impression of being on the inside by highlighting trivia, often at second hand.

I believe, instead, that each paper has got to unify and plan comprehensively its assault on the executive, as is the practice in America where, for example, I believe Mr. James Reston of the *New York Times* has a team of twenty-eight working with him. The senior political writer must have the authority and status that his position justifies, with a foot in Westminster as well as Whitehall, directing the political coverage (in the widest sense) of his paper and also writing himself and dealing with the major policy issues.

This suggests an end of the Lobby system as we now know it, or at least a merging of it in a bigger whole rather than retaining its monopoly. It would remain to review the important day-to-day routine of Westminster and to cover the party controversies. I would like to see the senior political writer on each paper retaining the right as a Lobby correspondent of access to Members at Westminster, but no longer based there; concerned with top-level policy and less with routine reporting; commanding greater respect than he now does. In his office he should be the head — the political editor — of a team co-ordinating the various writers covering Whitehall and Westminster, and only writing on major themes and issues from a position of authority.

Whatever arguments there may be about the precise form, the purpose must be clear: to enable the press to match, in its coverage of politics and government, the scale of modern government. Organization, calibre, status, and strength of staff are all involved in this. It must resist the cosy conventions, the easy devices of collective news-gathering, and other comfortable arrangements. It must challenge the atmosphere of secrecy that surrounds our public life, the desire to keep so much either off the record or 'just for background

[1] Anthony Howard and Richard West (London: Cape, 1965).

guidance' — devices which, valuable and essential as they are in many ways, enable the politician to avoid controversy and weaken democracy because they reduce informed public participation. Politicans must accept the need to get out into the open. The closed shop mentality must go.

THE 1964 GENERAL ELECTION ON TELEVISION

A BBC Audience Research Report

In assessing the influence of political propaganda disseminated by the mass media, it is more important to consider the
predispositions of the audience than the content, techniques,
and intention of the propaganda. The BBC's Audience Research Department has conducted studies of audience size
and audience response to pre-election television programmes
prior to the 1959 and 1964 general elections. Both surveys
have found, notwithstanding the difference in political personalities, in TV techniques and in party support between
the two elections, that the predispositions of viewers influence their evaluation of party political television programmes far more than the programmes influence party
identifications formed by a long-term process of political
socialization.

INTRODUCTION

THIS report falls into three parts. The first deals with the estimated
size of the audiences for the various election broadcasts, the second
with the reactions of audiences. The third part is a brief summary.

Estimates of audience *size* are derived from the continuous Survey
of Listening and Viewing in which representative samples of the
population of the United Kingdom (aged five and over) are questioned about their previous day's listening and viewing. A different
sample, numbering in total approximately 4,000, is questioned each
day, but as each day's sample is selected by the same procedure the
results for any one day are comparable with those of any other.

To be counted as a member of a broadcast's 'audience', an individual must satisfy the interviewer that he/she recalls having seen,
or heard, 'at least a half' of it. This criterion is consistently employed
so that all audience estimates in this respect may be regarded as
comparable one with another. (Other criteria might well produce
different estimates — smaller if the criterion defined listening/

Abridged from 'The 1964 General Election', an unpublished mimeograph
report prepared by the Audience Research Department of the British Broadcasting Corporation.

viewing more restrictively, larger if the definition were looser.) Since all the estimates are, of course, subject to the inherent limitations of sampling, small differences should be treated with caution.

A different method is used to assess audience *reactions*. They are arrived at by means of questionnaires sent to standing panels of ordinary viewers and listeners who have undertaken to report on those broadcasts which they happen to listen to. The questionnaires are designed to elicit relevant views (and to provide opportunities for 'free comment'), but they have one common feature — a 'five-point scale' on which the listener/viewer can 'sum up his/her reactions' to the broadcast as a whole. The use made of this scale forms the basis for the broadcast's Reaction Index (maximum 100, minimum zero).

It is important to emphasize that a Reaction Index does *not* purport to be a measure of the broadcast's 'quality' in any objective sense. It is intended to reflect how 'the audience' (or more exactly the 'average member' of the audience) felt about it, in the full knowledge that what they felt may owe as much to what they brought *to* the broadcast as to what the broadcast contained or how it was presented. (It is for this reason that steps were taken to classify those who answered the questions about the party broadcasts in terms of their party allegiance.) Finally, like estimates of audience size, assessments of audience reaction are based on sampling and therefore subject to the inherent limitations of this process. Once again it must be said: small differences must be treated cautiously.

The Size of Audiences

There were thirteen party election broadcasts on television. Each was transmitted simultaneously on BBC-1 and on ITV from 9.30 to 9.50 p.m. Their estimated audiences expressed as percentages of the population (excluding children under five) are reported in Table 1. The averages of these figures are: BBC 15·6 per cent and ITV 10 per cent, making a total of 25·6 per cent. Except for the last two which, like the last two in the 1959 series, had rather larger audiences than the rest, the variations in total audience are comparatively small. Such as they are, they appear to be related to the audiences of the broadcasts which they happened to follow. There was no significant variation in terms of party (in 1959 the Conservative average was slightly higher than that of Labour) nor was there any significant difference in party terms in the distribution of the audiences between BBC and ITV.

Had BBC-1 and ITV each been transmitting normal (and, of course, different) programmes it is likely that, to judge by the same

TABLE 1

Estimated audiences of the party election broadcasts on television

			BBC–1 %	ITV %	Total %
Sat.	26 Sept.	Conservative	14·9	*	*
Mon.	28 ,,	Labour	15·7	10·4	26·1
Tues.	29 ,,	Liberal	15·3	9·9	25·2
Wed.	30 ,,	Conservative	15·6	9·8	25·4
Fri.	2 Oct.	Labour	12·1	10·4	22·5
Mon.	5 ,,	Labour	15·3	10·4	25·7
Tues.	6 ,,	Conservative	15·6	9·5	25·1
Wed.	7 ,,	Liberal	17·6	7·5	25·1
Thurs.	8 ,,	Labour	16·8	7·5	24·3
Fri.	9 ,,	Conservative	14·9	10·5	25·4
Sat.	10 ,,	Liberal	12·3	9·4	21·7
Mon.	12 ,,	Labour	18·1	12·4	30·5
Tues.	13 ,,	Conservative	19·4	11·3	30·7

* No estimate available.

nights in 1963, the combined audiences would on most evenings have been considerably greater. The average audience for BBC and ITV together on these evenings in 1963 was 35 per cent — some 9 per cent more than on the evenings when the party election broadcasts took place. This suggests that the effect of transmitting party election broadcasts at 9.30 p.m. on both services was to reduce the viewing audience by about one-quarter. (This is a sharper reduction than was thought to have been sustained in the 1959 election, when the party election broadcasts went out at 10 p.m., for the reduction on that occasion was estimated at about one-fifth. But both in 1959 and in 1964 the evidence suggested that ITV viewing was reduced much more than that of the BBC.)

There were eighteen party election broadcasts on radio, ten in the Home Service following the 10 p.m. News and eight in the Light Programme at 7 p.m. Their estimated audiences are reported in Table 2. These figures are, of course, small compared with those for the television broadcasts, but they are no smaller than might be expected in view of the present balance between listening and viewing each night. The Home Service broadcasts' audiences, which averaged 0·6 per cent, were usually about half those of the preceding News. The Light Programme broadcasts followed 'The Archers' on Monday to Friday and 'Listen to the Band' on Saturdays and this undoubtedly accounts for the week-day figures (average 1·9 per cent) being so much higher than those for the two Saturdays (0·5 per cent and 0·7 per cent). Once again there is no convincing evidence that the size of the audience had much to do with the party broadcasting.

TABLE 2

Estimated audiences of the party election broadcasts on radio

Home Service				Light Programme			
			%				%
Sat.	26 Sept.	Labour	1·0	Thurs.	1 Oct.	Conservative	1·8
Mon.	28 ,,	Conservative	0·7	Sat.	3 ,,	Labour	0·5
Thurs.	1 Oct.	Labour	0·5	Mon.	5 ,,	Liberal	1·7
Fri.	2 ,,	Liberal	0·5	Wed.	7 ,,	Conservative	1·8
Sat.	3 ,,	Conservative	0·6	Thurs.	8 ,,	Liberal	2·2
Wed.	7 ,,	Labour	0·4	Fri.	9 ,,	Labour	2·1
Thurs.	8 ,,	Conservative	0·7	Sat.	10 ,,	Conservative	0·7
Sat.	10 ,,	Labour	0·5	Tues.	13 ,,	Labour	1·8
Mon.	12 ,,	Liberal	0·7				
Tues.	13 ,,	Conservative	0·7				

Table 3 is a comparison of the average audiences for party election broadcasts in 1964 and 1959. (Since in 1959 no statistics were collected about the listening and viewing of persons under the age of sixteen, assumptions have had to be made about the numbers of them in the election audiences.) The average television audience was, on this showing, 4,000,000 larger in 1964 than in 1959. About half this increase can be accounted for by the growth in the size of

TABLE 3

1964 and 1959

Party broadcasts		1964 Approx. av. aud.		1959 Approx. av. aud.	
Television	BBC and ITV	9·30 p.m.	12,700,000	10.00 p.m.	8,750,000
Radio	Home Service	10·10 p.m.	300,000	9.15 p.m.	950,000
	Light Programme	7·00 p.m.	800,000	7.00 p.m.	1,500,000

the 'television public' over these years. In the autumn of 1959 about 75 per cent of the population had television sets in their homes, but by the autumn of 1964 this had become 90 per cent (of a slightly larger population). The rest of the increase is almost certainly attributable to the change in timing, from 10 to 9.30 p.m. The decreases in the Home Service and Light Programme audiences are primarily due to the decline in the prevalence of evening listening in face of the increased competition of television, but the greater Home Service decrease is probably also attributable to the change in time from 9.15 p.m. to 10.10 p.m.

The three 'Election Forums', broadcast simultaneously on BBC–1
and the Home Service from 9.30 to 9.50 p.m. had the audiences reported in Table 4. The Labour and Conservative 'Forums' had

TABLE 4

Estimated audiences for 'Election Forums'

			BBC–1 %	Home Service %
Tues. 22 Sept.		Liberal	10·3	0·4
Wed. 23	,,	Labour	15·8	0·5
Thurs. 24	,,	Conservative	14·9	0·8

audiences which were similar to those obtained by the BBC transmissions of the party election broadcasts. They were in fact much as
might normally be expected for broadcasts of a serious kind at
9.30 p.m. in these services. The audiences for the Liberal 'Forum'
were rather less. The most probable explanation of this is that at the
same time the Light Programme was broadcasting a boxing commentary. Boxing commentaries normally draw exceptionally large
audiences and this was no exception; moreover they are one of the
few types of radio broadcasts for which substantial numbers of
people will forego viewing television.

The first 'Gallery' was at the usual time for this series and its
audience was in no way abnormal. The rest, and 'Question Time'
(on BBC–1) replaced 'Tonight' which normally has audiences of
about 10 per cent. The audiences for the 'Question Time' in the
Home Service resembled those normal for Home Service broadcasts
at this time. Two editions of 'Any Questions', falling into the election campaign period, dealt with political matters. Their audiences
were similar to those which might normally be expected.

By and large the average audiences for news bulletins during the
period of the election campaign were much the same as they were
during the comparable period in 1963. 'Election News Extra' was
transmitted late in the evening in BBC–1, but at variable times. The
size of its audience, as might be expected, tended to vary with that
of the programme immediately preceding it, for every one hundred
people viewing the preceding programme from twenty to twenty-five
would see 'Election News Extra'. As a result its audience varied
between 1·0 per cent to 6·6 per cent (the average being 4·0 per cent).

Audience Reaction

Those panel members who answered questionnaires about the party election broadcasts were asked to say whether they 'expected to agree' or 'to disagree' with its point of view. This was done in order to make it possible to analyse reactions in these terms. In what follows those who 'expected to agree' are referred to as the Pros, those who 'expected to disagree' as the Antis, and those who 'could not say' as the Uncommitted. Table 5 gives the mean Reaction Indices from each of these three groups.

TABLE 5

Mean Reaction Indices for party election broadcasts

	Pro	Anti	Uncommitted
TV broadcasts			
Labour (5)	72	42	57
Conservative (5)	66	38	53
Liberal (3)	71	53	58
Sound broadcasts			
10 p.m. Home Service			
Labour (4)	69	41	55
Conservative (4)	70	42	52
Liberal (2)	73	48	55
7 p.m. Light Programme			
Labour (3)	70	41	52
Conservative (3)	68	34	52
Liberal (2)	61	37	48
Summary (TV and Sound)			
Labour (12)	71	42	54
Conservative (12)	68	38	53
Liberal (7)	70	47	54

It will be seen that in every case the Reaction Indices given by the Pros far exceeds that given by the Antis, while that given by the Uncommitted falls between the two — though nearer that of the Antis than of the Pros. (Exactly the same thing happened in the 1959 election.) This pattern, moreover, showed itself not merely in the mean Reaction Indices but also in those for each of the thirty-one broadcasts. As the Summary at the foot of the table shows there is little to distinguish between the figures of one party and another, with the possible exception that people who were anti-Liberal were a little less critical of Liberal election broadcasts than were anti-Labourites of Labour broadcasts and anti-Conservatives of Conservative broadcasts.

Other questions were also asked about the party election broadcasts, but the answers to these, too, were clearly related to partisanship. Each broadcast tended to be rated as more interesting, more reliable, and even better presented, by those who supported the sponsoring party than by those who opposed it.

Within the limits of precision dictated by the amount of material available, it cannot be said that any of the individual broadcasts of any of these parties stand out conspicuously from the rest. Broadly, all of them tended to be well received by the supporters and adversely received by opponents. To judge by the reactions of the uncommitted the individual broadcasts, irrespective of party, were much of a muchness.

The Reaction Indices for the 'Election Forums' are shown in Table 6. The first point to note about these figures is that those

TABLE 6

Reaction Indices for the 'Election Forums'

| | | On BBC–1 | | | Home Service | |
	Pro	Anti	Uncommitted	Pro	Anti	Uncommitted
1. Liberal	70	62	62	64	50	59
2. Labour	78	56	65	72	50	58
3. Conservative	69	51	60	66	47	52

for the BBC–1 transmissions are consistently higher than those of the transmissions in the Home Service — a fact which presumably reflects the added impact of vision. Secondly, comparison with Table 5 shows that even though, in the 'Forums', the leaders had to answer questions which were not of their own choosing, the Pros reacted to them in much the same way as they reacted to the Party broadcasts — they liked the one devoted to their own party. The Antis, understandably, were less hostile and the Uncommitted also reacted more favourably to the 'Forums' than to the Party broadcasts.

There was some feeling that the Liberal leader was given a rougher ride than either of the other two (and this earned him some sympathy) while Labour supporters were better pleased with their leader's performance than Conservative supporters were with theirs. In the judgement of not only anti-Conservatives but also of the Uncommitted, the answers given by Sir Alec were a good deal less satisfactory than those given by either Mr. Grimond or Mr. Wilson.

All five 'Galleries' had Reaction Indices of between 61 and 63 — a satisfactory if unexciting level. They were, in general, considered

o

competent and well varied broadcasts, authoritative where authority
was called for, and careful to avoid bias — all qualities which viewers
had evidently come to expect from the series.

Reaction Indices are available for only three of the regionalized
'Question Times'. They were close together — 65, 66, and 67 —
and the tenor of the comment on the other broadcasts, limited
though it was, suggests that had it been possible to compute Reaction
Indices for them it is unlikely that they would have been of a
radically different order. The device of having journalists question
candidates of different parties in the same programme seems to have
commended itself, though naturally there were varied views about
the skill with which the candidates acquitted themselves. The chairmen and the journalists were, on the whole, thought to have dis-
charged their tasks satisfactorily. In general, the audiences seem to
have felt that 'Question Time' performed a useful, if rather unexciting, function.

The second of the two 'Any Questions' which took place during
the campaign, on 9 October had a rather higher Reaction Index
(63) than the first, on 2 October (58), largely because it was felt to
have been so 'pleasant and good-humoured'. Among habitual
listeners to this series there was evidence of resentment at its exclusive
preoccupation with politics. Even though the 'Any Questions' on
the day after Polling Day was also largely political it had a much
higher Reaction Index (74). Listeners seemed to enjoy it more because they felt the discussion benefited by being free from election
tension.

CHAPTER IV

THE ARTICULATION OF PRESSURE-GROUP DEMANDS

FEW individuals have the time, information, or status to communicate their political demands directly to officials in national government, whenever they wish their views considered on matters immediately affecting their interests. Pressure groups give political articulation to demands of their members, who are presumed to share a common interest in a particular area of public policy. Between elections, pressure groups provide the chief means by which ministers and Civil Servants are likely to obtain information and advice about the consequences of specific items of policy for particular groups into which society is divided.

Pressure groups are long established in Britain. S. H. Beer's study, *Modern British Politics*, has shown that their roots can be traced back long before the days of the democratic franchise. Some pressure groups, such as the Anti-Corn Law League, have expired once their purpose was achieved; others, such as the Trades Union Congress, founded in 1868, have grown in importance through the years. Today, approximately half the electorate belong to one or more organizations which sometimes seek to influence British government. The largest single category of pressure group in terms of membership is the trade unions. By international standards, pressure-group membership is high, and the groups are politically ubiquitous.

In many countries the absence of a single centre of governmental authority increases the strength of pressure groups in political bargaining. In Britain, by contrast, the Cabinet has the formal authority to impose legislation and administrative decisions upon society, free from constitutional restraints and free from parliamentary restraints, as long as the majority party is united. Notwithstanding this impressive formal authority, ministers and civil servants think it right that they should consult and negotiate with pressure groups before reaching decisions, and pressure-group spokesmen expect to be consulted and to bargain with the Government while its policy is being formed. In this process of consultation, Government spokesmen are likely to have their decisions influenced by the information, advice, and occasional threats of public attack advanced by pressure groups;

reciprocally, they try to get pressure-group leaders to accept and advocate Government policies to group members.

The extent to which pressure groups shape and restrain Government policy varies from issue to issue. Harry Eckstein's *Pressure Group Politics: The Case of the British Medical Association* concludes that in the introduction of the National Health Service the Government was most influential in terms of broad questions of policy, while the B.M.A. was most influential on narrow issues affecting doctors more strongly than patients. By contrast, H. H. Wilson's *Pressure Group* recounts the story of the introduction of commercial television by lobbyists who succeeded in 'capturing' Government authority to promote their special legislation. Given that pressure groups are important, it is a separate question whether they must or should be as important as they are at present. William Kornhauser in *The Politics of Mass Society* has argued that the existence of pressure groups strong enough to restrain Government influence upon social and economic life is a necessary bulwark against tendencies towards totalitarian government. Critics of party politics, such as R. T. McKenzie, have gone so far as to argue that pressure groups organized to advance specific and relatively narrowly defined interests of members are more qualified to provide guidance to public officials than M.P.s or party workers, who cannot be expert on the many interests affected by decisions of a multitude of Government departments. On the other hand, critics of pressure groups argue that interests are represented imperfectly; for instance, it is easier for a small group of prosperous producers to organize a lobby against consumer interests, than for a large number of scattered consumers to lobby against the producers. Furthermore, there is no necessary reason why the product of the demands of many different sectional groups in society should necessarily be in the long-term interest of the majority. On this basis it is argued that political parties should be strong in order that they may impose a broad pattern of policy upon pressure groups.

BIBLIOGRAPHICAL NOTE

The book-length literature on British pressure groups is large and growing. General surveys include: S. H. Beer, *Modern British Politics* (London: Faber, 1965); S. E. Finer, *Anonymous Empire* (London: Pall Mall, 1958); Allen Potter, *Organized Groups in British National Politics* (London: Faber, 1961); and J. D. Stewart, *British Pressure Groups* (Oxford: Clarendon Press, 1958). Harry Eckstein's *Pressure Group Politics* (London: Allen & Unwin, 1960) sets a case study of the

British Medical Association into a general theoretical context. Other case studies include James Christoph, *Capital Punishment and British Politics* (London: Allen & Unwin, 1962); Peter Self and Herbert Storing, *The State and the Farmer* (London: Allen & Unwin, 1962); H. H. Wilson, *Pressure Group: the Campaign for Commercial Television* (London: Secker & Warburg, 1961) and Graham Wootton, *The Politics of Influence* (London: Routledge, 1963). Theoretical perspective can be gained from two American classics of pressure-group theory, A. F. Bentley, *The Process of Government* (1st edition, 1908), and David Truman, *The Governmental Process* (New York: Knopf, 1951).

PRESSURE GROUPS IN BRITISH GOVERNMENT

By W. J. M. Mackenzie

THE familiar term 'pressure group' refers to a broad spectrum of organizations which differ in many politically important ways. W. J. M. Mackenzie's article provides a succinct and sophisticated introduction to important theoretical and practical points distinguishing different pressure groups, as well as an assessment of developments in the relationship between pressure groups and British government.

READERS of Professor Hancock's autobiography will remember that he refers to Disraeli's gambit — 'How is the old complaint?' — and says that if he ever meets a young social scientist whose name he has forgotten he opens conversation by asking, 'How is the conceptual framework?'[1] The subject of 'pressure groups' raises so many issues of social and political theory that one is tempted to treat it primarily as an excuse for the discussion of concepts. I think however that it would be unwise to push logical analysis very far until some attempt has been made to state the facts of the situation, and this is the primary object of the present paper. Criticism of it may provide a basis for further research and for better analysis.

Political scientists in Britain are challenged to enter this field both by the trend of academic interest in other countries and by the present state of British parties. Since 1949 we have entered a phase in which party programmes seem relatively unimportant. Parliament between 1944 and 1949 put on the statute book a programme of reconstruction which it will take at least twenty years of hard work to execute. No party is at present much tempted to look beyond the end of that period, so that the emphasis is on good administration, rather than on choice of policy. The issues in foreign policy are more profound, so profound that the public as a whole finds them hard to grasp except in terms of personalities, and is more ready to think about character and diplomatic skill than about principles. This phase might be cut short by events at any moment, but while it lasts

[1] Sir Keith Hancock, *Country and Calling* (1954), p. 223.

Reprinted from *The British Journal of Sociology*, vol. vi, no. 2 (1955), pp. 133–48.

we tend to think of politics as a continuous process of adjustment and not as a contest between alternative principles.

The British have not experienced this mood since the emergence of the Labour Party as a serious political force early in the 1920's. Before 1914 the more sophisticated and the more rebellious were agreed in regarding British parties, like American parties, as empty bottles bearing different labels, into which any political mixture might be poured. The composition of the mixture, it was assumed, was due to forces outside the parties, and political theory and empirical research both turned in that direction. The early work of the Webbs, on consumers' co-operation, trade unionism, and local government, was based on these assumptions, and they followed up their studies of working-class organization by investigating professional associations as they existed during the war of 1914–18.[1] All this was the background of their *Constitution of a Socialist Commonwealth of Great Britain*, published in 1920, which attempted to combine 'old' and 'new' constitutional principles into a single document. Events almost immediately turned in a different direction. Since 1920, both academic students and working politicians have discussed government primarily as a means of democratic choice between alternative policies, and not as a continuing social process.

In the historical circumstances of the time this emphasis was both inevitable and right: but its limits are indicated by the complete difference of development in the U.S.A. The theme was set by A. F. Bentley in 1908 in a book called *The Process of Government*, and his thesis was restated by D. B. Truman in 1951 in *The Governmental Process*, a book which takes account of the immense mass of description and analysis which has accumulated in the intervening years.[2] The political theory which emerges from all this research is not very coherent, and can accommodate various conflicting conclusions about ideal forms of government. But it is extremely effective as a tool of analysis, as may be seen in the recent assessment of our situation by Professor S. H. Beer of Harvard.[3] A good deal of research inspired by the same ideas is in progress in this country, and some of

[1] Published as a special supplement to the *New Statesman*, 21 and 28 April 1917. Professor W. A. Robson's early work on the local government service (*From Patronage to Proficiency in the Public Service*, Fabian Society, 1922) also belongs to this phase.

[2] A. F. Bentley's book was reissued in 1949 by the Principia Press, Bloomington, Indiana. The full title of Professor Truman's book is *The Governmental Process: Political Interests and Public Opinion* (New York, 1951). My debt to both these books will be obvious.

[3] 'The Future of British Politics,' *Political Quarterly*, vol. xxvi (January 1955), p. 61.

what follows is based on discussion with those concerned in it, to whom I am particularly obliged. There is however little published work on which to draw except for some studies of trade unions and professions, which generally pay more attention to internal structure than to political and social influence. The position in other countries of Western Europe is much the same. There is an excellent study of the position in Sweden (which preceded us on this road) by Professor Gunnar Heckscher:[1] and Professor Duverger[2] has recently drawn attention to the need for research in France. But there is still little comparable material except for the U.S.A., and it is obvious that parallels with America cannot be pushed very far.

One has therefore to deal with a subject which is wrapped in a haze of common knowledge. People everywhere are familiar with it and know a good deal about it, but they find it hard to see the situation in proportion and as a whole. It may therefore be a useful first step to seek for some agreement about what we already know, and that is the main object of the present paper. Its 'conceptual framework' is extremely amateurish, and can be justified only in so far as it arises naturally from the problem of compressing a mass of miscellaneous information into a manageable form.

A. Terminology of Definition

First, terminology. The phrase 'pressure group' is now well established, but its origin is a little obscure. A. F. Bentley's book was called *The Process of Government: A Study of Social Pressures*, and it is almost entirely concerned with the concept of 'group pressures' as a tool of analysis in politics. But I do not find that he reversed the phrase so as to make it 'pressure groups': indeed it would be out of line with his scheme of thought to do so. The reversal must have been made a little later by casual usage in politics and journalism,[3] and it has always had a flavour of political abuse.[4] As Bentley

---

[1] *Staten och Organisationerna*, Stockholm, 1946: there are also two articles in English by Professor Heckscher, which I have not seen: G. Heckscher, 'Group Organization in Sweden', *Public Opinion Quarterly*, vol. iii, no 4 (Winter 1939); G. Heckscher and J. J. Robbins, 'The Constitutional Theory of Autonomous Groups', *Journal of Politics* (1941).

[2] He refers to the work being done on the French employers' movement by Professor H. W. Ehrmann, of the University of Colorado, who has already published an interesting article on 'The French Trade Associations and the Ratification of the Schuman Plan', *World Politics*, vol. vi (July 1954), p. 453.

[3] The usage was well established by 1928: see P. N. Odegard, *Pressure Politics: The Story of the Anti-Saloon League* (Columbia U.P., 1928), preface, p. vii.

[4] E.g. 'We do not have pressure groups on this side of the House' — followed by an interruption (Mr. Anthony Hurd, M.P., in the Crichel Down Debate: *Hansard*, 20 July 1954, at col. 1217).

says,[1] there is an accepted view that politics should be conducted by reason alone — or perhaps by reason and sentiment: 'a pressure' is associated with 'power', and (like 'power politics') it is repugnant to most people, if only because they believe that 'power' is always exercised by someone else, and never by themselves.

The phrase 'interest groups' is used by Bentley, and is more legitimate than 'pressure groups'. But it has acquired some unpleasant overtones, and has to be used with care. I have sometimes preferred to use the phrase 'organized groups', in a rather narrower sense explained below: but ordinary usage is too strong to displace, and 'pressure groups' they remain.

Next, definition. We have no difficulty in recognizing a pressure group when we meet one, but this does not make definition any easier. One source of difficulty is that many groups important in politics are hazy organizations of a very informal kind, the members of which do not always recognize themselves for what they are. If we are to understand British politics we must know about such things as the Clapham Sect, the Benthamites, Benjamin Jowett, Crabbet, Bloomsbury, the Morant connection in the Civil Service, Cliveden, the pro- and anti-German factions in the Foreign Office in the 1930's, and so on. Groups of this sort are not beyond the reach of academic study, as one can see from works like Professor Finer's book on Chadwick, Mr. Annan's on Leslie Stephen, Mr. Harrod's on J. M. Keynes. But these instances suggest that the job is one for historians: such groups are highly individual and their operation is the pith and substance of the political history of a nation. There seems to be no hope of generalization about it except at the exalted level of talk about human groups in the abstract, which is exhilarating, but not very helpful to students of politics.

It is therefore necessary, as a matter of tactics rather than of principle, to reduce this unlimited field to something more manageable, and for a political scientist it is natural as a first step to cut out groups which do not possess a specified formal organization. Formal organization is a subject which we are accustomed to handle in dealing with the state and its organs, and we know what its problems are.

I think however that to make the subject manageable it must

---

[1] P. 447. There was a neat example of this recently in a statement issued by the National Coal Board, which included the words: 'The action taken at Markham Main and the sympathetic action taken at other collieries in Yorkshire is an attempt to use power instead of reason to solve disputes.' (*Manchester Guardian*, 6 May 1955.)

(handwritten margin notes: "demonstration of effects in market sq", "small group - loca - nat")

somehow be reduced still further. The number of distinguishable
organizations in this country is enormous — perhaps of the same
order as the number of adult inhabitants — and all organizations
may have some reference to politics in the sense that all are recognized or at least tolerated by the law, and that all have some
tendency to persist in their chosen course and to react against any
interference, including interference by public authority. How is one
to separate organizations which are politically significant from those
which are not? The difficulty is that there is no logical halting-place
between the least of the organized groups and the greatest. There
are circumstances in which the most harmless local dramatic society
or hiking club may find that it can only get on with its business if it
uses tactics in local politics (or in the politics of a greater group)
which are indistinguishable in principle from those used by great
organized groups in national politics. Similarly, one finds that the
problems of internal democracy and bureaucracy are much the
same at all levels, in spite of great differences of scale.

It may be, therefore, that if one wishes to find a model or models
for different types of organized groups, the best tactics will be to
begin by detailed study of small pressure groups rather than of great
ones. But what we are interested in as students of politics is the part
played by such groups in *public* decisions, and it is therefore fair to
exclude organizations which have only limited dealings with the
organization of the state. This is in its nature a shifting category,
since a shift in circumstances may bring almost any organization into
a public stituation. But at any given moment the number of organizations which are playing politics is relatively small. For instance
the Catholic Church only comes into our scope in so far as it is involved in politics by a row about voluntary schools or about the
persecution of Catholics in some foreign country. Trade unions may
sometimes be outside our scope, in so far as they are organizations
which exist to bargain with employers and to organize mutual
benefits for their members. But some trade unions are composed only
of the servants of public bodies, so that all their bargaining is bargaining with the public; and all unions are now much involved in
the public regulation of wages and conditions of work. It is therefore
impossible to exclude trade unions in general; the focus of trade-
union studies has traditionally been different, but it is sometimes
illuminating to consider them from the point of view of political
pressure, rather than from that of industrial democracy.

It may (finally) be wise to exclude various types of bodies which
are in law organized groups but which are in practice so constituted
that it is not easy to say who their real members are. I.C.I. and the

City of Manchester are in a legal sense organized groups, and they are certainly entities which exercise influence on government, but here the gap between formal and informal organization is so wide that we shall never get outside the lawyer's world if we start from the Articles and Memorandum of Association or from the Charter of Incorporation with the relevant Acts. We cannot avoid the issue by limiting ourselves to pressure groups whose members have a free choice whether to belong to them or not, for the question of the 'closed shop' in the professions, in industry and in trade is one of the central problems: but it will be wise to exclude cases in which legal membership of the legal organizations is no more than a matter of form.[1]

These exclusions leave a field which could be described as follows: *the field of organized groups possessing both formal structure and real common interests, in so far as they influence the decisions of public bodies*. This raises a difficulty about political parties, which is referred to below, and there are a number of terms in it which could be debated at great length; but it will perhaps serve as a starting-point. One can illustrate what is meant by a list; such a definition would include the influence on public policy of organized professions, trade associations and trade unions, of associations of local authorities and their officers, and of associations for the promotion of particular interests or of particular good objects: for instance, the B.M.A., the N.U.T., the Town Planning Institute, the Iron and Steel Federation, the Association of British Chambers of Commerce, the N.U.M., the N.U.R., the A.M.C., N.A.L.G.O., the Association of Education Committees, the Association of Medical Officers of Health, the N.F.U., the Sabbath Day Observance Society, the Africa Bureau, the Howard League, the Road Haulage Association, the Fish Friers' Association, the educational organization of the Catholic Church, a community association or tenants' association on a housing estate, a local Trades Council or Chamber of Trade, a golf club interested in protesting against the use of its land for building, a Mothers' Union offended by BBC talks about psychology and religion.

[1] Since this paragraph was written, I have come on the following, which illustrates how hard it is to draw a working distinction between groups that are politically active and those that are not: 'The Calico Printers' Association, Ltd., has issued a booklet to each of its ten thousand employees explaining the issues involved' (in the adverse report on C.P.A.'s trade practices by the Monopolies Commission) 'and urging them to write to their members of Parliament without delay, no matter to which party they belong.' 'We fear,' writes the chairman of C.P.A., 'that desire for immediate political gain has been a deciding factor in the decision to force us to abandon our measures to ward off depression and unemployment when trade slackens.' (*Manchester Guardian*, 30 April 1955.) There has also been discussion of the possible effects of I.C.I.'s profit-sharing scheme on electoral chances on Tees-side (*Manchester Guardian*, 18 May 1955).

The list is potentially enormous, yet it excludes many groups which are of great interest to sociologists. The next problem therefore is whether one can say anything important about the politics of these groups without becoming deeply involved in matters of social structure.

B. The Situation

In a field like this, one system of classification is bound to cut across another, and in the end the best tactics may be to choose one classification out of many, and relate everything else to it. But this will entail some sacrifices, and it may be best here to experiment briefly with various alternatives. These four seem to be the most obvious: by the type of body whose decision is influenced, by the type of interest at stake, by the internal structure of the organization, and by the methods which it uses. What I have to say about these is based on inquiry and discussion over a pretty wide field, but there are only scraps of material here and there which can be documented up to the hilt, and very little of this documentation could be published. This is a problem not of accident but of substance: it affects all research into current politics, and its implications have not perhaps been fully considered by social scientists.

The first heading, that of type of body influenced, raises only one point of interest. Public bodies are classified conveniently enough in the textbooks as central, local, and 'other': it is almost a commonplace that any public body has its penumbra of organized groups which form its particular public. Perhaps this is most familiar in the middle levels of administration: the cabinet or the full council of a large local authority are the centre of so many contending pressures that it is very hard for any single organization other than a political party to impinge on them effectively. But each permanent secretary in Whitehall has to know a good deal about the troop of big and little associations which move with and around his ministry: in a sub-department the attendant retinue may be quite small and it is the Civil Servant's job to know it intimately. Similarly, each committee of a local authority will have its own pressures, and both chairman and chief official will know them very well.

In this sense, the field of groups is organized (with much overlapping) into the clienteles of various decision-makers at various levels,[1] and this is one way in which one could organize material for research: for instance, a thesis about group pressures on the homing

[1] The Report of the Committee on Intermediaries (Cmd. 7904 of March 1950) did much to explore this.

pigeon sub-section of the pets section of the livestock division of the production department of the Ministry of Agriculture and Fisheries — or what you will. In our system the focus of decision is almost always somewhere in the field of 'administration'; an approach from this end would describe the British system in a fairly complete way, and there would scarcely be the necessity (which Professor Truman finds in the U.S.A.) to deal separately with pressure in the legislative process and on the judiciary.

This seems however to leave political parties out of the story altogether. As Professor Truman insists, the words 'political party' mean in the U.S.A. many different things in different circumstances. This is also true in Great Britain, but we tend in this country to draw a pretty sharp line between parties and pressure groups by defining party with some variant on Burke's formula: 'a body of men united for promoting by their joint endeavours the national interest upon some particular principle in which they are all agreed'.[1] This excludes a good many manifestations of party in the U.S.A., and it also excludes the conception of party dominant in the old German and Austrian Empires (and by no means extinct), which virtually identified parties with organized interests. We also tend at present to lay a great deal of emphasis on the hierarchical organization of the parties so well described by Mr. Robert McKenzie, and to bother less about the oddities of the informal structure. A party in this strict sense, 'Burkean' and hierarchical, may be a social class organized to transform society in its own interest: more prosaically, it may be an honest broker of many interests, a mediator between public opinion and public policy. On either interpretation of party, party is one important focus of pressure groups and channel for influence. Indeed, there is a strict view of the constitution which would assert that influence on decisions ought to be exercised *only* through parties prepared to submit to the judgement of the electors. I should guess that this is not what happens. Undoubtedly some pressure groups operate on one party or the other or on both parties, and all pressure groups are interested in M.P.s. But I do not think that the parties bulk very large in the day-to-day operations of the average honest pressure group; there are many ways of exercising influence nationally or locally which are accepted as proper and which do not pass through any party office.

The second line of classification is by the type of interest involved. This looks promising, but is very difficult to manage without introducing one's own judgement about the particular question at issue.

[1] *Thoughts on the Present Discontents* (1770): World's Classics edition, vol. ii, p. 82.

One could spot at once the bias of a researcher who classified the pressures regarding television into those based on private profit and those based on interest in public service. In theory there is a distinction between selfish pressure groups and 'do-gooders': in almost all cases there is a mixture of motives. Private financial interests will campaign by using arguments derived from widely held views about the public interest, and they may end (or even begin) by convincing themselves. On the other hand, even the most high-minded organization cannot last long or press very hard without recruiting and paying for permanent full-time employees: and there then arises the problem of the man whose job depends on his success in finding a case to make.

It would be a mistake therefore to build much on a classification of organized groups into 'self-regarding' and 'other-regarding'; and if any lines are to be drawn between types of interest it must be done more cautiously. There are for instance common local interests, such as those fostered and expressed by Industrial Development Associations.[1] There are common interests in manufacture, expressed by trade associations; there are common interests in setting standards of skill and maintaining a monopoly of jobs, expressed by professional bodies and by certain trade unions; there are common interests between the employees of one employer, expressed by the Civil Service unions or by industrial unions: and so on. This suggests some points of importance, but (at first sight) not many. There seems to be great similarity between all these bodies in so far as they have evolved working techniques of influence; there are also great differences of internal structure, and these seem to be related to the history and technical character of individual interests, rather than to any grouping by type of interest.

It may be convenient to take next this question of internal structure. There is a good deal to be said about this, but very little of it relates to the formal constitutional structure of the association. The constitutions of states are almost always interesting, the rules of associations are generally very dull, and contain much that is common form set out so as to conceal a sentence or two here and there on which the whole thing depends. It is therefore best to approach from the angle of informal organization: what questions does one ask first when one is trying to get on terms with a body that one does not know? Who runs it? Who are the active members? Where does it get its money? The answer to the first question almost always turns out to be one

[1] See Professor M. P. Fogarty, *Plan Your Own Industries: A Study of Local and Regional Development Organizations* (Oxford University Press, 1947).

man, full-time and paid for his services; the impression one gets is
not that there is an iron law of oligarchy, but that there is a new type
of entrepreneur or broker; the man who makes a living by finding
and focusing common interests and grievances and by pressing them
in the right way. This impression is to some extent due to the terms
of our inquiry: one of the main reasons why an informal group
acquires formal organization is that it has reached the scale of hiring
staff and spending money on a fairly large scale, and these are things
that cannot conveniently be done except in proper form. Probably
the two things develop together: the existence of a potential director
encourages formal organization, formal organization makes it possible to have full-time staff. Without research one can only say that
there is quite a large class of jobs which have much in common, in
spite of social and educational differences: jobs like those of a trade
union official, or secretary to the N.U.T., or the A.A., or the B.M.A.,
or the N.C.S.S., or the Howard League, or director of the F.B.I., or
of a Chamber of Commerce. It is hard to fit these men and women
into accustomed categories such as administrator or entrepreneur or
politician, and one must not call them 'lobbyists' because that suggests American analogies which are quite misleading. The category
is a new one, and perhaps specifically British.

There is much greater variety as regards membership. One comes
across organizations of all sizes and of all degrees of keenness, from
small groups of businessmen or philanthropists keenly interested in a
single topic to vast organizations which include many members
whose interest in the association is very slight and who contribute
nothing to it except subscriptions. There is perhaps a line to be
drawn between 'do-good' organizations, which are not interested in
increasing membership except to increase their funds, and may
prefer to work with a few large contributors; and 'occupational'
associations which will always tend towards the closed shop, because
their influence depends on the completeness of their membership
within the area which they attempt to control. This factor is expressed in familiar experience from standards of qualifications,
pressure to join, internal jurisdiction, lines of demarcation, and
growth of amalgamations, problems which have something in common at the level of the B.M.A., or that of the Chartered Institute
of Secretaries, or that of the A.S.L.E.F. But one must be careful
not to generalize too much, as the whole field except that of trade
unions is unexplored, and even trade unions are imperfectly
known.

The third problem is that of the link between management and
members. One can call this internal democracy, or one can call it the

problem of financial control: the two formulae mean much the same in practice. Trade-union studies have cast some light on the possible variety of constitutions and on different ways in which the same constitution may be worked.[1] There are some obvious points of importance in the formal drafting of a constitution: for instance, to give large powers to the annual general meeting of members will tend towards centralization, as A.G.M.s are generally ill-attended and easy to handle. A plebiscitary or pyramidal constitution may have the same effect. On the other hand, the reference of decision to a large number of branches acting separately is likely to delay action and also to weaken the central authority. This sort of proposition about comparative politics can be made *a priori* and confirmed by a few cases: but there is very little ground for generalization from recorded facts except about trade-union structure.

Much more could be said about classification by method; this is a point at which group politics fits into the whole structure of national politics, and one can see that there could be a book on this which would add enormously to our understanding of the character of British government, as distinct from American or French or Russian government. Here are some headings, incomplete and badly documented:

1. *Inducement to individuals*, in cash or kind: or pressure by threats, which is the correlative of this. The line drawn by law between honesty and corruption varies very much in different countries, and may have little practical significance. I do not know of any comparative study of the law about corrupt practices, but my impression is that British law, including law about financial support for candidates, is stricter in form than the law of most other countries. This is uncertain, but there is no doubt that British law is effectively applied. The trickle of insignificant cases in central and local government illustrates the small scale of such illegal corruption as there is, and makes it clear that the game is not worth the candle. I know of no case in which there has been even a suspicion of illegal corruption by an organized group: as will be seen later, the good reputation of a pressure group is one of its most effective means of influence, and it would be insane for any group to endanger it for small temporary gains.

There are however two important matters which are not illegal, and could scarcely be made illegal, but which raise controversy from time to time.

a. It is a familiar fact that particular M.P.s act regularly as

[1] See in particular V. L. Allen, *Power in Trade Unions* (London, 1954).

spokesmen of particular interests,[1] and indeed this is one of the most important parts of the work of the House of Commons. We badly need an analysis of types of M.P.s in the twentieth century on the lines boldly drawn by Sir Lewis Namier for the eighteenth century. Presumably all (or almost all) M.P.s now spend a good deal of time on the minimum of routine attention to constituency and to party which is necessary to keep a seat: and presumably there are still some who do this for reasons of social prestige and do not attempt to take a serious part in the business of the House. But probably the number who take some interest in public business is larger than it has ever been, and here there seems to be a workable distinction between those who speak mainly on specific matters related to some special interest or interests, and those who speak as potential leaders of opinion or spokesmen of opinion on large matters of public policy. The protagonists of special interests are not disqualified from reaching office, and one can think of well-known cases, that of Sir Reginald Dorman-Smith for instance:[2] but on the whole the way to office is not through identification with an interest, however powerful. Yet the interests are anxious to have their case stated on the floor of the House, in committees, and in the smoking-rooms, and it is in the interests of the House that this should be done. It raises its prestige as Grand Inquest of the Nation, and also contributes to the efficiency of business. The Committee stage of Bills 'upstairs' is rarely effective except when there is a discussion between one set of experts speaking through the Minister and other experts speaking through various back-bench M.P.s. Are the M.P.s who act as spokesmen bound in any way to the interests for whom they speak? By formal rule they are not bound and cannot be bound, without breach of privilege of the House: the matter was last thrashed out in the discussion in Mr. W. J. Brown's case in July, 1947.[3] In practice, a wide range of motives is involved; it may be the vain but human desire to have a good case and to do justice to it, the political desire to keep a good 'connection' or clientele, or some motive of social and financial ambition, honestly pursued.

   b. The other matter that has caused anxiety is the question of whether individual public servants are influenced by the idea of good jobs in industry when they leave the service of the Crown. This is raised sometimes about politicians: there was a considerable pother

---

[1] This has been excellently brought out in Sir Ivor Jennings' book on *Parliament*.

[2] There are also cases, like those of Mr. Ernest Bevin and Sir Andrew Duncan, of spokesmen brought straight into office from outside the House of Commons; but House of Commons opinion is unlikely to accept this except in serious emergencies.

[3] Report of the Committee of Privileges (HC 118 of 1947), and *Hansard* for 15 July 1947. Similar issues arose in other privilege cases about that time.

P

about naval officers and armament firms in the 1930's, when Senator
Nye and others gave currency to the idea that wars were due largely
to 'Merchants of Death':[1] and it is obvious now that retired air
marshals are seldom left to beg their bread or become golf club
secretaries. This is a point which requires vigilance, so long as the
emoluments of public service are less than those of private industry:
but it can affect only a very small part of the public service, and my
guess is that even there its effect on policy is negligible.[2]

2. *Direct Pressure on Political Parties.* Here the most obvious question
is that of party funds: this has attracted so much attention that it can
be passed over quickly. The position about the Labour Party is clear
enough, that about the Conservative Party is more obscure: all that
need be said here is that the sort of groups which subscribe to
political parties are very limited in numbers and type; they may be
very important to the parties, but they are only a tiny part of the
enormous world of organized groups.

It would be pleasant to be able to say more about pressure on
parties through elections, but there is not enough evidence to enable
one to be very positive. My general impression is that the plebiscitary
character of elections is squeezing this out; campaigns (like that of
the Catholic Church in 1950) to organize blocks of voters on particular issues are now reckoned to be a little disreputable, and in any
case they do not seem to have much effect. The old nineteenth-
century routine of putting specific questions to candidates also seems
to be dying. But in some ways the process of selecting candidates is
now more important in British politics than the process of election,
and there are certainly organized groups (not trade unions only)
which have an important influence at that stage; it is possible, but
more difficult, for them to depose a sitting member or an established
candidate.

3. *Appeal to Public Opinion.* Pressure through elections may be declining but there is no doubt that organized attempts to alter the
prevailing climate of opinion are still important in British politics.
A new Corn Law League is unthinkable: and the press Lords have
passed their peak: but public agitation is still worth trying. The
object perhaps is not so much to create public opinion, as to create

---

[1] Cf. Philip Noel-Baker, *The Private Manufacture of Armaments* (Gollancz, 1936),
vol. I, part ii, chap. 3: The Nye Report (74th Congress, Senate Report no. 944),
in particular part III of 3rd Part (April 1936) and part II, chap. iv, of 4th part
(June, 1936): Royal Commission on the Private Manufacture and Trading in
Arms (Cmd. 5292 of 1936), in particular at p. 57.

[2] The case usually quoted is that of Sir Christopher Bullock, Permanent Under
Secretary at the Air Ministry, who resigned after an inquiry in 1936 (Cmd. 5254);
but there is still a good deal of doubt about the true circumstances.

an opinion about public opinion; both politicians and Civil Servants are trained to be conciliatory, and like to move with opinion, more from habit than from any specific compulsion. Expressions of opinion in the House of Commons carry extra weight if they are known to be based on wide contacts, and the status of the parliamentary Question as an instrument of pressure depends on this. 'Write-in' campaigns of the American type may affect the atmosphere of the House of Commons a little, but under our system they rarely affect the actual vote; they may even defeat themselves by arousing suspicion and hostility. Public meetings are useful, but only if well attended and well reported in the press. Resolutions by a variety of ostensibly unconnected bodies are worth something: so are poster campaigns. But there is no doubt that the key position is held by the press, which decides what is 'news' and allocates space — editorial space, news space, and space in correspondence columns. The daily press is still held to be the best arbiter of public opinion, at its various levels, if only because its circulation figures are related in some way or other to public appreciation: but politicians are by trade pretty expert in taking the temperature of newspapers, and are not as easily deceived about public opinion as they were in the days when Northcliffe and others held the initiative. This in turn has moderated the use of stunting, and the general press is growing less important politically in relation to the various types of specialist journal, which relate to special public opinions, and belong to the next two sections of my paper as well as to this one. The BBC is of course a key point in British politics, but its importance is kept within bounds because it keeps as quiet as it can about public reactions to its programmes; ITA may prove to be more important as a sounding-board than the BBC if it has fewer inhibitions about giving publicity to what listeners and viewers think.

4. *The Best Information.* In spite of the implications of the word 'pressure', there is not much doubt that the most effective of all techniques is the appeal to reason, as the Webbs well knew. Some social and intellectual prestige is necessary in order to ensure that your information is what the best people believe to be the best: and there is an element of management in seeing that information is planted in places where it will reach decision-makers. But the essential thing is that the proper authority, whoever he may be, should be fed over a long period with relevant information which turns out to be correct. Those of us who were temporary Civil Servants during the war were fascinated at first by the discovery that every possible object of human consideration has its proper niche somewhere in Whitehall. But one soon discovers, when one traces the man

responsible for (shall we say) food for racing pigeons, that he is a chap who has never seen a racing pigeon, has only been in the job two months, and has an inquiry about pigeon-food (among his many other duties) to handle once a fortnight. But he is a conscientious chap and quite able — perhaps he got a First in Greats: he has the files: and it is easy to see from them which stories have in the past worked out right and which have worked out wrong. So he will be much influenced (for instance) by the *Pigeon Fanciers' Telegraph* if he knows that that journal has over the years been a reliable source of facts about pigeon-food.

Politicians are more accustomed than Civil Servants to talking generalities so as to conceal ignorance, and are vulnerable to various forms of appeal to sentiment rather than reason, which Civil Servants escape. But there is a vast area of decision in which politicians are concerned mainly to acquire a reputation for being right, and they too are very thankful to anyone who can keep them out of trouble.

5. *Administrative Necessity*. The organized groups are often as indispensable in the execution of policy as in the making of policy. This can be found at all sorts of levels. At one extreme is blackmail by the experts: 'organize it our way or we won't co-operate'. These were the tactics of the medical profession in 1911 and 1947. The doctors overplayed their hand and became a public laughing-stock on both occasions: but their pressure has undoubtedly been responsible for the rather syndicalist look of one section of the health service organization. At the other extreme are associations formed on the initiative of Government because there is a job to be done quickly and it is impracticable or politically undesirable for the Ministry to expand its own staff and issue orders through them. Perhaps the first famous case was the formation of the British Iron and Steel Federation under the pressure of tariffs in 1934: but the device of marketing boards was introduced at about the same time for somewhat similar reasons, and we are equally familiar with industrial research associations, with semi-official bodies with names like 'Bacon Importers National (Defence) Association, Ltd.', and with Development Councils under the Act of 1947.

Often the same result may be achieved less formally, with little said on either side; indeed it is a matter of form rather than of substance whether business is done by an association acting as sole agent for the Government, or by an official 'control' under a temporary Civil Servant seconded to the Ministry by the relevant trade association for the duration of the emergency. One is tempted to say that in a technological society, government is not possible except on this basis: the political master is necessarily a layman with reference to the experts, and he is taking grave risks if he attempts to rule them except by discussion. It is hard to imagine what happens in Russia in matters of this kind: certainly British government rarely takes the risk of trying to break down a united front of expert opinion. On the contrary, it is often tactically important for the Government to unify the experts and interests concerned in a problem, so as to be able to make a bargain which will stick, and (perhaps) so as to be able to shift the burden of responsibility to their shoulders if the scheme breaks down.

This is most marked at the lower levels of policy, since there are some matters such as defence and foreign policy for which the Government must accept full responsibility or abdicate. But similar considerations may have the same effect in great matters as in small ones. The Society of British Aircraft Constructors was reorganized during a defence crisis in January 1938, to strengthen the industry in dealing with the problem of rapid expansion: traditionally, various groups in the City of London have influenced foreign policy because of the excellence of their information about the financial situation in other centres; and we have recently seen, in the denationalization of steel, an instance of the difficulty of distinguishing precisely where the line comes between control by Government and control by an organized industry.

Certainly, the principle of action with and through organized groups is dominant in all ordinary affairs of government, and colours all British practice. Yet these relations are generally of a very informal kind and seem to be blighted by any attempt to tie organized groups into the formal machinery of government, on the lines familiar to theoretical reformers. In spite of Mr. Morrison's kindly references to them,[1] it is hard to believe that much collective influence is wielded by the Economic Planning Board, or the National Joint Advisory Council of the Ministry of Labour, or the National Production Advisory Council for Industry of the Board of Trade. Their members are individually important, but collectively weak. Other bodies, less official in character, the Association of Municipal Corporations and the County Councils Association for instance, have achieved unofficially a status which makes them something like sub-parliaments, and they often play a very important part in legislation. But apparently this semi-official status has been achieved at the cost of effectiveness as organized groups: the local government associations are much more effective in small matters affecting local government than in great ones. Their terms of reference are so wide,

---

[1] *Government and Parliament* (Oxford, 1954), p. 305.

their respectability so great, that they have become channels of
pressure rather than pressure groups.

C. Assessment

The preceding sections have raised some very general issues about
British government, and perhaps cross the frontier between fact and
judgement. It would be fair to end with some discussion of the
political theory of pressure groups. Are they good things? Or rather,
what standards do we use when we attempt to answer the question,
'Are they good things?' But my own assessment is implicit in my
statement of the situation, and it is scarcely possible to go beyond
this without tackling the subject again from a different point of view.
I can therefore only sum the matter up in a personal way.

The structure of British government includes besides the hierarchical world of public servants and the parliamentary world of
party politics a very complex world of organized groups: and public
decisions are the result of interplay between these three worlds. Does
the public get left out in this process? Perhaps, but then no public or
publics exist politically except in so far as they can express themselves through this process: access to it is open to all, and the entry-
fee can be paid in brains and energy as well as in cash. This may
sound a complacent conclusion, but it is one implicit in this method
of analysis. It is extremely illuminating sometimes to consider politics
as a process or equilibrium, in which decisions are taken not by men
but by the interrelation of events. But one can get no assessment out
of this analysis except that latent in its premises: 'The world is the
best of all possible worlds, and *everything* in it is a necessary evil.'[1]

The answer may be different if one is asked bluntly whether one
likes the thing. I think my own answer is that I don't like it very
much. It seems to be one symptom among many of a general reversal
of Maine's famous progress from status to contract. We are gradually
shifting back into a situation in which a man is socially important
only as a holder of standard qualifications and as a member of
authorized groups, in fact into the new medievalism which was the
promised land in the days from the younger Pugin to William
Morris. This seems a good deal less romantic now than it did in the
heroic age, when the English were wandering in the desert. The
system is egalitarian in so far as qualifications lie freely open to
talents: and its rigidity is mitigated by the fact that almost everyone

---

[1] F. H. Bradley, Preface to *Appearance and Reality*, quoted by Professor Oakeshott
in his inaugural lecture on *Political Education*. Richard Wollheim discusses the effect
of 'equilibrium theory' on Pareto's assessments, in a recent article in *Occidente*,
vol. x (November 1954), p. 567.

has many different statuses within separate but overlapping organizations, a matter stressed equally from different points of view
by Professor D. B. Truman and Mr. T. S. Eliot.[1] Group managers
are in general competent and clear-headed men who recognize the
existence of the public interest and are moderate in action, by
temperament or because in England moderation is a good way to
get what you want. The worst danger to the system is from external
shocks. Within its limits it is both sensible and humane, but it is
technologically conservative and its political horizon is limited to
problems familiar to the ordinary man in his daily business and to
the organizer who represents him. Unfortunately there are a good
many problems to be faced which are much wider in scope than that,
and it is no use thinking that there is some specially organized group
of experts which has capacity and power to deal with them. If great
problems are to be handled at all it must be by a government prepared to use its majority: it is this that still gives primacy to the party
system and to the traditional doctrines of the constitution.[2]

[1] *Notes towards the Definition of Culture* (London, 1948).

[2] Since this paper was written the same point has been put with an attractive
insularity by Mr. R. M. Jackson in quite a different context (an article on 'Ministerial Tribunals' in the *Manchester Guardian* of 22 April 1955): 'The underlying
assumption is that the Government must always get its own way if it thinks the
matter is sufficiently important, or cease to be the Government; that is a shocking
doctrine to Americans and Frenchmen and their camp followers, but it happens to
be our system and to work, like monarchy, because of the structure of convention
and understanding.'

THE POLITICS OF THE BRITISH MEDICAL ASSOCIATION

By HARRY ECKSTEIN

BECAUSE pressure groups have grown outside control by statutory legislation, each group has been left relatively free to develop its own form of internal organization and methods of making policy. In organizations divided into a large number of scattered members with little time for politics and a small number of full-time officials and part-time advisers concentrated in London, there is a tendency for the small, centralized group of officials to make many policy decisions without reference to rank-and-file members. Harry Eckstein's study of the lobbying activities of the British Medical Association is significant because he is able to document and explain the types of differences that arose between pressure-group officials and their members in the important negotiations leading up to the adoption of the National Health Service.

THE B.M.A. has a considerable reputation for playing politics, and playing it very one-sidedly. It is supposed to be as callously conservative as the American Medical Association, which is surely a paragon of callous conservatism. But it scarcely deserves its reputation. At any rate, I shall try to show here that the B.M.A.'s conservatism is something much less simple than its critics seem to think and something which, upon proper understanding, should appear much less reprehensible even to Mr. Bevan.

B.M.A. Politics to 1942

The ancient political history of the Association is innocent, even laudable, enough. Throughout the nineteenth century it took scarcely any interest in politics.[1] As the leading medical organization in the country it could not help becoming embroiled in the medical agitation of the 1850's, nor did its first three political committees — the Medical Reform Committee, the Committee on Medical Legisla-

[1] For analyses of the B.M.A. see Little, *The British Medical Association*; and Carr-Saunders and Wilson, *The Professions*, p. 90 f.

Reprinted from *Political Quarterly*, vol xxvi, no. 4 (1955), pp. 345–59.

tion, and the Medico-Political Committee — have a very sedentary career. But the Association's forays into politics were so half-hearted that it incurred the bitter enmity of Wakley, the stormy editor of the *Lancet*, and, indeed, had to put down an attempt (in 1900) to create a rival, more politically active medical organization. At the same time, it ran up an excellent record in the development of the public health services. It battled against some of the worst aspects of poor law medical practice and the old M.O.H. system; it fought for compulsory notification; it led the demand for the Vaccination Act and helped to create the School Medical Service.[1] One commentator concluded that 'the policy of the Association has in the main been in advance of public opinion' on medico-political matters.[2] Since this view comes from the B.M.A.'s own centenary history, it need not be taken as gospel, but there is at least a kernel of merited righteousness in it.

Indeed, in the 1930's and during the early war years the Association's views on medical policy were considerably ahead of general public opinion. In 1930 it published a remarkable document which asserted that every individual had a right to every form of medical treatment and could have it provided only through the application of a *planned national health policy*.[3] While it felt that an extension of national health insurance would serve the purpose, the sentiment and wording of the document were almost precisely those of the Beveridge Report. In 1942 — easily the most radical year in B.M.A. history — it contributed to an even more extraordinary report, that of the Medical Planning Commission, organized by the B.M.A. and the Royal Colleges.[4] The Commission recommended, in effect, that the provision of medical services should be centrally planned by public authority; that general practice should be organized on a 'corporate basis', i.e. in health centres (the pet proposal of the Socialist Medical Association); that hospitals should be organized in co-ordinated regional schemes; and it at least mentioned the possibilities of covering everyone, rich and poor alike, by a single medical scheme, financed out of taxation. Here were all the essentials of the National Health Service itself.

The profession received these proposals with great enthusiasm. The B.M.A.'s Representative Meeting endorsed most of the important recommendations[5] and the *British Medical Journal* approved

---

[1] This is a very incomplete list.   [2] Little, op. cit., pp. 137–8.
[3] B.M.A., *A General Medical Service for the Nation*.
[4] See 'Draft Interim Report of the Medical Planning Commission,' *Brit. Med. Journal* (1942), vol. i, pp. 743–53.
[5] Ibid., vol. ii, suppl., pp. 31–2, 35–6, and 41.

the scheme, even if it would involve '*some loss of professional freedom*'.[1] In the same year, the *Journal* was flooded with projects for medical reform, and indeed, one of the *Journal*'s correspondents thought that the B.M.A. would now have to exert pressure on the parties to get legislation out of them.[2] No doubt all this zeal for reform was brought on by the medical experiences of the war,[3] but it was certainly not unprecedented in the B.M.A.'s previous history.

Why then does the B.M.A. have such a bad reputation among the British socialists? For two main reasons (other than its reaction to the proposals for a National Health Service, which I analyse below): its tendency to put the vested, especially financial, interests of the doctors above all other considerations and its attempt in 1912 to boycott Lloyd George's health insurance scheme.[4]

The B.M.A. has never been able to fight down its trade-union impulse; indeed a great many of the public-spirited activities on which it now prides its conscience were more concerned with the bread-and-butter interests of the doctors than the medical needs of the public. The fight against Poor Law practice, for example, centred largely on conditions of practice and remuneration. So did the Association's battles on behalf of the Medical Officers of Health. Again, consider its attitudes towards the School Medical Service and public maternity clinics. It was heartily in favour of both, but only up to the point where the profession's pecuniary interests were likely to be affected. It favoured medical inspections in the schools, but opposed the provision of treatment by a salaried school medical service; it was all for maternity clinics, but it insisted that they be used for 'education' rather than for treatment. The reason is surely obvious. Medical inspections and education were bound to increase the need for private treatment while actual treatment, both in the schools and the clinics, was bound to diminish it.

The attempted boycott of Lloyd George's scheme is traceable to many causes, the most important being Lloyd George's incredibly misguided failure to consult the Association on any point until the main outlines of his scheme had been fully settled, the fact that medical services were to be controlled by organizations on which the profession would not be represented and that terms of service were to be dictated to the profession and not negotiated with it. Even Mr.

[1] See 'Draft Interim Report of the Medical Planning Commission,' *Brit. Med. Journal* (1942), vol. i, pp. 764–5.
[2] Ibid., vol. ii, p. 112.
[3] See, for example, R. M. Titmuss, *History of the Second World War: Problems of Social Policy* (H.M.S.O., 1950).
[4] The later attempted strike against the scheme was merely a response to a proposed cut in the capitation payment, not an attempt to ruin the system.

Bevan never treated the profession so cavalierly as this. The Association ultimately won out on every one of its objections before the scheme went into effect; nevertheless it did not withdraw its decision to boycott the system until a large-scale desertion of members to the 'panels' forced it to throw in its hand. Perhaps the kindest view to take of the incident is that of a writer in the *Westminster Gazette* who expressed the greatest admiration for people who don't know when they are beaten but thought that 'the trouble with the B.M.A. is that it doesn't know when it has won'.[1]

Despite all this we still cannot accuse the B.M.A. of being a politically reactionary force *per se*. What it feared in the insurance system was not public authority but the profession's subsumption to any sort of organization, i.e. the disintegration of the traditional pattern of medical practice. After all, the Association fought the profession's subsumption to private organization no less tenaciously than it fought against public control; the boycott incident merely followed a precedent established long before in the 'battle of the clubs'; the fight against 'contract practices', the friendly societies and the Medical Aid societies, all of which were non-medical organizations providing medical services. In fact, one of the Association's decisive objections against the compulsory insurance scheme was that the so-called Approved Societies were to administer medical benefit, i.e. that doctors' services were to be controlled by the same 'private' organizations which the B.M.A. had fought so bitterly in 'the battle of the clubs'. It insisted on the administration of medical benefit by public insurance committees and it won its point.

The crucial point to note here is that the B.M.A. was far more suspicious of private than of public control. Having had a long and bitter experience with the voluntary societies it chose to be controlled by the state, if there was to be any organizational control of doctors' services at all. Thus it is not ideological opposition to the positive state which underlies the Association's conservatism but — apart from the inevitable trade-union impulse — a general distrust of non-medical organizations and of any modifications of the traditional structure of independent practice. Its fight against the voluntary societies is only one of many instances of this point; perhaps the most famous is its long battle against the integration of army doctors into the regular military hierarchy and especially the command of field hospitals by line rather than medical officers. We owe the derogatory term 'army medicine' at least partly to this battle.

[1] For descriptions of the Health Insurance incident, see Little, op. cit, p. 324; Carr-Saunders and Wilson, op. cit., p. 95; and H. Levy, *National Health Insurance* (1945), *passim*.

Once it is realized that the B.M.A.'s conservatism in the past has been due chiefly to a fear of 'organization', its political history should be at once more comprehensible and less offensive, even to the extreme radicals. Effective medical practice does depend on a certain freedom from the sort of demands which any administrative organization, public or private, is likely to make on the doctors. There is no real difference between an unqualified practitioner and an unqualified administrator, if the latter is in a position to dictate clinical matters. The medical profession's distrust of organization is not due simply to cabalistic fears that its mysteries might be penetrated by the unanointed. It is due, above all, to the reasonable fear that the extremely tenuous organization of medical practice might be irreparably harmed by non-medical considerations; e.g. that the functionally indispensable privacy of the doctor–patient relationship might be infringed, that the secrecy of medical records might be violated, that patients might be deprived of their right to choose their doctors, and so on.

Seven years of socialized medicine have taught us that the clinical relationship need not be in the least upset even by the most ambitious organizational arrangements. But surely it was reasonable for the profession to distrust organizational innovations with a kind of instinctive defensiveness prior to such experience. Perhaps one ought to admit that the B.M.A. has sometimes allowed its just suspicions of non-medical interference to become a tool for the shoddier purposes of political factions; but that is really as far as one can go towards granting its critics' case.

Hysteria in Tavistock Square, 1943–6

The profession's zeal for reform in 1942 should now no longer appear as deviant behaviour. It falls into a very clear pattern. In 1942 nothing was likely to be done about any major schemes for medical reform; after all, Mr. Churchill had undertaken not to introduce controversial domestic legislation while the war lasted. For the moment, the profession could safely forget its vested interests and its terror of change and indulge its scientific interests in medical policy. But the doctor who wanted the B.M.A. to exert pressure on the parties need not have worried. It soon became clear that the Government was willing, indeed anxious, to act on the Medical Planning Commission's proposals and the Beveridge Report. And when this became evident the B.M.A.'s heat for reform cooled abruptly. Planning for medical reform now was no longer a professional enterprise and a paper enterprise. The prospect of reform was now imminent and concrete and the initiative was about to pass into the hands of politicians and bureaucrats. Acute anxiety now gripped B.M.A. House.

The Association was squarely on the horns of a very unfortunate dilemma. It favoured medical reform; it opposed, almost reflexively, the intrusion of non-medical organizations into medical affairs; but there could clearly be no reform without such intrusion. The B.M.A.'s politics after 1942 make sense only when one has understood this dilemma; its inevitable effect was constant wavering between the realization of the need for change and the dreadful implications of change.

The first indications of hysteria in Tavistock Square came soon after the publication of the Medical Planning Commission's report. The Beveridge Plan had been published and Sir John Anderson had announced the Government's intention to act on it. The Ministry of Health now embarked on a programme to translate Assumption B[1] of the plan into legislation. First, there were to be purely exploratory discussions with representatives of the profession; then a series of official proposals were to be published in a White Paper; then, draft legislation was to be introduced. The preliminary discussions were to be confidential and entirely non-committal on both sides;[2] certainly no one could have expected trouble at this stage of the proceedings. But serious troubles soon broke out when two London dailies reported that the Government intended to introduce a fully salaried service, a kind of medical civil service, controlled by the local authorities.

The medical representatives now themselves broke the secrecy of the discussions and convened an indignant mass meeting of the Metropolitan Counties Branch where Charles Hill revealed the Ministry's 'proposals'. They were received with great bitterness, the *British Medical Journal* producing a long verbal shudder.[3] At the meeting it was alleged that the doctors had been confronted with a *fait accompli*, maliciously designed to reduce the profession to the status of mere local authority functionaries. However, when the Minister of Health was questioned on the matter in the House, he was at a loss to explain all the fuss. Apparently the medical delegates had simply asked the Ministry what a salaried service for general

---

[1] 'A comprehensive national service will ensure that for every citizen there is available whatever medical treatment he requires, in whatever form he requires it . . .' Sir William Beveridge, *Report on Social Insurance and Allied Services* (H.M.S.O., 1942), para. 426.

[2] See *Parl. Deb.*, vol. 390, chaps. 971–3.

[3] *Brit. Med. Journal* (1943), vol. i, p. 670.

practitioners might be like. The Ministry had responded by producing a tentative plan to which it attached no authority; this was
the plan unearthed by the London rags and attacked so frantically at
the mass meeting.[1] Why then had the doctors violated the confidential character of the discussions?

It seems to me that delay for delay's sake was the B.M.A.'s chief
purpose at this point. Hence its proposal that the matter be deferred
to a Royal Commission — a measure unlikely to produce rapid
legislative results. The newspaper leak merely provided a convenient
pretext for bringing pressure to bear towards this objective. In any
case the incident of the mass meeting had all the earmarks of
hysteria. And when the official government scheme finally appeared[2]
the panic became even more acute.

The B.M.A. found little to criticize in the actual proposals of the
White Paper. It therefore directed its venom towards the 'hidden
implications' of the scheme rather than the concrete proposals. The
scheme was suspiciously above criticism; it was therefore simply a
clever device for seducing the profession into agreement and then
chaining it to Whitehall by means of the full-time salary. 'The ultimate intention,' said a correspondent, 'is brilliantly camouflaged ...
underlying the subtle phrases of the White Paper is the mailed fist of
bureaucratic control carefully wrapped in the velvet glove of political
diplomacy.'[3] 'If this interpretation is correct,' commented the
Journal, 'it is useless to deny that there is trouble ahead.'[4] The interpretation was not correct, but trouble still ensued. The doctors in
Tavistock Square simply had to find some sort of ground, correct or
incorrect, for venting the fears which the very fact of Government
intervention had created.

One could go on and on citing examples of this stark panic.[5] But
we must now ask a very serious question. Were the B.M.A.'s views
really representative of the sentiments of the profession in general?
They were actually stated by a select group of doctors: medical
practitioners in Parliament, the editors and correspondents of the
Journal, and — above all — the permanent officials of the B.M.A.
and of its Council. These were, of course, the articulate elements of
the profession; but did the articulate doctors speak with the authen-
tic voice of the profession?

---

[1] *Parl. Deb.*, vol. 390, chap. 974.
[2] Ministry of Health, *A National Health Service* (H.M.S.O., Cmd. 6502, 1944).
[3] *Brit. Med. Journal* (1944), vol. i, suppl., pp. 66–7.
[4] Ibid., p. 295. For similar comments see the *Journal* for 1944, vol. ii, suppl.,
pp. 36 ff., 50, 66, 110 and 125, and 1945, vol. i, suppl., p. 90.
[5] See, for example, ibid., suppl., p. 75, for an especially juicy one.

The Questionary on the White Paper

Fortunately, we know exactly what the rank and file's views on the White Paper were. Shortly after the appearance of the White Paper the B.M.A. drew up a 'Questionary' which was distributed to the entire profession and analysed by the British Institute of Public Opinion. The Questionary was very copious and the proportion of replies established an all-time record; the number of respondents was so large that it would be inaccurate even to speak of a 'sample'.[1] The most important results, broken down into some simple categories, are tabulated on p. 228. In gist, they show that a majority of the profession was opposed to the White Paper, taken as a whole. But they also show that this opposition was due only to some unpalatable and not at all crucial administrative proposals. On every substantive issue there was a clear majority for the scheme, and nearly 40 per cent of the profession were for the White Paper lock, stock and barrel. In view of the attitude taken by the profession's spokesmen, the results of the Questionary must be interpreted as a repudiation of the B.M.A. leadership.[2]

To see this more clearly, let us take four crucial issues covered by the Questionary. (1) The White paper proposed a free service for the entire population. This the profession approved by a vote of 60 to 37 per cent, while the B.M.A. leaders vehemently objected. (2) The White Paper recommended that a Central Medical Board be established with powers to keep doctors out of relatively over-doctored areas. The profession approved by 57 to 39 per cent, but the leaders thought that no other proposal so clearly revealed the Government's despotic intentions. (3) The rank and file approved the idea of group practice in health centres by 68 to 24 per cent. But the official view of the B.M.A. now was that the Centres should be tried only on a voluntary, experimental basis and kept out of any impending statute. (4) The abolition of the sale of practices was approved by a large majority; the leadership was vehemently opposed to the proposal.

But if the rank and file's outlook was so relatively radical, why did not a majority approve the White Paper as a whole? The chief reason should be obvious from certain preceding parts of the paper. The profession was not opposed to the scheme because of any concrete reason. It was simply instinctively opposed to the idea of public direction, however much it was in favour of specific reforms. This

[1] *Brit. Med. Journal* (1944), vol. ii, suppl., p. 25 f.
[2] For a good comparison of the results of the poll and the B.M.A. Council's views, published in a 'Draft Statement of Policy', see ibid, pp. 51-9.

point is clearly supported by the fact that all the negative votes were on administrative issues, i.e. issues which brought the idea of 'organization' to the foreground.

The B.M.A. Questionary on the White Paper
(selected questions, percentages)

Questions	All		Service doctors		Consultants		G.P.s		Salaried doctors	
	Pro	Con	Pro	Con	Pro	Con	Pro	Con	Pro	Con
1. For or against White Paper	39	53	53	41	36	58	31	62	60	33
2. A 100 per cent service (free, comprehensive)	60	37	73	26	54	44	54	43	74	23
3. Free and complete hospital service	69	28	79	19	58	40	66	32	84	15
4. Central administration by Ministry	35	51	45	41	30	57	29	57	49	39
5. Larger areas for hospital administration	63	24	67	23	64	27	58	26	74	17
6. 'Joint Authorities' for hospital administration	13	78	13	81	9	84	11	79	24	69
7. Remuneration of consultants by local authorities	37	40	40	40	50	34	30	41	39	44
8. Central Med. Board for G.P. services	55	31	62	25	50	31	54	35	64	21
9. Control over G.P.'s distribution	57	39	68	28	56	38	51	45	71	25
10. Health Centres	68	24	83	13	67	23	60	32	84	11
11. Health Centre Practititioners under contract to local authorities	31	53	35	50	29	48	23	63	45	39
12. Salaried Service in Health Centres; full or part	62	29	74	20	73	25	53	38	79	22
13. Abolition of sale of practices	56	33	60	28	57	29	53	39	66	19

To this one other point must be added. However much the doctors might have feared 'organization' as such, there is one form of organization — the local authority — which they seemed to fear above all. The idea that the new hospital service should be controlled by Joint Boards of the local authorities was rejected by 78 to 13 per cent, but the general notion of hospital planning within large regions was approved by 63 to 24 per cent. While there was a clear majority for the health centres there was a similarly clear majority against local authority control over the centres. Clearly the doctors did not fear nationalization as much as municipalization. Why was this the case?

One can think easily of some simple explanations. Memories of the long battle which the B.M.A. had fought against the maltreatment of Medical Officers of Health by the local councils may have lingered on. Local authority medical services were probably associated with the M.O.H. principle of employment — payment by salary and the integration of doctors into the regular bureaucracy — while national services were associated with capitation payments and the use of special administrative bodies like the Insurance Committees. One of the most clear-cut images to come to the doctor's mind when he thought of local medical services was probably the public hospital, more often than not in an atrocious state, perhaps a former workhouse, badly equipped and inhospitable, understaffed, doing relatively monotonous medical work, and offering few opportunities for professional distinction or affluence; no doubt many doctors thought this sort of thing was inherent in local institutions and not the result — as it was — of a vicious dualism in the old hospital system.

Nevertheless one has the feeling that deeper motives must be responsible for so manifestly bitter a distrust of local government. Perhaps the fundamental cause was class contempt. The operative upper-class stereotype of the councillor is pronouncedly *petit bourgeois*; he may have a perfectly decent understanding of sewerage and drainage but he is otherwise afflicted with a narrow and superficial outlook on life. He is still subjected to the contempt which the squirearchical society had for trade, especially petty trade. On this basis the doctors were less afraid of central control because Civil Servants of the administrative class and M.P.s are (again at least in popular mythology) a rather different species from their local counterparts: more *like* the doctors, you know.

The Internal Political Structure of the B.M.A.

The B.M.A.'s leaders at first reacted to the Questionary with stunned surprise, but like Shakespeare's rhyming lovers they did quickly reason themselves out again. It was now claimed that the rank and file had not understood the 'hidden implications' of the scheme, that the Socialist Medical Association had stuffed the ballot boxes, that salaried doctors should have been excluded from the poll because they had no understanding of private practice, and that, in any case, the Annual Representative Meeting of the B.M.A. was soon to meet

Q

and speak the 'real mind' of the profession. Needless to say the Representative Meeting repudiated most of the poll. But if this suggests anything it is surely that the representativeness of the Association's supposedly most representative body is extremely dubious.

The breakdown of answers to the Questionary should make it clear that the British medical profession is divided into a number of groups which have radically different political outlooks. The profession's 'leaders', i.e. the sort of people who go to Annual Representative Meetings, sit on the Executive Council, and find their way on to negotiating committees, come predominantly from the more conservative of these groups.

In the *first* place, there is a marked difference in attitude between the two main technical groups of the profession, specialists and general practitioners. The specialists, as the poll shows on almost every issue, are significantly less conservative than the G.P.s. This indicates that there is at any rate no simple correlation between medical incomes and medical politics. The only reasonable economic explanations for the relative radicalism of the specialists is a more complex one. Under the pre-Health Service system, a large proportion of medical services was rendered gratuitously by 'honoraries' working in the Voluntary Hospitals. It was fairly normal for a well-established specialist to do most of his work free of charge, as a sort of charitable contribution to the charitable hospital. The White Paper now recommended that all specialists be paid for all services rendered; this must have been a telling inducement to many of them to approve the scheme.

There is, however, an equally reasonable non-economic explanation for the specialists' radicalism, and one much more consistent with the basic argument of this paper; the fact that general practice has always been much more individualistically organized than specialization. The consultant's usual habitat is the hospital; hence, he necessarily has experience with 'organization' and, not least, with the impact of non-medical authorities (boards of governors, non-medical secretaries, stewards) on medical affairs. Ignorance and fear are always related, so that the specialists' experience must have given them a less defensive attitude towards a state medical service.

Secondly, a distinction must be made between young and established doctors. The young doctors were represented on the poll chiefly by the Service Doctors. These voted, in a clear majority, for the White Paper's proposals as a whole; they returned landslide majorities in favour of health centres, salaried general practice, and a 100 per cent free service, and they voted negatively on only two major proposals, both involving local authority administration.

The reasons for their radicalism are not difficult to find. One of them is surely that they expected a socialized medical service to solve the problems of secure establishment in practice, always a matter of great importance to young doctors. The other, I think, is that the White Paper recommended practice in health centres. The jump from the hospital into the private surgery must involve considerable disappointment. Private surgeries are necessarily underequipped in precisely those facilities, physical and human, to which the student becomes accustomed in hospital. They are also apt to be lonely places and intellectually deadening for those doctors who thrive on consultations. The health centre at least promised a sort of hospital atmosphere; in any case, the Service Doctors voted for them by 83 to 13 per cent; while medical students, in a poll of their own, endorsed the proposal even more overwhelmingly, by 89 to 8 per cent.[1]

The Service Doctors' vote on health centres also suggests that they had not been in the least disillusioned by 'army medicine'. When the B.M.A. was trying to delay legislative action on Assumption B of the Beveridge Plan one of its pet arguments was that it would be undemocratic to act while a large proportion of the profession was on service; after the results of the Questionary were revealed it was argued, for obvious reasons, that the Service Doctor should not have been given an equal voice in the plebiscite.[2] The Service Doctors had clearly found corporate practice rather congenial. Even more, they had got a full dose of 'organization'. No doubt they had realized what the whole profession should realize by now: that the doctor's clinical independence need not be in the least threatened by even the most ambitious non-medical organization.

Yet another, political distinction may be made between doctors in private and in public practice. The latter category includes salaried specialists, the M.O.H.s, School Medical Officers, and similar medical functionaries. They had no commercial vested interest in private practice and clearly little distrust of public organization. Hence, they were the most radical of the groups which responded to the Questionary, although even they were opposed to local authority administration.[3]

These rather simple distinctions in the political structure of the B.M.A. are directly suggested by the breakdown of replies to the Questionary. We can only guess as to other distinctions, although we

[1] *Brit. Med. Journal*, 1944, vol. ii, suppl., pp. 40–1.
[2] Ibid., p. 30.   [3] See items 6 and 7 in the table.

can probably make some fairly safe guesses. For example, it seems fair to rank the established general practitioners into four classifications: working class, 'Mayfair', suburban, and resort practitioners, in descending order on a 'radicalism scale'. On the basis of commercial motives, the working-class doctor stood to gain a great deal from a free national medical service; the Mayfair doctor stood to lose little, so long as private practice was still permitted; the other two categories stood to lose a great deal. On the basis of acquaintance with organization we would get roughly the same result; at any rate, working-class doctors had a much more intensive experience with insurance practice than the rest. In the case of consultants it is much more difficult to devise persuasive political categories, other than the one between salaried and private consultants. But no doubt certain specialists, e.g. obstetrician and gynaecologist, who practised their skills very largely in nursing homes (where really fabulous incomes were to be earned) tended to be rather more conservative than the less affluent species, i.e. eye, nose, and throat men or general physicians.[1]

As always, these general categories are not completely satisfactory. But at least they suggest the essential points: that there are great differences of political attitudes within the profession and that these differences are due to three factors: income, security of establishment, and familiarity with the impact of non-medical organizations on medical practice. The categories are also sufficiently detailed to explain the differences between the B.M.A.'s leadership and its rank and file on the most serious political issue which has ever confronted the profession.

Unestablished doctors do not tend to become successful medical 'politicians', i.e. the sort of people who go to the Representative Meetings or sit on the B.M.A.'s Council; nor do working-class practitioners struggling with large lists of public patients or Medical Officers of Health, with their load of committee work and routine administration. To exert one's weight in medical politics one must have a certain amount of money and, above all, time. The workload of a middle-class practice and the income derived from secure consultant status are eminently suited to participation in medical politics. 'Representative' medical bodies are therefore inevitably weighted in favour of age, affluence, private practice, and the suburb.

Indeed one can go further and question the representativeness of

---

[1] For a discussion of income differentiations among consultants and specialists, see Ministry of Health, *Report of the Inter-Departmental Committee on the Remuneration of Consultants and Specialists* (H.M.S.O., Cmd. 7420, 1948), Table 4.

all the doctors who frequent any political meetings. The medical profession's rate of participation in associative affairs is extraordinarily low, no doubt because of the sheer pressure of the doctor's work. Hence, medical 'politicians', even on the lowest levels, are peculiar types, and they get more and more peculiar as the level rises. Representativeness is difficult to achieve under any circumstances, but it is particularly difficult to achieve in a profession which makes such great demands on its young, overworks the vast majority of its practitioners, and has such a low rate of 'participation'.

To summarize my argument: the B.M.A.'s conservatism, even that of its 'leaders', is not the sort of simple and selfish conservatism which people like Mr. Bevan worry about. Rather it is a conservatism which grows almost naturally out of the traditional character of medical practice and traditional ideas about the clinical relationship. It is, in short, a peculiarly medical conservatism and its chief cause is a quite reasonable fear of the impact of non-medical organizations on medical practice. This fear is more pronounced on the part of the medical politicians simply because it is reinforced by other factors, e.g. income and security of establishment.

If this analysis is correct, then the B.M.A. should be decidedly less conservative today than it was seven years ago and it should become even less conservative in future. So far this is exactly what has happened. The B.M.A. has entirely accepted the Health Service; since 1948 its criticisms have been restricted to minor matters of administration and terms of service and even these criticisms are gradually diminishing. It has, inevitably, been more of a trade union than ever in the past; for example, it vigorously took up the case of the supposedly redundant registrars and it agitated for a long time against the Ministry's interpretation of the Spens Report. But all these were bread-and-butter issues which one would not expect any group to be high-minded about. On other matters the B.M.A. has indeed given indications that its radicalism of 1942 is flickering up again. Thus, at recent Representative Meetings it has increasingly deplored the current state of general practice and it now seems more anxious to get on with the Health Centres than Mr. Bevan was as Minister of Health.

One reason for the B.M.A.'s swift reconciliation to socialized medicine may be that it has got its way on so many issues. The profession is extremely heavily represented in the administrative structure of the Service; medical incomes are, to say the least, generous; there has been no wholesale sacking of Registrars; the recommendations of the Central Health Services Council have never, to my knowledge, been ignored — and one could go on in this vein for pages. The unkind view to take is that the B.M.A. has been 'bribed' into accepting the Service. But this view, in light of what we know of the Association's political past, would also be superficial. The fundamental reason for the B.M.A.'s reconciliation to the Service is simply that it is now clear that the clinical effectiveness of medical practice did not depend on its traditionally private organization and has not been harmed by socialization.

BRITISH PUBLIC RELATIONS: A POLITICAL CASE STUDY[1]

By Morris Davis

PRESSURE groups differ greatly in their internal organization, in their political skills and resources, and in their significance in national party politics. Many groups are neither large nor automatically successful in pressing their demands. Morris Davis's study of the British Trawlers' Federation is a reminder that a pressure group may suffer from internal divisions of opinion, and may also require the assistance of outside experts in order to press its political demands. It is important to note that the public relations firms engaged by the Federation found it easier to direct propaganda at the general public than at the Government. In the period under consideration here, the pressure group was not strikingly successful.

THE present importance of professional public relations in Britain is reflected in the frequency with which recent studies of other subjects have referred to the field in passing.[2] Only once, however, has British public relations been at the centre of a serious academic investigation;[3] and Aims of Industry, the firm that was studied in detail, is not typical of the profession. Unlike most P.R. firms it not only possesses technical expertise, but has an explicit — Conservative and anti-socialist — outlook on most matters of public policy. It is as much pressure group as public relations organization.

This article focuses on more usual client–firm relationships in

[1] Materials for this study were collected during 1960 under a fellowship from the Social Science Research Council. The Council, of course, neither supports nor opposes any statements of fact or interpretation made here. My thanks go also to individuals within the fishing and public relations fields and within the Government, who talked to me at length and pointed me often to unpublished or unprinted documentation.

[2] See, for example, H. H. Wilson, *Pressure Group: The Campaign for Commercial Television* (London: Secker & Warburg, 1961), pp. 94 ff., 151 ff., and 210 ff.; and Allen Potter, *Organized Groups in British National Politics* (London: Faber and Faber, 1961), part 6.

[3] H. H. Wilson, 'Techniques of Pressure', *The Public Opinion Quarterly*, xv. 2 (Summer 1951), pp. 225–42.

Reprinted from *Journal of Politics*, vol. xxiv, no. 1 (1962), pp. 50–71. Further details of the politics of fishing can be found in Morris Davis's *Iceland Extends its Fisheries Limits* (London: Allen & Unwin, 1963).

P.R. consultancy.[1] It considers the working arrangements that obtained between one British trade association — the British Trawlers' Federation (Distant Water Section) — and two of the public relations firms it has retained since the Second World War. The first section of the article considers the power structure of the British Trawlers' Federation as it existed generally from 1954 to 1960. The second discusses the activities performed for the Federation by Patrick Dolan & Associates, at one time its public relations consultant, and the causes and results of the Federation's decision to discontinue retaining that firm. The third section describes the activities performed by its present public relations firm, Galitzine and Partners. Finally, the fourth section considers some of the possible effects of P.R. consultancy on the British political system.

I

Though not of major importance like textiles or automobiles, the British fish industry still employs a large number of persons. About 24,000 are fishermen regularly and another 3,300 occasionally. In addition, over 11,000 are in port wholesaling, over 4,000 in inland wholesaling, 35,700 in fishmongering, and 38,500 in fish frying and fish frying/fishmongering.[2] Overlap in the last two figures is more than compensated for by the numbers in processing and transporting of fish and fish products, and in the building, repairing, and provisioning of fishing craft. Two large cities in England, Hull and Grimsby, are pre-eminently fishing communities; and many others, like Fleetwood and Lowestoft in England, and Aberdeen and Leith in Scotland, have a large stake in the industry.

The sea-fish industry, however, has not been a unified whole. Sectors of it often oppose one another — the retailers, for example, vocally attacking the prices and practices of wholesalers and trawler owners, and the wholesalers complaining about the increased vertical integration instituted by some trawler companies. Each sector, too, is with few exceptions composed of very small units.[3] On

---

[1] Professional P.R. activities are also, of course, commonly undertaken by internal P.R. departments; but even organizations with their own departments often employ a firm of consultants as well.

[2] On fishermen (figures for 1958) see Central Office of Information, *The Fishing Industry in Britain* (London, 1959), p. 2; on the others (figures for 1954) see White Fish Authority, *Report on Enquiry into the Costs of Distributing White Fish* (London, 1956), pp. 14, 23, 26, and 30.

[3] Among the exceptions are the trawler companies and the Mac Fisheries chain of fish shops owned by Unilever. In distributing there are some 2,000 coastal merchants, 1,000 inland wholesalers, 11,000 fishmongering businesses, and 20,000 fish-frying businesses. (F. M. G. Willson, *Government Services to the Sea-Fish Industry of*

the catching side of the business itself there is also considerable fragmentation. British sea-fishing is customarily listed under four heads: herring fisheries, distant water trawling, near and middle water trawling, and inshore fisheries. With the herring fisheries this article is not at all concerned.[1] Of British-caught white fish landed some £22·2 million was caught in distant waters (of which only £0·2 million was landed in Scotland), £18·8 million in near and middle waters (£6·9 million in Scotland), and £6·4 million in inland waters (£4·9 million in Scotland).[2] Inshore fisheries are clearly Scottish in the main and 'less an industry than a way of life . . . the sole *raison d'être* of many small communities, thus attracting a considerable degree of social and political sympathy'.[3] The near and middle water fisheries (fishing the waters about the British Isles to about as far as the Faroes) are about one-third Scottish, and the rest is scattered over much of the English and Welsh coast. The distant water fishing, on the other hand, is almost entirely English. Of the 248 distant water trawlers in service at the end of 1958, all but two (at Aberdeen) were English, and of these all but one were based at Hull, Grimsby, or Fleetwood.[4] Though it is easy, then, to find M.P.s who speak on and are interested in the fishing industry, most of them come from constituencies that have nothing at all directly to do with *distant water* fishing.[5]

In short, the distant water fleet is only one section of a relatively minor industry. Its catch may be largest of all the fishing branches; but its geographical concentration at only three ports and its being a business rather than 'a way of life' give it fewer potential friends in Parliament than have the smaller, more dispersed, and less economical, middle, near, and inshore fleets. And its political effectiveness has been further diminished by stresses that have existed even within this corner of the industry.

Despite the fact that all owners of English trawlers in the distant water fleet are members of the Distant Water Section of the British Trawlers' Federation (hereinafter we use 'B.T.F.' to refer to this

---

Great Britain (Rome: F.A.O., 1957), chap. i, sects. 6–10). A comparison with the employment figures above shows the small average size of these firms.

[1] The catch of herring is worth about a tenth of the total fish catch. The Herring Industry Board is headquartered in Edinburgh and the industry is largely Scottish. Its problems and regulations are somewhat idiosyncratic. See Willson, op. cit., chap. vi, sect. 1.

[2] White Fish Authority, *Annual Report and Accounts for the Year Ended 31st March 1959* (London, 1959), p. 4.

[3] Willson, op. cit., p. 18.   [4] White Fish Authority, op. cit., p. 38.

[5] See J. D. Stewart, *British Pressure Groups* (Oxford: Clarendon Press, 1958), p. 158 and 158n. His account is somewhat misleading on this point.

section of the Federation alone), as a going concern[1] the B.T.F. has often exhibited considerable tension. Three groups long have dominated the distant water catchers: Associated Fisheries (or the Bennett Group) with 25 per cent; Hellyer Brothers with 17 per cent; and the Ross Group with 14 per cent.[2] But because of uneasiness among the owners of these three groups, the presidency of the Federation and the officership of the Distant Water Section itself tended to go, as a compromise, to persons not identified with any of the big three.

Thus Mr. (now Sir) Jack Croft Baker, president of the Federation from spring 1944 to autumn 1957, came from a small firm and did not arouse the jealousies and mistrust of the larger owners. So, even more clearly, his successor, the late Major-General Sir Farndale Phillips, who had no connection at all with fishing prior to his appointment. As he saw it, the owners wanted an outsider with no axe to grind, who offered good leadership, and who (as a bonus) was supposedly familiar with Whitehall.[3] Mr. J. R. Cobley, then Vice-President of the Federation and Chairman of the Distant Water Section, did come from within the industry; but his firm, Rinovia Steam Fishing Company was, like Baker's, small in comparison to the three large groups.[4]

[1] We take Professor Mackenzie's advice ('Pressure Groups in the British Government,' *The British Journal of Sociology*, vi. 2 (June 1955), pp. 139–40) and do not recount here the formal constitutional structure of the Federation.

N.B. There is also a Near and Middle Water Section of the British Trawlers' Federation; but except for a very few matters affecting the organization as a whole (for example, the selection of a president) the two sections run themselves separately.

[2] Figures supplied me by Mr. Austen Laing in a letter dated 23 May 1960. More recent figures differ by a few percentage points.

[3] Interview in Grimsby, 20 May 1960. Personal factors also entered into his selection. From their military days of the Second World War he was known by John Bennett, son of the then chairman of Associated Fisheries. He was similarly acquainted with Major Patrick Wall, M.P. for a Hull suburb. Wall, it is said, suggested Phillips' name to Patrick Dolan, head of the P.R. firm then employed by the B.T.F.; Dolan then recommended Phillips to the Advertising Committee of the B.T.F., which in turn commended him to the full membership of the Federation.

[4] Recent events have now brought to a close this phenomenon of top officership in the B.T.F. not being given to persons associated with the big three groups. General Phillips died on 25 February 1961. Mr. Cobley was chosen to succeed him. Rinovia, the company Cobley used to direct, was absorbed by the Ross Group, and Cobley became director of Northern Trawlers, one of the companies of Associated Fisheries. As the result, then, of a death, a 'take-over,' and some shuffling of personnel, the President of the B.T.F. is now directly connected with the largest of the fishing groups. His successor as Chairman of the Distant Water Section is Mr. T. W. Boyd, also a director of Associated Fisheries.

Much evidence, in fact, suggests that some of the tensions within the B.T.F. are now abating. The rugged individualism and general *laissez faire* attitude of leaders in the industry has undergone considerable modification. But the account in the text is accurate for the period 1954–60; and these more recent changes are properly subject matter for another study.

Stress within the B.T.F. also had a geographical basis — a rivalry, or antipathy, between Hull and Grimsby.[1] Though only a leisurely ninety-minute drive from one another, including a ferry trip across the Humber, they have, in the opinion of many trawler owners, a different atmosphere about them. Hull owners, for example, see themselves as far more progressive and far less insular in outlook. The antipathy may be lessening now — with Ross and Bennett having interests in vessels of both ports — but many persons still spontaneously mention the difference.

Port loyalty and emphasis has been evident not only in the vitality of the port associations (Grimsby Trawler Owners' Association, Hull Fishing Vessel Owners' Association) but in the existence of an organization known as the Distant Water Development Scheme (hereinafter 'D.W.D.S.'). The D.W.D.S., of which all distant water trawler owners were members, aimed at limiting competition. By retiring old ships, restricting the number of new ships built, instituting minimum landing prices for fish, providing a system of fish allocation in time of glut, and laying up some ships in the summer if necessary to reduce 'overproduction,' it was hoped to rationalize the operation of the distant water fleet.[2] The D.W.D.S. began separately from the B.T.F. because at first not all distant water trawler owners would join the Scheme. But by 1954 at the latest, 'All companies have now joined the Scheme so that it is 100 per cent representative of the Industry.'[3] Why then was there need for the D.W.D.S. to continue as a separate organization when its membership was identical to that of the Distant Water Section of the Federation? And furthermore, why did the D.W.D.S. survive when it had, in fact, so little to do? For, as the White Fish Authority itself remarked: 'In 1959 there will be no lay-up at all under the scheme, and the freedom to sell the whole of the catch, within basic capacity, for freshing and curing is to continue.'[4] Probing makes evident that the D.W.D.S. has continued its separate existence because it has provided a ready-built organization for Hull interests in case they decided to secede from

[1] In 1958 Hull had 138 distant water vessels and 60·3 per cent of the distant water catch by weight; Grimsby, 84 such vessels and 34·1 per cent of the catch. Fleetwood, with only 23 such vessels and 5·6 per cent of the catch, can be omitted from consideration here. See B.T.F., *Fishing in Distant Waters* (Fleetwood, Grimsby, Hull, 1958), p. 39; and White Fish Authority, op. cit., p. 40.

[2] Minimum prices, lay-ups of ships, and regulations about allocation were set by the D.W.D.S. in consultation with the Government's White Fish Authority; but the Authority does not seem to have dissented from the rules made under the Scheme. See White Fish Authority, op. cit., pp. 8–9.

[3] Patrick Dolan and Con O'Brien, *Advance Copy, 1954 Annual Report: British Fishing Industry, Distant Water Section* (London, 1955), sect. 9 (mimeographed).

[4] White Fish Authority, op. cit., p. 9.

the Federation. The D.W.D.S. was founded by Hull owners.[1] It has continued to be Hull based and largely controlled by the strongest Hull companies. (The B.T.F. is headquartered in Grimsby.) It has its own Management Committee, Owners' Association, and Administrator (Austen Laing).

Closely allied with the D.W.D.S. is the Department of Economic Investigation, also headed by Laing. It collects and disseminates statistics on the fleet and the catch, and estimates the probable effect of various changes in fishing operations. In making such projections, it becomes in effect a planning agency — indeed, the only long-term planning office within the industry itself. As a Hull owner said in 1960:

> The General [Phillips] has no researchers, no paid thinkers. Laing is not B.T.F. The Department of Economic Investigation is essentially a Hull organization. It is all very wrong, but the ports are parochial in outlook and the B.T.F. is, in the owners' view, and in their actions, really subsidiary to the port associations. At any rate there is no one in the B.T.F. even working steadily on the business of fishing limit lines.

In short, while a few companies dominated distant water landings, this section of the industry during the time under consideration here evidenced much internal strain. Officership in the Federation went to persons not connected with the three largest concerns. Port loyalty and differences in outlook resulted in the D.W.D.S. being organized parallel to the Federation and potentially in rivalry to it.[2] There were other conflicts as well;[3] but these seem to have been the chief ones.

---

[1] Its roots go back to a marketing scheme of the 1930's. Owen Hellyer and the late Tom Hudson, both of Hull, were most instrumental in organizing the Voluntary Control Committee, as it was then known. Hull interests again led in instituting the D.W.D.S. after the Second World War.

[2] Landings of fish have steadily diminished over the last five years so that control schemes to limit the catch have become nugatory and the distant water fleet has now become dependent, for the first time, on governmental grants and subsidies. This and the recent diminution of internal tension (it would seem) within the B.T.F. make it likely that the D.W.D.S. may be wound up in the near future. Cf. footnote 4, p. 238 above.

[3] For example, many more traditional firms are apprehensive about the recent growth of the Ross Group and its branching out into such fields as the freezing and distribution of fish and of foodstuffs generally, and into the motor, transport, and engineering industries. There is also conflict between companies with quite old trawlers, like Consolidated in Grimsby and most companies operating out of Fleetwood, and those with more modern craft. In the long dispute with Iceland the former would not, because of the limited geographical range of their profitable operations, allow the sorts of compromise with Iceland that a few of the other firms seemed at times willing to entertain.

II

Stresses among distant water trawler owners help to account for the
B.T.F.'s change of public relations firms shortly before the 1958
United Nations' Conference on the Law of the Sea in Geneva.[1] At
the end of 1957 the Federation ended its relationship with Patrick
Dolan & Associates (hereinafter 'P.D.A.' or 'Dolan') and, after a
delay of over two months, hired Galitzine & Partners only a couple
of weeks before the Conference was to begin. It was obviously un-
suitable to a sustained programme for developing public interest and
sound governmental consultation to change firms at this time. As
mentioned above, the B.T.F. had no research staff at all; and the
Department of Economic Investigation at Hull, while concerned
with planning, was technologically oriented and politically inex-
perienced. Dropping one P.R. firm and hiring another so soon before
the Conference meant that nobody with the requisite political skills
in the industry, or *for* the industry, was giving serious and connected
thought to what advice to give the Government (about fisheries
zones and the like) or how to go about giving it.

In the three years that it had worked for the B.T.F., Patrick
Dolan & Associates performed many important economic and
political tasks. It was not the first public relations or advertising firm
to be employed by the B.T.F. Even in the late twenties there was a
small advertising programme.[2] And immediately before Dolan, the
B.T.F. had retained Pritchard, Wood and Partners (now a sub-
sidiary of Interpublic, the parent company of McCann Erickson),
mainly to improve journalistic contacts and to help establish better
relations with the fish fryers and thus sell more fish. But when the
need for a more active public relations campaign was felt within the
industry, particularly by directors of the larger companies,[3] the
B.T.F. switched its account to Dolan and greatly increased the
amount of money allocated to it. Dolan was selected largely on the
basis of a submission, 'Analysis of P.R. Problems and Recommendations', prepared for the fishing industry. P.D.A.'s general aim was

[1] The Conference dealt comprehensively with international sea law, with committees devoted to the continental shelf, the general régime of the high seas, fishing
and conservation on the high seas, access to the sea for land-locked states, and the
territorial sea and contiguous zone. Cobley and Phillips were present at the Conference as advisers to the official British delegation. Since trawling takes place in
shallow waters and British trawlers fish mainly off foreign coasts, the B.T.F. would
have been seriously affected by any increase deemed legal in the breadth of the
territorial sea or of exclusive fisheries zones. But the 1958 Conference failed to
muster the two-thirds vote necessary to decide what these breadths should be.
[2] Interview with Sir Jack Croft Baker in Grimsby, 21 May 1960.
[3] Interview with Mark Hellyer in Hull, 20 May 1960.

'to get a better public atmosphere for your industry and thereby
ultimately to sell more fish'.[1] It combated such charges as restrictive
practices, high prices and price rigging, and the exclusion of Icelandic fish from the country.[2] 'We took the initiative and we hit
right back,' publishing the first Annual Report of the industry, and
countering attacks by the fish fryers, the Cheap Food League, and
pro-Icelandic propaganda in the press and in Parliament.

Much of P.D.A.'s activities consisted of placing general human
interest stories in the newspapers — a process familiar to all P.R.
firms. A man was dispatched to Hull to 'translate the statistics com-
piled by the Department of Economic Investigation into terms
suitable for the Press and politics'.[3] Direct telecommunications were
set up between Hull and Fleet Street and stories sent out frequently
on such topics as skippers going long periods without sleep, rescues at
sea, exceptional catches of fish, or voyages imperilled by ice. The
aim was to portray fishermen as good British citizens doing a difficult
job well. In this publicity little attention was paid trawler owners as
such; emphasis was almost entirely on the trawlermen. Dolan also
arranged projects that would inspire a favourable ambiance about
the fishing industry.[4] 'Operation Pleasure Trip' (newsmen aboard
trawlers at sea) in summer 1955 provided, according to P.D.A.,
'almost saturation coverage in the national press'. A film was made
and shown on both the BBC and ITV. Schoolboys from Birmingham
and Leicester were given extensive trips on fishing vessels one summer under 'Operation Arctic Schoolboy'. Institutional advertising
(in Dolan's language, 'public relations/educational/political advertising') of distinguished quality was placed in papers like *The
Times*, *Daily Telegraph*, *Observer*, *Financial Times*, *Fishing News*, and
Yorkshire Post. Annual reports on the distant water fleet were produced and distributed each year (except the last), and became glossy
and picture-studded.

Dolan paid considerable attention to Parliament, and especially to
the Fisheries Sub-committees of the Labour and Conservative parliamentary parties. But there was in fact, in O'Brien's words, 'in Parliament no great interest in this dying industry (which is taking an

[1] 'The P.D.A./D.D.W.S. Activities November 1954–December 1957,' typed
inter-office memorandum of 12 December 1957 (hereinafter 'Memorandum
1957'), p. 1.
[2] A landing ban against Icelandic fish had come into effect in Britain after
Iceland had extended its fisheries limits from three to four miles (with new base
lines) in 1952. The ban was not lifted until 1956. On Iceland's extension to twelve
miles see pp. 247 ff. below.
[3] Interview with Conor O'Brien, then of P.D.A., in London, 19 February 1960.
[4] Memorandum 1957, pp. 3–4.

unconscionably long time in dying).' The late Edward Evans, M.P. for Lowestoft, was the most interested in the subject; but he cared mainly about inshore, not distant water, fishing. Contacts with Parliament were largely channelled through Lieutenant-Commander Christopher Powell, of Watney and Powell.[1] Also important, as already mentioned (see p. 238 n.), were the discussions between Major Patrick Wall, M.P., and Mr. Dolan before General Phillips was selected president of the Federation.

P.D.A. worked to improve communications channels with the Ministry of Agriculture, Fisheries and Food, but it is difficult to assess how effective and important these ministerial connections became. In the main, contacts dealt with such ordinary matters as checking figures for a report or clearing the wording of a press release.[2] Persons in the Ministry generally deny that they have any discussions, and certainly no important ones, with public relations men at all — rather only with the leadership of the fishing industry itself[3] — and in this they reflect what seems to be the official position on this point. For while there were special reasons why officials of the Ministry of Agriculture might have been somewhat cool towards P.D.A.,[4] the more important fact is that, while interest groups are accepted ideologically into the British political system by the

---

[1] P.D.A./D.D.W.S., 'Budget, Plans, Details, Propaganda Campaign: Distant Water Section, 1956' (hereinafter 'Budget, Plans 1956'), p. 18 (mimeographed). Watney is dead, and except for some secretarial assistance Powell is pretty much the whole of his organization. The general impression is that in briefing M.P.s or in arranging field trips for them his work is useful and probably marginally influential. As 'consultant and adviser on Parliamentary affairs to a number of trade associations and societies,' he deserves fuller study than he has yet received in the current literature. See S. E. Finer, *Anonymous Empire* (London: The Pall Mall Press, 1958), pp. 78–9; Stewart, *British Pressure Groups*, p. 165; and Potter, *Organized Groups in British National Politics*, pp. 257–8.

[2] Interview with Mr. Dolan in London, 2 May 1960. P.D.A. also helped the B.T.F. prepare for its negotiations with Icelandic trawler owners and was instrumental in the 1956 settlement, reached under the auspices of the O.E.E.C., that ended the landing ban. The settlement was between the trawler organizations of the two countries and not between their governments.

[3] Interview with Mr. Basil Engholm, Fisheries Secretary in the Fisheries Department of the Ministry of Agriculture, 29 April 1960; and with Mr. A. Savage, Principal in the same department, 2 May 1960.

[4] Interview with Mr. Conor O'Brien in London, 3 March 1960. The Government was supposedly angered at the publication in February 1956 of an advertisement in *The Times*, designed by P.D.A. for the B.T.F., which contained confidential information, i.e. the text of a memorandum from the B.T.F. to the Ministry of Agriculture. There is no question of P.D.A.'s legal right to quote the memorandum in the advertisement ('The Icelandic Fishing Dispute: A Statement by British Trawlermen'), but this was still felt in the Ministry to violate those standards of discretion needed for the smooth operation of the British system of consultation. See Stewart, op. cit., chap. iii.

Ministries, public relations firms employed by these groups are not. Public relations organizations obviously intrude into the workings of the political system, but they are not accorded recognition by the Ministries as having a political role to play.

Like most well-conducted public relations firms, P.D.A. mixed ballyhoo and inspiration. Its best-known publicity device was instituting a prize for the trawler skipper with the largest annual catch. The award, the Silver Cod Trophy, is given each year in the Fishmongers' Hall in London with considerable attendant publicity; it has three times been awarded by Ministers of Agriculture, but in the second year was presented by no less than the Duke of Edinburgh.[1] Representatives from all sections of the fish trade are present at the ceremony; and the attention given to the highest catch tends to counter-act charges of monopoly restraints. According to P.D.A.:

You will notice that there has been no criticism of landings since the institution of this award. Even the Fish Fryers are silent. . . . One of the many useful results has been the eagerness of the skippers themselves to win it. This, we consider, is an example of both good internal and external Public Relations.[2]

The trophy is a statuette of a cod jumping as a trout does. Cod, of course, are demersal fish that swim along the ocean's floor. They do not leap at all. The statue, like much publicity everywhere, subordinates accuracy to grace.

An outsider finds it difficult to assess P.D.A.'s work. What sounds callous may well have been effective and appropriate public relations: 'In January 1955 we helped bring home to the public the significance of the loss of the *Lorrela* and *Roderigo* in the so-called "Black Frost" disasters. Tragic as it was a disaster of this magnitude really brought home to the public at one blow just how dangerous and difficult long distance fishing is.'[3] A vague summary may actually refer to concrete and detailed operations: 'We arranged meetings with M.P.'s of all parties and the Ministry of Agriculture and Fisheries with such success that a protégé Pat Ward [Wall] was promoted P.P.S. to the Ministry.' It may even be true that as a result of 'Operation Pleasure Trip' almost every newspaper now has 'its fishing industry expert' who knows 'where to get his facts.' But it was rather bland to have said, as this memorandum does say:

We know that this has been a successful, almost classic campaign; we have lived with it for three years and got to know all of you and your interests; conflicting as they are. It has been great fun and well worth while.[4]

[1] In 1959 it was awarded by Admiral Lord Mountbatten.
[2] Budget, Plans 1956, pp. 21-2. It is to be doubted, in fact, that the fish fryers really were silent.
[3] Cf. Potter, op. cit., p. 328.   [4] Memorandum 1957, pp. 2, 3, and 6.

For within a few days the relationship between P.D.A. and the B.T.F. was ended.

Persons in public relations are not ungenerous in assessing Dolan's services to the Federation. As they see it, P.D.A.'s primary goal was to present the Federation as a body of important men; to bring them to public attention; to educate the public that fishing is a costly, highly technical, risk-laden business, and not, as popularly supposed, a row-boat operation. In this it did a good job in terms of both the general public and of parliamentary and Press relations. Secondly, P.D.A. tried to deal with the Icelandic dispute of that time and with the British landing ban against Icelandic fish. This problem was not clearly solved, even by the 1956 agreement; but it was not in Dolan's hands to do the ultimate solving. Thirdly, P.D.A. tried to sell more fish on a nation-wide scale. This last objective involved it in a clash of personalities reflecting the power distribution within the B.T.F., and led to the rupture between the two organizations.

Product advertising, even in 1956, had become a major item of expense to the B.T.F. Most of this advertising was handled by the firm of Dolan, Ducker, Whitcombe & Stewart (the 'D.D.W.S.' of the memoranda), sister firm to P.D.A.[1] For 1956 the budget for advertising and public relations was approximately as in Table 1.[2] Even at this time advertising comprised about 70 per cent of the combined advertising-public relations budget. With the so-called 'Choose Tuesday' campaign in 1957,[3] the advertising outlay was further increased.

The relatively high cost of P.D.A.'s services[4] and the coincident

[1] P.D.A. handled public relations work and D.D.W.S. did advertising; but the two often shared the same staff and submitted joint reports. D.D.W.S. has now been absorbed by the American advertising firm of Batten, Barton, Durstine & Osborn.

[2] Budget, Plans 1956, p. 1 (somewhat rearranged to better segregate product advertising and public relations).

[3] This campaign was totally P.D.A./D.D.W.S. in conception: 'what we believed was one of the boldest advertising schemes ever known'. It tried to induce housewives to serve fish not only on Friday but on Tuesday. To succeed would have required a massive change in consumer habits, and also a major reorganization in the distribution and merchandising of fish, since many shops used to (and now again do) close on Monday and Tuesday. As another P.R. man has put it, the campaign was 'an attempt to rewrite Scripture'. It was not marked by any quick, noteworthy success, though it might have done better with more time; unfortunately, however, the campaign also coincided with 'a turn in landings and the start of a progressive decline which has been almost inexplicable'. See Memorandum 1957, pp. 5 and 4.

[4] I do not imply that P.D.A.'s costs were high relative to its programme; just that they were high in an absolute sense, as far as many persons in the fishing industry were concerned.

R

TABLE 1

	£	£
A. *Advertising*		
1. Family and women's magazines in colour .	94,000	
2. Television (summer), Lancashire and Midlands only	30,000	
3. National dailies	47,000	
4. Provincial Press	9,000	
5. Press production	2,000	
6. Recipe books	10,000	
		192,000
B. *Public Relations*		
1. Political-educational campaign: nationals and opinion-forming Press throughout the year (i.e. institutional advertising)	55,000	
2. Public relations*	12,000	
3. Film	10,000	
4. Consumer research . . .	4,000	
5. Annual Report	300	
6. Silver Cod Dinner and Trophy . .	650	
		82,450
C. *Reserve*		2,550
TOTAL		£277,000

* This is the retainer fee.

decline in fish sales, together with the relatively blunt manner in which Mr. Dolan (personally) operates, made him and his companies a source of contention within the B.T.F. Personal antagonisms mainly reinforced the more deep-seated stresses outlined earlier. Dolan was favoured by one of the big three Groups, but on balance was more opposed than supported. Officership in the Federation, which was friendly to Dolan,[1] carried too little weight in the industry to help him. Especially crucial was opposition from the late William Bennett of Associated Fisheries. Though his companies dominated the fleet in terms of capital assets, Bennett, it is said, rarely asserted his power openly; but at this time he was severely critical of the advertising campaign in general and the 'Choose Tuesday' theme in particular. Since his company was also the largest contributor to the advertising fund, such criticism was bound to be effective.[2] With the ending of the advertising campaign, Dolan and the B.T.F. parted company.

Whatever the reason for the dismissal of P.D.A., it still left the

[1] See footnote 3, p. 238 above.

[2] Dolan himself agrees that the parting was due to the conflict between the heads of the three large groups, but states that there was no dissatisfaction with his advertising campaign. Interview in London, 2 May 1960.

Federation without any group doing concerted political thinking at a most dangerous time for the fishing industry. When Dolan left, no new firm was immediately selected to take its place. As one person remarked appositely: 'The Federation flopped about like a fish out of water.' It did want continued representation of itself to press, Parliament, and ministries. But until it should hire another P.R. firm, such representation would be sporadic at best because there was no office in the B.T.F. itself politically adept enough to accomplish that task. In short, between the time that P.D.A. left and Galitzine & Partners were hired — indeed, a longer time than this, for Dolan did only routine work during the last couple of months, and it took at least until April for the new consultants to get firmly in harness — there was no *systematic* thought given by the Federation or for the Federation to long range political problems. And this at a time when the United Nations Conference on the Law of the Sea was presenting the fishing industry with the evident possibility of an extension of the world's fisheries limits from three or four miles to twelve or more.

III

'B.T.F. appoints new P.R. officers,' the trade paper *Fishing News* headlined on 21 February 1958.[1] 'First major task being handled by the new consultants,' the article stated, 'is the public relations aspect of the British fishing industry's case to be presented at the nine-week conference on the International Law of the Sea, which will open at Geneva on Monday.' Colonel Stuart Chant — Director, Deputy Chairman, and co-owner of Galitzine & Partners (hereinafter 'Galitzine') — who heads the B.T.F. account does not exaggerate, then, in saying: 'the '58 conference began two weeks after we received the account. "We are going to a conference in two weeks at Geneva," they said. "What shall we do?"'[2] The fishing industry clearly was not prepared for the political forces at play in the

[1] No. 2340, 21 February 1958, p. 1.
[2] Interview in London, 3 May 1960.
Galitzine's activities are to be understood against this background of international events. The 1958 Geneva Conference did not settle limits for the territorial sea or for fisheries zones. In June Iceland announced an extension of exclusive fisheries limits to twelve miles effective 1 September 1958. Britain and other West European fishing nations protested, the British vaguely threatening to use force if necessary. On 1 September the extension took place, attempts at compromise within the ambit of NATO and elsewhere, having failed. British warships then protected British trawlers fishing within the twelve-mile limit. This 'cod war' cost no lives on either side; but the issues involved were not settled, if they really are settled now, until February 1961.

Conference.[1] Neither, it seems, was the British Government.[2] It is not surprising, then, that to persons in the B.T.F. the 1958 Conference 'passed like a bad dream'.

In searching for a P.R. firm to replace Dolan, the B.T.F. had been guided principally by two considerations.[3] First, it wanted no further part of product advertising, for 1958 at least; therefore, it sought a firm that was solely in public relations and not at all, itself or an associate company, in advertising. Secondly, it wanted its account handled by a principal of the firm and not just by an account executive. Galitzine & Partners met both requirements. Colonel Chant's military experience may also have stood him in good stead with General Phillips.

Much that Galitzine did for the B.T.F. was similar to what Dolan had done. It too set up a regional office in Hull in order to work closely with the industry heads and to disseminate news stories about the fishing fleet.[4] It reinstituted, after a year's lapse, the issuance of an annual report on the distant water fleet, and it also continued the award of the SILVER COD trophy. Similarly, it had routine contacts with officials of the Fisheries Department, clearing news releases, obtaining information on ministerial policy, and the like.[5] Galitzine also made contact with various M.P.s; unlike Dolan, it did this directly and not with Commander Powell as an intermediary.[6] Luncheon meetings were regularly held from time to time with members of the Fisheries Sub-committees of the two parliamentary parties — usually with members of both Sub-committees jointly. At these meetings General Phillips would make a speech and answer questions, some printed or mimeographed materials be handed out, and general discussions occur. Meetings were also arranged with the Conservative Fisheries Sub-committee alone, since it was always

[1] For the industry's view of the Conference see *Fishing News*, nos. 2341–50.

[2] Evidence on this point is too complex and prolix for presentation here. But certainly indicative is the fact that Britain thought at the beginning that it could save the three-mile rule, and ended by advocating 'six plus six'.

[3] Interview with Major-General Sir Farndale Phillips in Grimsby, 20 May 1960.

[4] *Fishing News*, no. 2354, 30 Man 1958, p. 1.

[5] Some contacts, though, were more than routine. The decision to protect British trawlers fishing within Iceland's twelve-mile limit in certain specified areas (later called 'warrens' or 'boxes') stemmed from consultations between B.T.F. officials and the Northern Department of the Foreign Office, the Admiralty, and the Ministry of Agriculture. So too, the decision to station ex-trawler skippers, at B.T.F. expense, aboard warships of the Fishery Protection Squadron in order to improve liaison between the fishing vessels and the warships guarding them. There were also later meetings with the Commander of the Squadron to work out details for different seasons of the year. At some of these various meetings officials of Galitzine were present.

[6] Interview with Colonel Chant in London, 3 May 1960.

easier for an owners group like the B.T.F. to establish rapport with Conservative than with Labour M.P.s — and anyway, the Conservative Party was in power.[1] Galitzine was able to pay more attention than had P.D.A. to intra-industry public relations. By introducing a news-sheet *Trawling Times*, it tried to improve the owners' lines of communication with the skippers, officers, and crew. It also tried to improve relations with wholesalers, fishmongers, and fish fryers.

More interesting was the public relations work Galitzine did for the Federation in international affairs.[2] Some of this was relatively conventional: for example, accompanying the B.T.F. delegation to a conference of European trawler owners at Scheveningen, near the Hague, on 14 July 1958, and helping to prepare press releases about the conference upon its conclusion.[3] Other work, though, came close to being reconnaissance operations.[4] For example, in late June of 1958 an official from Galitzine travelled, without advance publicity, to Reykjavik, Iceland, to ascertain Icelandic sentiment towards British fishing interests in view of the impending conflict between the two countries. He was there, however, only two days and spoke mainly to British embassy and consular officials and to a few pro-British Icelanders. The report he wrote for the B.T.F. reflected the opinions of these informants and was, as events shortly would demonstrate, far too optimistic.

More valuable information was unearthed during a second reconnaissance mission arranged by Galitzine & Partners for the autumn of 1958, just after Iceland's extension of fisheries limits to twelve miles. The visitor, a Scandinavian friend of a principal of the firm, moved about without attracting suspicion, spoke to Icelanders in a language with which even the common people were acquainted,[5] and sounded public opinion not just in the capital but in small towns. His findings were conveyed to Galitzine in a long memorandum, and through it to the B.T.F. His conclusions, more detailed and less roseate than his predecessor's, tally closely with my own

[1] Interview with Kenneth Younger, former M.P. for Grimsby, in London, 22 February 1960. Joint luncheon meetings are reported, for example, in *Fishing News*, no. 2356, 13 June 1958, p. 10, and no. 2372, 3 October, p. 1; and with the Conservative Sub-committee alone, ibid., no. 2346, 4 April 1958, p. 3.

[2] Galitzine's letterhead identifies it as 'International Public Relations Consultants'.

[3] Statements were not released for publication until 21 July; but the Government was informed on 16 July of the resolutions passed at the Conference.

[4] What follows is based on confidential documents and memoranda that cannot be cited in detail here. All data in the text, however, does come from authoritative printed, typed, or written materials.

[5] Danish is the second language of most Icelanders; and the other Scandinavian tongues are relatively similar.

made in Iceland during the summer of 1959; and I would like to think, therefore, that they are accurate and perceptive.

The activities performed for the B.T.F. at the United Nations General Assembly meeting in October and November of 1958 were more complicated and delicate. An official from Galitzine flew to New York with a list of questions from the Federation. For example: When are fishery limits to be discussed in the General Assembly or its Sixth Committee? What is the best form that 'lobbying' can take? Could B.T.F. representatives make direct contact with foreign delegates? Would one need to know languages other than English? What about pamphlets? In what layout? The official consulted primarily with members of the United Kingdom Delegation to the United Nations. As might have been expected, they strongly advised against lobbying 'in the Assembly area in the strict sense of the word', although they considered some press contact, and further discussions with members of the U.K. Delegation only, to be proper. Meeting with other delegates was virtually ruled out: 'I did not see any evidence of activity by the Icelandic delegation during my visit. According to reports Mr. Hans Anderson [Andersen] was in New York but the U.K. Delegation asked that I should not seek him out.'

In return for restricting its activities, Galitzine received advice and practical help from the British Delegation. Its official was informed that the U.N. would not discuss the issue before 7 November 1958; that a B.T.F. pamphlet might be of some use, especially if also printed in French and Spanish; and that the British Information Service and other such agencies would help in its distribution. This pamphlet would complement an official memorandum[1] submitted to the General Assembly in November 1958 by the Government of the United Kingdom.

After consultation with officials of the Ministry of Agriculture, Galitzine produced a pamphlet for the B.T.F. entitled *The Right to Fish on the High Seas*.[2] This rather garish 12-page effort — paragraph headings in red ink, all print 14-point type and larger, extremely repetitious — was sent, 1,000 copies of it, to the office of U.K. Delegation to the United Nations for distribution at a time and in a manner of its choosing. Other copies were similarly sent British Information Service. On the request of British officials, distribution of the pamphlet in Britain by the B.T.F. or Galitzine, was delayed several weeks, except 'to a close circle of Government officials and to the Trawler Owners', Galitzine further agreed to:

[1] *The Problem of the Fisheries Around Iceland;* this was the only pamphlet on the subject the British Government had published to Iceland's three.
[2] London, November 1958 (in English only).

leave the final decision concerning distribution to the Delegates of the U.N.O. in the hands of our own people who will be best able to judge the right moment. At the request of our Delegation we are asked to avoid any undue aggravation of the present position.

The B.T.F. also followed this advice.

Even without product promotion the Federation spent a good deal of money at this time on P.R. activities. Expenditures from February 1958 to March 1959 on items related solely to the question of fisheries limits are listed in Table 2:

TABLE 2

	£	£
Travel	1,100	
Entertainment and luncheon (Press and political) .	1,260	
S. H. Benson (artwork, institutional advertising) .	31,705	
Fee for Scandinavian visiting Iceland . . .	298	
Trip to U.N. autumn 1958	570	
U.N. booklet	1,130	
Telephone and telegraph	350	
TOTAL *		£36,413

* In addition, some £10,600 was spent during this time on liaison skippers.

Activities and expenditures, of course, did not end in March of 1959. For example, in preparation for the Second United Nations Conference on the Law of the Sea, held in March and April of 1960,[1] Galitzine arranged for the publication of several pamphlets to be given to the delegates attending. The most important of these — a slick, well designed, well written article of nine printed pages — was published not only in English (*Towards a Fisheries Settlement*) but in French (*Vers un règlement du différend au sujet de la pêche*) and in Spanish (*Hacia un acuerdo en las pesuerias*).[2] Galitzine also reprinted a rather legalistic article, 'The Icelandic Dispute in Perspective', from *The Oxford Lawyer*, and in addition had it translated into French ('Exposé du différend Anglo-Islandais').

The firm in addition, helped organize the trips made by officials of the B.T.F. in early 1960 to trawler federations in Western Europe and North America. Originally, General Phillips was to have led these visits, but at this time he fell seriously ill. Mr. William Letten,

---

[1] This Second Conference dealt almost exclusively with the question of the breadth of the territorial sea and of fisheries zones that the First Conference had failed to resolve. It too was unable to decide the issue.

[2] The text of this pamphlet is almost identical to that in the full-page B.T.F. advertisement that appeared in *The Times* of 5 February 1960, p. 5.

managing director of the Atlas Trawling Company (now a part of
Associated Fisheries), accompanied by Colonel Chant, filled in on
the visits to Spain, Portugal, Italy, and Greece; Mark Hellyer went
to Norway; Cobley and Boyd, accompanied by Prince Galitzine
himself (he is of White Russian nobility), went to Canada; and on
their return Cobley and Boyd also visited France.[1] In all these
countries the delegations from the B.T.F. met their opposite
numbers and some political figures. In Canada they even paid a
courtesy call on Prime Minister Diefenbaker. This tour was undertaken at the suggestion of Galitzine, which felt that co-ordination
among the leaders of the fishing industries of these countries might
increase the probability of co-operation among their governments.[2]
But the suggestion for such a trip also came later from one W. M.
Chapman, Director of Research for the American Tunaboat Association. Dr. Chapman had had considerable experience in both the
scientific and political aspects of fishing, from within the industry
and also as a high official of the American State Department. He
has, indeed, been rather ubiquitous in the international politics of
fishing.[3]

Taking into account these publications and conferences with
fishing vessel owners in Europe and North America, as well as
advertisements in British and continental papers and also a great
many meetings with persons in the British Government, it is fair to
assert that the B.T.F. and Galitzine went well prepared to the 1960
Geneva Conference. It was not their fault that the Conference was
again to fail, this time by only one vote, to decide limits to the
territorial sea and to fisheries zones.

IV

The B.T.F. spent a respectable amount of money on public relations
activities. The two budgets cited above (£82,450 in 1956 and
£36,413 for February 1958–March 1959[4]) average to well over
£55,000 a year. By some American standards this may be a modest
investment: in three and a half years, for example, the American
Medical Association spent $4,678,000 fending off governmental

[1] Letter to me from Colonel Chant, 24 May 1961, p. 9.
[2] The tour was *not* undertaken at the behest of the British Government; in fact,
it is supposed rather to have frowned upon the idea.
[3] Bernard C. Cohen, *The Political Process and Foreign Policy: The Making of the
Japanese Peace Treaty* (Princeton: Princeton University Press, 1957), chap. 12 ('Salt
Water Politics').
[4] And this latter figure does not include Galitzine's retainer or P.R. expenses not
directly connected with fisheries limits.

medical insurance.[1] But in British terms it is a considerable sum. It is far more than the British Medical Association's expenditure of £13,750 on its Public Relations Department in 1957.[2] It compares favourably with Aims of Industry's annual operating budget in the late forties of about £75,000.[3] If it is much less than the £260,000 budget for the Tate and Lyle 'Mr. Cube' campaign of 1949–50, this is due to Tate and Lyle's being interested in mass persuasion, while the B.T.F. mainly addressed its efforts to *élite* opinion.[4]

For its money the B.T.F. obtained a wide range of politically significant activities. Patrick Dolan & Associates washed away much of the mud that had caked on the Federation due to charges of business restraint and high prices. Through a distinguished series of institutional advertisements in the 'quality press' and through annual reports and trophy awards, it built an image of the B.T.F. as a group of important men in a highly complex industry. Its material, aimed at an educated but lay public, seems to have been highly successful: this is the consensus of opinion within the P.R. field and among trawler owners as well. It also developed good contacts with certain members of Parliament.

If Dolan dealt particularly with what may be phrased the public side of public relations, Galitzine & Partners concentrated more on its private side. Not only did it establish better and more thorough contacts with officials in the Ministry of Agriculture, but it also undertook a number of confidential assignments in the area of international affairs. It helped prepare the B.T.F. for the Hague trawler-owners' conference in July 1958, and arranged meetings with various foreign trawling officials in early 1960. It did reconnaissance work for the Federation in Iceland and some limited reconnoitring at the U.N. in New York as well. It not only accompanied the B.T.F. delegation to Geneva in 1960 but also produced a number of pamphlets for distribution to the delegates attending that conference.

Taken together, the work of Dolan and Galitzine impinged on most levels of political action. Some of it was domestic in application, ranging from use of the mass media to influence broad public opinion and combat hostile interest groups, to face-to-face discussions with Members of Parliament and officials in ministries; some of it was international, and included intelligence gathering, contact

---

[1] Stanley Kelley, Jr., *Professional Public Relations and Political Power* (Baltimore: The Johns Hopkins Press, 1956), p. 106.

[2] Harry Eckstein, *Pressure Group Politics: The Case of the British Medical Association* (London: George Allen & Unwin, 1960), pp. 73–4.

[3] About £150,000 in 1956. See S. E. Finer, *Anonymous Empire*, p. 79.

[4] On this campaign, against the Labour Government's intention to nationalize the sugar industry, see H. H. Wilson, 'Techniques of Pressure'.

work at international forums, and pamphleteering. All of it helped
bridge the gap between the fishing industry and the governmental
decision-making machinery.

Doubtless a politically adept trade association could have performed many of these activities for itself. In theory, the characteristics of an associational interest group surely include '. . . orderly
procedures for the formulation of interests and demands, *and transmission* of these demands to other political structures such as political
parties, legislatures, bureaucracies'.[1] But the B.T.F. would hardly
be alone among British trade associations (and corporations) in
lacking the skills to perform these functions properly.

P.R. consultancy is, of course, not a panacea for a group's political
problems. Tensions within an industry may still inhibit the development of a sustained and well-transmitted set of political aims; they
may lead, too, to changing the public relations firm employed often
or at an awkward moment. And, particularly when advertising is
done, P.R. costs, which are concrete and readily apparent, may
seem to some industrial leaders to outweigh its advantages, which
are often long range and intangible. But, in the main, hiring a
capable public relations firm permits an organization quickly to
increase its political capabilities. Even groups with their own internal
P.R. department to handle routine matters often find the retention
of a firm of consultants useful. Such a firm can not only bring fresh
perspectives to a group's difficulties but also, because it services
many clients, provide the specialization and flexibility that a particular problem requires.

Clearly, for interest groups adequately to 'man the boundaries
between polity and society', they must be conceptually bilingual.
But many economic groups themselves speak the language of politics
(particularly welfare state politics) badly if at all. By hiring public
relation firms, the B.T.F. obtained, as it were, the services of skilled
translators who could put economic facts into language suitable for
the press and Parliament — and for ministries and international
conferences, too. That the translators sometimes did the speaking
for the Federation is true and unavoidable. The alternative would
have been for the Federation to abdicate its appropriate political
role.

[1] Gabriel Almond in Almond and James S. Coleman (ed.), *The Politics of the
Developing Areas* (Princeton: Princeton University Press, 1960), p. 34 (italics mine).

PARTIES, PRESSURE GROUPS AND THE
BRITISH POLITICAL PROCESS

By R. T. McKenzie

ALTHOUGH parties and pressure groups are often studied
separately for reasons of analytic convenience, from the point
of view of the individual, these organizations offer alternative
and complementary channels of political influence. In
British Political Parties R. T. McKenzie has developed the
constitutional doctrine that the role of the political party in
policy making, particularly of the party activist, ought to be
severely limited. In the article reprinted here, McKenzie
expands the discussion to consider what are and ought to be
the complementary functions of parties and pressure groups
in Britain.

SAMUEL BEER, perhaps the ablest American student of British
politics, has commented: 'If we had some way of measuring political
power, we could possibly demonstrate that at the present time pressure groups are more powerful in Britain than in the United States.'[1]
The realization that this may be the case appears to have grown
rapidly in Britain in recent years and, in most quarters, the reaction
to it has been gloomy,[2] indeed, among many publicists the gloom has
given way to outright despair. Thus, according to Paul Johnson, of
the *New Statesman*, 'Acts of policy are now decided by the interplay of
thousands of conflicting interest groups, and cabinet ministers are
little more than chairmen of arbitration committees. Their opinions
play virtually no part in shaping decisions which they subsequently

---

[1] S. H. Beer, 'Pressure Groups and Parties in Britain', *The American Political
Science Review* (March 1956), p. 3.

[2] Thus even so well informed an observer as W. J. M. Mackenzie concludes that
the dominant role of organized groups in British public life means: 'We are
gradually shifting back into a situation in which a man is socially important only
as a holder of standard qualifications and as a member of authorized groups, in
fact into the new medievalism which was the promised land in the days from the
younger Pugin to William Morris.' W. J. M. Mackenzie, 'Pressure Groups in
British Government', *British Journal of Sociology* (June 1955), p. 146.

Reprinted in an abridged and slightly amended form from *Political Quarterly*,
vol. xxix, no. 1 (1958), pp. 5–16.

defend with passion. . . . When everyone's wishes count, nobody's opinions matter.'[1]

There are no doubt many explanations of this despairing (and, I would argue, belated) recognition of the powerful role played by interest groups in Britain. There can be no question that their activities and their influence have increased in recent decades. This surely was inevitable; once it had been largely agreed by all parties that the governments (national and local) should collect and spend over a third of the national income, tremendous pressures were bound to be brought to bear to influence the distribution of the burdens and benefits of public spending on this scale. And further: a new and powerful factor was injected into the equation when the trade unions, since the Second World War, won recognition, in Sir Winston Churchill's phrase, as an 'estate of the realm'. The highly articulate middle class (by whom, and for whom, so many of our journals of opinion are written) developed an acute sense of claustrophobia as they watched the giants around them, organized business, labour, the farmers, and the rest, struggling among themselves, and often with the government of the day, for an ever larger share of the national income.

The Respective Roles of Pressure Groups and Parties

A starting-point in clarifying the situation in this country is to examine the respective roles in the British political process of political parties and of pressure groups. One source of confusion about the role of party has arisen from Burke's much quoted observation that a party is 'a body of men united for promoting by their joint endeavours the national interest upon some particular principle in which they are all agreed'.[2] This remark has been leaned on much too heavily; it provides no explanation at all of the *function* of party in a democratic society; and even as a *description* of parties it is misleading because it places far too great a stress on the role of principle and by implication, on the role of ideology and programme.

Yet some exponents of democratic theory, starting, it would appear, from Burke's definition, have implied that political parties serve (or ideally ought to serve) as the sole 'transmission belts' on which political ideas and programmes are conveyed from the citizens

---

[1] P. Johnson, 'The Amiable Monster', the *New Statesman* (12 October 1957), p. 468. In the same vein, Bernard Hollowood has remarked that 'Parliament has become the abused referee of the big power game and . . . the unhappy millions on the terraces are powerless, almost voiceless spectators', in 'The Influence of Business and the City', *Twentieth Century* (October 1957), p. 253.

[2] *Thoughts on the Present Discontents*, World's Classics edition, vol ii, p. 82.

to the legislature and the executive. According to their ideal political model, a group of citizens first organize themselves into a political party on the basis of some principle or set of principles; they then deduce a political programme from these principles and their candidates proceed to lay this programme before the electorate; if the party secures a majority in Parliament it then implements the 'mandate' given it by the electors. If issues arise not covered by the 'mandate', then it is for the M.P.s to use their own judgement in deciding what to do; they are to deliberate, one gathers, in a kind of vacuum in which no external pressures (either from the constituencies or from organized interests) play upon them.

According to this democratic model, it is the exclusive function of the parties to canalize and to transmit the will of the citizenry to their elected representatives who then proceed to transmute it into positive law. The existence of organized groups of citizens, standing outside the party system and pressing the legislature and the executive to adopt certain specific policies, is either ignored or treated as an unfortunate aberration from the democratic ideal.

This conception of the democratic process is, in fact, completely inadequate and grossly misleading even if one applies it in this country, where parties are based on rather more specific sets of principles than they are in many other countries. (Although even in Britain it would not be easy to list the respective 'sets of principles' on which the members of the Conservative, Labour, and Liberal Parties 'are all agreed'.) Max Weber offered a better working definition of parties when he described them as 'voluntary associations for propaganda and agitation seeking to acquire power in order to . . . realize objective aims or personal advantages or both'. The 'objective aims' may be of greater or lesser importance in providing the basis of association and the motive force for the activity of a particular party. But there is little doubt that it is the 'collective pursuit of power' which is of overriding importance. It is obvious too that during the pursuit of power, and after it has been achieved, parties mould and adapt their principles under the innumerable pressures brought to bear by organized groups of citizens which operate for the most part outside the party system.

I would argue that the basic functions of parties in the British political system are to select, organize, and sustain teams of parliamentarians, between whom the general body of citizens may choose at elections. The 'selection' and 'sustaining' of the teams is mainly the job of the party outside Parliament; the 'organization' of the teams (and the allocations of roles, including the key role of party leader and potential prime minister) is the function of the party within Parliament. It does not matter whether the party is organized on the basis of a set of principles on which all its members are agreed, or whether, alternatively, it represents merely an organized appetite for power. In either case parties play an indispensable role in the democratic system by offering the electorate a free choice between competing teams of potential rulers. In Britain, the parties do profess their loyalty to differing sets of principles and these help to provide an element of cohesion for the parties themselves, and they have the further advantage of offering the electorate a choice, in very broad terms, between differing approaches to the social and economic problems with which governments must deal.

None the less, elections in this country are primarily rough-and-ready devices for choosing between rival parliamentary teams. Under our electoral system (with its disdain for the principles of proportional representation and its penalization of minor parties) the winning team of parliamentarians rarely obtains half the votes cast. (Indeed only three governments in this century have managed to do so.) And even when, as in 1951, the winning party, the Conservatives, obtained fewer votes than their Labour opponents, no one challenges their right to rule the country.

It is, in part, one suspects, because of the tacit recognition of the enormous and legitimate role played by organized interests that the public acquiesces in the apparent anomalies of our electoral system. It did not much matter that a Conservative Government took office in 1951, having obtained fewer votes than the Labour Party which it ousted; the Conservatives would be less sympathetic to the aspirations of the principal supporters of the Labour Party (the trade unions), but the new Government were bound to be aware that they could not administer the economic affairs of the country unless they paid very close attention to the demands and the opinions of the trade unions. The trade unions for their part showed no disposition to sulk in their tents when the party of their choice was defeated in the election (although it had obtained more votes than the victors). The trade unions could not expect to play a dominant role in determining the policies of the new Government; but they could be confident that most of the channels of communication between the trade unions and the newly elected executive would remain open and that their views would carry great weight with the new administration.

I have suggested that any explanation of the democratic process which ignores the role of organized interests is grossly misleading; I would add that it is also hopelessly inadequate and sterile in that it leaves out of account the principal channels through which the mass of the citizenry brings influence to bear on the decision-makers whom they have elected. In practice, in every democratic society, the voters undertake to do far more than select their elected representatives; they also insist on their right to advise, cajole, and warn them regarding the policies they should adopt. They do this, for the most part, through the pressure-group system. Bentley, in the first trail-blazing analysis of pressure groups written fifty years ago, no doubt overstated his case when he argued that individuals cannot affect governments except through groups; therefore, Bentley claimed, the 'process of government' must be studied as 'wholly a group process'.[1] But there can be no doubt that pressure groups, taken together, are a far more important channel of communication than parties for the transmission of political ideas from the mass of the citizenry to their rulers. It is true that a larger proportion of the electorate 'belongs to' political parties in this country than in any other democracy. (The Conservative and Labour Parties together claim a membership of over 9 millions, rather more than one in every four of the voters.) But the number of *active* members who do the work of the parties in the constituencies, who draft the resolutions debated in party conferences and so forth, is not more than a few hundred per constituency. This stage army of politically active, numbering 100,000 or so in each party, invariably claims to speak in the name of the millions of inactive members of the party and, indeed, on behalf of the 12 or 13 millions who normally vote for each party at an election. Further, they alone choose the candidates for their respective parties, and this is of course a vitally important function, since nomination is tantamount to election in two-thirds or three-quarters of the constituencies in Britain. But it is perfectly clear that when most citizens attempt to influence the decision-making process of their elected representatives, they do so through organized groups which we call 'interest groups' or 'pressure groups'.

Certain of the great sectional groups choose to work through one or other of the great political parties in addition to bringing external pressure to bear on them. Thus, a large proportion of the trade unions are directly affiliated to the Labour Party and a number of unions also sponsor Labour candidates. But, as was noted above, the Trades Union Congress as well as individual unions reserve the right to deal directly with governments, whether Labour or Conservative. The relations between the business community and the Conservative Party are more obscure, in part because the Conservatives do not permit direct affiliation of organized groups, and also because they

[1] A. F. Bentley, *The Process of Government.*

do not publish their accounts. It can be taken for granted, however, that businessmen, as individuals and in groups, provide the greater part of the Conservative Party's revenue.[1] Yet the great associations representing the business community, such as the Federation of British Industries, expect to be and are intimately consulted by Labour governments. The Federation explains its own purpose in these words: '*whatever the government in power*, [the Federation] seeks to create conditions in which each firm has the maximum opportunity to turn its own ideas and resources to the best account in its own and the national interest'.[2]

Certain other associations, such as the National Union of Teachers, have also sponsored individual candidates for one or other or both parties. But, as the experience of the National Farmers Union suggests, most interest groups in recent years have tended to avoid a too close association with a particular party. This is partly no doubt because both parties, during their terms of office since the Second World War, have shown their willingness to serve, up to a point, as brokers reconciling the interests of rival pressure groups.

There is no doubt widespread fear that parties will in fact degenerate into nothing more than brokers serving competing interest groups; and it is this fear which underlies much of the hostile comment on the activities of pressure groups, and which inhibits a realistic evaluation of the positive and legitimate function of these groups in the political process. It may well be that much writing on pressure groups too casually assumes a happy state of equilibrium (Bentley argued that 'the balance of group pressures *is* the existing state of society'.) There is no doubt that governments which indulge in 'piecemeal surrender to interest groups' become incapable of devising a coherent social policy. In the extremity, of course, government action could become merely the resultant of the forces that play upon the decision-makers.

But the danger can easily be exaggerated. Sweden can be described even more aptly than this country as 'a pluralist society' yet it is far from the 'pluralist stagnation' which some critics of the interest-group system fear. Gunnar Heckscher (who is both a professor of politics and a Conservative member of the Swedish Parliament) re-

[1] It is important to remember, however, as F. C. Newman has pointed out, that in the case of both parties, 'it is the programme that attracts the money; the money does not structure the programme', in 'Reflections on Money and Party Politics in Britain', *Parliamentary Affairs* (Summer 1957), p. 316.

[2] *The F.B.I., what it is, what it does*, p. 1 (italics mine). For a very valuable examination of the structure and functioning of the F.B.I., see S. E. Finer, 'The Federation of British Industries', *Political Studies* (February 1956), pp. 61–84.

cently commented that 'It is now regarded as more or less inevitable' in Sweden that certain of the powerful interest groups 'should exercise a power almost equal to that of Parliament and definitely superior to that of the parliamentary parties'.[1] Yet he does not see in this situation any really serious ground for concern; nor is there, he says, any demand in Sweden that action should be taken to curb the powerful organizations. Heckscher attributes the comparatively good health of the Swedish body politic to the 'strong sense of responsibility among group leaders' and the 'politics of compromise' which govern the relations between the great groups themselves, as well as their relations with governments.

Despite the political and social tensions in contemporary Britain, surely much the same comment can be made about the situation in this country? Vague as the phrase may be, the concept of the 'national interest' is still to the forefront in the course of almost every big sectional dispute in this country. Business, labour, the farmers, university teachers, still consider it expedient to argue their case, at least in part, in the terms of the national interest. Governments may from time to time give in to one or other of the great pressure groups, also in the name of the 'national interest'. But they also on occasion stand out boldly against the claim of pressure groups on the ground that to give way would be to *betray* the national interest.

There remains, however, the problem of the ill-organized (or even unorganizable) section of the community. Is there not danger that they will be either ignored or trampled upon by the really powerful interest groups? Certainly the danger is real. But it is the politicians' ultimate worry to see to it that the 'little men' (each of whom has as much political influence in the polling booth, at least, as anyone in the land) do not revolt against their policies in such numbers as to bring about their electoral ruin. This surely is one ultimate safeguard of the ill-organized. Indeed, it is arguable that in the long run governments are at least as frightened of the unorganized consumers (in their capacity as voters) as they are of the highly organized economic interests. None the less there is an area of public policy in which the absence of organized groups represents a serious

[1] G. Heckscher, 'Interest Groups and Sweden', a paper presented to the *International Political Science Round Table*, Pittsburgh 7–14 September 1957 (duplicated), p. 8. See also his 'Pluralist Democracy; the Swedish Experience', *Social Research* (December 1948), pp. 417–61. It should be noted, in connection with Hecksher's remark quoted above, that there are five parties in the Swedish Parliament, and in such circumstances it is perhaps less surprising than it would be here to remark that certain of the great sectional groups are more powerful than the parliamentary parties.

S

problem. Thus, for example, governments under pressure from shop employees and certain categories of shop-owners, may contemplate further restricting shop hours; there is no one to speak for the shoppers. Or again, governments may be fearful of liberalizing licensing hours because of the pressures they would set in motion against themselves from the highly organized temperance forces; there is no organized body to speak for the drinkers. Here, it seems to me, the public opinion polls have a legitimate and important role to play. The evidence they can produce of the shoppers' attitude to proposals for restricting shop hours, or the drinkers' attitude to licensing laws, should be *one* of the factors taken into account by the decision-makers, in addition to the views of the organized interests, in arriving at their policy decisions.

But with reservations such as these, it seems to me reasonable to conclude that the pressure-group system, with all its dangers, is both an inevitable and an indispensable concomitant of the party system. It provides an invaluable set of multiple channels through which the mass of the citizenry can influence the decision-making process at the highest levels. Is it possible that the widespread uneasiness about pressure groups in Britain today is really a result of the shift in the balance of power between the classes? Samuel J. Eldersveld has remarked that in 'the fluid politics' of America there is no longer 'a decisive ruling class' but rather a set of 'multiple élites'.[1] The same development has obviously occurred in this country; and it is clear that the new *élites* are struggling to assert their strength in part through the pressure-group system.

[1] S. J. Eldersveld, 'American Interest Groups', a paper presented to the *International Political Science Round Table*, Pittsburgh, 7–14 September 1957 (duplicated). The paper is reprinted in Henry W. Ehrmann, editor, *Interest Groups on Four Continents* (1958).

CHAPTER V

PARTY REPRESENTATION

BRITISH political parties have a history which is far older than that of the democratic franchise; the origins of the Conservative Party antedate even the 1832 Reform Bill. For generations the British party system has often been cited by foreign writers as a model of democratic politics, and this evaluation has also been widespread in Britain. By international standards, party membership today is very high; approximately one-quarter of the British electorate are members of a political party. The linking of party loyalties with deep social and family loyalties gives the parties extraordinarily stable support from sections of the electorate; in the six general elections since 1945, the Labour share of the popular vote has fluctuated only 2·5 per cent either side of its mid-point, and the Conservative share, only 5·0 per cent.

While it is customary to speak of a 'party system' and define parties in terms of functions within it, this is misleading, for parties do not form a system independent of other political institutions; they are integrally linked with a number of institutions, and they contribute to the performance of many political functions. Parties contribute to the development of distinctive sub-cultural attitudes, they socialize individuals into norms appropriate to active participation in politics, and they help recruit office-holders. Parties articulate principles on behalf of broad categories of the population, as well as aggregating the demands of pressure groups; by refusing some demands, they help to maintain the independence of political leaders from domination by economic and high-status groups. Albeit sometimes imperfectly, parties provide a communications network extending from leaders in Parliament down to ward organizations in the constituencies. At annual conferences and in Westminster party leaders deliberate on matters of public policy, and once policies are adopted, the machinery of the party is used to advance substantive and symbolic reasons why any abrupt shift in policy is legitimate in principle and right in practice.

From the viewpoint of the voter, parties are primarily important because they reduce an infinite combination of principles, policies, and teams of men to a very few alternatives; it is in the choice between two or three alternatives that voters most directly influence government. Because there are only two major parties competing for votes, the alternatives offered individual voters may be far from their first preference: the fewness of parties greatly circumscribes the actual choice before the voters. Because of the importance of the methods which parties employ to aggregate preferences, much analysis has concentrated upon the relationship between the political outlooks of voters and of parties.

From the viewpoint of the governors, parties are first of all important because party identification and discipline are necessary to sustain the fusion of authority in the hands of men who are Cabinet, parliamentary, and party leaders. The histories of parliaments and cabinets in other countries have shown that without disciplined majority parties, British institutions do not inevitably produce a fusion of authority. The difficulties of the minority Labour governments in the 1920's showed how the multiplication of divisions within and between parties can also lead to the weakening of Cabinet authority in this country. Because of the importance of party discipline in maintaining the predominance of the executive in Britain, it would perhaps be more accurate to speak of British government as 'party government' rather than parliamentary or Cabinet government.

BIBLIOGRAPHICAL NOTE

In the contemporary academic literature about British party politics, R. T. McKenzie's *British Political Parties* (London: Heinemann, 1st edn., 1955; revised edn., 1963) has a special place, because it contains a controversial thesis about the distribution of power within political parties, as well as a wealth of detailed information about party organization and history. Academic studies of parties include Martin Harrison, *Trade Unions and the Labour Party since 1945* (London: Allen & Unwin, 1960); J. D. Hoffman, *The Conservative Party in Opposition, 1945–51* (London: MacGibbon & Kee, 1964), and Jorgen Rasmussen, *The Liberal Party: a study of retrenchment and revival* (London: Constable, 1965). *British Politics in the Suez Crisis* (London: Pall Mall, 1964), by Leon Epstein, is a case study of the influence of party upon the workings of national government; A. H. Birch, *Small-Town Politics* (London: Oxford University Press, 1959), and Frank Bealey *et al.*, *Constituency Politics: a Study of Newcastle under Lyme* (London: Faber, 1965) are case studies of party politics at the local level.

In the literature of party politics, two old classics are specially relevant to British students: Robert Michels, *Political Parties* (1st

English-language edn., 1915) contains themes developed in R. T. McKenzie's study; M. I. Ostrogorski's *Democracy and the Organization of Political Parties* (2 vols.: 1st English-language edn., 1902) provides a comparative and theoretical analysis of the historical development of parties in both Britain and America. For an important reinterpretation of Michels, see John D. May, 'Democracy, Organization, Michels', *American Political Science Review*, lix. 2 (1965).

Comparative studies of political parties attempting to develop theories about parties and party systems applicable to England as well as other countries include: Maurice Duverger, *Political Parties* (1st English-language edn., London: Methuen, 1954); Avery Leiserson, *Parties and Politics* (New York: Knopf, 1958); Neil A. McDonald, *The Study of Political Parties* (Garden City, New York; Doubleday, 1955); Sigmund Neumann (ed.), *Modern Political Parties* (Chicago: University Press, 1956); Austin Ranney and Willmoore Kendall, *Democracy and the American Party System* (New York: Harcourt, Brace, 1956); and S. J. Eldersveld, *Political Parties: a behavioral analysis* (Chicago: Rand, McNally, 1964).

THE PARADOX OF PARTY DIFFERENCE

By D. E. BUTLER

A CONVENTION exists treating the policy differences between British parties in terms of 'left' and 'right'. If this distinction is pressed to its logical conclusion, as H. J. Laski tended to do in *Parliamentary Government in England*, it can produce a misleading picture of two mutually exclusive and cohesive monoliths facing each other across a wide ideological gulf. In practice, the differences in attitudes within political parties can be as significant as differences between parties. D. E. Butler's article points out the importance to the party system of different distributions of political attitudes along the left–right continuum, by suggesting comparisons between different periods in British politics, and between British and American and French politics. The author assumes, for purposes of discussion, that political opinions may meaningfully be placed along a continuum representing a single ideological dimension. Research conducted since suggests that more than one dimension is discernible in British political attitudes.

MOST teachers of politics in the United States and in Britain would agree that Lord Bryce's picture of the Republican and Democratic parties as 'two bottles, each having a label denoting the kind of liquor it contains, but each of them empty', has been too long with us. A rather smaller majority would agree that the picture offered by Professor Schattschneider and others of the clear contrast between the British parties has been much overstated. I do not wish to add to the controversies on the theme — many and profitable though they have been — but merely to offer a graphic device which has been used with some success before audiences on both sides of the Atlantic to illustrate the nature of the differences within and between the party systems of different countries.

For the purposes of this device, one assumption that admittedly begs the question must be made: that political positions can be explained in terms of a spectrum running from extreme left to extreme right and that everyone can be classified in terms of his particular place on that spectrum. This assumption is grossly

Reprinted from *The American Behavioral Scientist*, vol. iv, no. 3 (1960), pp. 3–5.

arbitrary, of course. A man may be to the left on some issues and to the right on others, while in relation to many issues the terms 'left' and 'right' are meaningless.

However arbitrary this notion may be, it is not altogether unrealistic. Some such view underlies a large amount of everyday political conversation and reporting. And a host at an academic or political cocktail party will be amazed at how rarely he has to tremble in indecision if he distinguishes between his guests' drinks by taking the glass of his more right-wing guest in his right hand. It is quite possible to make a rough estimate about where a politician or an elector stands along a spectrum from radical red to reactionary violet. Furthermore, with the use of the questionnaire and other techniques, more precise scaling can be achieved, as Angus Campbell, Herbert McClosky, and others have recently shown.

The popular picture of the spread of opinion between right and left in British and American parties is probably much like that

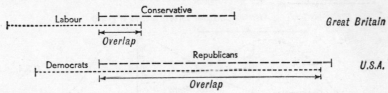

FIG. 1. The Popular Picture of Right and Left in British and American Politics

shown in Fig. 1. The overlap between the positions of Conservative and Labour M.P.s is very slight; the overlap between Republican and Democratic Congressmen is fairly complete. The grounds for believing in the total confusion of the American party system and the relative clarity of that in Britain are made blatantly plain.

But the picture is transformed if averages and not extremes are considered, if attention is focused upon the way in which opinion is *concentrated* in each party and not upon its potential range. Frequency distributions, showing how people holding right and left opinions are distributed within each party, would probably have the shape of Fig. 2. In this figure the distance between what may be loosely termed the centres of gravity, the positions of the median supporter of each party, are about the same in Britain and the United States. Indeed, if the right wing of the Democrats, so largely drawn from the South, was eliminated, the American contrast would be appreciably more striking.

Even without this consideration, however, it can be argued that there is in fact a greater difference between the two American

parties than between the two British parties. In some recent periods
the issues in the area between the party centres of gravity — for example, acceptance of the welfare state or of international involve-
ments — have been bigger and more genuinely controversial on
the western side of the Atlantic.

A simplified expository device must not be mistaken for an exactly
observed picture of reality. These curves are not based on precise
measurements. Different observers might have very different views
on how individuals and issues should be classified. It would be
possible to draw and defend curves that would illustrate the substantial identity or the total contrast between the parties in either
or both the countries. Each theorist must decide for himself the

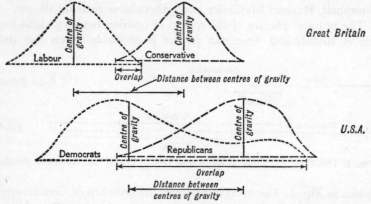

FIG. 2. Centre of Gravity in British and American Politics

extent of the paradox which the device is designed to explain — the
paradox that parties whose views seem very largely to overlap can
be so very different, while parties whose views seem quite distinct
can be so close to each other. Moreover, each theorist must decide
for himself how much of the political struggle can be explained within the terms 'right' and 'left', and how much must be regarded as
feuding between sections or interests of a kind that cannot be fitted
into any such ideological classification.

But if the concepts of 'right' and 'left' can throw light on any
area of party conflict, then this graphic device can be used to clarify
other problems. For example, the gap between the parties obviously varies with time. Fig. 3 suggests a possible interpretation of
recent British politics: the spread of opinion between the Conservative and Labour parties — and to some extent within the Conservative party — diminished greatly between 1935 and 1955.

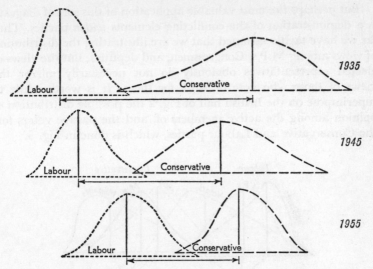

FIG. 3. The Diminishing Gap Between Labour and Conservative

Similar diagrams drawn for the United States would show the Republicans and Democrats overlapping greatly in the early 1920's, drawing widely apart with the coming of the New Deal, and overlapping greatly once more in the 1950's.

The complex dilemma of French politics under the Fourth Republic can be illustrated by another graph. Fig. 4 shows the position of members of the National Assembly after the 1951 election, which returned six roughly equal groups of deputies. It is true that the difficulties of explaining French politics in terms solely of 'right' and 'left' are particularly great, but a diagram such as this can help students to understand how much wider was the range of opinion in France than in English-speaking countries, and how much compromise was necessary to find a majority among the democratic parties of the Fourth Republic.

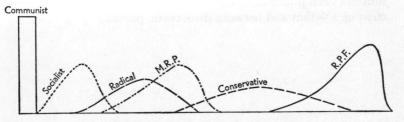

FIG. 4. The French National Assembly, 1951

But perhaps the most valuable application of this sort of diagram is a demonstration of the conflicting elements *within* parties. Thus far we have tacitly assumed that we are illustrating the distribution of views among M.P.s, Congressmen, and deputies. But the views of elected representatives obviously do not necessarily mirror the views of those who vote or work for them. It is worth while to superimpose on the British half of Fig. 2 the possible distribution of opinion among the active members of, and the passive voters for, the Conservative and Labour parties, which is done in Fig. 5.

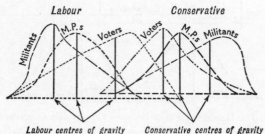

Fig. 5. M.P.'s, Militants, and Voters in British Politics

This diagram illustrates the essential dilemma of party leaders in Britain, and elsewhere: their most loyal and devoted followers tend to have more extreme views than they have themselves, and to be still farther removed from the mass of those who actually provide the vote. Party leaders have to conciliate those who support them with money or with voluntary work, without alienating that large body of moderate voters whose attitudes make them most likely to swing to the other party and thus to decide the next election.

These various diagrams are no more than pedagogic devices, arbitrarily drawn to illustrate propositions that must occur to any serious observer of party politics. In conjunction with voting records or survey-based indices of 'rightness' or 'leftness', they do offer a useful technique. They can help separate out, more clearly than has hitherto been practicable, the extent of present and past ideological cleavages within and between democratic parties.

PARTISANSHIP IN THE SUEZ CRISIS

By LEON EPSTEIN

MANY questions about the role of political parties in British government are treated in detail in Leon Epstein's book, *British Politics in the Suez Crisis*. The following excerpt concerns one question: to what extent did differences in party attitudes in the House of Commons conflict with, reflect, or influence differences in opinion among the general electorate? During the crisis and shortly afterwards, great publicity was given to remarks which indicated that at least a few partisans differed from national party policy; particularly this was alleged to be true among working-class Labour voters. Epstein's article does not rest upon casual observation or generalization from single instances, but rather upon a careful sifting of survey data collected by the Gallup Poll to assess the relationship between national party policy and the views of rank-and-file voters in this instance.

THE Suez issue has been presented almost entirely in terms of the conflict between the major political parties. This was true with respect both to the parliamentary conflict and to its extension to the constituencies. What about the opinions of the rest of the community? To what extent were the ordinarily less partisan Englishmen mobilized on one side or the other? In considerable degree, this is a way of asking how successfully each party was able to mobilize its own usual voters, not just its actual dues-paying membership, to support its Suez position.

There can be little doubt that the actions of political party leaders tended to extend the lines of partisan conflict to the general public. They were plainly fortified in doing so by their own zealous constituency activists. But party leaders needed and wanted to do much more than secure the support of their own usual following. For the Labour opposition, it was crucial to rally outside opinion sufficiently to cause Conservative M.P.s to waver in their loyalty to the Government, or more feasibly to lessen the Government's popularity for some future electoral occasion. Such objectives were what the

Reprinted from Leon Epstein, *British Politics in the Suez Crisis* (London: Pall Mall, 1964), pp. 139–51.

partisan conflict was really about. Without projecting the conflict beyond Parliament itself, Labour could hardly hope to accomplish anything. And on their side the Conservative leadership had every incentive to seek public agreement for its policy. To this end, Prime Minister Eden broadcast an appeal to the nation during the crisis itself.[1] The opposition answered, notably in a broadcast by Gaitskell.

The major public effort, however, was Labour's 'Law, Not War' campaign. Plans for this campaign were announced almost immediately after military action had begun. They were agreed upon jointly by the Labour Party's national executive, the Trades Union Congress' general council, and the National Council of Labour. These agencies announced demonstrations and meetings throughout the country. While specifically excluding a general strike or any such industrial action, the trade-union leaders did thus support their party's general campaign.[2] The most publicized feature of the campaign was a mass rally at Trafalgar Square, where an estimated 30,000 heard Aneurin Bevan and from which an estimated 10,000 went on to demonstrate at Number 10 Downing Street.[3] Strong and unparliamentary language was characteristic of speech-making at some of the protest meetings, particularly outside the main London arena. In one small community, for example, a Labour M.P. Denis Healey, asked the assembled crowd: 'What sort of people are you to allow a liar and a cheat to be your Prime Minister?'[4]

In exploring the extent to which this kind of partisan enthusiasm carried over to the rest of the nation, there are limited sources of information. First and most direct is the polling of opinion during and soon after the crisis, particularly in sample surveys but also in by-elections. Secondly, there is the press, through editorials as well as in news coverage. Thirdly, there are unsystematically gathered statements from a variety of opinion-makers besides the press.

Fortunately a considerable amount of data on popular responses to the Suez affair was collected by the sample surveys conducted by the reliable and well-established British Institute of Public Opinion (usually known as the B.I.P.O. or the British Gallup organization). Equally fortunate, from the author's viewpoint, the Institute has

[1] 'All my life,' Eden broadcast, 'I have been a man of peace, working for peace, striving for peace. I have been a League of Nations man and a United Nations man, and I am still the same man with the same convictions and the same devotion to peace.' *Manchester Guardian*, 5 November 1956, p. 6.
[2] Ibid., 2 November 1956, p. 1.
[3] *Daily Express* (London), 5 November 1956, pp. 1, 9.
[4] *Daily Telegraph* (London), 6 November 1956, p. 13.

TABLE 1

Polls by British Institute of Public Opinion on Military Action in Egypt
(per cent)

Interview Dates and Question	Opinion	Voting Intention				
		All	Con.	Lab.	Lib.	D.K.
16–24 Aug. 1956. If Egypt will not accept the decision of the conference, should we take military action against her, or confine ourselves to economic and political action?	Mil. action	33	43	30	24	20
	Econ.-pol.	47	44	52	61	39
	Don't know	20	13	18	15	41
5–6 Sept. 1956. If Egypt will not agree to international control of the canal, what should we do? Would you approve or disapprove if we were to give Egypt an ultimatum that unless she agrees to our proposals we will send troops to occupy the canal?	Approve	34	47	28	23	24
	Disapprove	49	41	54	55	54
	Don't know	17	12	18	22	22
1–2 Nov. 1956. Do you think we were right or wrong to take military action in Egypt?	Right	37	68	16	24	23
	Wrong	44	17	67	52	44
	Don't know	19	15	17	24	33
1–2 Dec. 1956. Do you think we were right or wrong to take military action in Egypt?	Right	49	81	22	30	43
	Wrong	36	10	62	49	34
	Don't know	15	9	16	21	23
27 Sept.–1 Oct. 1957. Looking back on Suez, do you think we were right or wrong to take military action in Egypt?	Right	48	79	30	40	33
	Wrong	32	10	51	41	23
	Don't know	20	11	19	19	44

generously made its data available for presentation here.[1] Much of what follows by way of analysis of sampled public opinion relies on such data. Only parenthetically is reference made to the results obtained by another poll (published in the *Daily Express*). Tables 1–3 and Figs. 1–2 are all based on B.I.P.O. data, and these presentations provide the best estimates of what Englishmen thought about Suez. These estimates do have limitations, but they are most revealing on certain points.

[1] I am grateful to Dr. Henry Durant and to his staff of the B.I.P.O. both for the data and for the facilities to transcribe the data.

274   LEON EPSTEIN

Immediately it can be observed that the B.I.P.O. polls never showed that a majority of all voters were in favour of military action. This was true before, during, and after the action itself (Table 1 and Fig. 1).[1] Even the *Daily Express* poll failed to show over 50 per cent supporting military action as it began (line 1 of Table 4), despite a spectacularly loaded question, and this source showed only barely over 50 per cent on 5–6 November favouring Eden's action generally. It is true, to return to the B.I.P.O., that slightly over 50 per cent did,

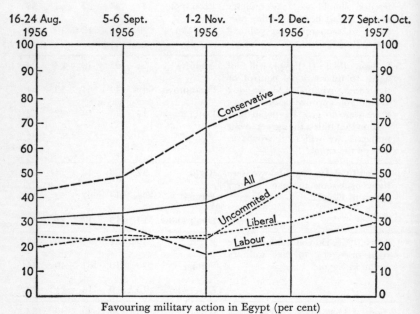

FIG. 1. Polls by British Institute of Public Opinion on Military Action in Egypt

on 10–11 November 1956 and on 1–2 December 1956, agree generally with the way Eden handled the Middle East situation (Table 2). But both these polls were taken after the conclusion of military action and it is possible that a little of the agreement with Eden derived from his decision to halt. The military action itself never received the approval of half the voters polled by the B.I.P.O. Even on 1–2 December 1956, when 51 per cent agreed generally with Eden's

[1] French public opinion was more favourable to the intervention, but it was not overwhelmingly so despite the absence of much party opposition apart from that of the Communists. In a French poll taken 2–3 November 1956, 44 per cent approved the Anglo-French action, 37 per cent were against, and 19 per cent had no opinion. *Revue française de l'opinion publique*, 1956, no. 4, p. 18.

policy (Table 2), only 49 per cent thought Britain had been right to take military action in Egypt. It is true that two percentage points either way are not especially significant. The vital point is that there simply was not anything like a substantial majority in favour of the use of force. This seems more important than the fact, on the other side, that there were never as many as 50 per cent clearly against military action. The 'don't knows' were always numerous enough, as Table 1 makes clear, so that neither the pros nor the cons were in a clear majority on any occasion.

TABLE 2

Polls by British Institute of Public Opinion on handling of Middle East situation
(per cent)

Interview Dates and Question	Opinion	All	Voting Intention			
			Con.	Lab.	Lib.	D.K.
7–18 Sept. 1956. Do you approve or disapprove of the way the Government has handled the Suez Canal incident?	Approve	42	71	21	31	36
	Disapprove	40	17	60	54	37
	Don't know	18	12	19	15	27
1–2 Nov. 1956. Speaking generally, do you agree or disagree with the way Eden has handled the Middle East situation since Israel marched into Egypt?	Agree	40	76	16	25	27
	Disagree	46	16	72	55	41
	Don't know	14	8	12	20	32
10–11 Nov. 1956. Speaking generally, do you agree or disagree with the way Eden has handled the Middle East situation?	Agree	53	89	20	46	50
	Disagree	32	4	63	33	24
	Don't know	15	7	17	21	26
1–2 Dec. 1956. Speaking generally, do you agree or disagree with the way Eden has handled the Middle East situation?	Agree	51	85	19	46	39
	Disagree	35	9	64	31	35
	Don't know	14	6	17	23	26

This much of the analysis is in accord with an earlier academic study of the polls that had been aimed particularly at contradicting the reports in the *New York Times* of a high degree of British public support for the Suez action.[1] No newspaper account of majority support could be based on the polls. Notably was this true as the

[1] Jean Owen, 'The Polls and Newspaper Appraisal of the Suez Crisis', *Public Opinion Quarterly*, vol. 21, pp. 350–4 (Autumn 1957).

military action began, since then a significantly smaller percentage of those polled thought the action right than thought it wrong (Table 2, third poll reported). Any newspaper reporter who at that time thought there was majority support for military force must have had a very different sampling method from the B.I.P.O.'s — perhaps the time-honoured 'sampling' of taxi-drivers and customers of public houses. But if a reporter detected increasing support during

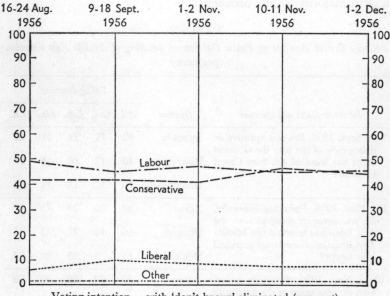

| 16-24 Aug. 1956 | 9-18 Sept. 1956 | 1-2 Nov. 1956 | 10-11 Nov. 1956 | 1-2 Dec. 1956 |

Voting intention — with 'don't knows' eliminated (per cent)

FIG. 2. Polls by British Institute of Public Opinion on Voting Intentions

and after the action he would have been decidedly in line with the trend reported by the B.I.P.O. and presented in Tables 1–2 and Fig. 1.

That trend is most sharply upward from 1–2 November to 1–2 December 1956, but it had also risen slightly in the earlier period (Fig. 1). Probably the early rise is less striking than the fact that only about one-third of all voters favoured military action in August and September. Moreover, the August result, as presented in Table 1 and Fig. 1, overstates the percentage willing at that time to support military action in a circumstance approximating that which actually occurred. Specifically, the interviewees who responded to the August poll by favouring military action were also asked whether they would still want the action if America was not prepared to support it.

Only 27 per cent (of all interviewees) stood for the go-it-without-America position.[1] Even with no such qualification, however, the number favouring military action before Eden made his move was markedly below the number opposing. The difference remained nearly the same as when the action began, and only turned around after the action was concluded. Eden's decision, therefore, was made without evidence of even a plurality in favour. He obtained his plurality only after the event. To be sure, it might be argued that thus the public supported him retrospectively, when leadership had been exerted and the case had been made. But this is the place to recall that even after the event the plurality was not a majority. Whether it would have been a majority if the military action had plainly

TABLE 3

Poll by British Institute of Public Opinion on effect of Suez on party voting inclinations (per cent)

Interview Dates and Question	Opinion	Voting Intention				
		All	Con.	Lab.	Lib.	D.K.
27 Sept.–1 Oct. 1957. Taking every-thing into account, has the way the Government handled the Suez situation made you more inclined to vote Conservative, less inclined to vote for them, or hasn't it made any difference?	More	10	26	2	5	3
	Less	26	9	40	41	16
	No difference	52	59	53	44	41
	Don't know	12	6	5	10	40

succeeded is in the realm of speculation. As far as the data go, they provide no basis for believing that Eden had a potential or incipient majority, any more than an actual majority, for military action.

A curious feature of the polls is the change in the nature as well as the degree of support for military action (Table 1 and Fig. 1). In the polls of August and September, support was not nearly so closely associated with party as later. Conservative voters, it is true, did favour military action in larger numbers than Labour and other voters, but the difference was much less great than it subsequently became (and it was somewhat less in August than in September).

[1] The specific wording of this question, not given in Table 1, was: 'If America is not prepared to support such military action, should we go ahead on our own, or not?' Four per cent answered negatively and 2 per cent answered 'don't know'. Thus 6 per cent of all the August interviewees shifted from an affirmative position taken in response to the first question noted in Table 1, reducing the total for military action from 33 per cent to 27 per cent.

T

Large numbers of Conservatives were still against military action, and large numbers of Labour voters were for it. This was the case even though party lines were more strictly followed, even in September, in response to the question of agreeing or disagreeing generally with Eden's handling of the Middle East situation (Table 2). This was likely to produce a nearly straightforward partisan response, while the military action question would not have done so in

TABLE 4

Polls by 'Daily Express' on Governments action in the Middle East
(per cent)

Interview Dates and Question	Opinion	Voting Intention			
		All	Con.	Lab.	Lib.
30 Oct.–3 Nov. 1956. As a result of Israel's invasion of Egypt, Sir Anthony Eden has sent British forces to occupy the Suez Canal zone to protect British interests and to guarantee freedom of transit through the canal by British ships and ships of all nations. Do you support or oppose this action?	Support	48·5	75	28	50
	Oppose	39·0	15	60	38
	Don't know	12·5	10	12	12
5–6 Nov. 1956. Do you favour or disfavour Sir Anthony Eden's Suez policy?	Favour	51·5	80	26	44
	Disfavour	36·0	11	60	32
	Don't know	12·5	9	14	24
17–21 Nov. 1956. In general, are you satisfied or dissatisfied with Sir Anthony Eden as Prime Minister?	Satisfied	60·5	95	25·5	48·5
	Dissatisfied	30·5	2	60·5	40·5
	Don't know	9·0	3	14·0	11·0

September. The Government had not yet made it clear that it would really use force. When it did employ force at the end of October, however, then the question of supporting military action was converted into a partisan question. A more usual way to say the same thing is that opinion about military action became polarized around party positions. What was, in August and September, far from a straight party issue in the minds of voters became much more nearly so in November and December 1956 (and even in September–October 1957). It was most so in December 1956 when the Conservative percentage of support reached its peak and the Labour

percentage of support had risen moderately from the low point of
1–2 November. Roughly the same high degree of party polarization
of opinion, during and after military action, is displayed by the
Daily Express data in Table 4.

The Conservative voters' support is really immense. Whatever
doubts many of them had had earlier about military action appear to
have been dissipated, or put to one side, once their leaders took the
action. Here, it seems probable, the leaders, particularly the Prime
Minister, could effectively lead. What Eden did seemed right to Conservatives either simply because he did it, in collaboration with his
Conservative Cabinet, or because his arguments for action became
persuasive. But for others, Eden's leadership appeared to produce a
negative result. By taking military action, against partisan opposition, Eden may have made such action less popular with Labour
voters than it was before. At least, the percentage of Labour voters
favouring military action went down between August–September
and November. This partisan loss, however, was not so great as
Eden's partisan gain among Conservatives.

The development of opinion so much along party lines, even
though less rigorously among Labour than among Conservative
voters, calls into question the frequently voiced view that Labour's
stand against Suez was unpopular with the party's own working-
class voters. The supposed unpopularity was later admitted by at
least one Labour M.P.,[1] and a large defection of working-class
sentiment to Eden was claimed by Conservatives. The assumption
was that the intellectual leaders of the Labour party were out of
step with ordinary Englishmen.[2] Partly this was a matter of patriotism, and it was thought possible that Gaitskell's heavily interna-
tionalist basis for opposition, as well as opposition itself, struck the
wrong note among party followers. Aneurin Bevan has been
quoted to this effect. He is supposed to have said informally, during
the crisis:

If we don't take care, we shall turn the working class against us. Of course
I am against Eden's crazy attempt to put the clock back. But there's no
reason why, in attacking the Tories, we should commit ourselves to the view

---

[1] R. J. Mellish said: 'We do not deny that many of our supporters in the country
supported the line taken by Sir Anthony Eden.' 570 *H.C. Deb*. 530 (15 May 1957).

[2] Working-class Englishmen, in particular, are supposed to cherish exaggerated
views of Britain's place in the world. Of these views, Richard Hoggart has written:
'Those which claim superiority for Britain are not "patriotic," in any proper
sense; they express an inherited assumption of national superiority. Though re-
peatedly told, especially during the last dozen years, about the change in England's
international position, the majority of working-class people have no realization of
it.' *The Uses of Literacy* (Harmondsworth: Penguin, 1958), p. 80.

that all United Nations decisions must be accepted and that all recourse to force must be opposed as aggression.

What makes the Labour Party go wrong in foreign affairs is that it takes its policies from middle-class intellectuals, devoid of antennae and with a dreadful habit of falling down and worshipping abstractions. In fact, there is only one motto worse than 'My country right or wrong' and that is 'The United Nations right or wrong'.[1]

It was also assumed that many Englishmen felt racially superior in such a way as to applaud rather than oppose a campaign to teach the Egyptians a lesson. This attitude was supposed to be related to residual imperialism. 'The contempt,' it has been said, 'which power breeds had been directed above all on to the Egyptians, just as in France it had been directed on to the Algerians. It is doubtful whether an attack on any other people in the world would have aroused as much enthusiasm in England as an attack on the Egyptians.'[2] Also stressed was the particular contempt for Egyptians which ordinary members of the British Eighth Army had brought back from the Second World War. None of this can be discounted completely. It may even explain a large part of the support that Eden's military action did receive. But not much of this, as has been shown, came from Labour voters, even though most but not all of the party's voters are known to have been working class. The plain fact is that during the crisis itself relatively few Labour voters were attracted by the military action — fewer than had been willing to support it beforehand. Afterwards, especially by September–October 1957, the percentage did increase. And always there were some Labour voters supporting the action. Evidently they were numerous enough to impress, perhaps to over-impress, the politicians of both parties. A good reason for this is that there were more such Labour defections in the pro-Suez direction than there were Conservative voter defections in the anti-Suez direction. Yet it must be emphasized that pro-Suez sentiment remained in a decided minority among Labour voters.

A question closely related to the degree of party polarization is one concerning the effect of the Suez affair on subsequent party fortunes. Because the military action was of very limited popularity originally and a failure ultimately, it might seem reasonable to hypothesize that the Conservative political cause would have suffered. But this does not seem to have been the case. Certainly the

---

[1] The words were attributed to Bevan by R. H. S. Crossman, presumably relying on his memory of a conversation over five years earlier. *Manchester Guardian Weekly*, 28 December 1961, p. 6.

[2] A. H. Hourani, 'The Middle East and the Crisis of 1956', in St. Antony's Papers No. 4, *Middle Eastern Affairs No. 1* (London: Chatto & Windus, 1958), p. 10.

Conservatives did not suffer in the 1959 general election, since they improved their position over 1955. More meaningful here, however, are estimates of voter responses nearer to the Suez crisis. These estimates also do nothing to establish significant political damage to the Conservatives from Suez. Instead the B.I.P.O. polls show that Conservative fortunes took a turn for the better during the crisis itself (Fig. 2). In mid-November 1956 the Conservative percentage was higher than Labour's for the first time in a year.[1] The fact was that the Conservative's support had slumped below Labour's a year before Suez, and mainly stayed there until just after mid-1958.[2] The mid-November rise was exceptional and temporary. A good case might thus be made that Suez briefly helped the Conservatives regain some of their lost popularity. On the other hand, they dropped down even further by early 1957 than they had been before Suez, and it is possible that this drop was caused in part by the ignominious withdrawal from Suez and the resignation of Eden. It would be stretching matters, however, to think that the subsequent low level of Conservative standing in the B.I.P.O. poll, through the middle of 1958, was caused significantly by Suez. A likelier explanation is that a variety of domestic economic irritations against the government was responsible for the party's political slump in 1957–58 as in 1955–56.

B.I.P.O. data provide one other method of trying to estimate directly the effect of Suez on political party fortunes. Almost a year after the event, voters were asked what effect Suez had had on their party preferences. The answers, revealed in Table 3, do indicate the possibility of lessened Conservative support. No more than a possibility, however, is indicated, and that may fairly be regarded as dubious. True, significantly more voters did say that Suez had made them less inclined to vote Conservative than the number who said that Suez had made them more inclined to vote Conservative. But most of those in the first category were Labour and Liberal voters, whose existing party preferences were simply strengthened by Suez. The poll does not mean that those less inclined, as a result of Suez, to vote Conservative would ever have voted Conservative anyway.

By-elections provide another source for trying to understand the effect of Suez on voting behaviour. All of the by-elections of 1955–59 that permit meaningful comparisons with the 1955 general election are listed in Table 5, and the relative Conservative gain or loss is

[1] *News Chronicle* (London), 15 November 1956, p. 4.
[2] D. E. Butler and Richard Rose, *The British General Election of 1959* (London: Macmillan, 1960), p. 40.

282 LEON EPSTEIN

shown. The most relevant by-elections are just before and after
Suez. Here it can be seen that, as in B.I.P.O. polls, the Conservatives were doing poorly before Suez and continued doing so, at
about the same level, just afterwards. The sharpest slump came in

TABLE 5

*List of by-elections of 1955–59 in which results can be compared with 1955
general election**

Date	Constituency	Conservative gain or loss in percentage of poll
7 Dec. 1955	Gateshead West	− 1·2
8 Dec. 1955	Greenock	− 2·3
15 Dec. 1955	Torquay	− 9·4
2 Feb. 1956	Blaydon	− 3·4
9 Feb. 1956	Leeds North-east	+ 1·8
14 Feb. 1956	Hereford	− 7·5
7 June 1956	Tonbridge	− 8·4
27 Sept. 1956	Chester-le-Street	− 4·5
		————Suez
15 Nov. 1956	Chester	− 5·0
19 Dec. 1956	Melton	− 7·6
7 Mar. 1957	Warwick and Leamington	−12·2
7 Mar. 1957	Bristol West	− 5·1
21 Mar. 1957	Beckenham	− 6·1
21 Mar. 1957	Newcastle upon Tyne North	− 3·6
27 June 1957	Dorset North	− 7·0
28 Nov. 1957	Leicester South-east	− 3·2
13 June 1958	Ealing South	− 9·3
13 June 1958	St. Helens	− 0·4
13 June 1958	Wigan	− 5·7
8 Nov. 1958	Morecambe and Lonsdale	− 5·9
8 Nov. 1958	Chichester	+ 0·1
28 Nov. 1958	Shoreditch and Finsbury	− 2·5
29 Jan. 1959	Southend West	− 8·6
19 Mar. 1959	Harrow East	− 1·6
11 June 1959	Reniston	− 1·8
18 June 1959	Whitehaven	− 0·5

* The list includes only 26 of the 52 by-elections held between the 1955 and 1959
general elections. The other half mainly did not have candidacies politically comparable with those of 1955, usually because a third-party candidate was present to
receive a substantial number of votes in one election but not the other. A few
constituencies had to be excluded because of the absence of the regular party
competition.

March 1957, but that may have been the result of the special fact
that Warwick and Leamington, then contested, was the seat from
which Eden had just resigned. At any rate, from this list no case can
be made that Suez directly hurt the Conservative party. Nor can

anything conclusive by way of harm to the Conservative cause be drawn from the manner in which the same data are presented in Table 6. It is true that the Conservatives did do least well in the group of elections in the year after Suez, but the difference is hardly sharp. Left out of all these by-election comparisons, because of non-comparable candidacies, are the four more spectacular cases of Conservative decline sufficient to lose seats previously held by the Government. But these, even if they could be compared, would not necessarily show greater decreases in Conservative voting percentages. They simply happened to be in marginal constituencies where Conservative decreases usual in the 1956–8 slump would

TABLE 6

Three groups of by-elections of 1955–59 in which results can be compared with 1955 general election

Group	Ave. (mean) Conservative loss in percentage of poll
Eight by-elections from 7 Dec. 1955 to 27 Sept. 1956 .	−4·4
Eight by-elections from 15 Nov. 1956 to 28 Nov. 1957 .	−6·2
Ten by-elections from 13 June 1958 to 18 June 1959 .	−3·6

cause loss of the seat. Certainly this seems applicable to the one Conservative loss of seat that occurred in the year after Suez. The constituency was Lewisham North, in whose by-election of 15 February 1957 the Conservative percentage dropped from 54 to 46·5, with an Independent Loyalist capturing 4 per cent (mainly, it can be assumed, former Conservative voters),[1] as against the Labour increase from 46 per cent to 49·5 per cent. If the Loyalist vote is added to the 1957 Conservative total, then the party's loss is less than usual before and after Suez. And even without thus treating the Loyalist vote, the Conservative percentage loss of 7·5 percentage points is lower than the loss in three pre-Suez by-elections. In so far as the Lewisham North loss has been attributed to any specific issue, it was not Suez but rent control, just then being reduced by the Conservative Government, that claimed the most attention.

Despite an obligatory uncertainty, it can be said that neither B.I.P.O. nor by-election data have established that the Conservative political cause suffered from Suez. Nor can it be proved that the

---

[1] The Loyalist candidacy represented an imperialist rebellion against the Government partly because of its withdrawal from Suez, certainly not because of its earlier intervention.

party's cause was helped even though the polls do show that the Suez action gained in popularity in the year after the event. What is more definite and also more significant is that the Suez action became, during the crisis, a distinctively partisan issue for the voters, as it was for party activists and for M.P.s. It did not start so much that way for the voters, but it so developed and then largely remained an issue dividing voters according to their party preferences. The likelihood is that these party preferences, existing first, determined the voters' responses to Eden's military action. The available data, however, do not clearly carry this message, and it is possible that some party preferences were fixed by attitudes towards Suez rather than the other way around.[1] A heavily partisan division was the result in any case.

[1] The high degree of coincidence between party voting and foreign policy views may be compared with American findings concerning this relationship. George Belknap and Angus Campbell, 'Political Party Identification and Attitudes Toward Foreign Policy', *Public Opinion Quarterly*, vol. 15 (Winter 1951–2), pp. 601–23, and Warren E. Miller, 'The Socio-Economic Analysis of Political Behavior', *Midwest Journal of Political Science*, vol. 2 (August 1958), pp. 239–55. The latter, in particular, appears at odds with the British data on Suez, since Miller found that foreign policy positions were not associated with partisan affiliation.

THE POLITICAL IDEAS OF ENGLISH PARTY ACTIVISTS

By RICHARD ROSE

ANNUAL party conferences are one of the chief channels
through which rank-and-file party workers can make their
views known to party leaders. Discussions of the role that
party conferences ought to play in making party politics
have often assumed that the views presented there are extremist. The following article is an attempt to provide evidence about the views of the party activists by analysing the
resolutions put forward by constituency parties to the annual
conferences of the Conservative and Labour Parties. On the
basis of this intensive analysis of conference resolutions, the
author is able to refute and reformulate propositions about
the opinions and motivations of the party workers who constitute a link between national politicians and those who only
vote for a party.

IF a democracy is to function successfully, the great mass of the
population need instruments for communicating their views to
political leaders. The chief channels for communication are parties
and pressure groups. English politics provides much scope for study
of these conduits, because both parties and pressure groups are
highly organized and well articulated. Although the part played by
party activists in policy formulation is only one small aspect of this
network, the study of that part throws considerable light upon the
interplay of parties and pressure groups, and challenges as well some
prevailing notions about the policy demands of party activists.

Party activists in Britain have only comparatively recently been
regarded as potentially capable of participating in discussions of
public policy. Both the Conservatives and Liberals originated as
small coteries of parliamentary notables who controlled, or were independent of rank-and-file party workers. Writing in 1908, A.
Lawrence Lowell characterized the two party organizations as
shams — the Liberals, with their formal devices for rank-and-file
policy-making as an opaque sham, and the Conservatives as

Reprinted from the *American Political Science Review*, vol. lvi, no. 2 (1962), pp.
360–71.

transparent shams.[1] He noted that in 1903 Conservative Party members were so deferential that when the Cabinet was split on tariff reform the annual membership conference 'shrank from saying what it thought'. Both Conservative and Liberal parties have maintained this aloofness from activists in matters of policy discussion up to the present day. The official report on Conservative Party reorganization prepared after the 1945 debacle noted that the size of the annual party conference made it 'a demonstration of strength and enthusiasm' and made impossible 'the more intimate circumstances necessary to thoughtful debate'.[2] Since the farcical intervention of activists in policy-making at the 1958 Liberal Assembly, Jo Grimond has successfully emphasized the need to keep Liberal policy-making in the hands of a small circle.

The Labour Party, in theory and to some extent in practice, has always stood for participation by rank-and-file party members in policy-making. A current party pamphlet states: 'The right to a voice in determining policy is important to any member . . . The individual member has a chance to use the machinery of the party to secure support for ideas on every aspect of party politics.'[3] In recent years a harassed Labour leadership has begun to stress Robert T. McKenzie's thesis that it is unconstitutional for party members to make policy to which M.P.s are bound, because M.P.s must be responsible to those who elect them and not to that allegedly unrepresentative fraction who constitute active party members. The Labour leadership is reverting to the Burkean position maintained by many Conservatives, that an M.P. owes his constituency party supporters nothing more than his informed and independent judgement.[4] Except for Ralph Miliband, who has argued that the influence of the active Labour minority should not be reduced because of the apathy of the majority,[5] there is a consensus among

[1] A. L. Lowell, *The Government of England* (London, 1921 ed.), vol. i, pp. 578, 584. See also M. Ostrogorski, *Democracy and the Organization of Political Parties* (London, 1902), vol. i, pp. 161 ff.; J. L. Garvin, *The Life of Joseph Chamberlain* (London, 1932), vol. i, chap. 14; W. S. Churchill, *Lord Randolph Churchill* (London, 1906), esp. chaps. 6–8.

[2] *Final Report of the Committee on Party Organization* (National Union, London, 1949), p. 27.

[3] S. Barker, *How the Labour Party Works* (London, 1955), p. 6.

[4] See R. T. McKenzie, *British Political Parties* (London, 1955), esp. chaps. 1, 10; *Report of the Fifty-Ninth Annual Conference of the Labour Party* (London, 1960), pp. 159 ff., and Morgan Phillips's *Memorandum on the Constitution of the Labour Party* (London, 1960).

[5] 'Party Democracy and Parliamentary Government,' *Political Studies*, vol. vi (1958), pp. 170–4. Wilfrid Fienburgh, then research secretary of the Labour Party, implicitly took this position in 'Put Policy on the Agenda,' *Fabian Journal*, no. vi (1952), pp. 25–27.

students of British politics that party activists cannot and should not make party policy, or even influence it greatly.

It does not follow, however, that the views of party activists are of no interest. There are several reasons for analysing them. First, activists may be mobilized to support a faction within the *élite* when there occurs what Michels treated as 'The Struggle Among the Leadership Themselves'.[1] Sometimes, a section of the counter-*élite* and of the activists appear to work together and respond to a common stimulus. Secondly, activists are a major channel of communication between M.P.s and party leaders and the electorate at large. Thirdly, they are presumed to be the last stronghold of ideologues within the party system. Last but hardly least, there has never been any systematic study of the policy views of activists in Britain, although there has been no lack of generalizing on this subject.

Many students of political parties, most notably Duverger, have claimed that the views of activists differ significantly from those of most party voters; hence, the description of an activist as a militant.[2] (American experience would suggest that many active party workers are far from being ideologically militant, but this has not until recently been thought relevant to European politics.) Such leading writers on British politics as Bagehot, Lowell, and McKenzie have also argued this with reference to Britain.[3] Leon Epstein has explained the alleged extremist views of these activists as follows:

> The voluntary and amateur nature of these associations ensures that they attract zealots in the party cause, and particularly so at the local leadership level, where there are many routine political chores which only the devoted are likely to perform. Principles, not professional careers, are what matter here.[4]

Nigel Nicolson, the victim while a Conservative M.P. of a constituency association which disowned him because of his centrist views, has argued that the extremist outlook of activists threatens to en-

---

[1] *Political Parties* (Dover ed., New York, 1959), p. 164 ff. McKenzie ignores this phenomenon.
[2] *Political Parties* (London, 1954), p. 101 ff. Cf. A. Leiserson, *Parties and Politics* (New York, 1958), pp. 191, 274.
[3] Bagehot, quoted in N. Nicolson, *People and Parliament* (London, 1958), p. 166; A. L. Lowell, *Public Opinion and Popular Government* (New York, 1914), p. 92; R. T. McKenzie, op. cit., pp. 196–7, 506. See also T. E. M. McKitterick, 'The Membership of the [Labour] Party,' *Political Quarterly*, vol. xxxi (1960), p. 316 ff.
[4] 'British M.P.s and their Local Parties: The Suez Case,' *American Political Science Review*, vol. liv (1960), p. 385. Epstein wrongly suggests that rank-and-file extremism strengthens the position of party leaders. This is because he generalizes from the extremist position of the leadership on Suez; the instance is, however, exceptional.

danger parliamentary government, because Parliament is losing power to Cabinet and Cabinet is dominated by party. Nicolson claims that parliamentary leaders rightly see problems in terms of 'the intrusive grey', whereas activists see things in black and white terms. Political activity only intensifies their militant beliefs. Hence, in the constituencies, warfare between the parties is 'a grim reality'.[1]

To use the terminology of Martin Lipset in *Political Man*, the influence of activists in party policy-making is said to give heavy emphasis to ideological cleavage without a compensating statement of consensus, whereas both the theory and practice of British government value consensus much more than cleavage. It is theoretically possible that constituency parties may act as a safety valve through which extremist pressures escape, but this argument has not been advanced. It is the crux of Nicolson's case that the steam being generated by extreme-minded activists threatens to scald the engine-drivers of democracy and endanger all the passengers.

I

Party activists have the same formal method of influencing policy in both parties — sending resolutions to the annual party conferences.[2] This is not sufficient proof of policy concern, but it is almost certainly a necessary condition which activists must meet if they wish their views to be considered by the national party leadership. The other major channel — lobbying one's M.P. — is informal and indirect. Furthermore, half the constituencies have an M.P. from the opposition party. There are no inhibitions surrounding conference resolutions. If anything, there is an expectation that resolutions will be used by extremists to voice complaints to and about leaders.

The circumstances in which policy resolutions are drafted, debated, and approved differ widely from constituency to constituency. Resolutions are likely to originate in committee meetings of local parties; alternatively, suggestions or amendments may be made at party meetings, where attendance will invariably be only a small fraction of a constituency party's membership, and an extremely small fraction of the party vote in the constituency.[3] Thus,

[1] N. Nicolson, op. cit., p. 169. His fear is not new. Cf. Ostrogorski, op. cit., vol. i, p. 493 ff.

[2] See S. Barker, op. cit., p. 7 ff.; *Party Organization* (Conservative and Unionist Central Office, London, 1961), p. 23 ff.; R. T. McKenzie, op. cit., pp. 231–58, 532–46.

[3] Cf. reports of low participation by trade unionists in discussions of union policy, in B. C. Roberts, *Trade Union Government and Administration in Great Britain* (London,

the method and setting facilitate domination by a small group determined to foster a particular set of ideas. The extent to which policy is discussed in local parties appears to vary considerably.[1] Motives for tabling resolutions may be mixed and several. Expressions of opinion may spontaneously originate within the local caucus from concern with an immediate event in the news. M.P.s or candidates may stimulate resolutions favouring views they wish to advance. Sometimes resolutions are presented in efforts to gain publicity, either for the local party or for the person who may be chosen to move it in a hall crowded with delegates.

The resolutions analysed herein are those submitted to Conservative and Labour annual party conferences from 1955 to 1960 inclusive. No list of resolutions was published for the cancelled 1959 Conservative conference. The omission of one year's total from the sample is offset by the fact that there is no limit on the number of resolutions which a Conservative constituency may forward. In the Labour Party, a constituency normally may send only one resolution, and occasionally an amendment. Because of alterations to constituency boundaries prior to the 1955 election, the analysis could not be accurately carried farther back in time.

Each resolution has been assigned to one of four categories — Right, Left, Partisan, or Non-partisan. Resolutions in the first three categories contain a distinctive element of partisan ideology; those in the last tend to reflect pressure group concerns or general cultural values not integrally a part of party ideology. The definitions follow, with examples taken from conference programmes.

Partisan

Enunciation of an agreed party policy which is opposed to that of the other party and which has an ideological basis.

Conservative example: 'That this Conference congratulates the Government on its economic policy, which has resulted in full employment, stable prices and the highest standard of living in our history, but urges the removal of the many impediments still hindering the spread of ownership throughout the community.' (No. 177, 1960)

Other favoured Conservative themes include: requests for maximum economy in public expenditure, denunciation of further

---

1956), p. 95 ff.; M. Harrison, *Trade Unions and the Labour Party Since 1945* (London, 1960), chap. 3.

[1] Cf. D. V. Donnison and D. E. G. Plowman, 'The Functions of Local Labour Parties', *Political Studies*, vol. ii (1954), p. 156 ff.; A. H. Birch, *Small-Town Politics* (Oxford, 1959), p. 44 ff.

nationalization, protection of property rights in land compulsorily acquired by the State, support for the Commonwealth, and approval of the tripartite divisions of secondary education.

Labour example: 'This Conference believes that a substantial measure of public ownership is essential for the nation's well-being. It therefore instructs the NEC to prepare for presentation to the 1961 Annual Conference a practical programme of public ownership for the next Labour Government, based on the needs of the economy, workers and consumers' interests.' (No. 203, 1960)

Labour resolutions in this category often deal with: world disarmament through the United Nations, support for colonial freedom and attacks upon the Conservative colonial policy, attacks upon advertising, the need for economic planning and controls, demands for an end to profiteering in land prices, and support for a comprehensive secondary education system.

Non-partisan

Enunciation of a policy which is not the subject of controversy along party lines, either because it reflects the views of pressure groups working within both parties or because it is generally regarded as desirable within the culture. A non-partisan resolution is not necessarily non-political.

Conservative example: 'That this Conference is of the opinion that in view of the statement made at the time of the General Election that old age pensioners were to share in the prosperity of the country, an increase in their pensions should now be made.' (No. 126, 1960)

Other popular themes for non-party resolutions at Conservative conferences include: assistance for particular industries or for agriculture, calls for more teachers and smaller class sizes, demands for more roads and safer roads, tax relief for home-owners, changes to strengthen local government in its work, changes in electoral law to simplify the job of party workers, and improvements in party organization.[1]

Labour example: 'This Conference urges the Government to grant an immediate increase for old age pensioners.' (No. 344, 1960)

Among a welter of Labour themes that were basically non-ideological were: assistance for shipbuilding, coal, other industries

[1] Resolutions dealing with the mechanics of party organization have been scored non-partisan because they show bureaucratic rather than ideological concerns. Interestingly, a number of resolutions ostensibly dealing with party principles are also non-ideological. They simply stress the need for unity on principle, or promoting principles, without any indication of which particular principles (if any) should be emphasized.

and for agriculture, calls for more teachers and smaller class sizes, requests for more hospitals and removal of alleged anomalies in welfare services, changes to strengthen local government in its work, more roads and safer roads, better railway services, and relief of the housing shortage and need for slum clearance.

Right-wing Conservative

A policy statement which calls for widening the gap between the two parties through adoption of a reactionary variant of party policy.

Example: 'That in the opinion of this Conference the monopoly of omnibus transport in large cities and towns should be abolished and that responsible operators be allowed to compete, thereby giving the public a better service.' (No. 48, 1960)

Right-wing Conservatives concentrate upon: pleas for weakening taxes which tend to redistribute income, requests for laws to curb trade unions and strikers, demands for a return to flogging and heavy reliance upon capital punishment to fight crime, the absolute reduction of government spending and services, the denationalization of various industries, and reducing benefits available through welfare services.

Left-wing Labour

A statement calling for a radical transformation of the domestic mixed economy welfare state, or of the existing system of international relations, in order to make the breakthrough to a Socialist society. Such statements are usually out of harmony with the declared policy of the leadership.

Example: 'This Conference instructs the National Executive Committee to appoint a sub-committee to investigate and report to the 1961 Annual Conference the most practical way in which all the means of production, distribution and exchange can be brought under public ownership, ensuring that the workers and consumers alike can participate in the management of each industry.' (No. 206, 1960)

Under this heading come resolutions: asking for unilateral nuclear disarmament, demanding large-scale extension of nationalization and/or workers' control, reaffirming Socialist principles in terms of root-and-branch rejection of a capitalist-influenced society, and those calling for compulsory closure of the public boarding schools.

Left-wing Conservative/Right-wing Labour

Statements of policy which deviate so markedly from conference policy that they tend to be in harmony with the policies of the opposing party.

Conservative example: 'That this Conference requests the Minister of Housing and Local Government to examine the position of the tenants of furnished accommodation with a view to introducing legislation to guarantee an adequate standard of furnishings and fittings, and a reasonable security of tenure.' (No. 331, 1960)

Labour example: 'This Conference moves that the Labour Party, being a social and democratic movement, seeks to determine by means of a social-political survey, such questions as the image of the party in the minds of the electorate, their social habits and background, and their wishes concerning the fundamental issues of the day, with the aim of studying the results of such an enquiry and deciding to what extent they should influence future party policy.' (No. 424, 1960)

The number of these resolutions is so few that one cannot generalize much. In the Conservative Party, left-wing resolutions seemed to come either from constituency parties in working-class areas, which voiced Labour-inclined views on social services and economic policy, or from constituencies where progressive Conservatives had some sympathies with Labour's overseas policy. Labour deviation seemed largely motivated by a desire to repudiate traditional Socialist ideology, with an occasional repudiation resulting in virtual alignment with Conservative positions.

Any system of categorizing data is open to criticism. The headings here employed have been designed to group together views which signify, either explicitly or by their nuance, association with one or another faction within the two parties. This is the standard used by many speakers on resolutions at party conferences, who discuss them in terms of left/right tendencies, and the same standard is characteristically employed in descriptions of conference debates by journalists.

II

The analysis immediately reveals that the description of local parties as a force constantly pressing extremist views upon national party leaders is false. The total proportion of ideological (i.e., left-wing, right-wing, and partisan) resolutions is 54 per cent; those which are non-ideological constitute 46 per cent of the total (Table 1a). In other words, constituency parties are nearly as apt to be

voicing views derived from general cultural values or from interest group links as they are to voice those clearly associated with a
partisan ideology.

When the scores are analysed according to parties, one finds that

TABLE 1a

Total scores for all constituency resolutions

Type	No.	%
Extremist (Rt., Con.; Left, Lab.) .	1398	30
Partisan (Con. and Lab.) . .	1013	22
Misplaced partisanship (Left, Con.; Rt., Lab.)	97	2
Non-partisan (Con. and Lab.) .	2090	46
TOTALS	4598	100

TABLE 1b

*Total scores of Conservative constituency resolutions**

Year	Right	Partisan	Left	Non-Partisan	Total
1955	50	52	17	173	292
1956	137	109	10	137	393
1957	130	60	6	216	412
1958	90	141	12	204	447
1959	(No resolutions published)				
1960	98	41	17	259	415
Totals No.	505	403	62	989	1959
Per cent	26	21	3	50	100

* This table, like 1a and 5a, includes resolutions filed by Welsh constituency
parties and minor federated bodies, as well as those from English parties. Welsh
resolutions are omitted from all other calculations because the party system there is
not quite the same as in England; minor parties are twice as strong. The federated
bodies are omitted because they are not comparable to Labour ones. Omitted
groups have similar scores to those fully analysed. Scotland and Northern Ireland
are not included in any Conservative tabulations, because these parties are separate
and have their own conferences.

the Conservatives are more inclined to press non-partisan resolutions on their leaders than are Labour constituencies. But the
differences are not great and Labour parties do not show strong
partisanship; 42 per cent of their resolutions are non-partisan, compared with 50 per cent of Conservative ones (Table 1b, 1c). The

U

variation in the number and orientation of resolutions from year to year appears to reflect the temper of the times. A party's adversity would seem to stimulate extremist views.

An analysis of the number of resolutions submitted by individual constituency parties reveals the existence of wide variations in concern with policy. Approximately one-third of Conservative constituency parties did not present a single resolution in the five-year period studied; only 26 per cent forwarded an average of one resolu-

TABLE 1c

Total scores of Labour constituency resolutions*

Year	Left	Partisan	Right	Non-Partisan	Total
1955	123	98	5	198	424
1956	109	119	5	169	402
1957	127	140	4	172	443
1958	173	89	6	160	428
1959	152	73	3	186	414
1960	209	91	12	216	528
Totals No.	893	610	35	1101	2639
Per cent	34	23	1	42	100

* This table, like 1a and 5b, includes resolutions from Welsh and Scottish constituency parties, and from trade unions and other affiliated bodies. There is no significant variation in scores as between those groups fully analysed and those omitted elsewhere.

tion or more a year (Table 2a). This disinterest in pressing policy views cannot be attributed to poor party organization, because virtually all English Conservative constituencies are sufficiently well organized to have a full-time party agent. It may well be related to the deferential relationship which exists, socially as well as politically, between party leaders and members. Balfour is reported to have said that he would as soon take orders from his valet as from a Conservative Party annual conference.[1] Perhaps some party members would equally regard it as wrong to depart from the obligations of their station in life.

In the Labour Party, concern with matters of policy is more widely diffused, as one might expect from a party which has always boasted of its ideological basis. The gap between individual constituency parties is not so great, because of the limit of one resolution

[1] Quoted in McKenzie, op. cit., p. 82. See also Earl Balfour, *Chapters of Autobiography* (London, 1930), p. 158 ff.

TABLE 2a

Frequency distribution of resolutions filed by Conservative constituency parties

No. of resolutions	No. of parties*	% of all parties	Cumulative percentage†
0	165	32	32
1	90	18	50
2	49	10	60
3	42	8	68
4	29	6	74
5	23	5	79
6	22	4	83
7	14	3	86
8	15	3	89
9	12	2	91
10	7	1	92
11–20	33	6	98
21–30	4	0·8	98·8
31–40	3	0·6	99·4
46	1	0·2	99·6

* Bolton West and Huddersfield West are omitted from this and subsequent calculations because they do not nominate parliamentary candidates, standing aside in favour of the Liberals.

† Percentages do not add up to 100 because of rounding off.

TABLE 2b

Frequency distribution of resolutions filed by Labour constituency parties

No. of resolutions	No. of parties	% of all parties	Cumulative percentage*
0	28	6	6
1	48	9	15
2	62	12	27
3	72	14	41
4	94	18	59
5	102	20	79
6	96	19	98
7	7	1·4	99·4
8	2	0·4	99·8

* Percentages do not add up to 100 because of rounding off.

and one amendment for each party at each conference (Table 2b). Although the Labour Party has more constituencies which will sometimes file a resolution, there is little difference in terms of heavy activity, in so far as different regulations permit of comparison. Among Conservative constituencies, 74 per cent file resolutions less than once a year on average; in the Labour Party, the proportion is 79 per cent.

Concern with questions of policy is not the same as partisanship. In order to isolate those constituencies which reflected particularly strong partisanship, the groups were divided into four categories, according to the extent to which they varied from the average party score. In the Conservative table, partisan views are those scored right or partisan; in the Labour table, those scored left or partisan.

TABLE 3a

Partisanship in Conservative constituency parties*

Category	No.	%
No partisan resolutions . . .	164	35
Low (1–34%) partisanship . .	113	24
Average (35–64%) partisanship .	120	26
High (65% or more) partisanship . .	71	15

* Constituencies which submitted only one resolution in the period, and that one partisan, have been omitted, because this was regarded as insufficient evidence for categorization.

TABLE 3b

Partisanship in Labour constituency parties*

Category	No.	%
No partisan resolutions . . .	88	18
Low (12·5–40%) partisanship . .	83	17
Average (41–75%) partisanship† .	208	42
High (above 75%) partisanship .	113	23

* Constituencies presenting only one resolution, and that partisan, have been omitted from this table.

† This category is not as large as it appears, for only seven parties could have scored between 41–49·9 per cent.

From this we find (Tables 3a, 3b) that the proportion of constituency parties which regularly press partisan views is less than one-quarter in each party. There is a skewed distribution among the Conservatives, for 59 per cent of the constituencies show less than average partisanship. Absence of partisanship does not, of course, mean absence of ideological commitments; it is evidence that parties so labelled are little interested in advocating ideological views. There is more interest in proclaiming partisan views in the Labour parties.

The incidence of ideological partisanship is certainly no cause for concern; few could criticize party activists for pressing party policy upon their leaders, when the leaders accept the ideas, as well as many voters. Ideological extremism is a far greater force for social cleavage, but it is extremely limited in both parties (Tables 4a, 4b). Even though the definition of high extremism in the Conservative Party does not require a constituency to express extremist views as much as half the time, only 11 per cent qualify for that appella-

TABLE 4a

Extremism in Conservative parties*

Category	No.	%
No extremist resolutions . .	314	66
Low (1–16·5%) extremism . .	20	4
Average (16·6–37·4%) extremism .	92	19
High extremism (37·5% or more) .	52†	11

* Those constituencies submitting one extremist resolution and filing only one or two in the period are omitted.

† Consists of 24 parties submitting up to 5 resolutions each in the period and 28 parties submitting more than 5 resolutions each in the period.

TABLE 4b

Extremism in Labour parties*

Category	No.	%
No extremist resolutions . .	191	38
Low extremism (20% or less) . .	47	9
Average (25–50%) extremism .	172	35
High (above 50%) extremism .	87	18

* Those constituencies submitting only one resolution, and that extremist, have not been categorized.

tion — and only 6 per cent are both extremist and quite active in pressing views. Although more Labour constituencies are extremist than Conservative, they form only 18 per cent of the total. The median Labour constituency will only forward one extremist resolution in a six-year period, and the median Conservative one will not even forward a single extremist resolution in a five-year period.

The foregoing tables indicate that party workers on opposite sides of the political fence are not so partisan as electoral contests suggest, and not so extremist as some theorists suggest. A breakdown of resolutions by subject matter and by policy orientation

provides a list of areas of common agreement within both parties
(Tables 5a, 5b). A notable feature of Conservative resolutions is
concentration upon domestic issues, notwithstanding the importance
of international affairs to the Government and to the electorate.
Only 3 per cent of resolutions concerned foreign policy and defence
questions, compared to 29 per cent in the Labour Party. The latter
devotes less attention to politically important domestic questions.

TABLE 5a

Topics for Conservative resolutions

Topic	Right	Partisan	Left	Non-Partisan	Total
Economic affairs . .	121	142	28	64	355
Housing . . .	22	35	4	107	168
Industrial relations . .	73	37	7	16	133
Party organization . .	5	8	3	112	128
Education . . .	33	18	2	72	125
Pensions . . .	6	2	..	104	112
Taxes	56	17	..	29	102
Compulsory purchase .	16	79	..	4	99
Crime	63	13	4	11	91
Transportation . .	5	1	..	82	88
Election law . . .	..	..	..	85	85
Commonwealth; colonies .	31	14	4	7	56
Local government . .	..	..	..	51	51
Welfare services . .	21	..	..	29	50
Agriculture . . .	5	..	..	42	47
Foreign policy . .	6	16	5	5	32
Defence . . .	1	18	2	7	28
Immigration . . .	21	..	..	..	21
Party principles . .	9	2	..	6	17
Miscellaneous . . .	11	1	3	156	171

The virtual absence in both parties of expressions on highly ex-
plosive racial, religious, and constitutional questions should not be
overlooked.

Analysis by topics suggests that the partisanship and extremism of
party activists is not so strong in several fields as the pull of interest
group or general cultural standards.[1] In four areas of public concern
— education, welfare services, transport, and pensions — partisan
standards are applied less than half the time by activists in both
parties. When facing these questions they may ask for 'more
schools' or 'higher pensions'; this is a cry of beneficiaries and bene-

[1] Cf. S. H. Beer, 'Pressure Groups and Parties in Britain', *American Political
Science Review*, vol. 1 (1956), pp. 1–23.

factors, not of ideologues. This non-party emphasis is the more striking because there are clear ideological differences between the parties on education, welfare, and transport. For instance, although the method of organizing secondary education is a point of sharp difference between the parties and affects the whole electorate, 64 per cent of Labour resolutions and 56 per cent of Conservative ones steer clear of all partisan controversy on education. The proportion of ideological resolutions rises in areas of economic policy, where interest group and ideological standards are likely to be the same for most activists; partisan ideology is thus intensified. For instance, all of the 19 Labour resolutions on industrial relations were partisan,

TABLE 5b

Topics for Labour resolutions

Topic	Left	Partisan	Right	Non-Partisan	Total
Foreign policy, defence .	594	145	14	20	773
Economic affairs . .	117	141	10	188	456
Housing and land . .	10	85	..	80	175
Party organization . .	14	4	1	130	149
Pensions . . .	2	1	..	143	146
Welfare services . .	7	31	..	94	132
Education . . .	17	19	..	64	100
Commonwealth; colonies .	8	82	3	1	94
Local government . .	7	43	..	44	94
Socialist principles . .	57	15	2	5	79
Transportation . .	4	3	..	56	63
Party unity . . .	18	2	1	31	52
Industrial relations . .	6	13	..	..	19
Miscellaneous. . .	32	26	4	245	307

and only 12 per cent of the 133 Conservative resolutions on this topic were non-partisan.

Some activists appear more concerned with the mechanics of party organization than with party policy. This shows in Conservative resolutions on party structure and on election law, and in organizational resolutions in the Labour Party, and resolutions asking for party unity — without any sign of preference concerning the programme upon which unity should be based.

III

Examination of conference resolutions has shown that constituency parties differ considerably in their political attitudes. The question is then raised: Do they differ in relation to other measurable social or

political factors? Unfortunately, the data available for cross-
tabulation is strictly limited,[1] but sufficient exists to test several
important hypotheses.

One hypothesis concerns the relationship between party strength
and attitudes of activists. It has been argued[2] that in areas where
the strength of both parties is nearly equal, policies will tend to
converge. In safe seats, extremist policies may be more readily
found. The most important index of party strength is the margin by
which a constituency is won or lost at the general election. A safe
seat may conveniently be defined as one in which the winner had a
majority of more than 10 per cent; a marginal seat as one in which
the majority is less than that; and a hopeless seat one as in which a
candidate lost by more than 10 per cent.[3] Nearly 85 per cent of
English seats were the same, safe, marginal or hopeless, at both
1955 and 1959 elections. In what follows only these three major
groups are discussed, because the numbers in the others are so small
as to be of negligible significance. Safe Labour seats may be assumed
to be heavily working-class; safe Conservative seats are likely to be
disproportionately middle class, though manual workers may still
form a numerical majority in the constituency. It is probable that
these differences in turn are reflected in the composition of party
activists in different areas, although there is no conclusive evidence
on this point.

The analysis shows no relation between partisanship in policy
outlook and safety of seat in Conservative constituencies, and only a
limited relationship in the Labour Party (Tables 6a, 6b). In both
parties there is a clear but strictly limited relationship between
ideological extremism and electoral support. In the Conservative
Party, safe seats display on average 9·1 per cent more extremist
resolutions than hopeless seats. In the Labour Party, hopeless seats
adopt 9·2 per cent more extremist resolutions than safe seats. A
further check was made to test this finding because of its importance.
Constituency parties were divided according to degrees of partisanship and extremism, as in Tables 3a–b, 4a–b, to see whether each
group had a fair cross-section of parties with strong, medium, and
weak electoral support. This was the case.

In both parties the variation between these two factors was of the

[1] For instance, census data cannot be related to parliamentary constituencies
because of boundary differences.
[2] E.g., Sir Ivor Jennings, *The Queen's Government* (Harmondsworth, 1960), pp.
60–1.
[3] On electoral swing and margins of victory, see D. E. Butler, *The British General
Election of 1955* (London, 1955), p. 202 ff.; D. E. Butler and Richard Rose, *The
British General Election of 1959* (London, 1960), p. 236.

order of one resolution in ten. But it takes a Conservative constituency party on average about fourteen years to submit ten resolutions, and a Labour party about twelve years. The major conclusion must be that policy views are randomly distributed among constituency parties without regard to their electoral strength, for the statistical differences are of negligible political significance. One may note but hardly stress that parties in the most markedly middle-class

TABLE 6a

Partisanship, extremism, and electoral support for Conservative constituency parties

Category	No. of seats	Total Reso- lutions	% Parti- san	% Ex- treme
Safe . .	213	788	48·4	29·3
Marginal .	123	512	49·8	25·0
Hopeless .	110	193	49·7	20·2

TABLE 6b

Partisanship, extremism, and electoral support for Labour constituency parties

Category	No. of seats	Total Reso- lutions	% Parti- san	% Ex- treme
Safe . .	110	383	50·6	28·2
Marginal .	123	462	55·2	32·7
Hopeless .	217	829	60·0	37·4

areas are slightly more extremist on both sides than in working-class areas.

The author began his investigation with the hypothesis that the smaller a constituency party's membership, the higher the incidence of extremism. This was based upon the assumption that the number of extremist party supporters is very small, and that they could more easily dominate a small party. This hypothesis could only be tested for the Labour Party. There are 140 English parties which affiliate to headquarters on the minimum membership of 800; the extremism score for this group averaged 36 per cent. For the 61 parties with above average memberships ranging from 2,000 to 3,000, the extremism score averaged 34 per cent; for the 35 parties reporting membership above 3,000, the figure was 30 per cent. Similarly, parties with high extremism scores average 22 party members for every 1,000 electors, compared to a figure of 26 for those with average scores, and 25 for those with no extremist resolutions. The differences are hardly of a size to lend much support to the hypo-thesis.

Constituency parties may also seek to influence policy by pressing M.P.s or prospective candidates to act as spokesmen for the local party caucus. Candidates are selected by small groups representing less than 1 per cent of the electorate, and these nominations cannot be effectively challenged. In a normal election, nomination is tantamount to election in at least three-quarters of the constituencies; nomination is virtually tantamount to election for life in upwards of half the constituencies. Most students of British politics have com-mented upon the failure of constituency parties to exercise their considerable potential powers over candidates in such a way as to produce M.P.s with views like their own.[1] This generalization needs testing by reference to extremism scores because these writers have usually assumed that constituency selection committees are dominated by extremists. The wide range of opinion within both parliamentary parties might reflect an absence of policy concern in the selection process — or it might reflect a tendency for constitu-ency parties to adopt candidates with views compatible with their own.

The emergence of unilateral nuclear disarmament as a major factional issue within the Labour Party provides one test for the coincidence between extremism in candidates and in parties. We find that there is some relationship between extremism in a constituency party and a candidate who is extreme on this issue. Parties showing high extremism constitute 18 per cent of all local parties, but 29 per cent of those nominating unilateralist candidates. Unilateralist candidates are least likely to be found where extremism is low or non-existent (Table 7). Like many statistical findings, this one is only important if it is an indication of a trend. Further checks showed no tendency for unilateralist candidates to be nominated particularly for hopeless seats, nor were they especially favoured in the adoption of new candidates. Counter-balancing this absence of association was the tendency of constituencies with trade-union sponsored can-didates to score below average on extremism. Of 102 constituencies categorized, only 5 per cent were extremist, and 55 per cent had submitted no extremist resolutions in the period.

A similarly meaningful issue was not available for testing Con-

---

[1] See especially John Biffen, 'The Constituency Leaders', *Crossbow*, vol. iv. no. 13 (1960), p. 30.

servative M.P.s. A rundown of the 16 Conservative M.P.s who took
extremist positions on the Suez affair showed that two-thirds of their
constituency parties scored below average on extremism. A check
was made on Conservative parties which had Privy Councillors as
M.P.s; it was assumed that the responsibility of these M.P.s, and
their closer identification with generally moderate government
policies, would damp down party extremism. In fact, the distribution of extremism scores among the 46 parties categorized was virtually identical with the distribution for all Conservative constituency parties. The most significant relationship found had on the

TABLE 7

*Extremism and the nomination of unilateralist candidates
by constituency Labour parties*

Category*	No. Candi- dates	No. Unilat- eralist	% Unilat- eralist
No extremism.	191	14	7
Low extremism	47	5	11
Average extremism	172	31	18
High extremism	87	20	23
TOTALS	497	70	14

* Constituency parties submitting only one resolution, and that one extremist,
have not been categorized.

face of it no connection with policy. It was that safe Conservative
seats choose 84 per cent of their candidates from those with expen-
sive public school educations, and only 31 per cent of the time take
men with local connections. In hopeless seats, only 44 per cent have
been at public schools, and 60 per cent of candidates have local
connections. Marginal seats fall between these two groups. (No
such pattern exists in the Labour Party). One might speculate that
the return of members of a national social-political *élite* by safe
constituencies tends to increase the independence of M.P.s from
constituency parties, for such persons are more likely to be independently minded, or influenced by a national peer group, than
to submit to pressure from lower status activists.

IV

The fundamental conclusion which arises from this study is that
attitudes on questions of policy are randomly distributed among

constituency parties and, it may be tentatively assumed, among party activists as well. One cause of the diversity would appear to be the plurality of motives leading individuals to become active in party politics, together with the plurality of functions which local parties may perform.[1] The following list of motives is not exhaustive, nor is any particular one meant to exclude the operation of others within the same individual.

Motives for volunteer political work

A. Overtly political
    Desire to advance party programme
    Desire to modify party programme to bring it more into line with one's own ideological beliefs
    Desire to modify party programme to bring it more into line with the programme of one's interest group
    Local government concerns
    Sense of civic duty
    Ex officio involvement — e.g. as trade union official.

B. Non-political
    Occupational careerism
    Status seeking
    Gratification of desire for power
    Pleasure from group activities
    Pleasure from a 'sporting' contest
    Friendship with active party workers.

The functions which constituency parties fulfil are also numerous. Some have a bearing on national party policy, but others do not:

Functions of English constituency parties

Propagate national party policy
Advise upon national party policy
Organize and conduct election contests
Nominate parliamentary candidates
Manage local government affairs
Act as pressure group for local interests
Provide social facilities for the community
Finance and maintain local party office

An immediate consequence of this diversity is the flexibility which it gives to party leaders. At annual party conferences leaders are not

[1] A. Leiserson, op. cit., is notable for the allowance he makes for diversity. See also Robert E. Lane, *Political Life* (Glencoe, 1959), for much evidence on motives for political participation.

faced with a mass of extreme-minded activists, demanding the adoption of socially divisive policies as the price of continuing to do menial work.[1] Opposition comes from only a fraction of the rank and file. Another portion is likely to support the leadership and a significant group may have no clear views, or even interest, in questions of party policy. In such circumstances support of the rank and file assembly may be gained simply by giving a clear policy lead. Lacking firm anchorage in an ideological position, constituency parties may be willing to trust their leaders wherever they lead. The pressure from above, the effect as it were of the gardener's lawn-mower upon the grass roots activists, is considerable. The classic illustration occurred when the Conservative Government was able to keep the party virtually united behind it when it unexpectedly attacked Egypt, and again when it abruptly accepted a cease-fire there in 1956. This flexibility is less in the Labour Party; a small contributing factor is the greater attachment which activists have to ideological standards.

Robert T. McKenzie has suggested that representative democracy presupposes a near identity in views between persons at different levels in parties, and half-suggested that democratic parties should have views tending towards identity.[2] Hence, his polemics against the participation of alleged extreme-minded activists in party policy-making. But on the basis of their resolutions, constituency parties do not seem to be pulling the parties apart. While recognizing the simplifications involved, one might consider party differences as being ranked on a scale from 0 to 100, with 0 being extreme right-wing and 100 being left-wing extremism. Simple consensus based upon an identity of views within and between parties would occur if all opinion rested at 50; more realistically, consensus would result if the centre of gravity of opinion[3] within both parties was at 50. But a situation of balanced disagreement would operate if one of the parties centred at 60 and the other at 40, assuming a normal distribution frequency. An imbalance would result only if one party tended towards the centre while the other balanced near an extreme.

---

[1] Some British politicians still regard local party organizations with the respect they received in the days of open voting and bribery. The Nuffield studies find no evidence to support this. See most recently D. E. Butler and R. Rose, op. cit., pp. 143, 232 ff.

[2] See especially 'Parties, Pressure Groups and the British Political Process', *Political Quarterly*, vol. xxix, no. 1 (1958), p. 12 f.; and 'The "Political Activists" and Some Problems of "Inner Party" Democracy in Britain' (mimeo, International Political Science Association, Paris, 1961), p. 5 ff.

[3] Cf. D. E. Butler 'The Paradox of Party Difference', *American Behavioral Scientist*, iv. 3 (1960), pp. 3–5, where the concept of centres of party gravity is developed.

Balance, of course, is not a good in itself. Theoretically, a balance would occur if one party rested at 90 and another at 10. Furthermore, balance could produce stagnation when a radical shift in one direction was required by objective social circumstances. If we distribute resolutions along such an axis, we see that much of the weight of constituency views is closer to the centre than to the extremes. The leftward bias is largely the result of the greater frequency of Labour resolutions. When a correction is made for differences in submitting resolutions as between the parties, the point of balance turns out to be 3 per cent to the left of centre.

There has been no systematic investigation of political attitudes in an effort to find out what differences, if any, exist between voters, activists, M.P.s, and leaders in parties. There is evidence to indicate that the spread of opinion is wide at all levels of both parties. For instance, a 1959 national survey found that 45 per cent of Conserva-

TABLE 8

Distribution of the policy views of activists*

Scale:	0 Right Con.	25 Parti- san Con.	50 Non- parti- san	75 Parti- san Lab.	100 Left Lab.
No. of resolutions . .	505	438	2090	672	893
Per cent of resolutions .	11	10	45	15	19

* Resolutions showing misplaced partisanship are assigned to the partisanship category for the other party.

tive sympathizers accepted the *status quo* in the nationalized industries, and 40 per cent wished to denationalize one or more industries. In addition, 42 per cent of Labour sympathizers were opposed to further nationalization, whereas 36 per cent supported it.[1] In 1960, when 34 per cent of constituency party resolutions were extremist, 33 per cent of Labour M.P.s voted against Hugh Gaitskell in a contested election for the parliamentary party leadership. During the past decade the resignations of such leading Cabinet ministers as Aneurin Bevan, Lord Salisbury, and Peter Thorneycroft have pro-

[1] See D. E. Butler and R. Rose, op. cit., p. 244, and also p. 71. The opinion surveys regularly reported in the monthly *Gallup Political Index* (London) by the British Institute of Public Opinion, and by Mark Abrams, in M. Abrams and R. Rose, *Must Labour Lose?* (Harmondsworth, 1960) also bear out the point that party sympathizers are divided into partisans, extremists, deviants, and indifferents on almost all issues. Cf. also S. E. Finer, H. Berrington and D. Bartholomew, *Backbench Opinion in the House of Commons 1955–59* (London, 1961).

vided public evidence of the frequent suspicions of sharp divisions within a theoretically united Cabinet. Thus, it appears that the dilemma which David Butler has posed for party leaders — 'their most loyal and devoted followers tend to have more extreme views than they have themselves, and to be still farther removed from the mass of those who actually provide the vote' [1] — does not really exist. Differences in policy exist within parties, and conflict is sometimes great, but this is not conflict between a monolithic *bloc* of activists and a monolithic leadership. Rather, it would seem that factional disputes divide parties vertically, joining some Privy Councillors, M.P.s, lobbyists, activists, and voters into a faction which is in conflict with another which also contains members drawn from all ranks of the party.

[1] D. E. Butler, op. cit., p. 5.

CONSERVATIVE CONSTITUENCY LEADERS

By JOHN BIFFEN

THE system of nominating parliamentary candidates leaves considerable discretion to officers of local constituency associations. Nigel Nicolson, a Conservative M.P. disowned by his association following the Suez crisis, argued in *People and Parliament* that the existing form of nominating M.P.s was threatening to increase the number of extremists in the House of Commons. John Biffen's article, written a year before he himself became an M.P., reports findings from an investigation of constituencies in the West Midlands. The number of constituencies surveyed is small, but large enough to illustrate the dangers of generalizing from a single case; Nicolson's experience is shown to be exceptional rather than the rule.

IN leftish mythology the Conservative constituency associations are packed with hatchet men (and women) who are all anxious to cut down the faintest Tory Liberal, and to ensure a rabid orthodoxy — with permissible right-wing deviations. This is nonsense. Constituency associations are rarely concerned with the finer points of party policy. Parliamentary candidates are frequently chosen on an almost charmingly non-political basis. Willingness to live in the constituency or to support the activities of the association, is often of much more moment than a 'correct' attitude to Schedule A or the Common Market. A sample of eight constituencies in the West Midlands (all Labour held in 1955) helps to illustrate this point (see Table 1). The constituency associations were asked the questions. The answers recorded suggest very little attempt by constituency associations to cast M.P.s in their own or in any particular image. Apart from Suez no political issue seems to have roused the selection committees.

Moreover, Tory Members of Parliament normally have little difficulty in securing readoption, even when they have pursued a markedly independent line. This is a very fashionable viewpoint: but most of the serious clashes between a Member and his association have arisen from a conflict of personalities rather than on issues

Reprinted as an excerpt from *Crossbow*, vol. iv, no. 13 (1960), pp. 29–32.

of policy — although the latter inevitably become invoked. The marriage between Nigel Nicolson and the East Bournemouth Conservative Association was never matched in heaven. More typically all three Tory M.P.s in the West Midlands who showed sharp signs of disagreement with the Government in the last Parliament were re-adopted and re-elected. These were Mr. Enoch Powell (Wolverhampton S.W.), who resigned from the Government over the Budget

TABLE 1
Questioning of candidates

Were candidates asked to give views on	Yes	No
Suez	3	5
Hanging/birching	1	7
Mr. Thorneycroft's resignation . .	1	7

Viewpoint	Would have prejudiced selection	Would not have prejudiced selection
It was wrong to *start* the Suez operation	3	5
It was wrong to *stop* the Suez operation	2	6
Mr. Thorneycroft's resignation was justified	2	6
Greater use should be made of corporal/capital punishment . . .	1	7
Mr. Butler is right to resist wider use of corporal punishment . . .	1	7

estimates, and Sir Edward Boyle (Handsworth) and Mr. William Yates (the Wrekin), who were demonstrable opponents of the Suez venture. Like Abbé Siéyès in the French Revolution, all have survived.

It is, therefore a particularly unbalanced judgement to suggest that local associations are militantly hostile to minority Tory opinion; the problem when it does arise is generally due to the manner in which a minority opinion is held and propagated. The really significant thing about the constituency associations' choice of candidates is not the political power this gives them, which is unquestionable but the largely a-political manner in which their power is exercised. It certainly has not produced a preponderance of recognizably conformist-type Tory M.P.s. This point is also the more striking when one realizes that after 1945 the relationship between a constituency association and its M.P. was sharply altered. Before the war there were no limits on the subscription of an M.P. to his association; and it would be no exaggeration to say that some M.P.s practically carried their associations. The Maxwell Fyfe reforms after the 1945

x

election put stringent limits on the extent to which an M.P. could finance his association, so considerably increasing the authority of associations in relation to their M.P.s. If the constituency associations were really the homes of reaction, they would have had an excellent chance to assert their stronger position by selecting right-wing candidates. The post-war Tory M.P., especially the 1950 vintage, is by common consent more liberal and reform conscious than his inter-war predecessor. I am not concerned to argue why this should be, but only to show that the stronger position of constituency associations has not been employed to pack the Tory benches with right-wing conformists. That Conservatives, at all levels, should expect political loyalty is reasonable. (The present confusion of the Labour Party, or of the Liberals after the First World War, is warning enough to underline this.) The steadfastness of Tories after the Suez debacle illustrates a commendable and mature instinct for political survival rather than the lifeless unanimity of the graveyard. The constituency associations made a very real contribution to that steadfastness.

Resolving Policy

Constituency associations may also seek to influence policy by submitting resolutions either to area conferences or to the annual party conference. Resolutions discussed at area level are passed to London, but normally receive little publicity. On the other hand, resolutions submitted to the national conference are published and widely discussed in the political Press. However, interest centres not on the few that are actually chosen for debate — which are often depressingly eulogistic — but on the tone of the resolutions not chosen, for these may reflect considerable dissatisfaction with the leadership. The best recent example of this was the Brighton conference in October 1957. The preceding year had included Suez, the Rent Act, and finally the 7 per cent Bank Rate. The conference skilfully avoided a direct clash between the platform (the Government) and the floor (the constituency associations), but the critical tone of the resolutions left no doubt about the uneasiness the latter felt about the Government. There are, however, very clear limits to the influence of constituency associations working through the conference. Decisions of the conference are not mandatory; and resolutions chosen for debate can rarely be represented as a direct assault upon government policy. The greatest opportunity for constituency associations to exercise a real influence on party policy might arrive in the event of a sharp and fairly equal division of opinion in the party over a major issue. It is, for example, just conceivable that this might happen over British participation in the Common Market — but even then only if the Government had given no clear indication of what was considered a desirable policy.

If the influence of constituency associations through the use of resolutions is limited, their influence as contributors to the finances of Central Office is probably nil. Each constituency is asked to pay a 'quota' to the national finances of the party, but it seems probable

TABLE 2

Sources of finance

Source	Listing in order of importance				Nil or Negligible
	1	2	3	4	
Branch quotas	9	1	1	3	2
Private individual subs. direct to Association Treasurer . . .	3	5	5	3	..
Private business subs. direct to Association Treasurer . . .	5	..	3	5	3
Constituency functions i.e. fêtes, raffles	7	5	3	1	..

that this represents only a fairly small proportion of the party's central fund. An examination of the source of constituency income suggests that constituencies are very largely concerned with raising money to support themselves. The sample of sixteen constituencies were asked to list in order of importance four possible sources of income (see Table 2). The answers shown place emphasis on 'collective fund raising' rather than individual subscriptions. It seems more than likely that individual subscriptions predominate in the financing of Central Office activities. This is hardly surprising; but it does put into some perspective the financial role of local associations. This is to finance party activities locally, with a contribution, which may or may not be token, to national finances.

All this is in sharp contrast to the position in the Labour Party, where the vote of constituency organizations may effectively decide conference policy when the trade union cohorts are divided. Labour's constituency associations have for long provided a redoubt for extremist, reactionary and unrepresentative Socialism — a thesis cogently argued by T. E. M. McKitterick in *The Political Quarterly*, vol. xxxi, no. 2.

The Controller

If the constituency Labour parties are in the control of unrepresentative political zealots, who control the Tory associations? Tory association officers appear, on a fairly limited sample (see Table 3), to be overwhelmingly middle class, with only a small admixture as yet of the 'new' middle class whose advent since 1950 has buttressed Conservative electoral success. This helps to explain the support that constituency associations have given to the 'housing lobby' in the campaign for '300,000 houses' or 'the Abolition of Schedule A', and similar measures.

TABLE 3

Occupation and religion of executive officers of sixteen West Midland Conservative Associations

Occupation		Religion	
Company directors	. 18	Church of England	. 58
Other business executives	. 9	Roman Catholic	. 4
Professions	. 17	Nonconformist	. 4
Housewives	. 14		
Others*	. 27		
TOTAL	. 85	TOTAL†	. 66

* Almost entirely middle-class occupations — except 2 factory workers.
† The smaller figure arises because fewer answers were given to this question.

One thing still seems clear — the shop floor trade unionist has had little more success in winning a significant place in the local hierarchy than he has in being elected to Westminster. On the other hand, it is likely that a similar sample carried out before 1939 would have shown a far larger number of landed gentry and, perhaps, of professional people. Their places may well have been taken by the growing number of business executives. Confessional politics are almost entirely absent in the West Midlands, and only operate very marginally in local government. Even so, the very poor showing of Roman Catholics and Nonconformists on association executives is a little depressing.

However competitive politics may become in the higher reaches, there is an almost debilitating lack of scramble for office in the constituency associations. This gives the lie to a recent offensive article in the *New Statesman* which suggested that the honours list provided a powerful spur to Tory local organization. The sample constituencies were asked if association executive officers observed the three-year limit on tenure of office, which is recommended by Central Office. In addition, associations were asked questions on the ease of filling executive posts. Their answers are shown in Tables 4 and 5.

There appears to be rather more competition for office among the

Tory ladies. Certainly anyone who has experienced working in and with a constituency association will testify to the much more active role played by women than men in fund raising and indeed in most of the pedestrian political activities. Alas for the fun of politics, these matronly militants hardly measure up to the Giles or Vicky cartoons of themselves.

TABLE 4
Limited tenure

Suggested three-year limit observed	
Totally . . .	5
Generally . .	5
Quite often . .	1
Generally not . .	6

TABLE 5
Finding the officers

Question	Yes	No
Is there competition for top constituency jobs? . .	3	12*
Is there difficulty in dislodging holders of top constituency jobs?	1	14*
Is there difficulty in finding holders of top constituency jobs .	9*	5

* In each case an exception to the general rule is provided by the Women's Branches: this involves three separate constituencies.

The sad truth is that two-thirds of the Tory associations always have the problem of wondering from where the next suitable executive officers will come. In fact, if there is a challenge and a problem for the Conservative Party in the state of the local associations it is certainly not their harshly unrepresentative or reactionary nature — that is Labour's difficulty. The danger is not that the production manager, washing his Ford Zodiac on Sunday morning (a truly Anglican sacrament), is conspiring another assault on Schedule A or State education but that he is giving up the unequal struggle with his wife — and promising that this *will* be his last year as ward chairman.

PARTIES, FACTIONS AND TENDENCIES
IN BRITAIN

By RICHARD ROSE

THE statement that Britain has a two-party system character-
izes a complex political activity in terms of a single variable —
the number of parties that successfully compete in general
elections. When Liberal strength is significant, it is even
inaccurate on that basis. Views on policy are represented by
more than two positions within the general electorate, within
the ranks of party activists, and within the ranks of national
politicians. The following article shows that concentrating
attention simply upon the electioneering function of parties
gives a partial and distorted picture of the internal dynamics
of British party politics; it is necessary to distinguish more
groupings in order to relate differences within and between
parties to the formulation of public policy.

IN studies of party politics, Britain is often cited as the leading
example of a two-party system. The purpose of this essay is to challenge the utility of labelling the whole of party politics by a term
which describes only one aspect of national party politics — electoral
competition. British parties have many functions beside that of supporting competing teams of leaders at general elections. The most
salient characteristics of the entities called 'parties' shift as functions change and attempts are made to reconcile the conflicting
pressures arising from the bundle of roles, individuals, and institutions normally lumped together under one omnibus heading. Distinguishing between parties as electoral institutions and as policy
institutions may reduce some of the confusion caused by use of the
broader term, as well as explaining how parties place restraints
upon government today.

A. The Functions of Parties

Definitions of party systems usually emphasize the function of parties
qua electoral institutions. In consequence, systems are distinguished
by the number of parties competing at the polls: this provides a
means of classifying parties, although it hardly provides a 'syste-

Reprinted from *Political Studies*, vol. xii, no. 1 (1964), pp. 33–46.

matic' description of the workings of parties within a political
society, as the term 'system' is now used by political sociologists.[1]
Parties function only intermittently as electoral institutions, and
much of the long-term work of attending to elections is delegated to
relatively unimportant bureaucrats. This is particularly true in
Britain where elections occur only once in every four or five years.
Electoral considerations are usually in the middle distance. In the
short run, the parties, especially the governing party, are confronted
with national problems upon which positions must be taken in
Parliament. Most policy decisions cannot be taken on the basis of
electoral preferences, because of the narrow range of electoral
concerns and the vagueness of preferences. Public opinion polls may
show that voters want peace and prosperity; such information is
virtually worthless to ministers and potential ministers attempting to
choose between alternative economic and international policies
concerned with means to these ends. *Élitist* traditions in the political
culture emphasize the duty of governors to be unpopular in the short
run, if they think they are right, and most party leaders are sophisticated enough to appreciate that temporarily unpopular policies
may produce popular consequences by the date which the governing party chooses for the general election.

In terms of shaping public policy, the party *qua* Government is
much more significant than, and significantly different from, an
electoral party. Politicians in office have both party and Government roles, and the claims of these roles are not always identical.
Priority out of office can be given to the demands of groups within
the extra-parliamentary party. In office, priority must usually be
given to administrative exigencies and to intractable dilemmas
which cannot be glossed over simply by means of a party conference
resolution. Civil Servants are ever present, proffering administrative objections to policies which are acceptable or desired by sections of the party outside its ministerial membership. The goodwill of
pressure groups is important to the success of some Government
policies, even when these groups may be supporting the opposition
party at elections. Duties of a departmental nature reduce the time
politicians have for meeting partisans outside government. In so far
as role conflicts lead to transparent differences between previous
party policy and the policy of the party as Government, then party
members excluded from the Government may follow their principles
and ambitions and make an issue of such discrepancies. Since the

[1] Cf. the sociologically systematic discussion of parties in R. K. Merton, *Social
Theory and Social Structure* (Glencoe: Free Press, revised edition, 1957), pp. 71 ff.,
and the approach of Maurice Duverger, *Political Parties* (London: Methuen, 1954).

leaders of the governing party can give immediate effect to their decisions, differences within the party can be intensified. Behind the façade of unity maintained by the conventions of parliamentary government, M.P.s can differ privately with each other and with ministers, and ministers may differ with each other. Conflicts in personalities or in personal ambitions can stimulate or intensify differences arising either from conflicts on party principles or conflicts based upon contrasting departmental concerns.

The party *qua* Opposition is organized differently and subjected to other pressures. An Opposition leader, immediately after an electoral defeat, in theory may be a potential prime minister, although only three times in this century has a new prime minister stepped directly from a position as leader of the Opposition. Normally, a new prime minister comes into office between elections after a long apprenticeship in Cabinet. The Opposition leader is after defeat a potential scapegoat for the disappointed within his party, lacking the resources of a prime minister for stifling public controversy. *Ex hypothesi*, a party as Opposition concentrates upon victory at the next general election, however distant. But in practice, there are often disagreements as to what are the best means to this end, and in the Labour Party there have always been some who have rejected electoral success as an irrelevant standard by which to determine party actions. And it is the Labour Party which has usually provided the Opposition in the past forty years.

Perhaps the greatest degree of cohesiveness can be found in the party *qua* organization.[1] Both major parties have stable, hierarchical institutions which deploy full-time bureaucrats at all levels from constituencies to national headquarters. Party employees enjoy pensions and may refer to themselves as Civil Servants. Their status as pensionable party servants depends in part upon their ability to serve the leadership while keeping free from identification with factions inside the party. Much of the day to day work of party bureaucrats is free from controversy. When policy statements are required, the officials can draft them so as to concentrate fire upon the electoral opponent, thus avoiding factional disputes. This, for instance, has normally been the tactic of the international secretary of the Labour Party, even though this makes such statements ineffectual with regard to the long and important dispute about foreign affairs within the electoral party.

The foregoing sketch of the structures and functions of political parties is illustrative, not exhaustive. Political parties are also instruments of pressure groups, vehicles of men seeking power and

[1] See Richard Rose, 'The Professionals of Politics', *New Society* (8 August 1963).

status, centres of social activity, vehicles for individuals seeking to reduce psychological tensions, and agencies involved in local government and local life. Parties are all these things at once, and these many functions are not always harmoniously combined. That is why it is necessary to use modifying terms with the word 'party' in order to avoid confusion.

B. *Parties in the Policy Process*

The focus of this essay is upon the party *qua* Government and the party *qua* Opposition, that is, upon parties as policy parties, participating with pressure groups, Civil Servants, and others in the making of public policy. From this perspective, it is important not only to ask which electoral party has a parliamentary majority but also which policy party predominates in the victorious electoral party? In this way recognition is given both to the differences *between* electoral parties and to the differences *within* electoral parties. The latter differences are at least as important as the former, because most general elections since 1900 have not resulted in a formal change in party government but in a confirmation of the combination in office. Often differences within electoral parties are treated as much less significant than differences between electoral parties. For instance, Austin Ranney and Willmoore Kendall define a party as 'a large-scale organization whose purpose is to control the personnel and policies *of the government*' and a faction as 'an element inside a party whose purpose is to control the personnel and policies *of the party*'.[1] But when a faction attempts to control the governing party, then it is, by this definition, both a party and a faction.

In modern British political history, the realignment of policy groups within and across electoral lines has been as significant, if not more significant, than shifts in government caused by general elections. Since 1885, only the elections of 1906 and 1945 may be said to have directly precipitated major realignments in government policy. More often, major changes have arisen from divisions within electoral parties: the Liberal Unionists split from the Liberals in 1886; the Conservatives divided on tariff reform after 1900; the Lloyd George Coalition was formed by a split in 1916 and ended in one in 1922; the Labour Party split in 1931, the Conservatives divided in 1940, and Labour split in 1951. The Conservatives' unwillingness to divide in public has not sustained continuous harmony in private. The Labour Party is federal or confederal in policy as in structure; since its origins it has combined groups in basic

[1] *Democracy and the American Party System* (New York: Harcourt, Brace, 1956), p. 126. Italics in the original.

disagreement on policy.[1] The Liberals have split, split, and split again since 1886.

Contemporary evidence of divisions within the electoral parties may be drawn from many sources, and from many sections of parties. The Government of Harold Macmillan experienced the resignation of three senior ministers on policy grounds; one can only speculate about how many resignations have been threatened and forestalled in the course of dividing, then coalescing on policy. Hugh Dalton's memoirs document divisions on Cabinet policy in the 1945–51 Labour Government. The volumes of *Hansard* are full of expressions of differences between M.P.s nominally in the same party. Signatures to parliamentary motions offer additional substantiation. Of the resolutions sent by activists to annual party conferences, about half of those which are overtly partisan stress internally divisive policies. Among voters, disagreements on policy among those supporting the same party cover a wide range of issues.[2]

Policy parties emerge between elections and concentrate attention upon the literal and metaphorical centres of policy-making, the Cabinet and Shadow Cabinet. Policy parties do not seek absolute control of government; a realistic aim is predominance. Because questions of policy usually do not affect the nomination of parliamentary candidates, there is little scope for policy factions to operate within the electoral process. Studying them involves both conceptual and empirical problems. In analysing parties as policy institutions, three elements are of special importance — factions, tendencies, and non-aligned partisans.[3] These three elements have been of importance over a very long period of time. Clarity can be gained by analysing these elements separately, although actual policy parties mix the three elements. The difference in the proportions mixed remains of major operational significance.

A political *faction* may be defined as a group of individuals based on representatives in Parliament who seek to further a broad range of policies through consciously organized political activity. Factions are thus distinguished from other influence groups by having mem-

---

[1] See, for example, R. T. McKenzie, *British Political Parties* (London: Heinemann, 1955), chap. 3; and Henry Pelling, *The Origins of the Labour Party, 1880–1900* (London: Macmillan, 1954).

[2] See especially S. E. Finer, H. B. Berrington, and D. J. Bartholomew, *Backbench Opinion in the House of Commons, 1955–59* (London: Pergamon, 1961); Richard Rose, 'The Political Ideas of English Party Activists', *American Political Science Review*, lvi, 2 (1962); R. S. Milne and H. C. Mackenzie, *Marginal Seat, 1955* (London: Hansard Society, 1958), chap. 8.

[3] The author is indebted to S. H. Beer for the formulation of the difference between a faction and a tendency.

bership based in Parliament, rather than in the Civil Service or
elsewhere. Because they persist through time, factions can be distinguished from the *ad hoc* combinations of politicians in agreement
upon one particular issue or at one moment in time. Factions may
be distinguished from pressure groups because the former are
concerned with a wide range of political issues, including foreign
affairs, colonial policy, and defence, as well as economics and social
welfare. Factions may be distinguished from exponents of a political
tendency because factions are self-consciously organized as a body,
with a measure of discipline and cohesion thus resulting. Identification with a faction usually increases an individual's commitment
to a programme, as well as creating the expectation that the politician will consistently take the same side in quarrels within an
electoral party. These expectations are a form of discipline operating
socially and internalized by an individual. To abandon a faction
is to risk appearing publicly as a renegade, as well as causing tension in the personal relations of the defector with his political
associates. The existence of recognized lines of conflict can become
the cause of policy disagreements, as factional opponents transfer
old enmities to new issues.[1]

By contrast, a political *tendency* is a stable set of attitudes, rather
than a stable group of politicians. It may be defined as a body of
attitudes expressed in Parliament about a broad range of problems;
the attitudes are held together by a more or less coherent political
ideology. One may speak of right-wing and left-wing tendencies
within both British parties because of the extent to which political
differences in this country may be placed along a single left-right
axis. The number of M.P.s who adhere to a tendency varies from
issue to issue. Adherents are often not self-consciously organized in
support of a single policy and they do not expect, nor are they expected, to continue to operate as a group supporting the same tendency through a period of time. This makes it easier for M.P.s to
shift positions from tendency to tendency. Individuals may be
attached to conflicting tendencies, resolving the resulting cross
pressures in different ways in differing contexts. For instance, many
M.P.s will at some time or another show a reform tendency with
regard to a particular measure. But this will not make them all
members of a reform faction, supporting a wide range of changes.
In so far as an electoral party is primarily characterized by factionalism, then cleavages within the party tend to be stable and follow
predictable lines. In so far as groups of politicians do not self-

[1] See on this point, J. S. Coleman, *Community Conflict* (Glencoe: Free Press, 1957),
chap. 2.

consciously band together, then party divisions are fluid and less easy to anticipate.

Non-alignment is identification with positions supported by the whole of the electoral party, rather than with factions or tendencies. This is a real and important alternative for M.P.s and activists.[1] Non-alignment may result from an active concern with only the gross differences between electoral parties, from a passive attitude towards policy issues, or from a calculated desire to avoid identification with particular tendencies or factions in order to gain popularity within the whole electoral party. At times of intense differences on policy within an electoral party, non-aligned partisans represent a slack resource which disputants attempt to mobilize in order to shift the balance.

Policy parties are not pure factions, tendencies, or collections of non-aligned partisans. For instance, the Bevanites combined the stable core of a faction with occasional support from those supporting a left-wing tendency on one issue. The right-wing of the Conservative Party, by contrast, has in recent years been unorganized; a few Conservatives frequently follow right-wing tendencies, but many come and go in accordance with circumstances and issues. The complex nature of this scheme of analysis, juxtaposing groups of individual politicians and analytic categories, is intended to correct the over-simplifications arising from concentration on electoral parties. Yet it is in turn an over-simplification. Groups and categories could be further divided and sub-divided until one was left only with individual politicians — each divided within himself and divided in his sympathies with others. But then, a process of building up patterns would have to be begun again.

C. Policy Parties in Electoral Parties

The policy parties formed by an amalgam of factions, tendencies, and non-aligned partisans have a relatively simple and somewhat fluid structure, which may operate only intermittently within the electoral parties, as the cohesiveness of the electoral party and its salience varies. The chief features of a policy party, particularly a consciously organized faction, appear to be an ideology, leadership, limited technical expertise, *cadres*, a communications network, and rewards, whether material or psychological.

Ideology is important in so far as a common adherence to shared political values may cause politicians to act together. Adherence to ideological principles, presented as the essence of the electoral

---

[1] Cf. the analysis of constituency party resolutions in Richard Rose, 'The Political Ideas of English Party Activists', op. cit., pp. 362 ff.

party's beliefs, can be used by factions to justify activities which might be judged to harm the party electorally. Whether the principles have much intellectual content, or are purely symbolic, they can none the less cause shifts within an electoral party, as the dispute within the Labour Party on repealing Clause IV demonstrated in 1960–61. Leadership gives a recognized focus and stature to what may otherwise be a collection of second-string politicians. With a leader of national stature, disputes are no longer between front bench and back bench, but are fought out within the ranks of front-bench M.P.s. The resignation of Aneurin Bevan from the Labour Government in 1951 provides a classic illustration of how the emergence of a leader can help a tendency to crystallize into a recognized faction. But, as Bevan's *rapprochement* with Hugh Gaitskell in 1957 demonstrated, factional leaders, if they are not to become intransigents and politically isolated, face the difficult task of leading a faction and acting as a broker in negotiations with opposing political groups.[1] Technical expertise is important in so far as a faction is pressing detailed proposals. But the various parliamentary elements often appear less concerned with matters of detail than with general principles, seeking to influence the evaluation of detailed claims and counter-claims, rather than to originate proposals based upon expert knowledge. For instance, the development of opinion among M.P.s on the European Common Market appears to have far outpaced the assimilation of expert and detailed knowledge on the Market. *Cadres* are necessary to support and implement the programme of a faction, giving to a small body of men the semblance of a 'mass' movement with widespread electoral support. In Maurice Duverger's terms, factions are *cadre* parties without rank and file members and with only a limited number of devotees.[2] The habitual supporters of a tendency are usually so loosely associated as not to constitute *cadres*, but they can provide the *cadres* for a new faction. The communications networks of groups are informal and intermittent, relying upon face-to-face contacts around the Palace of Westminster. The Press can be manipulated in order to stimulate private conversations and combinations, but printed publicity is not a necessity. Editors themselves often appear more interested in supporting one or more tendencies than in supporting a single faction or giving blanket endorsement to an electoral party. Factional leaders or M.P.s representative of a tendency may

---

[1] The excellent discussion of this problem in another context by Myron Weiner, *Political Parties in India* (Princeton: University Press, 1957), pp. 241 ff., contains insights which can be applied to Britain.
[2] Op. cit., pp. 62–70.

enjoy the reward of office, being given ministerial appointment in order to decapitate potential opponents within the electoral party. The careers of many leading ministers indicate that a period of association with a minority faction or tendency is no barrier to reaching the highest offices. M.P.s whose limited talents or whose psychological characteristics disqualify them from high office may find that eminence within a faction or tendency is the highest position they may realistically hope for. The satisfactions which M.P.s seek are sufficiently varied so that official or shadow patronage will never bring into line all the nominal supporters of the electoral party leader.

The Conservative electoral party is pre-eminently a party of tendencies. The chief tendencies towards which politicians may gravitate can be approximately labelled reaction, defence of the *status quo*, amelioration and reform. The existence of these several tendencies without the firmness of factional groupings means that alignments within the Conservative Party are usually temporary and in flux. The authors of the Keele study of early day motions conclude of Conservative M.P.s: 'Such disagreements as arise are struggles between *ad hoc* groups of members who may be left or right on specific questions; but as new controversies break out, the coherence of the former groups dissolves, and new alignments appear, uniting former enemies and separating old allies.'[1] Since this fluidity is usually combined with a high respect for electoral party leaders, the Conservative Prime Minister has wide scope for manipulating his followers — though he cannot rely upon the same hard core of support available to a factional leader such as Hugh Gaitskell. But the Conservative Party is also notable for the fact that its dissidents have normally confined public complaints against the leadership to a single issue or, like Peter Thorneycroft in 1958, have refrained from efforts to rally a faction and found themselves later readmitted to the Cabinet. Conservatives in favour of amelioration and reform would appear to constitute the nucleus of a political faction. Yet this collection of individuals has not coalesced into a cohesive and self-conscious group, and the leading extra-parliamentary spokesmen, the Bow Group, have gone to some lengths to repudiate the idea that they are a 'party within a party' in the sense familiar within the Labour ranks.[2]

Reformism may be described as a tendency supporting change for its own sake, or 'left' views on issues which are, in Anthony Cros-

---

[1] S. E. Finer, *et al.*, op. cit., p. 106.
[2] See Richard Rose, 'The Bow Group's Role in British Politics', *Western Political Quarterly*, xiv. 4 (1961), pp. 869 ff.

land's terms, 'left–right issues which are not socialist–capitalist issues'.[1] Reformism is a tendency which cuts across electoral party boundaries. Many individuals will support a particular reform through a special-purpose pressure group with 'non-party' sponsorship. Some reformers — the Webbs up to 1914 being a notable example — have preferred to work through more than one electoral party, rather than narrow their influence by concentrating upon factional activity within a single electoral party. Conflicts between the policies and symbols of reform and those which provide the traditional basis of the unity of the Conservative and Labour parties inhibit conscious organization of reform factions. The Liberal electoral party has embraced the symbols of reform — but, as the debate on a possible Liberal–Labour merger in the winter of 1962–3 illustrated — the Liberals were unable to convince more than a handful of politicians in the major parties that support for reform could better be given outside the two major parties rather than inside it.

The Labour electoral party has been since its foundation a party of factions, although it is not exclusively composed of factions and the left-wing faction has been notoriously schismatic. Notwithstanding many differences, conflict between right and left has been stable — whether between Aneurin Bevan and the supporters of Clement Attlee in 1951, between Sir Stafford Cripps and Transport House in the 1930's, or, as in the 1920's between the I.L.P., formally a party within a party, and the official party leadership. Hugh Gaitskell's period as party leader began by his accession to office as the chief spokesman of a recognized faction; during most of his time in office he not only acted as leader of a faction divided from another faction in the electoral party, but also as the nominal symbol of electoral party unity. (The contrast with Clement Attlee, who did not allow himself to become a symbol of controversy and disunity, is marked.)[2] The fight within the Labour Party on nuclear disarmament from 1959–61 brought into relief the inconsistency in Gaitskell heading the electoral party and the Campaign for Democratic Socialism faction. The Labour left as a faction shares a desire to transform Britain into a completely socialist society, and the need to act together, notwithstanding schismatic influences, in attacking the leaders of the Labour moderates. The persistence of left factions from generation to generation shows the deep roots of the left in the Labour Party. In the days of the Bevanites, the left held regular caucuses in the Palace of Westminster, with an agenda and

---

[1] Anthony Crosland, *The Future of Socialism* (London: Cape, 1956), pp. 520–1.

[2] A point that Harold Wilson appears to have noticed. See his remarks in an interview with Kenneth Harris, the *Observer*, 16 June 1963.

minutes. It conducted a propaganda campaign through *Tribune* and held meetings in the constituencies. At present, the *New Left Review* and the Campaign for Nuclear Disarmament perform the important functions of recruiting new adherents and providing an institutional focus for activity. The use of extra-parliamentary groups indicates the relative weakness of a faction now leaderless in Parliament. Parliamentary weakness can hardly deter many members of the left, however, since they have spent their whole political lives far from the centres of power.

The strength of factionalism in the Labour Party has placed a high premium upon non-aligned partisans. Their importance was dramatically demonstrated after the 1959 general election. First, this categoric group appeared to have been decisive in defeating Hugh Gaitskell's proposal to repeal Clause IV in the party constitution, a clause which embodied an important symbol of the electoral party. Secondly, the victory of Hugh Gaitskell in his fight against the nuclear disarmers appeared to have come from the mobilization by the moderate faction of non-aligned partisans in support of loyalty to the leadership and collective security. It remains to be seen whether or not the election to the leadership of Harold Wilson represents a re-emergence of Attlee's conception of the leader as a non-aligned politician, or whether the policies of Wilson and the problems the party faces will lead to the re-emergence of old factional differences, the emergence of new factions, or the conduct of intra-party disputes by *ad hoc* collections of men rallying to different tendencies.[1]

D. *Consequences for the Political Process*

The existence of varied, unstable policy parties within the formally united governing party maintains and strengthens a number of restraints upon the exercise of power by the Cabinet, which today is secure against defeat in the House of Commons because of the acceptance of the discipline of the two-party system by M.P.s and electors.

Policy parties act as a counterweight against pressure groups. The co-operation of pressure groups is important for the success of a government. But because pressure group allegiances have not been demonstrated to be strong enough to affect voting behaviour significantly, organized group leaders can rarely succeed in punishing a recalcitrant government at the polls. But members of policy

---

[1] Conflict cutting across factional lines had begun to show itself in the debate on the European Common Market at the 1962 Labour Party Conference, a few months before Hugh Gaitskell's death.

parties opposed to particular pressure groups may create trouble in Cabinet, in speeches leaked from private party meetings and on the floor of the Commons itself. For instance, the Attlee Government's nationalization of the steel industry was persevered in against the wishes of affected pressure groups and of important Cabinet members because of the strength of the left-wing tendency on this issue, including several ministers who had jumped outside their usual factional positions.[1]

A united Cabinet can fend off criticism from the opposition party indefinitely. (Concessions are more likely to be made to disaffected potential voters than to partisan opponents: witness the announcement of the repeal of the Schedule A tax on home-ownership following the Liberal victory at Orpington in 1962.) But the protest of a policy party within the governing party is immediately felt, especially if it involves sharp divisions during the private deliberations of the Cabinet. In at least four cases in this century — 1905, 1923, 1931, and 1951 — policy divisions have been notable as major causes in a government in office defaulting, and going down to electoral defeat shortly thereafter. The possibility is always present, as the lobbying within the Conservative Party, including the Cabinet, showed in the week before the division in the Profumo debate of 17 June 1963. The threat to expel a group of several dozen M.P.s who vote against a party whip is meaningless, because such an expulsion would hurt the electoral party by making more clear cut divisions within the ranks.

By voting together in Parliament, M.P.s in different policy parties reaffirm their common identification with a single electoral party. Voting together shows a degree of cohesion which political parties in many countries lack. But it does not provide continuously cohesive support for a party leader. Rather, the division lobbies represent only one phase in a lengthy process, a phase far distant in time from the one in which the most substantial decisions will be made about a problem. When problems arise salient to factions, ministers can anticipate to a considerable extent the nature of support and opposition to alternative policies under consideration. But lacking factional guidelines, ministers can only note the tendencies associated with policy alternatives, without being able to estimate so well the numbers of M.P.s who will associate themselves with the several tendencies. Only after the front bench takes a line can it find out whether the hints and threats of M.P.s lobbying them are in fact accurate predictions of opposition or part of the complicated game of bluff involved in situations of political uncertainty. Because public

[1] See Hugh Dalton, *High Tide and After* (London: Muller, 1962), pp. 248 ff.

Y

dispute within an electoral party can harm both sides in the dispute, a high premium is placed upon accurate information which can be used to anticipate and forestall policy disputes. This accounts for the importance of party whips; they provide the two-way flow of information between the party leader and back bench M.P.s. Individual ministers have parliamentary private secretaries to warn them of impending difficulties. The object of this communication, from the point of view of a nominally impregnable leadership, is to keep the leadership informed about possible sources of discontent, and threats of factions forming around tendencies opposed to those prevailing among the dominant leadership group. In this way, the appearance of unity can be maintained by aborting public controversy. This was, for instance, the technique that Clement Attlee used when informal collections of M.P.s began discussing his replacement, by Sir Stafford Cripps or Ernest Bevin, during the 1947 economic crisis. Retention of Cripps in the Cabinet was essential at this point in order to forestall the conversion of a left-wing tendency into a strong left faction with a potential prime minister at its head.[1] More recently, Harold Macmillan has demonstrated in successive Cabinet changes since the 1959 general election an awareness of the importance of keeping his political associates divided and balanced against one another by the distribution of Cabinet posts.

The need to balance factions, tendencies, and individuals against one another acts as a major restraint upon the power of the party leader, whether in Opposition or as Prime Minister.[2] The recurring polemical discussion about the 'constitutional' position of the leader of the Labour Party *vis-à-vis* extra-parliamentary followers, with emphasis given to affirming the pre-eminence of Parliament, has drawn attention from the question of what restraints might be needed upon the Prime Minister. One wonders whether British prime ministers are always so wise and dispassionate in their actions that they need no restraints. History suggests not, and provides recent examples. In practice, restraints are often imposed by divisions within the electoral party. Three Prime Ministers, Neville Chamberlain, Lloyd George, and Asquith, were forced from office by defections of nominal supporters. Eden, Attlee, MacDonald, and Balfour retired after intense strife within their parties. It is impossible to demonstrate the extent or the weight of Attlee's self-denying

---

[1] See H. Dalton, op. cit., ch. 29; and Leslie Hunter, *The Road to Brighton Pier* (London: Barker, 1959), pp. 18 ff.

[2] The restraints upon the party leader are discussed in detail in Richard Rose, 'Complexities of Party Leadership', *Parliamentary Affairs*, xvi, 3 (1963).

approach to the potential power of his office — but this does not deny the significance of the limitations upon his influence due to his self-effacing approach and the dispersion of power during most of his period in that office.

Policy divisions help to maintain flexibility and diversity in a political system in which large nominal grants of power are made once every four or five years to one of two parties in duopolistic competition. Flexibility is desirable inasmuch as many major problems which face a government cannot be foreseen at a general election, by candidates or by electors, and during a crisis, an election is likely to be avoided by the party in office. But because a governing party contains a wide diversity of tendencies, a range of policies is likely to have some political support within a single electoral party. Since supporters are not united in their views, leaders have room for manoeuvre in choosing between alternatives. By manipulating the tendencies, and appealing for the loyalty of the non-aligned, a leader, especially a Conservative, may bring off a major public reversal of policy, as in Harold Macmillan's 'winds of change' speech on colonialism in 1960, or his Common Market policy subsequently. If the Conservative Party had been monolithic, it would have proven less adaptable in both instances — and if divisions had been as long-lived and deep as those in the Labour Party's factions, shifts would have been far less easily and quietly accomplished.

In times of crisis, the British party system has shown flexibility by the making of new coalitions across electoral party lines, as in 1940, 1931, 1916, and 1886.[1] Electoral parties split in times of crisis not because they have suddenly lost a previously maintained unity, but rather in part because of pre-existing divisions which crises serve to heighten in intensity. The process is illustrated in slow motion by the gradual collapse of the Liberal Party and its replacement by the Labour Party, with Labour assimilating one section of the Liberals and the Conservatives another. Even without the formation of new parties from the amalgams of old factions and tendencies, Britain has often enjoyed coalition government. In the seventy-eight years since 1885, the country has been governed by a combination of parties for thirty-four years. Major policy problems, such as Ireland, the Depression of 1931 and total mobilization in 1940, have been handled by coalition governments, and the foundations for the present mixed economy Welfare State were laid in the Coalition of 1940–5. The *ad hoc* building of coalitions within the limits of a single electoral party or between electoral parties has

[1] See the insightful discussion of cross-party ties in R. Bassett, *The Essentials of Parliamentary Democracy* (London: Macmillan, 1935), especially chap. 3.

important consequences for consensus in the political culture — that is, the acceptance by more than one party of important innovations in public policy.

Coalition governments do not endure in Britain, because once great hurdles have been taken, disagreements upon other policy issues become dominant, and the points of disagreement between electoral parties reassert themselves or else new points of difference become permanent as old differences disappear. The party system is dynamic, involving periods of coalition across electoral party lines as well as periods of competition; both are necessary elements in what has aptly been described as a 'moving consensus.[1]' Movement is as important as consensus. The existence within the British party system of a large number of policy parties, whether tendencies or factions, facilitates movement. (E.g. the domestic and international policies of the 1940–5 Coalition Government were not those of the dominant policy groups within the Conservative and Labour parties prior to 1940.) Non-aligned partisans are important in this process too, sometimes cushioning conflicts within electoral parties and sometimes resolving them. Since the government is not under the absolute control of any one policy party it is always able, potentially at least, to readjust its alliances. The surface cohesion of British parties reflects an equilibrium between forces pulling in different directions, not a unity obtained by a single, united thrust.

Divisions within electoral parties also serve to reduce the distance between electoral parties. Some Labour M.P.s have supported tendencies more in accord with those also claiming adherents within the Conservative Party than they have those in accord with their nominal colleagues of the Left. The closeness evidenced can cause confusion to the voter and friction between electoral party colleagues. It also makes it easier for ideas to be assimilated across electoral party boundaries. For instance, domestic policies enacted by Labour from 1945–50 were first accepted by reformist Conservatives, and have then gradually been diffused through the electoral party from sources of influence inside Conservative ranks. In a complementary fashion, non-Socialist critiques of Socialist economic doctrines and principles of foreign policy have been diffused within the Labour Party.

Because of the areas of agreement which cut across electoral lines (though rarely reaching from the extremes of the Conservatives to those of Labour), the stakes at general elections in Britain are not

---

[1] See Arthur W. Macmahon, 'Conflict, Consensus, Confirmed Trends and Open Choices', *American Political Science Review*, xlii. 1 (1948), pp. 2 ff.

such that either party actively fears the consequences of defeat. Election results and the accession of new governments involve shifts in the emphasis given to certain political tendencies as against others, by changing the label and the personnel of those engaged in holding together the governing party. The electorate is not defrauded or alienated in exercising its franchise by being asked to choose between two parties which are either interchangeable in programmes or mutually exclusive. The mixture of policy parties within the electoral parties means that there is something for all sorts of people to attach themselves to, whichever party wins an election or is given their vote. It also means that those who find themselves at the apex of the structure of 'winner-take-all' party government in Britain cannot govern without regard to a number of restraints built into the party system.

A BIBLIOGRAPHY OF ARTICLES

THE following bibliography is intended to provide a comprehensive guide to serious articles about contemporary political behaviour in England. Since the academic study of political behaviour only began to develop after the Second World War, bibliographical searches were largely confined to post-1945 volumes of periodicals; many journals in the field were not founded until after the end of the Second World War. Material of primarily historical interest has not been included.

The bibliography was accumulated by a systematic search of the following British and American academic journals: *Political Studies*, *Political Quarterly*, *Parliamentary Affairs*, *Public Administration*, *Public Law*, *British Journal of Sociology*, the *Sociological Review*, the *American Political Science Review*, *Journal of Politics*, *World Politics*, *Public Opinion Quarterly*, *Western Political Quarterly*, *Midwest Journal of Political Science*, and *Political Science Quarterly*. In addition, several 'quality' periodicals such as *The Listener*, which publish some articles of political interest, were also examined systematically.

The bibliography concerns only the topics covered in this reader. It therefore excludes articles primarily concerned with Parliament, the Civil Service and many other subjects; hence, exclusion of an article is not meant to reflect against its merits. Within the topics chosen, the bibliography is intended to be exhaustive. Because the value of an article to a particular reader depends in part upon the insight of the author, and in part upon the interests of the reader, the bibliography lists all articles in academic journals which might be of interest by their subject matter to some students of political behaviour. In order to avoid cluttering the list with numerous references to descriptive and ephemeral articles, the practice has been to exclude all but exceptional contributions to serious but non-academic periodicals.

Since books in the field are frequently cited in the text, the bibliography concentrates exclusively upon articles. The Hansard Society published in 1960 an annotated bibliography by John Palmer, *Government and Parliament in Britain*. S. E. Finer has also prepared a detailed bibliography of books, appended to his article, 'Research in Political Science in Britain', *Politische Forschung*, Band 17 (1960), pp. 22–37, 218–24. These bibliographies of books may be brought up to date by consulting the reviews and review notes in subsequent issues of *Political Studies*.

Abbreviations

APSR   *American Political Science Review*
BJS   *British Journal of Sociology*
PQ   *Political Quarterly*
PS   *Political Studies*

(Articles reprinted in this volume are indicated thus: *)

I THE POLITICAL CULTURE

ALLEN, V. L., 'The Ethics of Trade Union Leaders', *BJS*, vii. 4 (1956), pp. 314–36.

ANDERSON, P., 'Origins of the Present Crisis', *New Left Review*, no. 23 (1964), pp. 26–53.

BIRNBAUM, N., 'Monarchs and Sociologists', *Sociological Review*, iii. 1 (1955), pp. 5–23. See also SHILS, E. A., and YOUNG, M.

HACKER, A., 'Political Behaviour and Political Behavior', *PS*, vii. 1 (1959), pp. 32–40.

JONES, E., 'The Psychology of Constitutional Monarchy', *New Statesman*, 1 February 1936, pp. 141–2.

McKENZIE, R. T., 'Laski and the Social Bases of the Constitution', *BJS*, iii. 3 (1952), pp. 260–3.

McKENZIE, R. T., 'Bagehot and the Rule of Mere Numbers', *The Listener*, 19 November 1959, pp. 870–2.

*ROTHMAN, S., 'Modernity and Tradition in Britain', *Social Research*, xxviii. 3 (1961), pp. 297–320.

SHILS, E. A., and YOUNG, M., 'The Meaning of the Coronation', *Sociological Review*, i. 2 (1953), pp. 63–81.

YOUNG, M., see SHILS, E. A.

II FACTORS IN POLITICAL SOCIALIZATION

A. *Social and Psychological Influences*

ABRAMS, M., 'The Home-centred Society', *The Listener*, 26 November 1959, pp. 914–15.

ABRAMS, M., 'Social Class and British Politics', *Public Opinion Quarterly*, xxv. 3 (1961), pp. 342–51.

*ALEXANDER, K. J. W., and HOBBS, A., 'What Influences Labour M.P.s?', *New Society*, 13 December 1962, pp. 11–14.

*BALNIEL, LORD, 'The Upper Class', *Twentieth Century*, no. 999 (1960), pp. 427–32.

BOTT, E., 'The Concept of Class as a Reference Group', *Human Relations*, vii. 3 (1954), pp. 259–85.

EYSENCK, H. J., 'Primary Social Attitudes as Related to Social Class and Political Party', *BJS*, ii. 3 (1951), pp. 198–209.

FLETCHER, R., 'Social Change in Britain', *PQ*, xxxiv. 4 (1963), pp. 399–410.

GOLDTHORPE, J. H., and LOCKWOOD, D., 'Affluence and the British Class Structure', *Sociological Review*, xi. 2 (1963), pp. 133–63.

*HALL, R., 'The Status Seeker's Guide to the Eton Home Counties', *Time & Tide*, 28 December 1961, pp. 2087–92.

*HOBBS, A., see ALEXANDER, K. J. W.

LOCKWOOD, D., see GOLDTHORPE, J. H.

MARTIN, F. M., 'Social Status and Electoral Choice in Two Constituencies', *BJS*, iii. 3 (1952), pp. 231–41.

MINCHINTON, W. E., see PLOWMAN, D. E. G.

PLOWMAN, D. E. G., MINCHINTON, W. E., and STACEY, M., 'Local Social Status in England and Wales', *Sociological Review*, x. 2 (1962), pp. 161–202.

RAISON, T., 'Towards a Tory Sociology', *Crossbow*, vii. 25 (1963), pp. 45–9.

RUNCIMAN, W. G., '"Embourgeoisement", Self-Rated Class and Party Preference', *Sociological Review*, xii. 2 (1964), pp. 137–54.

SAMUEL, R., 'The Deference Voter', *New Left Review*, no. 1 (1960), pp. 9–13.

STACEY, M., see PLOWMAN, D. E. G.

TURNER, R., 'Sponsored and Contest Mobility and the School System', *American Sociological Review*, xxv. 6 (1960), pp. 855–67.

WILKINSON, R., 'Political Leadership and the Late Victorian Public School', *BJS*, xiii. 4 (1962), pp. 320–30.

WILLMOTT, P., see YOUNG, M.

*WILSON, H., 'Harold Wilson: a broadcast interview', *The Listener*, 29 October 1964, pp. 653–6.

*YOUNG, M., and WILLMOTT, P., 'Social Grading by Manual Workers', *BJS*, vii. 4 (1956), pp. 337–45.

B. *Voting and Elections*

*ABRAMS, M., 'Social Trends and Electoral Behaviour', *BJS*, xiii. 3 (1962), p. 228–42.

BARTHOLOMEW, D. J., see BEALEY, F.

BEALEY, F., and BARTHOLOMEW, D. J., 'The Local Elections in Newcastle-under-Lyme', *BJS*, xiii. 3, (1962) pp. 273–85; xiii. 4 (1962), pp. 350–68.

BENNEY, M., and GEISS, P., 'Social Class and Politics in Greenwich', *BJS*, i. 4 (1950), pp. 310–27.

BERRINGTON, H., 'The Future of the Liberal Party', *The Listener*, 6 October 1960, pp. 550–1.

BENYON, V. H., and HARRISON, J. E., 'The Political Significance of the British Agricultural Vote', University of Exeter *Report*, no. 134 (1962), pp. 1–59.

BIRCH, A. H., 'The Habit of Voting', *Manchester School of Economic & Social Studies*, xviii. 1 (1950), pp. 75–83.

BIRCH, A. H., see also CAMPBELL, P. W.

BIRCH, A. H., and CAMPBELL, P. W., 'Voting Behaviour in a Lanca-shire Constituency', *BJS*, i. 3 (1950), pp. 197–208.

BIRCH, A. H., CAMPBELL, P. W., and MACKENZIE, W. J. M., 'Partis Politiques et classes sociales en Angleterre', *Revue française de science politique*, v. 4 (1955), pp. 772–98.

BONHAM, J., 'The Middle Class Elector', *BJS*, iii. 3 (1952), pp. 222–30.

BOW GROUP, 'The 1959 Election; a Survey of 57 Parliamentary Candidates', *Crossbow*, iv. 10 (1960), pp. 27–31.

BRAINARD, A. P., 'The Law of Elections and Business Interest Groups in Britain', *Western Political Quarterly*, xiii. 3 (1960), pp. 670–7.

BROWN, J. C., 'Local Party Efficiency as a Factor in the Outcome of British Elections', *PS*, vi. 2 (1958), pp. 174–8.

BUTLER, D. E., 'Trends in British By-Elections', *Journal of Politics*, xi. 2 (1949), pp. 396–407.

BUTLER, D. E., 'The Redistribution of Seats', *Public Administration*, xxxiii. 2 (1955), pp. 125–47.

BUTLER, D. E., 'Voting Behaviour and its Study in Britain', *BJS*, vi 2 (1955), pp. 93–103.

CAMPBELL, P. W., see also BIRCH, A. H.

CAMPBELL, P. W., and BIRCH, A. H., 'Politics in the North-West', *Manchester School of Economic and Social Studies*, xviii. 3 (1950), pp. 217–44.

CAMPBELL, P. W., DONNISON, D., and POTTER, A., 'Voting Behaviour in Droylsden in October, 1951', *Manchester School of Economic and Social Studies*, xx. 1 (1952), pp. 57–66.

CROSSLAND, F. E., see HARRISON, L. H.

CLEARY, E. J., and POLLINS, H., 'Liberal Voting at the General Election of 1951', *Sociological Review*, i. 2 (1953), pp. 27–41.

CRAIG, J. T., 'Parliament and Boundary Commissions', *Public Law* (Spring 1959), pp. 23–45.

CRICK, B., 'Some Reflections on the Late Election', *Public Law* (Spring 1960), pp. 36–49.

DONNISON, D., see CAMPBELL, P. W.

GEORGE, W., 'Social Conditions and the Labour Vote in the County Boroughs of England and Wales', *BJS*, ii. 3 (1951), pp. 255–9.

GEISS, P., see BENNEY, M.

GRUNDY, J., 'Non-Voting in an Urban District', *Manchester School of Economic and Social Studies*, xviii. 1 (1950), pp. 83–100.

HARRISON, J. E., see BENYON, V. H.

HARRISON, L. H., and CROSSLAND, F. E., 'The British Labour Party in the General Elections 1906–1945', *Journal of Politics*, xii. 2 (1950), pp. 383–404.

JONES, C. O., 'Inter-Party Competition in Britain — 1950–1959', *Parliamentary Affairs*, xvii. 1 (1963), pp. 50–6.

KENDALL, M. G., and STUART, A., 'The Law of the Cubic Propor-tion in Election Results', *BJS*, i. 3 (1950), pp. 183–96.

LELOHE, M. J., see SPIERS, M.

McCallum, R. B., 'The Study of Psephology', *Parliamentary Affairs*, viii. 4 (1955), pp. 508–13.

Mackenzie, H. C., see Milne, R. S.

Mackenzie, W. J. M., 'The Export of Electoral Systems', *PS*, v. 3 (1957), pp. 240–57.

Mackenzie, W. J. M., see Birch, A. H., *et al.*

March, J. C., 'Party Legislative Representation as a Function of Election Results', *Public Opinion Quarterly*, xxi. 4 (1958), pp. 521–43.

*Milne, R. S., and Mackenzie, H. C., 'The Floating Vote', *PS*, iii. 1 (1955), pp. 65–8.

Morris-Jones, W. H., 'In Defence of Apathy: Some Doubts on the Duty to Vote', *PS*, ii. 1 (1954), pp. 25–37.

Newman, F. C., 'Money and Election Law in Britain — Guide for America', *Western Political Quarterly*, x. 3 (1957), pp. 582–602.

Pear, R. H., 'The Liberal Vote', *PQ*, xxxiii. 3 (1962), pp. 247–54.

Pennock, J. R., 'The Political Power of British Agriculture', *PS*, vii. 3 (1959), pp. 291–6.

Pollins, H., 'The Significance of the Campaign in General Elections', *PS*, i. 3 (1953), pp. 207–15.

Pollins, H., see Cleary, E. J.

Potter, A., see Campbell, P. W., *et al.*

Rae, S. F., 'The Oxford By-Election: a Study in the Straw Vote Method', *PQ*, x. 2 (1939), pp. 268–79.

Rose, R., 'Money and Election Law', *PS*, ix. 1 (1961), pp. 1–15.

Ross, J. F. S., 'The Incidence of Election Expenses', *PQ*, xxiii. 2 (1952), pp. 175–81.

Spiers, M., and LeLohe, M. J., 'Pakistanis in the Bradford Municipal Election of 1963', *PS*, xii. 1 (1964), pp. 85–92.

Stuart, A., see Kendall, M. G.

III Political Communication

Abrams, M., 'Public Opinion Polls and the British General Election', *Public Opinion Quarterly*, xiv. 1 (1950), pp. 40–53.

Abrams, M., 'The Impact of Admass', *The Listener*, 18 July 1957, pp. 82–3.

Abrams, M., 'Why the Parties Advertise', *New Society*, 6 June 1963, pp. 6–7.

Abrams, M., 'Public Opinion Polls and Political Parties', *Public Opinion Quarterly*, xxvii. 1 (1963), pp. 9–18. See also Moss, L., 'Comment', *ibid*, xxvii. 4, pp. 611–13.

Abrams, M., 'Opinion Polls and Party Propaganda', *Public Opinion Quarterly*, xxviii. 1 (1964), pp. 13–19.

Birch, A. H., Campbell, P. W., and Lucas, P. G., 'The Popular Press in the British General Election of 1955', *PS*, iv. 3 (1956), pp. 297–306.

Blumler, J. G., 'British Television — the Outlines of a Research Strategy', *BJS*, xv. 3 (1964), pp. 223–33.

*BUTLER, D. E., 'Political Reporting in Britain', *The Listener*, 15 August 1963, pp. 231–3.

CAMPBELL, P. W., see BIRCH, A. H., *et al.*

CHRISTOPH, J. B., 'The Press and Politics in Britain and America', *PQ*, xxxiv. 2 (1963), pp. 137–50.

DOWSE, R. E.,'The MP and His Surgery''*PS*, xi. 3 (1963), pp. 333–41.

DURANT, H., 'Public Opinion, Polls, and Foreign Policy', *BJS*, vi. 2 (1955), pp. 149–58.

ELDERSVELD, S. J., 'British Polls and the 1950 General Election', *Public Opinion Quarterly*, xv. 1 (1951), pp. 115–33.

HENNESSY, D., now WINDLESHAM, LORD, *q.v.*

LEYS, C., 'Petitioning in the 19th and 20th Centuries', *PS*, iii. 1 (1955) pp. 45–64.

LUCAS, P. G., see BIRCH, A. H., *et al.*

MACKENZIE, W. J. M., 'The Plowden Report: a Translation', *Guardian*, 25 May 1963.

*McLACHLAN, D., 'The Press and Public Opinion', *BJS*, vi. 2 (1955), pp. 159–68.

PLOWMAN, D. E. G., 'Public Opinion and the Polls', *BJS*, xiii. 4 (1962), pp. 331–49.

ROGOW, A. A., 'The Public Relations Program of the Labour Government and British Industry', *Public Opinion Quarterly*, xvi. 2 (1952), pp. 201–24.

ROSE, R., 'The Influence of Mass Media', *Crossbow*, iv. 13 (1960), pp. 33–6.

ROSE, R., 'Political Decision-Making and the Polls', *Parliamentary Affairs*, xv. 2 (1962), pp. 188–202.

SAMUEL, R., 'Dr. Abrams and the End of Politics', *New Left Review*, no. 5 (1960), pp. 2–9.

SILVEY, R., 'Election Broadcasting and the Public', *The Listener*, 26 November 1959, pp. 934–7.

WALLER, I., 'The "Lobby" and Beyond', *Encounter*, no. 141 (June 1965), pp. 73–80.

WATT, D. C., 'Foreign Affairs, the Public Interest and the Right to Know', *PQ*, xxxiv. 2 (1963), pp. 121–36.

WINDLESHAM, LORD (formerly HENNESSY, DAVID), 'The Communication of Conservative Policy, 1957–1959', *PQ*, xxxii. 3 (1961), pp. 238–56.

*WINDLESHAM, LORD, 'Can Public Opinion Influence Government?', *The Listener*, 22 August 1963, pp. 259–61.

WINDLESHAM, LORD, 'Television as an Influence on Public Opinion', *PQ*, xxxv. 4 (1964), pp. 375–85.

YOUNGER, K., 'Public Opinion and Foreign Policy', *BJS*, vi. 2 (1955), pp. 169–75.

IV PRESSURE GROUPS

BEER, S. H., 'Pressure Groups and Parties in Britain', *APSR*, l. 1 (1956), pp. 1–24.

BEER, S. H., 'Representation of Interests in British Government', *APSR*, li. 3 (1957), pp. 613–51.
BEER, S. H., 'Group Representation in Britain and the United States', *The Annals of the American Academy of Political and Social Science*, cccxix (1958), pp. 130–40.
*DAVIS, M., 'British Public Relations: A Political Case Study', *Journal of Politics*, xxiv. 1 (1962), pp. 50–72.
DAVIS, M., 'Some Neglected Aspects of British Pressure Groups', *Midwest Journal of Political Science*, vii. 1 (1963), pp. 42–53.
*ECKSTEIN, H., 'The Politics of the British Medical Association', *PQ*, xxvi. 4 (1955), pp. 345–59.
FINER, S. E., 'The Political Power of Private Capital', *Sociological Review*, iii. 2 (1955), pp. 279–94; iv. 1 (1956), pp. 5–30.
FINER, S. E., 'The Federation of British Industries', *PS*, iv. 1 (1956), pp. 61–84.
FINER, S. E., 'Transport Interests and the Roads Lobby', *PQ*, xxix. 1 (1958), pp. 47–58.
FINER, S. E., 'The Anonymous Empire', *PS*, vi. 1 (1958), pp. 16–37.
*MCKENZIE, R. T., 'Parties, Pressure Groups, and the British Political Process', *PQ*, xxix. 1 (1958), pp. 5–16.
*MACKENZIE, W. J. M., 'Pressure Groups in British Government', *BJS*, vi. 2 (1955), pp. 133–48.
MACKENZIE, W. J. M., 'Pressure Groups: the "Conceptual Framework"', *PS*, iii. 3 (1955), pp. 247–55.
MILLETT, J. H., 'The Role of an Interest Group Leader in the House of Commons', *Western Political Quarterly*, ix. 4 (1956), pp. 915–26.
MILLETT, J. H., 'British Interest-Group Tactics: a Case Study', *Political Science Quarterly*, lxxii. 1 (1957), pp. 71–82.
PENNOCK, J. R., 'Agricultural Subsidies in England and America', *APSR*, lvi. 3 (1962), pp. 621–33.
POTTER, A., 'The Equal Pay Campaign Committee', *PS*, v. 1 (1957), pp. 49–64.
POTTER, A., 'Attitude Groups', *PQ*, xxix. 1 (1958), pp. 72–82.
SANDERSON, J. B., 'The National Smoke Abatement Society and the Clean Air Act, 1956', *PS*, ix. 3 (1961), pp. 236–53.
SELF, P., and STORING, H., 'The Farmers and the State', *PQ*, xxix. 1 (1958), pp. 17–27.
STORING, H., see SELF, P.
TIVEY, L., and WOHLGEMUTH, E., 'Trade Associations as Interest Groups', *PQ*, xxix. 1 (1958), pp. 59–71.
WALLER, I., 'Pressure Politics', *Encounter*, xix. 2 (1962), pp. 3–15.
WILSON, H. H., 'Techniques of Pressure: Anti-Nationalization Propaganda in Britain', *Public Opinion Quarterly*, xv. 2 (1951), pp. 225–43.
WOHLGEMUTH, E., see TIVEY, L.
WOOTTON, G., 'Ex-serviceman in Politics', *PQ*, xxix. 1 (1958), pp. 28–39.

V Parties

Arditti, C., see Mackenzie, W. J. M.

Beer, S. H., 'The Conservative Party of Great Britain', *Journal of Politics*, xiv. 1 (1952), pp. 41–71.

/ Beer, S. H., 'The Future of British Politics', *PQ*, xxvi. 1 (1955), pp. 33–43.

/ Beer, S. H., 'Democratic One-Party Government for Britain', *PQ*, xxxii. 2 (1961), pp. 114–23.

*Biffen, J., 'The Constituency Leaders', *Crossbow*, iv. 13 (1960), pp. 27–32.

Birch, A. H., Donnison, D., and Jahoda, G., 'Ward Labour Parties: An Analysis', *Fabian Journal*, no. 6 (1952), pp. 27–33.

Blondel, J., 'The Conservative Association and the Labour Party in Reading', *PS*, vi. 2 (1958), pp. 101–19.

Bulpitt, J. G., 'Party Systems in Local Government', *PS*, xi. 1 (1963), pp. 11–35.

Burns, J. M., 'The Parliamentary Labour Party in Great Britain', *APSR*, xliv. 4 (1950), pp. 855–72.

Butler, D. E., 'American Myths About British Parties', *Virginia Quarterly Review*, xxxi. 1 (1955), pp. 46–56.

*Butler, D. E., 'The Paradox of Party Difference', *American Behavioral Scientist*, iv. 3 (1960), pp. 3–5.

Casstevens, T. W., 'Party Theories and British Parties', *Midwest Journal of Political Science*, v. 4 (1961), pp. 391–9.

Christoph, J. B., 'Capital Punishment and British Party Responsibility', *Political Science Quarterly*, lxxvi. 1 (1962), pp. 19–35.

Davis, M., and Verba, S., 'Party Affiliation and International Opinions in Britain and France, 1947–1956', *Public Opinion Quarterly*, xxiv. 4 (1960), pp. 590–604.

Donnison, D., see Birch, A. H.

Donnison, D., and Plowman, D. E. G., 'The Functions of Local Labour Parties: Experiments in Research Methods', *PS*, ii. 2 (1954), pp. 154–67.

Dowse, R. E., 'The Parliamentary Labour Party in Opposition', *Parliamentary Affairs*, xiii. 4 (1960), pp. 520–7.

Dowse, R. E., and Smith, T., 'Party Discipline in the House of Commons', *Parliamentary Affairs*, xvi. 2 (1963), pp. 159–64.

Epstein, L., 'Politics of British Conservatism', *APSR*, xlviii. 1 (1954), pp. 27–49.

Epstein, L., 'Cohesion of British Parliamentary Parties', *APSR*, l. 2 (1956), pp. 360–78.

Epstein, L., 'British Mass Parties in Comparison with American Parties', *Political Science Quarterly*, lxxi. 1 (1956), pp. 97–125.

Epstein, L., 'Candidate Selection in Britain', *P.R.O.D.*, ii. 4 (1959), pp. 16–18.

Epstein, L. 'British M.P.s and their Local Parties: the Suez Cases', *APSR*, liv. 2 (1960), pp. 374–91.

EPSTEIN, L., 'Partisan Foreign Policy: Britain in the Suez Crisis', *World Politics*, xii. 2 (1960), pp. 201–24.

/ EPSTEIN, L., 'British Class Consciousness and the Labour Party', *Journal of British Studies*, i. 2 (1962), pp. 136–50.

EPSTEIN, L., 'Who Makes Party Policy: British Labour, 1960–1961', *Midwest Journal of Political Science*, vi. 2 (1962), pp. 165–82.

EPSTEIN, L., 'New MPs and the Politics of the PLP', *PS*, x. 2 (1962), pp. 121–9.

GOULD, J., '"Riverside": a Labour Constituency', *Fabian Journal*, no. 14 (1954), pp. 12–18.

GRAINGER, G. W., 'Oligarchy in the British Communist Party', *BJS*, ix. 2 (1958), pp. 143–58.

HANHAM, H. J., 'The Local Organization of the British Labour Party', *Western Political Quarterly*, ix. 2 (1956), pp. 376–88.

HARMAN, N., 'Minor Political Parties in Britain', *PQ*, xxxiii. 3 (1962), pp. 268–81.

HARRISON, M., 'Political Finance in Britain', *Journal of Politics*, xxv. 4 (1963), pp. 664–85.

HENNESSY, B., 'Trade Unions and the British Labour Party', *APSR*, xlix. 4 (1955), pp. 1050–67.

HINDELL, K., and WILLIAMS, P., 'Scarborough and Blackpool: An Analysis of Some Votes at the Labour Party Conferences of 1960 and 1961', *PQ*, xxxiii. 3 (1962), pp. 306–20.

JAHODA, G., see BIRCH, A. H., *et al.*

JENKINS, P., 'Labour's Election Machine', *New Society*, 28 May 1964, pp. 12–15.

LEYS, C., 'Models, Theories and the Theory of Political Parties', *PS*, vii. 2 (1959), pp. 127–46.

LIPSON, L., 'The Two-Party System in British Politics', *APSR*, xlvii. 2 (1953), pp. 337–59.

LIPSON, L., 'Party Systems in the United Kingdom and the Older Commonwealth', *PS*, vii. 1 (1959), pp. 12–31.

LIVINGSTON, W. S., 'British General Elections and the Two-Party System, 1945–1955', *Midwest Journal of Political Science*, iii. 2 (1959), pp. 168–88.

LIVINGSTON, W. S., 'Minor Parties and Minority MPs, 1945–1955', *Western Political Quarterly*, xii. 4 (1959), pp. 1017–38.

LOEWENBERG, G., 'The British Constitution and the Structure of the Labour Party', *APSR*, lii. 3 (1958), pp. 771–91.

LOEWENBERG, G., 'The Transformation of British Labour Party Policy Since 1945', *Journal of Politics*, xxi. 2 (1959), pp. 234–57.

McKENZIE, R. T., 'Power in British Parties', *BJS*, vi. 2 (1955), pp. 123–32.

McKENZIE, R. T., 'The Wilson Report and the Future of the Labour Party Organization', *PS*, iv. 1 (1956), pp. 93–7.

McKENZIE, R. T., 'Policy Decision in Opposition: a Rejoinder', *PS*, v. 2 (1957), pp. 176–82. See also MILIBAND, R., and ROSE, S.

MACKENZIE, W. J. M., 'Mr. McKenzie on the British Parties', *PS*, iii. 2 (1955), pp. 157–9.

MACKENZIE, W. J. M., and ARDITTI, C., 'Co-operative Politics in a Lancashire Constituency', *PS*, ii. 2 (1954), pp. 112–27.

McKITTERICK, T. E. M., 'The Membership of the Labour Party', *PQ*, xxxi. 3 (1960), pp. 312–23.

MARTIN, L. W., 'The Bournemouth Affair: Britain's First Primary Election', *JP*, xxii. 4 (1960), pp. 654–81.

MILBURN, J. F., 'The Fabian Society and the British Labour Party', *Western Political Quarterly*, xi. 2 (1958), pp. 319–39.

MILIBAND, R., 'Party Democracy and Parliamentary Government', *PS*, vi. 2 (1958), pp. 170–4. See also McKENZIE, R. T., and ROSE, S.

NEWMAN, F., 'Reflections on Money and Party Politics in Britain', *Parliamentary Affairs*, x. 3 (1957), pp. 308–32.

NICHOLAS, H. G., 'Are Electoral Bargains Disreputable?', *The Listener*, 1 January 1959, pp. 3–5.

NOONAN, L. G., 'The Decline of the Liberal Party in British Politics', *Journal of Politics*, xvi. 1 (1954), pp. 24–39.

OSTERGAARD, G., 'Parties in Co-operative Government', *PS*, vi. 3 (1958), pp. 197–219.

PLOWMAN, D. E. G., 'Allegiance to Political Parties: a Study of Three Parties in One Area', *PS*, iii. 3 (1955), pp. 222–34.

PLOWMAN, D. E. G., see DONNISON, D.

POTTER, A., 'British Party Organization, 1950', *Political Science Quarterly*, lxvi. 1 (1951), pp. 65–86.

POTTER, A., 'The English Conservative Constituency Association', *Western Political Quarterly*, ix. 2 (1956), pp. 363–75.

RASMUSSEN, J., 'The Implications of the Potential Strength of the Liberal Party for the Future of British Politics', *Parliamentary Affairs*, xiv. 3 (1961), pp. 378–90.

ROCHE, J. P., and SACHS, S., 'The Bureaucrat and the Enthusiast: An Exploration of the Leadership of Social Movements', *Western Political Quarterly*, viii. 2 (1955), pp. 248–61.

ROSE, R., 'The Bow Group's Role in British Politics', *Western Political Quarterly*, xiv. 4 (1961), pp. 865–78.

*ROSE, R., 'The Policy Ideas of English Party Activists', *APSR*, lvi. 2 (1962), pp. 360–71.

ROSE, R., 'Complexities of Party Leadership', *Parliamentary Affairs*, xvi. 3 (1963), pp. 257–73.

ROSE, R., 'The Professionals of Politics', *New Society*, 8 August 1963, pp. 10–12.

*ROSE, R., 'Parties, Factions, and Tendencies in Britain', *PS*, xii. 1 (1964), pp. 33–46.

ROSE, S., 'Policy Decision in Opposition', *PS*, iv. 2 (1956), pp. 128–38. See also McKENZIE, R. T., and MILIBAND, R.

SACHS, S., see ROCHE, J.

SMITH, T., see DOWSE, R. E.

THOMPSON, J., 'Square Deal for Agents', *Crossbow*, iv. 13 (1960), pp. 37–40.

TRETHOWAN, I., 'The Tory Strategists', *New Society*, 21 May 1964, pp. 13–15.

VERBA, S., see DAVIS, M.

WILLIAMS, P., see HINDELL, K.

WOOTTON, G., 'Parties in Union Government: the AESD', *PS*, ix. 2 (1961), pp. 141–56.

Printed in Great Britain by Richard Clay (The Chaucer Press), Ltd., Bungay, Suffolk